Morning at Willoughby Run

July 1, 1863

Morning at Willoughby Run

July 1, 1863

Richard S. Shue

THOMAS PUBLICATIONS
Gettysburg PA 17325

Printed and bound in the United States of America

Published by THOMAS PUBLICATIONS, P.O. Box 3031, Gettysburg, Pa. 17325

Softcover: ISBN-0-939631-74-1
Hardcover: ISBN-0-939631-79-2

Cover design by Ryan C. Stouch

To

Lois

"Best image of myself and dearer half."

CONTENTS

	Introduction	ix
	Prologue	xi
I	Invasion	1
II	Prelude To Battle	24
III	The Fateful Morning Begins	48
IV	Buford Hangs On	70
V	Reynolds To The Rescue	99
VI	Rebels Flank Yankees	115
VII	Yankees Flank Rebels	126
VIII	Counterattack!	148
IX	A Larger Battle Looms	169
X	An Assessment	199
XI	Controversies	211
	Epilogue	233
	Appendices	242
	Notes	250
	Bibliography	304

MAPS

1 Confederate cavalry and Pennsylvania militia clash west of Gettysburg 12

2 Tactical situation confronting Meade when he accepted command of the Army of the Potomac – June 28, 1863 ... 20

3 Routes and bivouac positions, June 23 to June 30, of the three divisions that opened the battle of Gettysburg 27

4 Location of Union and Cornfederate infantry on the night of June 30, 1863 34

5 Buford's picket and patrols, June 30-July 1, 1863 55

6 Heth's Division march, morning of July 1, 1863 60

7 Buford's dismounted line 79

8 Situation at 9:30 a.m., July 1, 1863 91

9 Confederate attack south of the Chambersburg Pike 111

10 Confederate attack north of the Chambersburg Pike 116

11 Repulse of Confederate attack south of the Chambersburg Pike 134

12 Union counterattack at the railroad cut 153

13 Position at 10:30 a.m. of Union and Confederate troops approaching Gettysburg 173

14 Situation at 12:30 p.m., July 1, 1863 191

INTRODUCTION

Surely every American must know that the Battle of Gettysburg ended in Confederate defeat after the total failure of Pickett's Charge. How it began, two days earlier, is not nearly so well known. In fact, authors, in their concern to keep their narrative moving, have generally tended to short change the critical opening hours. Warren W. Hassler Jr.'s *Crisis at the Crossroads* (which describes only the first day's battle) is a notable exception. But even here the observation of Civil War historian Alan T. Nolan doubtless applies; namely, that "the presentation of the big picture requires such a broad brush that much of significance is unreported."[1]

It seemed promising, therefore, that an exhaustive study of just the first morning of the Gettysburg battle would uncover much worthwhile information that had not seen the printed page in a very long time, if ever. I determined to find out.

Research proved rewarding; indeed there was a great deal of engaging, long-forgotten material out there. And, because I had limited the scope of my study, nothing of real significance would have to be eliminated in the writing process.

The wealth of material available even on my circumscribed subject was not an unalloyed blessing, however. The more accounts I read the more points of disagreement I encountered. Some of these involved only minor details, but others presented sharp differences of opinion on vital issues. In February of 1882, Captain John H. Bassler of the 149th Pennsylvania Regiment wrote to Colonel John B. Bachelder, then assiduously collecting first-hand reports on the battle. After supplying the information the colonel had requested, Bassler made this gratuitous comment: "What a herculean task to separate the truth from the falsehood in the multitude of reports that have rained down upon you since 1863."[2]

Early on, I realized that becoming thoroughly familiar with who wrote what was just the beginning. I had to take into account the purpose and predisposition of the participant turned writer. Neither Yankee nor Confederate could be wholly objective; innate loyalty to his own side and his own particular unit precluded that. Then, too, some wrote out of a perceived need for self-justification; some had animosities to vent; some made errors in judgement purely through ignorance of the total picture.

The time element—*when* an account was written—also had to be considered. Obviously the shorter the span between an event and the recording of it, the more likely the account would be accurate, and vice-versa. While veterans' memories, as a rule, were remarkably keen, essential facts did become twisted and important details did slip away after a considerable passage of time. Also, it was not uncommon for actions in which the writer himself had taken part to be magnified in valor and significance when he got around to writing about them.

For the drama of the first morning of the Battle of Gettysburg to be fully understood, first the stage had to be set. I had to tell how certain elements of the Army of the Potomac and the Army of Northern Virginia happened to be in the vicinity of Gettysburg on the morning of July 1, 1863. This, along with introducing the huge cast of characters, is the substance of the first two chapters. Chapter III begins at 4:00 a.m. on that fateful morning.

Around noon there was a lull in the fighting, thus providing a felicitous end-point for the narrative.

One further comment. As I began my research I was aware that the cataclysmic events of the first morning had generated some controversies. What came as a surprise to me was that there were so many. Before completing my research I had identified no fewer than sixteen. Chapter XI consists of a discussion of these controversies, together with my conclusion for each. It may be useful to refer to this chapter when the controversial issues initially appear in the text.

I want to express my deep appreciation to Kathleen Georg Harrison, Chief Historian at Gettysburg National Military Park, for her gracious help and encouragement; for clarifying problems that had me puzzled; for sharing, from her awesome store of knowledge about the battle, obscure items of interest, as well as valuable insights, relating to my area of study. I also want to thank all those who helped me in so many ways. Most notably: Robert Prosperi, Scott Hartwig, and Gregory Coco of the National Park Service at Gettysburg; Dean Thomas, Mary Hush, and James Thomas of Thomas Publications; Dr. Richard Sommers of the U.S. Military History Institute, Carlisle Barracks in Carlisle, Pennsylvania; and Ryan Stouch, who prepared the maps from my sketches.

Finally, I want to thank my wife Lois for her patience and unfailing support throughout the eight-year period of this project. I also want to thank her for lending a critical ear. The ultimate test of any piece of writing, in my view, is to read it aloud. Consequently, she was called upon countless times to listen to a sentence, a paragraph, many paragraphs, a whole chapter. In every instance I relied on her to be the arbiter as to whether the writing was effective, whether it sounded "right."

Richard S. Shue
York, Pennsylvania
August 17, 1994

PROLOGUE

Three-quarters of a mile west of the Gettysburg Lutheran Seminary, the traveler headed toward Chambersburg on U.S. Route 30 crosses a stone bridge. Beneath it a placid stream wends its way southward. Narrow and shallow, it is certainly unprepossessing, ordinary. There is not even a signpost beside the highway to inform the traveler of its name.

And yet this seemingly insignificant stream played a central role in the action that opened the great battle at Gettysburg. On the hot, sultry morning of July 1, 1863, amid a hail of small arms and artillery fire, Confederates and Federals alike crossed and recrossed it as the tide of battle shifted. It was wider and deeper than usual that day, swollen after a week of heavy rains. Until the initial attack it functioned as a dividing line, or barrier, equidistant from the Rebel infantry coming onto Herr Ridge, west of the stream, and the Yankee cavalry lying in wait atop McPherson's Ridge on the east side.

It is called Willoughby Run, after the first name of the 18th-century settler whose land it bordered. Little known though it may be, the Pennsylvania stream deserves recognition comparable to that of Virginia's Bull Run or Maryland's Antietam Creek.

Sometime prior to November 28, 1740, Willoughby Winchester started farming a plot of land he had cleared west of the stream. On that day he presented his claim to the Penns' agent for a huge tract stretching from the then-unnamed stream westward to Marsh Creek.[1] Evidently his claim was in good order as it was subsequently approved. The new landowner's neighbors, naturally enough, soon began referring to his eastern boundary as Willoughby's Run. In time the possessive form disappeared.

The visitor to the battlefield today sees McPherson's Ridge much as it appeared in 1863. Edward McPherson's farmhouse burned down in 1895,[2] but his splendid stone-and-timber bank barn is still there. In first-rate condition, too, thanks to periodic restoration by the U.S. Park Service. Down the slope from it, on the south side of Route 30 and near the run, stands the Johns house, which was a toll station at the time of the battle. And Herbst's Woods (often mistakenly referred to as McPherson's Woods) still blankets a large portion of the ridge south of the highway. North of the highway and running parallel to it, the steep railroad cut is virtually unchanged.

Herr Ridge, on the opposite side of Willoughby Run, is a different story. Developments since 1900 have vastly altered the site where Confederate General Heth launched the first major assault in the historic battle. Instead of seeing an untrammeled expanse of open fields sloping down to Willoughby Run, the battlefield visitor today is confronted by modern suburban homes, a complex of condominiums with adjacent swimming pool and playground, and an 18-hole golf course.

The one bright note about this ridge is that the original Herr Tavern of 1815 still stands near the crest. Moreover — renovated as a restaurant in 1986 but keeping the same name and retaining as much as possible of its Victorian ambiance — it is once again in the business of serving food and drink.[3]

Willoughby Run broadens considerably as it meanders southward. But here on both sides of the Route 30 bridge it is normally only a few feet wide. Sunlight filtering through the overarching trees dapples its smooth surface. Minnows swim in its clear water; wild flowers dot its banks.... One looks in vain for a clue that this peaceful setting once resounded with all the sound and fury of battle.

Morning at Willoughby Run

July 1, 1863

Chapter I

INVASION

"...our best chance for success."

The mood of the Army of Northern Virginia after the Battle of Chancellorsville was positively euphoric. Despite odds of more than two to one against them, the Confederates had defeated "Fightin' Joe" Hooker's Army of the Potomac and sent it scuttling off like a whipped dog with its tail between its legs. The credit, as they were quick to acknowledge, was largely due to the leadership of Robert E. Lee and Thomas "Stonewall" Jackson. When the titanic struggle between North and South was finally over, many on both sides would claim that Chancellorsville was Lee's best-fought battle. For Jackson, accidentally shot by one of his own men, it was his last.

One of Lee's colonels boasted that after that battle in May of 1863 the Army of Northern Virginia was "as tough and efficient as any army of the same number ever marshaled on this planet."[1] It was, according to another Southern officer, "a compact, mobile army, well officered...and in splendid morale."[2] A British Army observer, Colonel James A. L. Fremantle, was impressed by the troops' esprit de corps, by the splendid elan evident even in their wearing their toothbrushes "like roses in their buttonholes."[3]

Henry Heth, division commander in A. P. Hill's Third Corps, stated that, before the Battle of Gettysburg, "there was not an officer or soldier in the Army of Northern Virginia, from General Lee to the drummer boy, who did not believe...that it was able to drive the Federal army into the Atlantic Ocean."[4] Just as laudatory, though less colorful, was Lee's pronouncement: "There were never such men in an army before. They will go anywhere and do anything if properly led."[5] Even James Longstreet, the phlegmatic commander of First Corps, concurred that at this juncture they were "capable of undertaking anything."[6]

In the Army of the Potomac, on the other hand, morale was at its lowest ebb. The lost battle had cost some 17,000 casualties, and in the ensuing weeks the ranks would be further depleted by the departure of 20,000 troops whose short-term enlistments had expired.[7] Of even greater import to the still vast Army of the Potomac was the crushed spirit of all those who remained. They were discouraged, despondent; their pride had been wounded and their confidence badly shaken. One chagrined infantry officer charged that the army had been "caused to retreat without the consciousness of having been beaten."[8] Another reported that after Chancellorsville there was "no confidence in Hooker, in either his honesty or ability."[9] Still another complained bitterly about the "heap of marching, with defeat after defeat emblazoned on our banners." He attributed the blame, at least in part, to the "successive changes" in the army's commander (Hooker being the fifth in two years).[10] The colonel of a Massachusetts regiment later frankly admitted: "We felt some doubt whether it was ever going to be our fortune to win a victory in Virginia...."[11] Perhaps the most striking testimony came from a cannoneer in Battery B, 4th United States. Augustus Buell wrote: "The prevailing idea among the old soldiers—and it formed the staple of camp talk—was that the army was being murdered by inches."[12]

With Hooker's army demoralized and his own bursting with confidence, Lee was convinced that the time was ripe for a successful invasion of the North. He proposed to enter Pennsylvania by way of the Shenandoah and Cumberland Valleys and strike at Harrisburg, the state capital. With the capitulation of that city and control of the Susquehanna River at that point, he could proceed eastward or southward, threaten Philadelphia or Baltimore and Washington.[13]

It was a bold plan, but totally characteristic of Lee, whom Henry Heth declared the most aggressive general in the Confederate army, not excepting Jackson.[14] Lee was not unaware of the risks involved, but these, he felt, were greatly outweighed by the military advantages and the bright prospect for achieving important political ends.[15]

In the first place, an invasion would completely disrupt the enemy's plans. The Army of the Potomac would be forced to leave its base on the Rappahannock River, follow the Southerners, and eventually give battle. Lee anticipated that it would be under circumstances favorable to his army and on ground of his choosing.

The second advantage was no less significant. Lee's army could subsist nicely in the rich farmland of the North, thus eliminating the critical problem of shortages, especially of food and forage. Moreover, with military operations shifted to enemy country, Virginia—so badly battered in two years of almost constant warfare—would gain a respite, a much-needed chance to recuperate.[16]

Besides these assured benefits, there were some very enticing possibilities. First: If a decisive victory were gained in the East, it would serve to counterbalance the defeats in the West. Furthermore, the invasion of Pennsylvania could conceivably cause Union troops to be diverted from the Western theater, thus reducing the pressure on the Confederate troops there.[17] Second: With strong anti-war sentiment already rampant among Northerners, the trauma of destruction and bloodshed on their own soil might be just the tinder needed to ignite such an outcry for peace that the Federal government would be forced to concede independence to the Southern states. Third: A successful campaign could lead to recognition of the Confederacy by England and France. Material support, including ordnance and ships, would surely follow.[18]

Initially, President Davis and his Secretary of War, James Seddon, opposed Lee's plan. Concerned about the fate of Vicksburg, both favored sending reinforcements to the Confederate troops there while maintaining a defensive stance in Virginia. General Longstreet advocated still another course of action: Augment Bragg's army in Tennessee, defeat the Union army under Rosecrans, then march into Kentucky, invest Louisville, and ultimately besiege Cincinnati, Ohio. The proposal had merit, and Lee certainly gave it due consideration. But he still believed his invasion plan had better prospects and, if successful, offered greater rewards. After his brilliant victory at Chancellorsville, he had sufficient clout to win the debate.[19]

With hindsight, a Union general would condemn the ill-fated campaign as "the last desperate throw of a gambler who recklessly stakes all his remaining fortune on a single cast of the dice."[20] And a Union sergeant would write: "...the audacity of the rebels in leaving their base and going so far into the enemies [*sic*] country, we could hardly beleive [*sic*] it."[21]

Among Lee's generals, however, there was staunch approval of his decision to invade the North. Major General Jubal A. Early, for instance, pronounced it "wise...our best chance for success."[22] Major General Isaac Trimble was even more emphatic. "But there is no question," he wrote, "that, as General Lee hoped and believed, a successful battle in Pennsylvania would have secured Southern independence."[23]

For many weeks before the Chancellorsville battle, Joe Hooker had continually bragged how he was going to annihilate Lee's army.[24] When he lost that battle, and lost it badly, his credibility vanished. No one was more discouraged than President Abraham Lincoln. Three months earlier he had entreated the cocky commander of the Army of the Potomac to "go forward and give us victories."[25] As Hooker did neither, Lincoln began to think seriously about replacing him.

On June 2—four weeks after the Chancellorsville debacle—Major General John F. Reynolds called at the White House to see the President. Who initiated the meeting is unclear. According to Colonel Charles S. Wainwright, Reynolds told him he was "summoned" by the President. But there are indications that Reynolds, having heard the rumor that Hooker was about to be replaced, requested an interview in order to express his views on the matter. In either case, Reynolds may have anticipated that Lincoln would offer him command of the Army of the Potomac. And that is exactly what happened.[26]

Meeting Reynolds face to face, Lincoln must have been impressed with his quiet dignity and handsome appearance, his dark eyes, suntanned face, black hair, neatly-trimmed mustache and beard. Certainly Lincoln came to the meeting already knowing a great deal about Reynolds' reputation—that he was reliable, efficient, courageous, modest, and highly esteemed by his men. But what probably counted most with the President was Reynolds' record: In every situation he had proved to be an *aggressive* leader.[27]

John Fulton Reynolds was born on September 21, 1820, in Lancaster, Pennsylvania.[28] Upon graduation from West Point in 1841, he was assigned to the 3rd U. S. Artillery.[29] Over the next twenty years he served at army posts in nine states from Maine to California.[30] During the Mexican War he was twice brevetted for bravery.[31] The start

Major General John F. Reynolds

of the Civil War found him at the U. S. Military Academy at West Point, where he served as Commandant of Cadets.[32]

Within a month after Fort Sumter fell, Reynolds returned to field duty, as lieutenant colonel of the 14th U. S. Infantry.[33] Promotion to brigadier general followed, in August 1861, and with it command of a brigade of Pennsylvania Reserves engaged in the defense of Washington. In the spring of 1862, he and his brigade moved to Fredericksburg, Virginia, for the purpose of establishing a military government with himself as governor.[34] In June he led his Pennsylvanians in the battles of Mechanicsville and Gaines' Mill. The morning after the latter engagement he was captured by Confederate pickets and sent to Libby Prison in Richmond. There he languished for six weeks until a prisoner exchange (for Confederate Brigadier General William Barksdale) was arranged.[35] On his return to duty, he was given command of 3rd Division, Third Corps. In the Second Battle of Bull Run, his division was caught in an enemy fire so severe that the men were on the verge of fleeing. Before that happened, Reynolds seized the flag from the colorbearer and galloped up and down the entire division line, waving the flag and exhorting his men to renewed efforts. His men not only rallied but drove back the Rebels in their front.[36] Overall, however, the Federals were defeated and Lee's army pushed on into Maryland.

Pennsylvania's Governor Andrew G. Curtin, fearful of his state being invaded next, made an urgent appeal for Reynolds' services. Painfully aware that the 50,000 men in his state militia were almost totally untrained, he wanted Reynolds to do what he could to get them ready for combat. General in Chief Henry W. Halleck, over the objections of Generals McClellan and Hooker, acceded to the governor's request. So Reynolds traveled to Harrisburg and took up the task. After the Battle of Antietam on September 17, however, the threat of invasion evaporated and Reynolds returned to the Army of the Potomac.[37] On September 29 he was given command of the First Corps; promotion to major general followed.[38] In the battles at Fredericksburg and Chancellorsville he demonstrated his thorough competence in directing the actions of an immense fighting force.

Nevertheless, when Lincoln offered him command of the Army of the Potomac, his response was less than enthusiastic. In fact, it was tantamount to refusal. Reynolds said he would accept only on one condition: that he be given free rein, without interference from Secretary of War Stanton or General in Chief Halleck. This, as Reynolds certainly realized, Lincoln could not grant. He could not thus hamstring the two men whom he had charged with the primary responsibility for the prosecution of the war.[39] Lincoln, swallowing his disappointment, then asked Reynolds whom he thought would be a good choice. Reynolds named his long-time friend and associate George Gordon Meade.[40]

"...to end the war if Providence favors us."

Before embarking on his daring invasion plan, Lee reorganized his army into three corps, each with three large divisions. James Longstreet retained command of the First Corps; Richard S. Ewell succeeded Jackson in command of the Second Corps; and Ambrose Powell Hill was put in charge of the newly-formed Third Corps. Since Chancellorsville, the army had been in a defensive position on the south bank of the Rappahannock at Fredericksburg.

The relative inactivity ended on June 2 (the same day Lincoln interviewed Reynolds). Before dawn the following morning Lafayette McLaw's First Corps division broke camp and was soon marching west, then north. Presently it was followed by the rest of the First Corps and all of the Second Corps. Lee's bold campaign had begun! By June 8 the two infantry corps, along with "Jeb" Stuart's cavalry division, had concentrated at Culpeper, Virginia.

The next day, at nearby Brandy Station, "Jeb" Stuart and his troopers suffered a sharp rebuff. They had been disdainful of their Union counterparts, who, in truth, up to this point had not given them much to worry about. Hooker, suspecting the Rebels were up to something, had sent Alfred Pleasonton's cavalry corps to investigate. As it turned out, the reconnaissance developed into a bloody encounter, with the Union cavalrymen giving a good account of themselves, much to the embarrassment of Stuart.[41]

The First and Second Corps plodded "down" the Shenandoah Valley toward Maryland. The men maintained remarkably high spirits, considering how poorly they were fed and clothed. "Their dress," one observer noted, "was a wretched mixture of all cuts and colors." Those who had shoes, however rundown, could count themselves lucky.[42] As to the shortage of food, Henry Heth indicated just how bad the situation was. Even though as a general officer he received a double ration, he confessed that "frequently to appease my hunger I robbed my horse of a handful of corn which, parched in the fire, served to allay the cravings of nature." Then he added, significantly: "What must have been the condition of the private?"[43]

On June 14 Ewell's Second Corps scored a smashing victory against Union General Milroy's forces at Winchester. Also that day, Hill's Third Corps finally left Fredericksburg to catch up with the rest of the invasion army. On June 15 Longstreet moved the First Corps east of the Blue Ridge to cover the passes, but also in the hope that Hooker would be deceived into thinking Washington might yet be Lee's objective. Even more noteworthy, that day Jenkins' cavalry brigade, riding in advance of the Second Corps, reached the Potomac River, crossed over, swept through Maryland and on into Pennsylvania. News of the sudden appearance of Rebel cavalry in Chambersburg, fifteen miles north of the Mason-Dixon Line, circulated swiftly. Farmers and townspeople throughout the region feared that this was not just an isolated foray.[44]

They were right.

Over the next week and a half some 75,000 Confederate infantry entered Maryland and pushed on to Pennsylvania.[45] They had begun the long trek from Culpeper in the middle of a heat wave. But, after a thunderstorm on June 18 dispelled the enervating heat and humidity, the marching had been easier.[46] North of the Potomac, the Rebel infantry—accustomed as they were to seeing desolation everywhere—reveled in the beauty of this unspoiled region.[47] "You never saw such a land of plenty," 56th Virginia's Colonel William S. Christian wrote home. "We could live here mighty well for the next twelve months, but I suppose old Hooker will try to put a stop to us pretty soon."[48]

All three Third Corps divisions crossed the Potomac on June 24 at Shepherdstown.[49] (Exactly one week later one of them would inadvertantly bring on the Battle of Gettysburg.) Shortly before the crossing, corps commander Hill addressed his troops, proclaiming that they would wrest from the Yankees a "glorious peace on their own soil."[50]

The following day, during a heavy rain, Lee crossed the river at Williamsport.[51] With him were Generals Longstreet and Pickett. Awaiting them on the far bank was a group of Maryland ladies, Confederate sympathizers, huddled under their umbrellas. For the three generals there was no recourse but to submit to protracted introductions all around—to protest would have been unthinkable for a Southern gentleman—though all the while rain dripped from their faces and uniforms. One lady slid a huge wreath over the head of Lee's horse, Traveler, which, it was reported, "objected to it seriously."[52]

To this point the campaign had gone exceptionally well. Lee was greatly encouraged and cautiously optimistic about the future. Just the day before, at Berryville, he said to Major General Isaac Trimble, "We have outmaneuvered the enemy, who even now don't know where we are or what are our designs. Our whole army will be in Pennsylvania the day after tomorrow, leaving the enemy far behind and obliged to follow us by forced marches. I hope with these advantages to accomplish some signal result and to end the war if Providence favors us."[53]

General Robert E. Lee

There was a fairly widespread belief in Lee's army that during its march through Maryland, where a large segment of the population espoused the Southern Cause, many able-bodied males would be moved to join the ranks and fight for the Confederacy. The expectation was never fulfilled.[54]

Although the South had suffered severe depredations at the hands of the Union armies, Lee was determined that there would be no retaliation in kind while his men were on enemy soil. The high-principled army commander would, in any case, have opposed such action; but it so happened there was a very practical reason for him to do so. Anti-war sentiment in the North was growing, as he was well aware, and obviously it was in the South's best interest to foster it.[55] Gross misconduct by his troops would have had exactly the opposite effect, would have so inflamed the North that the groundswell for peace would have completely evaporated.

Accordingly, the destruction of private property was strictly prohibited. This caused considerable grumbling, for many embittered Rebs felt the Yanks should be given a taste of their own medicine. But, with rare exceptions, the order was obeyed.[56]

Lieutenant Francis Dawson of Longstreet's staff proudly declared: "The army behaved superbly in Pennsylvania."[57] And that was true, provided the sole criteria was the low incidence of vandalism. There was, however, a dark side to the invaders' conduct in Pennsylvania.

While, for the most part, the soldier in the ranks refrained from destroying or even damaging enemy property, he had almost no compunction about taking it. Officers, confronted daily with evidence of petty thievery by their men, tended to look the other way. Colonel William Christian's attitude was typical. In the same letter to his wife quoted earlier, he wrote: "Pigs, chickens, geese, etc., are finding their way back into our camp; it can't be prevented, and I can't think it ought to be."[58] Probably most galling to Pennsylvanians was the wholesale theft of their horses. In possibly the worst instance, on June 21, in two hours, the town of Fairfield was virtually stripped of these prized possessions by a squadron of Rebel cavalry.[59]

In the main, however, the Army of Northern Virginia obtained its provisions by honorable means. Farmers, millers, and shopkeepers were either paid in Confederate scrip or given a receipt acknowledging the indebtedness. Ewell, whose Second Corps was the first to enter Pennsylvania, was elated by the overwhelming success his troops had in collecting everything from medicine to flour to cattle and horses.[60]

Yankee sellers, forced to accept dubious Confederate money or a mere receipt, were naturally quite unhappy. Captain E. A. Marye, whose battery fought at Gettysburg on the first morning, recalled buying a pair of boots: "The price was thirty dollars, and I'll never forget that merchant's blank expression when I handed him Confederate bills and walked out."[61]

After Brandy Station, Stuart's cavalry tangled with Union cavalry, successively, at Aldie, Middleburg, and Upperville. But these contests proved indecisive, the Southern cavaliers failing to restore the prestige lost in the earlier battle. Then, on the night of June 23, Stuart received Lee's consent to the bold plan he had proposed. It involved making a wide swing around Hooker's army, all the while conducting raids, disrupting enemy communications, and, in general, causing alarm, confusion, and fear. Lee's reply on the subject:

> You will, however, be able to judge whether you can pass around their army without hindrance, doing them all the damage you can, and crossing the [Potomac] river east of the mountains. In either case, after crossing the river, you must move on and feel the right of Ewell's troops, collecting information, provisions, etc.[62]

Stuart doubtless had already decided that he could do what he proposed, despite any attempted interference by the Federals. And he did, advancing with his three brigades almost to the outskirts of Washington. In the end, however, the free-wheeling raid was not worth the consequence. For Lee was deprived of the greater part of his cavalry when their presence could have made a crucial difference.

On June 12, amid bristling rumors of the imminent invasion of Pennsylvania, Governor Andrew G. Curtin called for volunteers to serve in a home guard for the duration of the war. Response was poor. Three days later (the same day Jenkins' cavalry rode into Chambersburg), the governor issued another call, this time for 50,000 men to enlist in the militia, with discharge after six months or when the emergency ended, whichever came first. Again, there was a weak response. On June 26, with more and more enemy troops streaming into Pennsylvania every day, Curtin made a final plea, asking for 60,000 men to defend the Commonwealth for ninety days. At last a great many men answered the call, but the total was still far short of the requested number.[63] Patriotism, evidently, was not a strong virtue among Pennsylvanians in the 1860s.

Concern for their own material possessions seems to have been a much more powerful trait.[64] This certainly applies to the most populous group in the invaded counties—the Pennsylvania Germans. The British observer with Lee's army, Colonel James A. L. Fremantle, declared: "They are the most unpatriotic people I ever saw...they don't care which side wins, provided they are left alone."[65]

Even so, they did not toady to the enemy nor aid them. They were, in fact, quite tight-lipped, steadfastly refusing to divulge what they knew about Federal troops in their vicinity. One Rebel, frustrated in the attempt to gain information, wryly remarked: "It is a strange thing you people know so little."[66] For the most part they did not bother to hide their disdain for the Southern troops.[67] The deeper feeling of hate they suppressed—but not always. The same Lieutenant Dawson who extolled the behavior of Lee's army in Pennsylvania was one who felt its sting. As he was riding through Chambersburg, his horse stumbled and he was thrown off. In that moment he heard a lady exclaim from the sidewalk, "Thank God, one of those wicked Rebels has broken his neck." But Dawson was only shook up; remounting, he rode over to the lady and politely told her that "the pleasure she anticipated was, at least, postponed."[68]

While Richmond newspapers in late June were prophesying Confederate victory, the Northern press, instead of instilling courage and determination in their readers, was adding to their fear by painting the blackest possible picture of the military situation.[69] One civilian, recalling the last days of June 1863, said bluntly: "The newspapers were in hysterics."

> Business [he went on] came to a standstill. Treasure was hidden or spirited away. The streets of the great cities were filled with pallid, nervous men who eagerly watched the bulletin boards and anxiously feared for the morrow. Churches were thronged with solemn and tearful worshippers.[70]

In endangered areas, he might have added, most schools were closed and mail delivery suspended.[71]

As Ewell's troops moved up the Cumberland Valley, many families whose farms lay in their path grew panicky and fled. The result was a steady stream of refugees, livestock, and overloaded wagons flowing eastward through Carlisle to Harrisburg.[72]

Gettysburg, a quiet college town in south-central Pennsylvania, had the advantage of not being in the Cumberland Valley and thus was not on the main invasion route. The townspeople nonetheless had every reason to worry: The gap in South Mountain which opened into that valley was scarcely ten miles west of their town. And beyond the gap, to the north, south, and west, were countless thousands of Confederate soldiers.

Gettysburg's high degree of vulnerability did not escape the notice of Major General Darius N. Couch, commander of the Department of the Susquehanna. Anxious that the town be as prepared as possible for any encounter with the enemy, he dispatched an aide to hold a public meeting there. Thus, on June 20, Major Granville Haller addressed the large crowd gathered at the Court House. He stressed the seriousness of the situation and called for every able-bodied man to arm himself and stand ready to defend his home and his state.[73] Certainly Haller's speech cast a pall of anxiety and fear over his audience; yet, in essence, it only confirmed what everyone must have suspected—that the war might come, literally, to their doorsteps.

A local innkeeper (perhaps after hearing the major's speech) decided he had better do something about the large quantity of expensive liquor he had just bought. Fearing confiscation by the enemy, he buried the bottles end to end in a long ditch. But he was still not satisfied—a sharp-eyed Rebel might detect the recent excavation. So, on top of the precious hoard he planted a row of cabbages. The ruse worked. When the Rebels came, they seized the few bottles of inferior liquor he had purposely kept in full view. Then, not believing his assertion that that was all he had, they searched the premises. But they never found the good stuff.[74]

Like the innkeeper, everyone in the town and on the outlying farms took precautions: weapons were cleaned and checked, supplies were laid in, valuables were hidden. But all knew, as a professor at Pennsylvania College put it, that they "could do but little to repel a powerful invading army, unless also supported by a strong military force."[75]

As it was, the only force at hand was a small troop of mounted militia under Captain Robert Bell. These were local men, only recently organized as Company B, 21st Pennsylvania Cavalry. Almost totally untrained, they would be scant protection in an emergency. Thus Gettysburg residents felt a bit more secure when the Philadelphia City Troop rode into town on June 21. The forty Philadelphians were headed west with orders to patrol the area around South Mountain, to report any enemy activity they discovered, and, above all, to warn of a Confederate advance in strength. When they departed, Captain Bell's troop rode with them.

For three days the cavalrymen kept a sharp lookout for the enemy. Although they ranged as far south as Monterey Pass, they found nothing alarming to report. One of those days they came upon a small band of Rebels and a few shots were exchanged; that was all.[76]

But the threat still remained that any day Confederate hordes might pour through the South Mountain gap. On June 24, General Couch, expecting just such a move, rushed the 26th Pennsylvania Militia by train from Harrisburg to Gettysburg. Pinched as he was for manpower, he could not be concerned that these men had only been mustered in six days before. It could not be helped that they were practically devoid of military training; in fact, some had never fired a musket. Prudence dictated that he get troops, however ill-prepared, into the endangered area.

The 743 officers and men were blithely riding along when, suddenly, they heard the screech of brakes. The next moment they were jolted out of their seats. The engineer, in a futile attempt to avoid hitting a cow on the tracks, had stopped the train so abruptly that several cars were derailed. As the regiment was then only six miles from its destination, its commander, Colonel William W. Jennings, decided to make camp in a woods nearby. Some of his men, incidentally, had very fresh beef for supper.

The following afternoon Jennings picked one hundred of his best riflemen to investigate reports of Rebels seen to the east of South Mountain. The detachment had advanced only as far as Gettysburg when a driving rain forced the militiamen to take refuge in the town. The rest of the regiment joined them there in the morning. For many Company A lads, it was a homecoming. Until recently, they had been students either at Pennsylvania College (now Gettysburg College) or the Lutheran Seminary.

Needless to say, the sight of so many soldiers in their midst greatly reassured the townspeople. And they showed their gratitude by plying them with sandwiches, pies, and coffee.

The pleasant interlude was, alas, soon over. At 10:30 the 26th Pennsylvania Militia, accompanied by Bell's cavalry, marched out Chambersburg Street and continued west on the Chambersburg Pike. Three miles from town the procession halted, pickets were sent across Marsh Creek, and the rest prepared to confront any enemy advance from the west. Little did they know that even then seasoned enemy troops—White's cavalry battalion and Gordon's infantry brigade—were headed directly toward them. Around 3:00 the inevitable clash occurred.

As might be expected, the "green" troops fared badly. But it might have been worse. Had they been caught unawares or had they disputed the Confederate advance, the encounter surely would not have been bloodless. Fortunately, however, Jennings and Bell had ridden to high ground and had seen the large enemy force coming. Perceiving the folly of making a stand, the two unit commanders agreed that the cavalry troop should try to divert the Rebels long enough for the infantrymen to make good their retreat. It was too late, apparently, to recall the pickets. All forty of them were captured.[77]

After overrunning the pickets, Colonel E. V. White's 35th Virginia Cavalry Battalion—the "Comanches"—spurred on toward the line of enemy cavalry in the distance. True to their nickname, they came yelling like savages and firing their pistols wildly. Before there was any real danger of them hitting anyone, Bell's troopers wheeled their horses around and galloped off. The Comanches, pressing on, quickly reached the rear of Jenning's fleeing militiamen. These men, according to one Rebel trooper, "threw down their bright, new muskets, and begged frantically for quarter." After that, the Comanches gave up the pursuit and returned to the Chambersburg Pike.[78]

Meanwhile, the rest of Jenning's regiment had disintegrated into three mobs, all running in the general direction of Hunterstown.[79] Confederate Major General Jubal Early, in Mummasburg, learned of the skirmish on the Chambersburg Pike and the

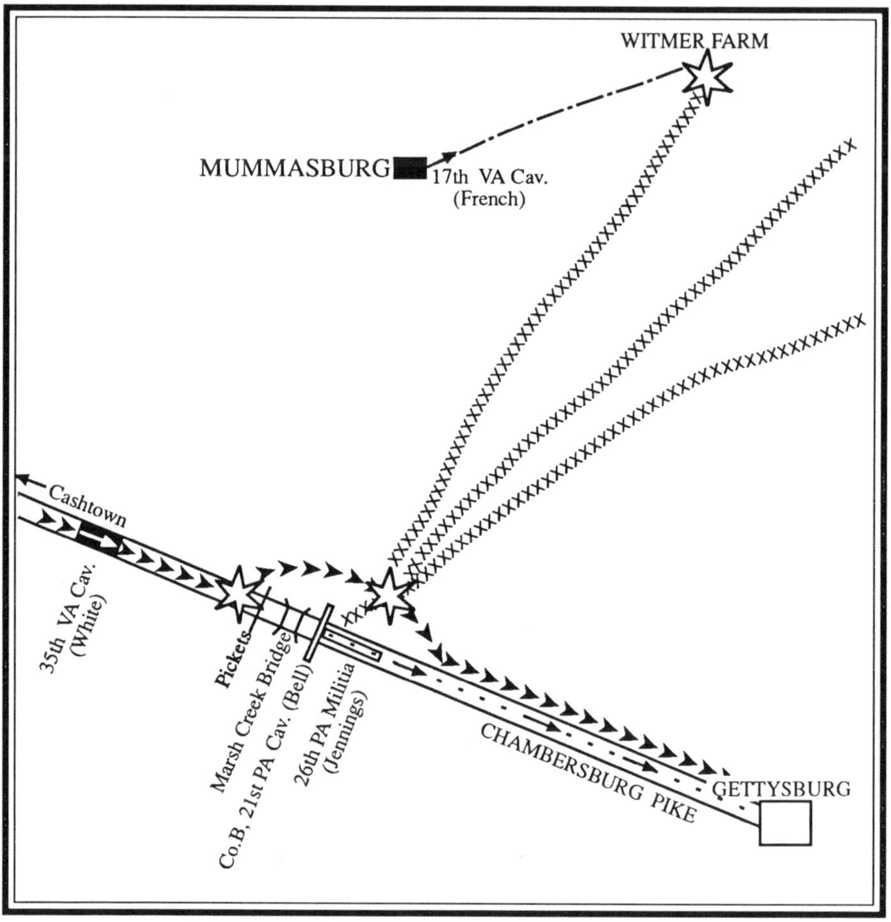

Confederate cavalry and Pennsylvania militia clash west of Gettysburg June 26, 1863

subsequent flight of the Yankee militia. He immediately sent Colonel W. H. French's 17th Virginia Cavalry in pursuit. The hard-riding Virginians soon caught up with about a third of Jenning's command crossing the fields of the Henry Witmer farm, 4-1/2 miles north of Gettysburg. In short order the troopers corralled and captured more than a hundred enemy militia.[80]

In the meantime, White's cavalry had entered Gettysburg. For two hours the citizens cringed in terror as the unruly Comanches raced up and down their streets, yelling and shooting with no regard for what they might hit. To placate the wild men, townspeople gave them everything they wanted. This naturally included strong drink, which only made them more obstreperous. The spree ended shortly after General Early arrived in Gettysburg. On being informed of Comanche behavior, the division leader felt their excess energy could be better utilized and therefore sent them out on a scouting mission.[81]

By then Gettysburg teemed with Confederates—not only White's cavalry but half of Early's large infantry division. Gordon's Brigade had followed the Comanches into town and Hay's Brigade had come down from Mummasburg. Some of these men were barefoot, most were exceedingly dirty, and all were bedraggled from marching most of the day in the rain.

Mayor Kendlehart was most certainly shocked when Early enumerated all that he required of the town: shoes, hats, coffee, flour, bacon, and much more. The mayor protested that his 2,100 constituents could not begin to meet the demands. Early's troops did find 2,000 food rations in some railroad cars, but little else. The truth was, prudent storekeepers had already carted much of their stock out of town, anywhere they thought it would be safe.

In the morning, Early's division set out for York, 27 miles to the east. Gordon's brigade followed the York Pike; Hay's brigade joined the other two brigades that had remained in Mummasburg on a parallel road farther north. Before leaving Gettysburg, Early paroled all the 26th Pennsylvania militiamen taken prisoner the previous day.[82]

Gordon's men halted eight miles west of York and pitched their tents for the night. Before long, Brigadier General John B. Gordon had unexpected visitors. Several of York's most influential citizens had taken it upon themselves to drive out in their carriages and make the Confederate commander an unprecedented offer. Their city would voluntarily surrender, they said, if they were assured there would be no harrassment of civilians and no destruction of property. Gordon readily accepted, giving his word of honor that his troops would abide by the conditions. (There can be no dodging the fact that York sold out to the enemy. Whether this was a cowardly act or a sensible one—surrender was inevitable, anyway—is still a matter of debate.)

General Early, riding to York the following morning, was not about to let its 9,000 residents off lightly just because they had capitulated without a fight. He requisitioned all the things he had tried and failed to get in Gettysburg, increasing the quantity of some items. On top of all this, he demanded $100,000. An ad hoc citizens' committee scurried about collecting supplies and money. They did well on the former, less well on the latter. As a result, Early received most of the clothing and food he wanted but only $28,600 in cash.[83]

In the meantime, Gordon's Brigade had pushed on to Wrightsville on the Susquehanna River. Whoever held the bridge at that point would control traffic on the main road to Lancaster and Philadelphia. Hence, Gordon's orders were to seize and hold that vital link. He was foiled, however, by a mixed group of Pennsylvania militia. These emergency troops quickly retreated across the mile-long bridge, but in the process hastily set it on fire. Gordon's men might have put out the blaze in the early stage if they had had buckets, but the villagers all claimed they didn't have any! So the Southerners could only watch as flames engulfed the wooden structure. That there was no shortage of buckets became manifest after the wind shifted and sparks ignited a number of fires in the village. Then men, women, and children streamed from their homes—all armed with buckets and tubs—intent on preventing a general conflagration. Gordon's men, putting aside their chagrin at being so blatantly lied to, joined the long lines of people passing buckets of water from the river to the fire sites, and thus helped save the village. By that time the bridge they had hoped to take intact was a smouldering ruin.[84]

The same day Gordon was thwarted at Wrightsville—Sunday, June 28—some fifty miles to the west, Confederate Major General William D. Pender wrote to his wife: "I hope we may be in Harrisburg in three days."[85] This was no idle dream; it certainly appeared that he and his Third Corps division would be able to do so. Even as Pender wrote his wife, Jenkin's cavalry was in Mechanicsburg, eight miles south of Harrisburg. And that very day, the cavalrymen had skirmished with some militia at a place called Oyster Point, only three miles from the capital city.[86]

In the city itself tension had been mounting for nearly two weeks. On the 28th, with the enemy so close and the nerves of every citizen strained almost to the breaking point, the mayor of Harrisburg wisely ordered all bars and taverns closed.[87] Gettysburg citizens could not have been any less apprehensive that day, for they now had Confederates on three sides—north, east, and west. In her diary entry for that date, a Gettysburg housewife named Sarah Broadhead reflected the terrible uncertainty everyone felt. She wrote: "Some say we may look for a battle here in a few days, and others say it will be fought near Harrisburg. There is no telling where it will be."[88]

"If Harrisburg comes within your means, capture it." Thus wrote Robert E. Lee from Virginia to Major General Richard Ewell in Pennsylvania, on June 21.[89] Exactly one week later, Lee ordered the Second Corps commander to press on and attain the goal.[90] With only untrained militia guarding the city, its surrender seemed certain, only a matter of time.

In the meantime, Lee had entered Pennsylvania. Arriving in Chambersburg on the 26th, he chanced to meet his Third Corps commander, A. P. Hill, in the town square. As curious townspeople looked on, the two Confederate leaders exchanged greetings, then, withdrawing from their staffs, rode to a corner of the square for a brief conference. That same day, Rodes' Second Corps division, which had been in town two days, marched out the Harrisburg Pike and Heth's Third Corps division passed through on its way east to Fayetteville.[91]

The next day Lee issued General Order No. 73, in which he commended all his troops for their fine conduct on Northern soil, though not overlooking what he politely termed "instances of forgetfulness." He went on to exhort his troops to continue "to abstain with most scrupulous care from unneccessary or wanton injury to private property." Lastly, he instructed every officer to mete out "summary punishment" to any offender in his command.[92]

That afternoon, in the privacy of his tent, Lee confided his feelings, plans, and expectations to Major General Isaac Trimble. Wounded at Second Manassas, Trimble had rejoined the Army of Northern Virginia as a supernumerary; at age 61, he was Lee's senior by five years. "I have not yet heard that the enemy has crossed the Potomac, and am waiting to hear from General Stuart," Lee told the older officer. This was a matter of no small concern, and, clearly, Lee was unhappy with his cavalry chief. He was well satisfied, however, with the condition of his army—"in good spirits," he summarized, and "not overly fatigued." If the need arose to concentrate his forces, he believed he could do so within twenty-four hours. But, with no word from Stuart, Lee could only guess at Hooker's intentions; indeed, he did not even know the location of the Union army. Nevertheless, he outlined the future course of events with such utter confidence that, years later, Trimble claimed he could still quote him almost verbatim. According to Trimble, Lee said:

> When they [the Army of the Potomac] hear where we are they will make forced marches to interpose their forces between us and Baltimore and Philadelphia. They will come up, probably through Frederick, broken down with hunger and hard marching, strung out on a long line and much demoralized when they come into Pennsylvania. I shall throw an overwhelming force on their advance, crush it, follow up the success, drive one corps back on another, and by successive repulses and surprises before they can concentrate, create a panic and virtually destroy the army.[93]

On the 28th, as stated earlier, Lee ordered Ewell on to Harrisburg. To virtually assure the fall of the capital city, Lee ordered Longstreet to move the First Corps in support of the Second Corps. Also that day, he ordered Hill's Third Corps to follow Early's route through Gettysburg and York to Wrightsville, to cross the Susquehanna, and, heading north, to cut the railroad tracks linking Harrisburg and Philadelphia. He had not counted on the enemy burning the Wrightsville bridge.[94]

Before the day ended Lee received startling news. It would completely change his plans, negate the orders he had just issued, and ultimately deny him the capture of Harrisburg.

Late that night a strange, rather furtive-looking man in a rumpled suit was ushered into his tent. He was thin, bearded, stoop-shouldered, and far from clean. His name was Henry Harrison, and he had come to repeat what he had just told General Longstreet. His occupation: Confederate spy. At least a fortnight earlier, Longstreet had engaged Harrison to go to Washington, discover what the enemy was up to, and report back to him. To facilitate the mission, Longsteet had given him a bag filled with gold coins. The spy went to bars frequented by Federal officers and, in that relaxed millieu, struck up conversations with them, bought them drinks. His free spending eventually paid off. When it did, he left Washington with electrifying news for his employer.

After an exhausting journey on foot to Frederick and from there on horseback to Chambersburg, Harrison entered Longstreet's tent and gave his report.[95] Lee, meanwhile, had been notified of Harrison's arrival but was disinclined to see him, having no confidence in secret agents. But he knew Longstreet had great faith in Harrison, and since he had heard nothing from Stuart, he decided he had better hear what the spy had to say.[96]

Harrison told him: *The Union army has crossed the Potomac and is now concentrated around Frederick.*

Lee was astounded...but also skeptical. Surely Stuart would have informed him if such were the case! Yet, as he quickly realized, he could not afford to ignore Harrison's words. To do so could prove diastrous. His widely scattered forces would have to be consolidated in a hurry.

Harrison had another bit of intelligence equally startling. *General Hooker has been relieved of command and General Meade has replaced him.*[97]

Lee had been impressed with George Meade's leadership ability on a number of battlefields. Once he mastered the transition from corps to army command, he would, in Lee's opinion, be a tougher opponent than Hooker. "General Meade will commit no blunder in my front," Lee remarked after the spy departed, "and if I make one he will make haste to take advantage of it."[98]

On the night of Harrison's visit, Brigadier General Stephen D. Ramseur, brigade commander in Rodes' Division, wrote his fiancée: "We are surprised that we have met with feeble resistance thus far. We feel sure however that we will have some stern and bloody work to do before this campaign is ended."[99]

He was absolutely correct.

"Well, I've been tried and condemned...."

Colonel James A. Hardie did not relish the task he had been assigned by Secretary of War Stanton and General in Chief Halleck. How would the volatile Meade react when he learned he had been appointed commander of the Army of the Potomac? Hardie wondered. Meade had not sought the post and in all probability would try to refuse it. When informed that he did not have that option, would he fly into a rage? Even more ticklish was the matter of telling General Hooker that he had been relieved of army command. Although "Fightin' Joe" had requested, in writing, that very day (June 27) that he be allowed to resign his position, he hardly expected his offer would be snapped up without the slightest dissent. What he probably expected was the denial of his request together with conciliation in some degree of his ongoing disputes with Lincoln, Stanton, and, most particularly, Halleck.

Hardie, knowing only that Meade and Hooker were somewhere in the vicinity of Frederick, Maryland, set out for that town by train from Washington. He wore civilian clothes, presumably to forestall questions from fellow officers about the purpose of his mission. Arriving after dark, he found Frederick astir with the boisterous antics of soldiers who had imbibed too much Maryland whiskey. Through persistent inquiry he eventually learned the approximate location of Meade's headquarters. As it was several miles outside town, Hardie again made repeated inquiry, this time to hire someone to drive him there. Finally, he found a man with a buggy willing to make the trip. It took far longer than either man expected because of wagon trains and carousing soldiers blocking the road.

But at last Hardie reached Meade's tent. It was then 3:00 a.m. The general had to be awakened, and was then told that an officer from the War Department was there on urgent business. Meade's first thought was that he was going to be arrested...but he could not imagine why. The notion was promptly banished when he read the Presidential order Hardie handed him. He, George Meade, had been elevated to command of the Army of the Potomac! The promotion was as unwelcome as it was unexpected. He grew more and more agitated as he vented his objections: the responsibility was too great; he did not even know the present positions of the various army corps; to change leaders at the height of a campaign would be a grave mistake; the army would expect Reynolds to succeed Hooker, not himself; it was a blatant injustice not to award top command to Reynolds. In short, he simply did not want the job.

When Meade finished ranting, Hardie calmly explained that his reaction had been anticipated and that he had been instructed to inform him that the decision was final.[100] Later, in better mood, Meade would jest: "Well, I've been tried and condemned without a hearing, and I suppose I shall have to go to execution."[101] Still, the letter from Henry Halleck that Hardie gave him during their meeting should have boosted his ego and dispelled his rampaging self-doubt. The General in Chief wrote: "Considering the circumstances, no one ever received a more important command; and I cannot doubt that you will fully justify the confidence the Government has reposed in you." And

Major General George G. Meade

these reassuring words: "You will not be hampered by any minute instructions from these headquarters." Halleck's only admonition to the new chief of the Army of the Potomac was that he safeguard Washington and Baltimore.[102]

At daybreak Hardie and Meade went to tell Hooker he had been relieved of command. As his headquarters was several miles away, Hardie was furnished a horse. During the ride neither officer spoke; both were dreading the coming ordeal. When they entered Hooker's tent, he took one look at their solemn faces and intuitively knew the reason for their visit. Hardie's announcement merely confirmed what he already surmised.[103]

Perhaps, in that moment, the irony of the situation struck Hooker. Ever since the Confederate army left Fredericksburg, he had been thwarted at every turn by his superiors in Washington. Now, with dizzying alacrity, they had granted his half-hearted request to resign, which, had it not been for their refusals of a number of prior requests, would never have been made.

Only a day or so earlier, Halleck had denied him the use of the garrison at Harpers Ferry.[104] But that was only the "last straw," the one that caused him to write the resignation letter. Hooker would later complain "that it was no use for me to make a request, as that of itself would be sufficient cause for General Halleck to refuse it."[105] After Chancellorsville, both the President and the Secretary of War were arrayed against him as well.

In early June, with two-thirds of Lee's army in or near Culpeper and one-third in Fredericksburg, Hooker proposed that his army cross the Rappahannock River at a point between those towns, turn east, and advance on the smaller force. Lincoln disagreed: "In a word I would not take the risk of being entangled upon the river like an ox jumped half over a fence and liable to be torn by dogs front and rear, without a fair chance to gore one way or to kick the other."[106] When part of Lee's army moved north and it appeared the rest would follow, thus leaving Richmond exposed, Hooker felt the best strategy was to threaten the Confederate capital. The Washington triumvirate—Lincoln, Stanton, Halleck—thought otherwise.[107] The President, writing to Hooker on June 10, enunciated their common position:

> ...I think Lee's army, and not Richmond, is your sure objective point. If he comes toward the Upper Potomac, follow on his flank and on his inside track, shortening your lines while he lengthens his. Fight him, too, when opportunity offers. If he stays where he is, fret him and fret him.[108]

Lee's legions did move toward the Potomac, Hooker dawdled, and it was Lincoln who began to fret. On the 14th he wrote Hooker: "If the head of Lee's army is at Martinsburg and the tail of it on the plank road between Fredericksburg and Chancellorsville, the animal must be very slim somewhere; could you not break him?"[109]

Two days later Lincoln dropped his colloquial style when he again wrote Hooker. Clearly, by then he was much put out with the army commander, with his lethargy and arrogant disregard of orders. Hooker needed to be put in his place and Lincoln did so, emphatically, as follows:

To remove all misunderstanding, I now place you in the strict military relation to General Halleck of the commander of one of the armies to the General-in-Chief of all the armies. I have not indicated differently; but as it seems to be differently understood, I shall direct him to give you orders, and you to obey them.[110]

Given this history of continual dispute, Hooker's reception of his successor on Sunday morning, June 28, was understandably less than cordial. And Meade did not help matters when he tactlessly expressed his disapproval of the army's scattered positions. He somewhat atoned for his faux pas, however, by insisting he be treated as a guest at headquarters as long as General Hooker was present and by requesting that Major General Daniel Butterfield (a crony of Hooker's) stay on as the army's chief of staff.[111]

After the meeting Meade and Hardie rode back to Meade's tent. At 7:00 a.m. Meade wired Halleck: "The order placing me in command of this army is received. As a soldier, I obey it...." He pledged to do his best; then, professing "ignorance of the exact condition of the troops and position of the enemy," he added, "I can only now say that it appears to me I must move toward the Susquehanna, or if he [the enemy] turns toward Baltimore, to give him battle."[112]

Unquestionably, Meade was in a most difficult position, and he was a worrier by nature, anyway. While he was uptight primarily about how to accomplish the herculean task of suppressing a full-scale invasion, no doubt (being Meade) he also worried about another aspect of his new role. How would the Army of the Potomac react to him as its new leader? Would morale suffer?

Major General Carl Schurz (Eleventh Corps) and Brigadier General James S. Wadsworth (First Corps) both commented that Hooker had forfeited the confidence of the rank and file when, after all his boasting, he lost the Battle of Chancellorsville. Consequently, as Schurz pointed out, Meade's assumption of top command had no unsettling effect on the troops.[113] Artillery Colonel Charles S. Wainwright wrote in his journal that the news of Meade's promotion was "very favorably received," though he personally felt it was a risky business to swap generals when battle was imminent.[114] An infantry lieutenant agreed the timing was off but contended that the removal of Hooker "should have been done long before." As to the choice of successor, the lieutenant acknowledged that Meade was not nearly so well known as some other corps commanders, but he approved of his "great modesty, with none of those qualities, which are noisy and assuming, and hankering for cheap newspaper fame."[115] An artillery lieutenant called Meade "a rattling fighter," adding that he would "give old Lee a bellyfull before he got through with him."[116]

The momentous news reached John Reynolds, at Middletown, just as he was getting up. He put on his dress uniform, hastily recruited an escort, and rode to pay his respects to his new commander. Meade was glad to see him, glad for the chance to air his frustration, to clarify his thinking. Reynolds would be sympathetic, helpful. Moreover, Meade needed to be reassured that he had the complete support of his most valued officer. Taking Reynolds' arm, he led him off to one side and at once began to pour out his feelings—his surprise at his promotion, his aversion to it, his fervent wish that

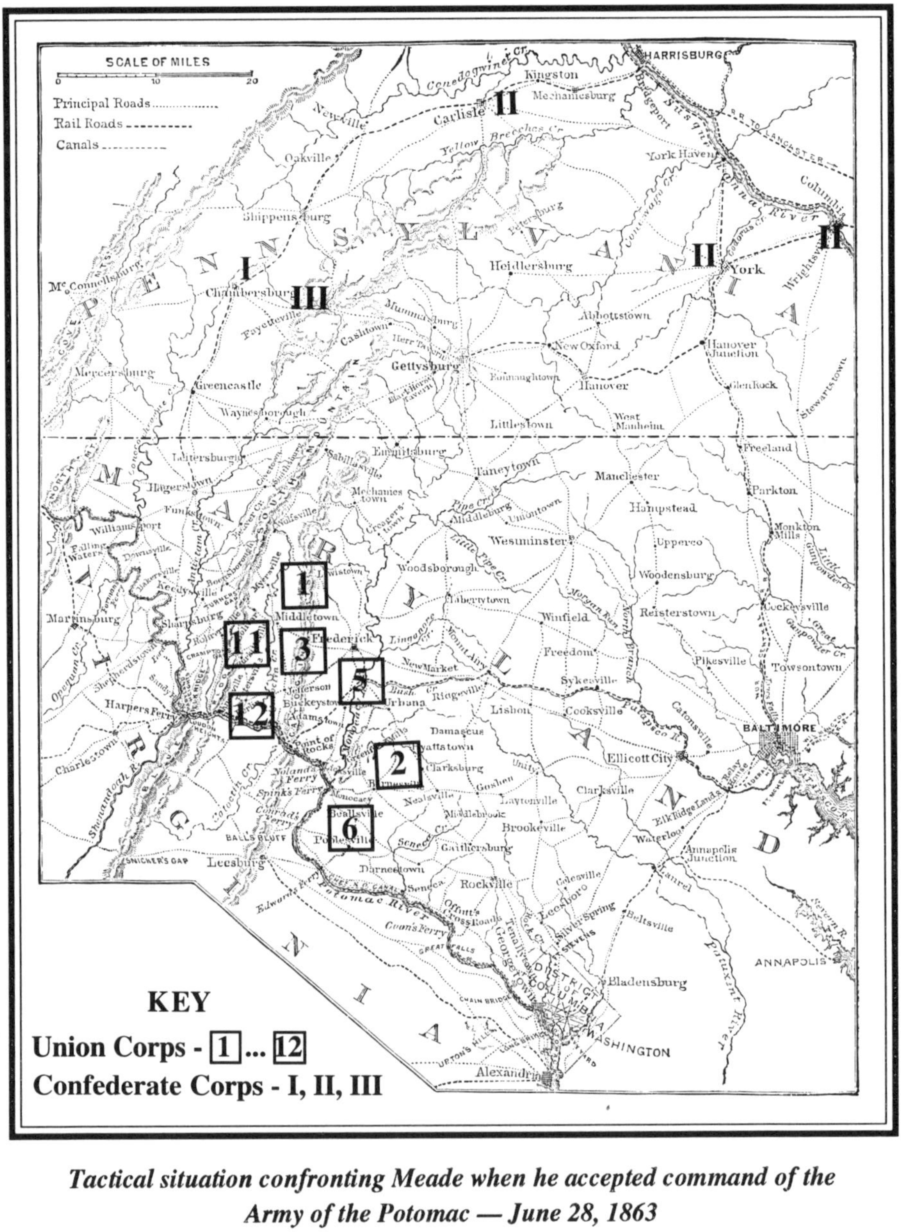

Tactical situation confronting Meade when he accepted command of the Army of the Potomac — June 28, 1863

it had come to Reynolds instead. Reynolds was quick to respond that, in his opinion, Meade was the right man for the job and that, personally, he was thankful not to have the heavy responsibility. Further, he assured Meade of his full support and cooperation.

Once both men knew exactly where the other stood, they could focus exclusively on the exigent military situation. All that the new army commander had just learned from Hooker about the positions and movements of the Union and Confederate armies, he now passed on to Reynolds. As for Hooker's recent reorganization of the army, Meade would have indicated he wanted Reynolds to continue in command of the left wing. (This he confirmed in writing in his dispatch of June 30 to Reynolds) Thus Meade replaced Hooker in directing the day-to-day operations of the four corps on the right, while Reynolds continued to direct First, Third, and Eleventh Corps on the left. The generals discussed plans and their implementation at some length. In addition, at Meade's request, Reynolds helped him draw up the general order officially announcing the change of command.[117]

After the long meeting Reynolds rode to his cousin's home in Frederick. He owed her an apology. The previous morning he had stopped to see Mary Reynolds and promised to return for "late tea." Thinking he would be hungrier than that, she had made him "a nice dinner." She had waited for hours, but he never showed up that night. When he did come the following afternoon, he explained that he had been obliged to go to Jefferson (a town southwest of Frederick) and regretfully had gotten back too late.

On June 28 and again on July 1 Mary wrote to Reynolds' sister Harriet about these events. John "looked very well," she said, "was quite communicative" (which surprised her) and "laughed heartily when I told him that I had told Ellie [another of Reynolds' sisters] it did not seem fair for her to have four brothers and me to have none."[118]

Mary's comments reflected the marked change in General Reynolds that occurred right after Meade replaced Hooker. His staff noticed it immediately. Ever since Chancellorsville their chief had been glum, taciturn, almost unapproachable. Behind his back, they spoke of him as "the Old Man." With Hooker gone, however, it seemed as though he had cast off a heavy burden. Once again he talked and even joked with his subordinates.[119]

"Joe" Hooker had not heeded Lincoln's express desire that he break the line of Lee's advance. Under Hooker's direction, the Army of the Potomac had simply shadowed the Southern army, keeping well to the rear and on the opposite (east) side of the Blue Ridge Mountains. During the second week of June the seven Union corps had set out from their camps on the heights across the Rappahannock River from Fredericksburg. Three of them marched north through Dumfries; the other four followed the Rappahannock westward for some distance before branching off on various roads leading north.[120] The same heat wave that afflicted Lee's army was just as cruel to Hooker's troops. The Federals plodded along in clouds of dust, sweating unmercifully. The ranks became thinner as one soldier after another dropped out, too exhausted to go on. Sunstroke claimed a number of lives.[121] Depression as well as weariness held the troops in thrall; they were, as one officer summed up, "morose, silent and sullen."[122] The spirits of those whose path lay across the old Bull Run battlefield surely sank even lower as they beheld a ghastly sight — the skeletons of soldiers who died there in '62, were hastily buried in shallow graves, and whose bones had since been uncovered by heavy rains.[123]

All seven corps eventually converged at Leesburg, Virginia, only a few miles from the Potomac River. For those troops that arrived first, it meant a most welcome respite for a few days. One night some First Corps men going on picket duty were serenaded by Southern belles at the window of a nearby home. If they intended to make a point by singing only Rebel songs—"Bonnie Blue Flag," for one—it was lost on the Yanks. Captivated by the sweet music, they could not have cared less about the secessionist lyrics.[124]

In two days, June 25-26, the Army of the Potomac crossed the river of that name at Edwards Ferry, just east of Leesburg. With the aid of two pontoon bridges, the operation went smoothly.[125] The only drawback was the weather—it rained continuously both days.

And still more rain the next day, though it had tapered off to a drizzle.[126] The result of all this precipitation was, of course, deeply muddy roads, which made the long marches through Maryland an even more fatiguing chore. Yet, oddly enough, the army completely reversed its previous gloomy mood. Instead of being sullen and silent as they had been in Virginia, the soldiers now were in high spirits, full of banter and fun.[127] The euphoria of those days stuck in the minds of the participants; they were still talking and writing about it years afterward. Fairly typical is this recollection of the 150th Pennsylvania: "Their step was never more elastic, and the live-long day their spirits effervesced in a fine spray of humor, or found vent in joyous outburst of song."[128]

How can the Federals' exuberant morale be reconciled with the miserable weather, the muddy roads, and, for many, an exhausting trek over the Catoctin Mountains? No doubt they were glad to leave enemy country, and probably they preferred cooling rain to blistering heat, but what really cheered them was the warm reception they received from Union sympathizers in Maryland. "Day after day," wrote a Massachusetts soldier, "we were met on the way by women in front of their homes with pails of fresh water, milk, bread, cake and pies, which they freely distributed among us."[129] A Michigan soldier, marching through Poolesville, was cheered by the sight of "the glorious Stars and Stripes waving from every window and doorstep."[130] Nature herself had a treat for the troops: luscious ripe cherries. According to Colonel Wainwright's journal entry for June 27, "half the [First] corps have been eating cherries all day, and stand a very good show for an attack of stomach ache tonight."[131]

On June 28—the day Meade replaced Hooker—both the Second and Third Corps marched at least fifteen miles. The other corps marched shorter distances. It was a clear day for a change. By evening five corps encircled Frederick. These were the First, Second, Fifth, Eleventh, and Twelfth. The Third Corps was about ten miles to the north, between Walkersville and Woodsborough; the Sixth Corps, ten miles southeast, at Hyattstown.[132] Altogether, the Army of the Potomac numbered some 85,000 troops. At the beginning of June it had exceeded 100,000; but the weeks of hard marching had taken a heavy toll and, on top of that, entire regiments, on the expiration of their nine-month or two-year enlistment, had gone home. Even so, the army Meade inherited from Hooker exceeded Lee's forces by roughly 10,000 men.[133]

Hooker, on his last full day as army commander, had directed his chief of staff to issue orders for the cavalry to move "in the direction of Gettysburg and Emmittsburg, and see what they can of the movements of the enemy."[134] Apparently no action was taken before Hooker found himself out of a job. During that trying meeting with his successor, he probably thought to inform him of his intention regarding the cavalry. In any case, Meade consulted his cavalry chief that same day. Like Reynolds, Major General Alfred Pleasonton first had to listen to Meade bemoan the fate that had thrust him into such a difficult position. The reluctant army commander then solicited Pleasonton's support and asked for his views on what course of action Lee would take. The cavalryman stated his firm belief that Lee would move on Gettysburg. And "if he seized that position before we could reach it we would have hard work to get him out." To prevent that from happening, he said, "would depend more on the cavalry than anything else."[135]

The conversation was interrupted by the arrival of a dispatch informing Meade that "Jeb" Stuart's raiders had cut the telegraph line to Washington. The news brought a hearty laugh from Pleasonton. The battle could now be fought, he said, without interference from that quarter. Meade failed to see the humor. Washington would expect the service to be restored, and therefore he wanted Pleasonton to eliminate the threat posed by enemy cavalry roaming at will between the Union army and the nation's capital. Pleasonton was quick to point out that Stuart, in his present location, virtually isolated from the Southern army, was of absolutely no use to Lee. Consequently, in his opinion, it would be wrong "to interfere with the enemy when he was making a false move."[136] Meade, persuaded by his subordinate's reasoning, discarded the idea of chasing Stuart. Between them, they decided the best course was to employ the entire cavalry corps in protecting the army's flanks.

Pleasonton's marching orders went out to his three division commanders the next day, June 29. Brigadier Generals David M. Gregg and Judson Kilpatrick, with their 2nd and 3rd divisions, respectively, were to guard the Army of the Potomac's right flank. The more critical assignment of the left flank—the one nearest the enemy—went to the 1st Division, commanded by Brigadier General John Buford. There were good reasons for Pleasonton's choice. One: This was his largest division, well-disciplined and battle-hardened. Two: This was his best leader and his toughest, most tenacious fighter. These qualities, Pleasonton believed, would be greatly needed.

The corps commander's orders were explicit (even specifying the precise routes to be followed). Buford was to detach one brigade to serve as rear guard while accompanying the division wagons to Mechanicstown (now Thurmont), Maryland. He, with his other two brigades and a battery of horse artillery, was to set out for Gettysburg and arrive there by the evening of June 30.[137]

The requirement was met with several hours to spare. Buford himself arrived about noon. Before long he received an urgent message from Pleasonton: Hold Gettysburg "at all hazards" until the army arrives![138]

It would be the supreme test of his mettle.

CHAPTER II

PRELUDE TO BATTLE

"The enemy are on our soil."

June 28, 1863, marked a turning point in the fortunes of both armies. For better or worse, the Army of the Potomac had a new leader. In the Army of Northern Virginia, after the revelations of the spy Harrison, Lee felt impelled to abandon his immediate plans and hastily concentrate his scattered forces.

Most distressing to the Confederate leader was the need to pull back the Second Corps troops just when Harrisburg lay within their grasp. Lee's withdrawal order reached corps commander Ewell, at Carlisle, in mid-afternoon of the 29th. All Second Corps divisions, Ewell noted, were to proceed at once to "Cashtown or Gettysburg, as circumstances might require." With a final reconnaissance of Harrisburg's defenses already underway and an attack, whose success was virtually assured, in the offing, Ewell was naturally highly displeased. In his frustration, he may even have questioned his superior's judgement as to the necessity for immediate withdrawal, thus giving up a chance to strike a telling blow. In any case, the order put Ewell in a bad mood.[1] An engineer on his staff stated he was "quite testy and hard to please" for the rest of the day.[2] Nevertheless, Ewell lost no time in getting his whole corps in motion.

His divisions threatening Harrisburg withdrew by different routes. Leaving their encampments at Carlisle, Robert Rodes' division followed the road south to Heidlersburg and Edward Johnson's division headed southwest on the road to Shippensburg. The other Second Corps division, under Jubal Early, marched due west from York on the road to East Berlin. The First and Third Corps divisions began moving eastward via the Chambersburg Pike.[3]

In due course Lee's whole army would be concentrated at Cashtown. There—with his three corps facing east and the natural fortress of South Mountain behind them—Lee believed he could score a decisive victory.[4] But would Meade take up the gauntlet, accept battle in that place? Lee could only wonder, since he had still heard nothing from General Stuart and consequently had no inkling as to Meade's intentions.

The cavalry chief had been unaccountably derelict in not keeping him informed of the enemy's movements, and while it was not in Lee's nature to openly criticize any subordinate, he was irritated nonetheless.[5] One detects a note of bitterness in his remark to General Heth: "If the enemy does not find us, we must try and find him, in the absence of our cavalry, as best we can!"[6]

Meade, as we shall see, also favored a particular site (quite far from Cashtown) and proposed to fight there if occasion offered. Thus, the two army commanders were playing the same game: Each wanted to lure the other into fighting on a field he himself had selected because it offered his side the greatest tactical advantage. In this, both were to be disappointed.

On the 29th Meade moved his headquarters from Frederick to Middleburg, Maryland. As telegraph service with Washington had not yet been restored, he dispatched a courier to General in Chief Halleck. "If Lee is moving toward Baltimore," he wrote, "I expect to get between his main army and that place. If he is crossing the Susquehanna, I shall rely upon General Couch, with his [militia] force, holding him until I can fall upon his rear and give him battle...."[7] Before leaving Frederick he wrote his wife: "I shall pray for strength and power to get through with the task assigned me." That evening, from Middleburg, he wrote her again: "We are marching as fast as we can to relieve Harrisburg," adding with grim resolve that he was going to "settle this thing one way or the other."[8]

The next day Meade moved his headquarters to Taneytown, five miles below the Pennsylvania line. But evidently the greater part of the day was spent in dictation: a dozen detailed dispatches—to Halleck, Couch, Reynolds, and several corps commanders—in addition to general and circular orders. The keynote in all of these was caution. Clearly Meade's aim was to be prepared, to be ready for action, not to seek it. In a circular order to his corps commanders he stated: "It is the intention to hold this army pretty nearly in the position it now occupies until the plans of the enemy shall have been more fully developed."[9] However, as he notified Reynolds, he was resolved that "if they advance against me, I must concentrate at that point where they show the strongest force."[10]

A wire the previous day had put his mind at ease about the security of Harrisburg. General Couch had written him that, in his opinion, the primary aim of the enemy's operations in his area was not offensive; rather it was to prevent his militia from cooperating with the Army of the Potomac. But this reassurance only reinforced Meade's basic wait-and-see policy, as his general order of June 30 attests:

> The general believes he has relieved Harrisburg and Philadelphia, and now desires to look to his own army, and assume position for offensive or defensive, as occasion requires, or rest to the troops.
>
> It is not his desire to wear the troops out by excessive fatigue and marches, and thus unfit them for the work they will be called upon to perform.[11]

Facing an inevitable showdown with Lee's army, Meade naturally wanted his troops in the best possible physical condition. But he was concerned that they be fit psychologically, as well. A circular order of June 30 addressed this concern. Exhibiting a fervor and eloquence quite unusual for the prosaic Union leader, it read, in part:

> The enemy are on our soil. The whole country now looks anxiously to this army to deliver it from the presence of the foe. Our failure to do so will leave us no such welcome as the swelling of millions of hearts with pride and joy at our success would give to every soldier of this army. Homes, firesides, and domestic altars are involved.

Meade requested that commanders at all levels speak to their men in this vein, to impress on them "the immense issues involved." And, if such motivation should fail to elicit the intended response, he prescribed the sternest remedy. All commanders, he said, "are authorized to order the instant death of any soldier who fails in his duty at this hour."[12]

In the meantime, Meade had sent out engineers to survey the region between Pipe Creek and Parr's Ridge, in northern Maryland. Impressed by their favorable report, on July 1 he ordered the army, if attacked, to withdraw and establish a defensive line there. While he allowed that the tactical situation could cause him to assume the offensive, what he intended, if at all feasible, was to remain on the defensive, tempting Lee to initiate battle on ground where he knew his Union forces would enjoy a decided advantage.[13]

In the first three days of his new command, Meade had advanced his army on a broad front across Maryland. On the last night of June Reynolds' First, Third, and Eleventh corps were clustered on both sides of the Mason-Dixon line in the vicinity of Emmitsburg. The right-wing corps were widely scattered. The Twelfth Corps had reached Littlestown just across the Pennsylvania line; the Second, Fifth, and Sixth Corps were still in Maryland, at Uniontown, Union Mills, and Manchester, respectively.[14] On Meade's order every infantryman then carried three days' rations in his haversack and sixty rounds of ammunition.[15]

The Army of the Potomac was ready to engage the enemy. If Meade had his way, it would be in his pre-selected position behind Pipe Creek.

"...a great battle will be fought."

Soon after entering Pennsylvania on June 29, John Buford called a meeting of his officers. "Within forty-eight hours," he predicted, "the concentration of both armies will take place upon some field within view, and a great battle will be fought."[16] And that is precisely what happened.

His 4,000 cavalrymen and a battery of horse artillery had started out from Leesburg, Virginia, two days before. Crossing the Potomac at Edwards Ferry, they had ridden all that day through the Maryland countryside and bivouacked near Jefferson. The next day had been easier—a short ride to Middletown, Maryland, with the rest of the day spent in shoeing horses and refitting equipment. Early on the morning of the 29th, Brigadier General Wesley Merritt's brigade set out with the division wagons for Mechanicstown. At the same time, Buford, with the artillery and the other two brigades, set out for Pennsylvania.[17]

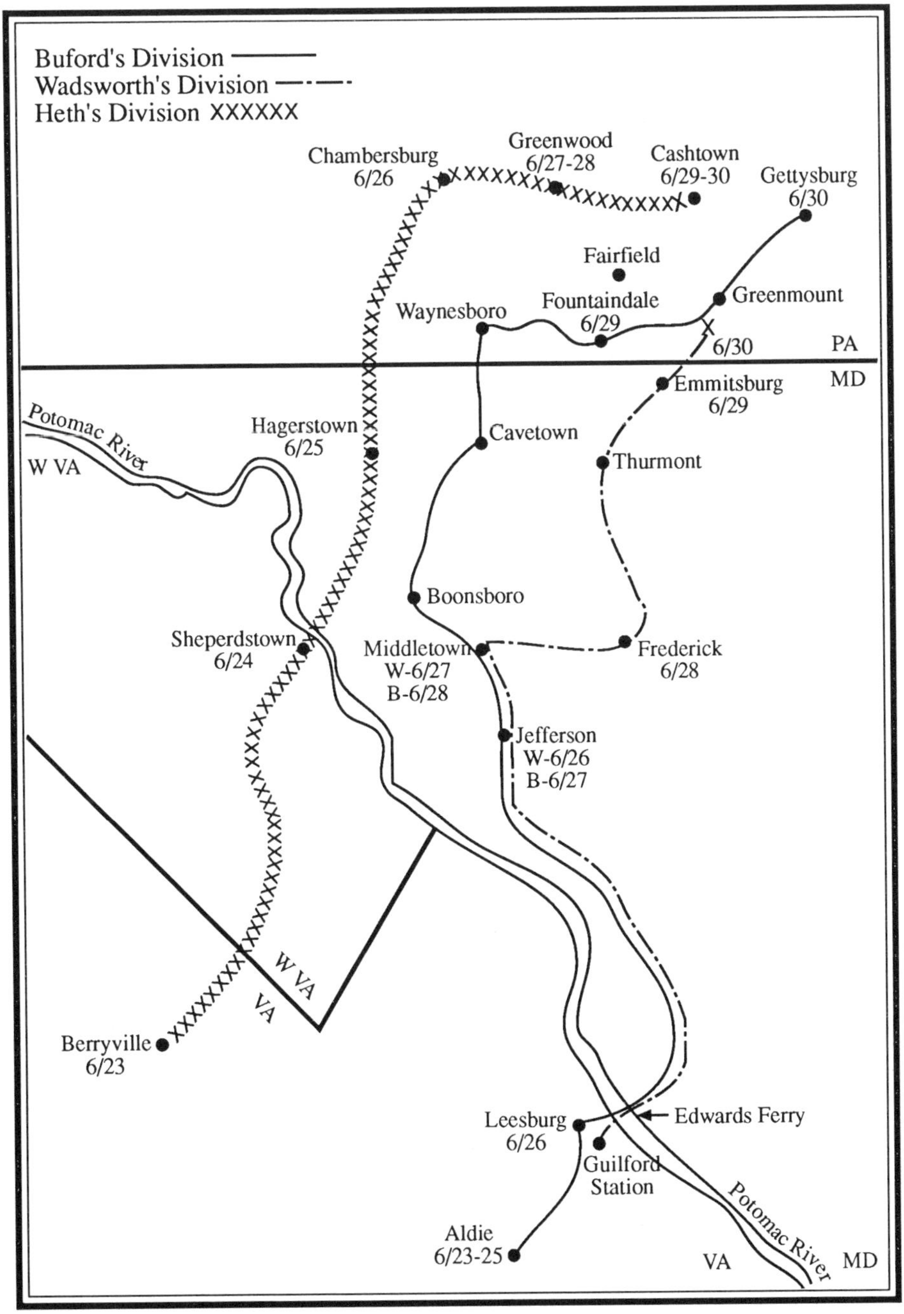

Routes and bivouac positions, June 23 to June 30, of the three divisions that opened the battle of Gettysburg

The commanders of these units were: Lieutenant John H. Calef (2nd United States Artillery, Battery A); Colonel William Gamble (1st Brigade); Colonel Thomas C. Devin (2nd Brigade). Calef was a recent West Point graduate; Gamble, a Regular Army man, who had come up through the ranks; Devin, a former infantry officer in the New York State militia.[18]

The march that next-to-last day of June was punishing for men and horses alike—forty-plus miles of hard riding.[19] The column, with Calef's battery bringing up the rear, had headed west over the South Mountain spur to Boonsboro, north through Cavetown to Monterey Pass, just over the Pennsylvania line, then east to Fountaindale.[20] Along the way, in every town and village, men, women, and children came out to cheer Buford's men, to give them food and drink.[21] These were exhilarating moments, a much-needed stimulant to flagging spirits. Another bright moment was crossing the Pennsylvania line. How glad they all were just to be back in the North, and none more so than the members of the 17th Pennsylvania Cavalry. An officer of that regiment's Company G stationed his guidon bearer on the boundary line, with the instruction to inform each company as it came up that it was entering Pennsylvania. As the cavalrymen rode by the trooper with the streaming red banner, they raised their caps and gave a lusty cheer.[22]

Buford finally halted his command for the night at Fountaindale, just north of the Mason-Dixon line.[23] Having little regard for physical limitations, the 37-year-old general had kept his weary men in the saddle until they were within a few miles of Reynolds and the two left wing corps encamped at Emmitsburg, Maryland. The

Brigadier General John Buford

cavalry leader required of his men the same toughness, pugnacity, and dedication to duty he himself possessed in high degree. As one officer succinctly put it, he was "not to be trifled with."[24] He had not hesitated, for instance, to hang a Confederate spy captured near Frederick. Irate citizens branded him a "Northern brute," but in his strict sense of justice, the heinous offense—which could result in the death of Union soldiers—called for the supreme penalty.[25]

Yet John Buford was neither brute nor tyrant. True, he demanded much of his men, but always with good reason. Logic and commonsense—never whim nor temper—dictated his every action. As his men came to realize this, he reaped their unstinting loyalty. This was already amply demonstrated the previous summer at Thoroughfare Gap, just prior to the second battle at Bull Run, when his 3,000 troopers delayed the advance of Longstreet's 27,000 infantrymen for six hours.

Like Lincoln, Buford was born in Kentucky and later moved to Illinois. After his graduation from West Point in 1848, he served with the U. S. Cavalry on the western frontier. In the Indian wars he quickly realized that the time-honored practice of the massed cavalry attack was largely outmoded, ineffective, and very costly. A far better tactic, he found, was to dismount his horsemen and have them fight as infantry.[26] The experience thus gained in battling Indians would later prove invaluable in fighting Rebels. After a melee with Sioux warriors, in 1855, at Blue Water Creek in the Nebraska Territory, Buford was commended for his "conspicuous gallantry."[27] But, as he and all Regular Army officers were acutely aware, commendation was one thing and promotion quite another. By the spring of 1861, after thirteen years' service, Buford had only attained the rank of captain. Two years later he was a major general. In the interim he had served with distinction in four major battles—Second Bull Run, Antietam, Fredericksburg, and Chancellorsville. He had, in addition, played a leading role in the cavalry engagements at Brandy Station, Aldie, Middleburg, and Upperville.[28]

In temperament and, indeed, in appearance, Buford was not unlike a bulldog. He had the square face, brooding eyes, and blunt nose of that breed; and certainly he was both aggressive and tenacious. While most generals of that era sported luxuriant beards, he was content with a trim mustache. He was moderately tall, smoked a huge pipe, and wore "ancient" corduroy pants tucked into a pair of ordinary cowhide boots.[29]

At Fountaindale Buford and his two brigades were only twelve miles from Gettysburg. They were even closer to the Confederates, whose campfires they could dimly see off to the north and northwest.[30] Buford tried to obtain information about the enemy from the mostly German population but failed utterly. The standard response to his inquiry was, "The rebels will destroy our houses if we tell anything." Buford was disgusted, for he would have liked to surprise the Rebels, send them packing. But without a local guide or any idea as to the size, nature, or disposition of the enemy force, that was obviously out of the question.[31] During the night his 3rd Indiana Cavalry pickets north of Fairfield had a brush with a company of 52nd North Carolina infantrymen, also on picket duty. The exchange of fire was brief, neither side wanting to risk a wider engagement in the dark against an unknown foe.[32]

At dawn the next morning a farmer and his daughter drove into the camp of the 17th Pennsylvania with a wagonload of bread and cakes, which they and the farmer's wife had stayed up all night to bake. The delighted troopers gave them three resounding cheers as they helped themselves.[33] Some of their number had just returned from an overnight visit to their homes in the Waynesboro area. Permission had been granted on the condition that they be back in camp by sunrise, and everyone in the group had kept his promise.[34]

Pleasonton had directed Buford to take the Emmitsburg road to Gettysburg. But Buford evidently decided he should first investigate the enemy force around Fairfield—determine, if possible, its exact position and approximate size—even though this meant additional miles and the likelihood of a hostile encounter.

He and his troopers rode toward Fairfield through fog so thick that they came upon enemy pickets unawares. The Rebels were no less surprised.[35] A few shots from the Yankee cavalry sent them racing back to their main force, which turned out to be two Mississippi regiments of Heth's division.[36] In the ensuing skirmish one Mississippian was killed and three wounded. No Union casualties were reported, though one trooper was knocked off his horse by a minie ball that ricocheted off "some hard substance," thereby averting a serious, probably fatal, stomach wound.[37]

The skirmish was soon over. Buford saw to that. His objective, after all, was intelligence, not battle. The foe, which also included some artillery, was obviously too strong to be routed. And, having already departed from the prescribed route, Buford also realized he could not afford further delay. He therefore ordered his troopers to withdraw by countermarch through Fountaindale to Emmitsburg. There (in tardy compliance with Pleasonton's order) they turned onto the Emmitsburg road and headed north to Gettysburg.[38]

Meanwhile, some fifteen miles to the east, two other cavalry divisions—one Confederate, one Union—were also marching north. Since the roads Stuart's and Kilpatrick's troopers had taken converged at Hanover, a clash was almost bound to occur there. And, about ten o'clock, it did, when the head of Stuart's column suddenly struck Kilpatrick's rear regiment just as it reached the edge of town. The attack split the Union regiment in two. The forward segment dashed into Hanover, with two Confederate regiments in hot pursuit. The rear segment fled across fields in the direction of McSherrystown. The only other Union cavalry regiment in Hanover at the time counterattacked. Presently two of Kilpatrick's regiments beyond the town turned back and entered the fray. Ironically, just minutes before Kilpatrick learned of the Confederate assault, he had received a warning from Pleasonton to watch out for Stuart!

The fight in Hanover was brutal. Dozens of troopers, Rebel and Yankee, were toppled from their horses and lay dead or wounded in the streets. The Yankee cavalrymen gained the upper hand, however, and drove the enemy out of town. In the process they captured a Rebel battle flag, a lieutenant colonel, and a number of men.[39]

"Jeb" Stuart himself narrowly escaped capture. Almost hemmed in by the enemy, he got away by vaulting his horse over a perilous ditch. A Rebel officer who saw the spectacular jump judged the ditch to be ten to fifteen feet across and three to four feet deep.[40]

The fight dragged on well into the afternoon, as each side brought up artillery and more troops. Eventually two Union and three Confederate brigades ringed the town. Neither side ventured a massed charge, however, and the action, apart from a one-hour artillery duel, was confined to intermittent skirmishing.[41]

Finally, with Hanover still in Union hands, Stuart gave the order to withdraw. Unaware that Lee was concentrating his army at Cashtown, he set out for Carlisle, where he expected to find Ewell's Second Corps engaged in a siege of Harrisburg. To bypass Kilpatrick, he took a roundabout route: east to Jefferson, north to Dover, northwest to Carlisle. The exhaustion of his men and horses, not to mention the encumbrance of 125 Union army wagons captured in Rockville, Maryland, precluded a rapid pace. By the time Stuart and his command arrived in Carlisle, Union troops occupied the town. Ewell's corps had long since departed and the battle at Gettysburg had already begun.[42]

Had Stuart maintained close contact with Ewell's Corps, as Lee had specifically ordered him to do, he would not have wasted precious time going in the wrong direction. And, had he and his formidable cavalry been at Gettysburg when the battle opened—as they could have[43]—the whole course of the action might have been vastly different.

"There's thousands of rebels here...."

On June 30, at 6:15 p.m., Secretary of War Edwin Stanton received a startling message from the militia commander in Harrisburg. The enemy in his front had suddenly pulled out! These troops of Ewell's corps were reported marching south. In his wire, General Couch also informed the Secretary that Ewell's troops in York had pulled out, as well, and were marching west. Thus it appeared the two forces would unite. General Meade should be advised at once.

Couch sent a second wire to President Lincoln. Its content was almost identical to the first except that Couch included the observation of his scouts that the Rebels seemed "a good deal agitated about some news they had received."[44] No doubt Lincoln puzzled over what the "news" might be. But it was quite apparent that, for whatever reason, Lee had changed his plans and was now concentrating his forces. The nagging question was: Where?

That morning Robert E. Lee moved his headquarters to the village of Greenwood, with the intention of moving again the following day to Cashtown. He fully expected most of his army would be concentrated there by then.[45] (According to legend, Cashtown derived its name from the inflexible policy of a local tollgate keeper. The man never accepted livestock, produce, or any other commodity in payment of a toll—only cash.)[46]

Lee's confidence in his foot soldiers was not misplaced. Considering they had to cope with rain and muddy roads, they performed exceptionally well.[47] By the night of the 30th, one division had reached Cashtown, another was practically there, and all the rest were within a day's march of the concentration point. In Longstreet's First Corps, Hood's and McLaw's Divisions bivouacked that night at Fayetteville, seven miles east of Chambersburg; Pickett's Division remained in Chambersburg, waiting to be relieved by Imboden's cavalry. In Ewell's Second Corps, Rodes' and Early's Divisions were at or near Heidlersburg, ten miles north of Gettysburg; Johnson's Division was at Scotland, a short distance from Fayetteville. In Hill's Third Corps, Anderson's Division halted just west of South Mountain; Pender's Division pushed on to its east slope, within sight of Cashtown. Heth's Division was already there, having arrived the day before.[48]

Henry Heth, aged 37, was a career soldier. Over the past twenty years, he had risen from West Point plebe to Confederate major general. He was a trim, compact man, with prominent forehead, straight dark hair, deep-set eyes, and bristling mustache. Naturally gregarious, he had an openness, a conviviality, not often encountered in a general officer.

Heth grew up on the family plantation near Richmond, Virginia. After attending exclusive schools in Washington and New York, he entered the United States Military Academy on an appointment secured by President Tyler, no less.

At graduation, in 1847, Henry ranked last in his class. He freely admitted his scholastic performance was "abominable." Yet he did excel in one thing: the accumulation of demerits. His offenses included frequenting an off-limits tavern, smoking in a restricted area, cooking in his room, laughing in ranks, and indulging in "vulgar and offensive language." Once, he and a classmate stole a roast turkey intended for the officers' mess. The officer- instructors were the enemy, he rationalized, and he and his friend were "simply foraging...which in all wars is commendable." Another time he barely avoided court-martial and, most likely, dishonorable discharge. The superintendent of the academy relented on his original intention only because he wished to save a local family embarrassment. Heth, it seems, had taken French leave one night to keep a date with his girlfriend. The breach of regulations might have gone undetected if he had not kept the girl out so late that her mother, becoming frantic, called the police. Years later, musing on his West Point escapades, he would say: "My thoughts ran in the channel of fun."[49]

The hostilities in the Mexican War had ended by the time the newly-commissioned lieutenant came on the scene; consequently, the only action he saw was of the amorous kind. But dalliance with fun-loving senoritas soon gave way to the tedium of garrison life on the American frontier. To relieve the monotony, Heth and his fellow officers played whist and read aloud the plays of Shakespeare.[50] Occasionally there were bloody fights with the Indians, such as the one at Blue Water Creek, in which Buford (as noted earlier) served with distinction. Heth fought there, too, and apparently was missing for some time afterward, for it was erroneously reported that he had been killed. "It is a very pleasant thing," he later wrote, "to be *killed,* if you live to read the nice things your friends say about you."[51]

Major General Henry Heth

On leave in 1853 Heth married Harriet Selden, his first cousin. On April 17, 1861—four days after Fort Sumter surrendered—he resigned from the U. S. Army and wrote that same day to Jefferson Davis, offering his services to the Confederacy. Over the next eighteen months he held various commands—regiment, division, military district—in Kentucky, Tennessee, and western Virginia. In November of 1862, after a humiliating defeat at Lewisburg, Virginia, he requested transfer to the Army of Northern Virginia. His longtime friend Robert E. Lee was glad to oblige and Heth was given command of First Brigade in A. P. Hill's "Light" Division. At Chancellorsville, after Hill was wounded, he led the division in a series of assaults that ultimately drove the Yankees from their works. In the reorganization which followed that battle, Hill became corps commander, Pender was given Hill's old division, and Heth was put in charge of one that had just been formed.[52]

While almost all of Lee's army was busy marching on that last day of June 1863, Heth's men were free to go foraging. The most ambitious expedition involved most of Pettigrew's Brigade. As we shall see, it turned out to be a complete bust. Conversely, in the other three brigades, efforts on a smaller scale seem to have been generally successful. Substantial quantities of flour and grain were collected. Beef cattle was seized.[53] In the Third Corps artillery battalion under Major W. J. Pegram the need for fresh horses had become critical. Upon arrival at Cashtown that day, "Willie" Pegram ordered parties sent out from every battery to procure them. For one battery commander, at least, it proved a soul-wrenching experience. "It appeared to be my fate," wrote Captain E. A. Marye, "that every other animal seized should be the especial

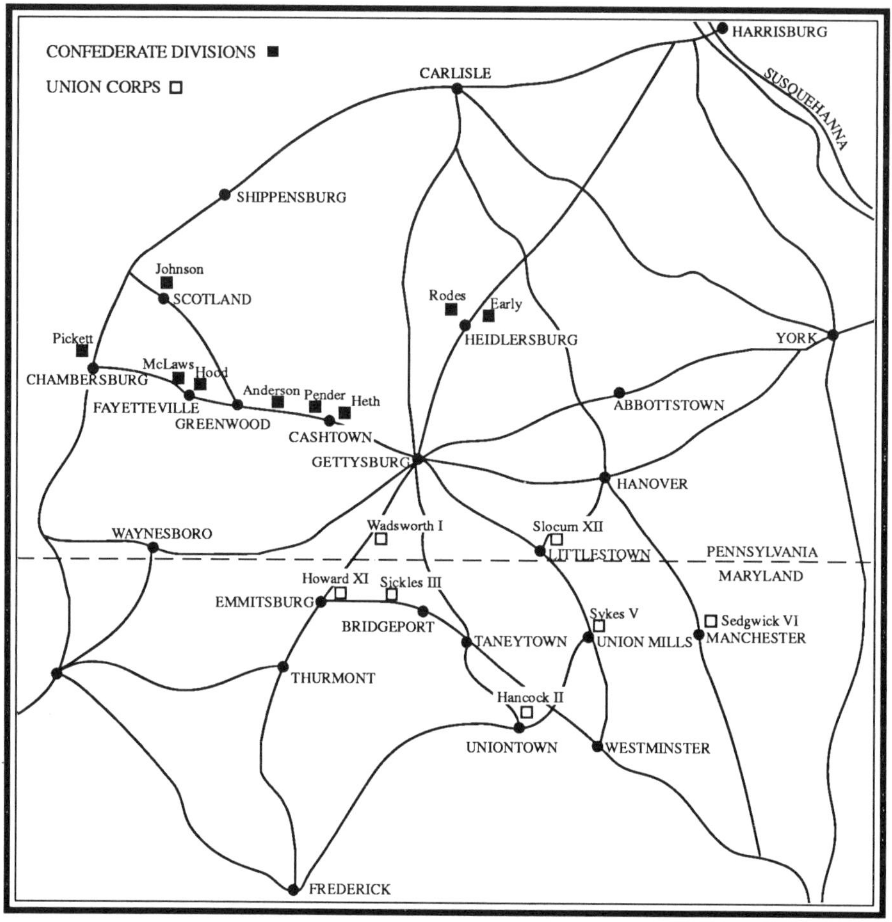

Location of Union and Confederate infantry on the night of June 30, 1863

favorite of the women and children of the family, who, with wailing and crying, begged that their 'pets' be spared."[54]

Apparel of all sorts was the object of intensive search and, when found, was either requisitioned, paid for (in the despised Confederate currency), or simply taken. Probably the most appreciated windfall was the one that benefitted the 7th Tennessee. Tipped off by a civilian, Colonel John Fite and some of his men uncovered a sizeable cache of shoes in the cellar of a private residence. The colonel reported he then "sent one of the boys for a wagon and we loaded it up...and everybody got shoes that wanted them."[55]

Henry Heth acquired a brand new hat. Previously he had asked his quartermaster to look for one for him. When that officer found a Cashtown store with more than a dozen men's felt hats on its shelves, he requisitioned the whole lot. Heth tried them on, but they were all too large. At that point, Heth's orderly, who been watching the procedure, spoke up: "General, I think I can fix one for you." First, he folded some foolscap paper into strips. Then, picking up a hat with a leather band, he inserted the strips behind the band. The result was a decent fit—and a pleased general.

It may be, as Heth claimed ever afterward, that the hat saved his life. When a minie ball struck him in the head the very next day, the worst that happened was that he was temporarily knocked out. The ball had sliced through felt, leather, and wadding, had scratched his scalp, but had not penetrated his skull.[56]

Early on the morning of the 30th, on Heth's order, Brigadier General James J. Pettigrew with three of his North Carolina regiments set out for Gettysburg. As a number of his men were barefoot, there was no question of its top priority. But many other items were also greatly needed.[57] And Pettigrew obviously expected to make a big haul, as he had a fleet of army wagons (27, by one account) accompany his troops. In addition, although he thought the most opposition he might run into would be a local militia unit, he still considered it prudent to take along a few artillery pieces—just in case.[58]

When troops, wagons, and guns all got underway, Pettigrew's column stretched for a mile and a half on the Chambersburg Pike.[59] As the 11th North Carolina drew near Gettysburg, its colonel stopped a civilian on horseback and asked him about Federal troops in the area. The man—a physician on his way to visit a patient—replied that there were four or five thousand in the vicinity and a larger force a few miles farther on. Was he merely repeating a false rumor, or did he exaggerate purposely to deceive the Rebels?[60]

About 9:30 the skirmishers in advance of Pettigrew's column halted on the eastern slope of Seminary Ridge. The houses on the western edge of Gettysburg lay directly ahead. Atop the ridge, Pettigrew and his staff officers peered through field glasses for any sign of enemy activity. Far to the south they detected what appeared to be cavalry supported by infantry. They were mistaken about the infantry, but they had indeed discovered Buford's troopers coming up the Emmitsburg road.[61]

The sudden appearance of Rebel soldiers on Seminary Ridge cast a pall of fear over Gettysburg. West end residents watched the enemy from second-story windows. "We had a good view of them from our house," wrote Sarah Broadhead, "and every moment we expected to hear the booming of cannon, and thought they might shell the town. As it turned out, they were only reconnoitering...."[62]

Pettigrew's officers sharply questioned civilians about Yankee troop activity in the area. No doubt much that they heard was hearsay, distorted or embellished through repetition. Nevertheless, one inescapable fact emerged: Federal troops, probably in strong force, were nearby.[63] The distant sighting of enemy troops together with the affirmations of townspeople were enough to convince Pettigrew that—in the present situation, at least—discretion was the better part of valor. Facing the risk of being confronted by a superior force, he was (as Lee put it) "unwilling to hazard an attack with his single brigade."[64] Pettigrew ordered an about face and his disheartened men began to retrace their steps. It was 10:30.[65]

View of Gettysburg from Seminary Ridge as seen by General Pettigrew and members of his brigade on June 30, 1863.

A half hour later, Buford rode into Gettysburg at the head of his division. The town, he noticed immediately, was in "a terrible state of excitement."[66] The reason became clear when he was informed that a menacing Rebel host had stood on the edge of town for about an hour and had just left. The fears of the townspeople abated, however, as regiment after regiment of Union troopers rode into town. Out of sheer relief and gratitude, the crowds lining the main streets greeted each new arrival with cheers, flag waving, and patriotic songs.[67] A 17th Pennsylvania private recalled hearing one group sing "The Star Spangled Banner," another, "Rally 'Round the Flag, Boys," and still another, "We'll Hang Jeff Davis on a Sour Apple Tree."[68] In yet another group, Tillie Pierce and her girlfriends essayed a tune called "Our Union Forever," but soon found themselves in trouble — they couldn't remember all the words. So they repeated the chorus, over and over again. (One of the troopers who heard them happened to run into Tillie after the battle. He told her he very much enjoyed their singing but would have liked to hear more than just the chorus!)[69]

When the 8th Illinois halted in town, a little girl watching from the sidewalk stepped up to the trooper who had reined in directly in front of her. She held a small bouquet, which she wanted to pin on him. She tried but could not reach high enough. Seeing the instant dismay on her face, the trooper dismounted. After pinning the flowers to his jacket, she handed him a purple ribbon, saying, "Soldier, I want you to wear this ribbon in the next fight you're in, the one you're going to have now."

"Thank you, my little lady," said the trooper, "and I will, if there is a fight, but I don't think we will have one."

"Oh, yes, you will, soldier," she replied gravely. "There's thousands of rebels here, and you will surely have a fight."[70]

Buford himself thought so. Convinced that the enemy would soon return, but not knowing from which direction, he split his forces, sending Devin's Brigade north of town and Gamble's west of it. In addition to the usual pickets, he ordered hefty patrols be sent out in every direction. He realized all the horses were "fagged out," but that could not be helped. Extreme vigilance, in his view, was absolutely necessary.[71]

Devin's cavalrymen followed Washington Street through Gettysburg and camped a short distance beyond Pennsylvania College, in fields beside the Mummasburg Road. Gamble's troops also rode north on Washington Street but at Chambersburg Street, they turned left and headed west.[72] The selection of a defensive position west of town had been left up to Colonel Gamble, Buford specifying only that it be farther west than the Lutheran Theological Seminary.[73] When Gamble arrived on the crest of McPherson's Ridge—a half mile beyond the seminary—he quickly realized he need not look any further. Here his men would have a clear view in every direction, a commanding field of fire, concealment in woods, and, if needed, cover behind a farmhouse, outbuildings, and a massive fieldstone barn.

The farm belonged to one Edward McPherson, a newspaper editor turned politician. Twice elected to the United States Congress, he was defeated in his bid for a third term in 1862. Presently he was Chief Clerk of the House of Representatives, a position he obtained through the influence of Thaddeus Stevens.[74]

John and Eliza Slentz, the tenants who ran the farm, probably saw little of their absentee landlord. Theirs was no small responsibility: 95 acres of wheat, corn, and oats; 30 acres of pasture and woodlands; apple orchard and vegetable garden; cows, horses, pigs, turkeys, and chickens. Not to mention five children under the age of twelve. When Gamble's cavalry inundated the farm, the couple could only look on helplessly as horses trampled the standing grain and troopers tore down fences for firewood or possible use as breastworks.[75]

Meanwhile, the Rebels were making a clean getaway. When they had countermarched about four miles, Pettigrew posted a strong line of pickets to resist any belated pursuit by the Federals. The rest of his troops moved on a little farther and established their camps.[76] Later on, Buford's patrols discovered Pettigrew's position but were careful to keep their distance; they had been cautioned not to provoke an engagement.[77]

For Buford's men not assigned to patrol or picket duty there was a treat in store. A number of thoughtful citizens brought delicious food to the regimental camps. There was fresh-baked bread and jam, pie and cake, meat and fruit. Some troopers even had the good fortune of being invited by a kind family into their home for supper.[78]

In the 9th New York, trooper A. R. Mix got permission to ride into Gettysburg to look for boots; his were "just about gone." There, presumably after repeated inquiry, he came across a town resident who said he had a brand new pair at home that he thought would fit the cavalryman. Come with me, he said, and we shall see. But Mix, due back at camp, could not spare the time. So the man gave him his address and told him to come back tomorrow. Mix, not forseeing any problem, assured him he would return.[79]

"...with beating drums and flying colors."

When Reynolds was elevated to wing command, Major General Abner Doubleday succeeded him as commander of the First Corps. In reality, however, Reynolds was still in charge. On June 30 Colonel Wainwright, chief of the First Corps artillery, noted in his journal: "Though Doubleday is supposed to be in command of the corps, all our orders come from Reynolds direct, and he looks as closely as ever after everything himself."[80]

Reputedly, Doubleday laid out the first baseball diamond and gave the game its name when he was still in his teens. He also had the distinction of firing the first gun in defense of Fort Sumter. Before assuming corps command, he had led the Third Division, First Corps. Brigadier General Thomas A. Rowley moved into the vacated position. Doubleday, Rowley, and the commander of Second Division, Brigadier General John C. Robinson, were professional soldiers; all had seen action in the Mexican War.[81] In contrast, the First Division commander, Brigadier General James S. Wadsworth, had had no military training whatsoever prior to the outbreak of civil war.

His chief interests were politics and the management of his large estate in New York's Genesee Valley. Like Henry Heth (his adversary at Gettysburg), he was no scholar. He attended Harvard and Yale but did not graduate from either institution. In 1856, when he failed to be picked as New York's Republican gubernatorial candidate, he rejected the counteroffer to run for the office of lieutenant governor. Shortly after the Civil War began, he personally chartered and paid for a boat to transport provisions to isolated Federal troops in Annapolis, Maryland. At age 53 (and already graying), he could have avoided military service; instead he lost no time in applying to Brigadier General Irvin McDowell for a staff position. Accepted as an aide-de-camp, he saw action in the First Battle of Bull Run. Three weeks later he was commissioned Brigadier General. In March 1862 he was appointed military governor of Washington. A few months later, while serving in that capacity, he reluctantly agreed to run for governor of his state but refused to campaign. This, coupled with the anti-war sentiment then rampant in New York State, undoubtedly led to his defeat by Democrat Horatio Seymour, a staunch Copperhead. Probably Wadsworth's disappointment was slight because what he really wanted at that time was field command. And that desire was soon fulfilled by the appointment to lead the First Division of the First Corps.[82]

Conscientious and intelligent, Wadsworth proved to be an able leader. What he lacked in military expertise he compensated for by a scrupulous concern for the welfare of his troops. One night during the march through Maryland the division's bivouac area

Moritz Tavern, located on the Emmitsburg Road, served as the headquarters of Major General John F. Reynolds on June 30, 1863.

was extremely wet from the recent rains. Wadsworth, with his own money, bought a farmer's haystack so that every man could lie on a dry bed of hay and get a good night's rest. Another night, after a rain, he paid a farmer $250 for his rail fence so that his men could dry out around a campfire and enjoy some hot coffee. On yet another occasion, when his troops were thoroughly exhausted, he allowed them to stow their rifles and knapsacks in the division ambulances, which was against regulations.[83]

In those last days of June, rumors circulated in Wadsworth's Division of an imminent clash with the Johnny Rebs. Such talk would unnerve new recruits; but these were seasoned troops. A 24th Michigan private expressed what was surely the sensible reaction of the majority. "All we can do," he wrote, "is to let it go in one ear and out the other."[84]

On Monday, June 29, the First Corps marched some 25 miles on muddy roads from Frederick to Emmitsburg. Doubleday, in his report, described the march as "long and toilsome."[85] A weary lieutenant in the 147th New York, writing in his diary that night, summed up the experience in two words: "Hard work."[86] Even so, the First Corps men apparently maintained the highest morale. The 150th Pennsylvania's historian related that "the hills and woods resounded with patriotic lays which were taken up by regiment after regiment, until the whole army seemed to have been metamorphosed into a vast singing society."[87] Lieutenant Loyd G. Harris always remembered this delectable incident. During the Sixth Wisconsin's march "a beautiful girl scarcely twenty...[came] down to the gate in front of an elegant mansion and stood waving a large American flag." Harris ordered his Company C troops to shift muskets to the right shoulder. Grasping their commander's intention, the men kept their heads high and their ranks straight. Then, "as we were just opposite the maiden, I commanded 'Carry arms.' Down came every bright shining musket. The next company did the same, and all the companies of the 'Iron Brigade' as they passed gave her the salute as if she were the general of the army."[88]

Finally, "with beating drums and flying colors," the First Corps marched through Emmitsburg and on to the high ground just north of town.[89] For the 147th New York, which had a late start, the day's march did not end until 11:00. Most regiments, however, arrived in their bivouac areas before dark.[90] The exhausted infantrymen sought relief from sore feet and aching backs in blessed sleep.

The demands on them the next day were far less strenuous. In fact, the two brigades comprising the Second Division did not march at all on the 30th. Neither did the Third Division brigade under Brigadier General George J. Stannard. The rest of the First Corps marched only three to six miles. Shortly after crossing the Pennsylvania line, these troops set up their camps in the vicinity of Marsh Creek.

The head of Wadsworth's First Division halted just short of the village of Greenmount, north of that stream and only five miles from Gettysburg. His two brigades and Captain James Hall's Battery B, 2nd Maine Light Artillery, set up their camps along the Emmitsburg road around noon. The First Brigade (the renowned "Iron Brigade") was commanded by Brigadier General Solomon Meredith; Second Brigade, by Brigadier General Lysander Cutler.

That afternoon Rowley's Third Division brigades under Colonels Chapman Biddle and Roy Stone bivouacked south of Marsh Creek, near the junction of the Emmitsburg and Fairfield roads. With Rebels known to be in Fairfield, it was obviously mandatory that Rowley's brigades be alert for any Confederate advance from that quarter. Captain James H. Cooper's Battery B, 1st Pennsylvania Light Artillery, and Lieutenant James Stewart's Battery B, 4th United States, were both close by, in the event artillery support was needed.[91]

When the 150th Pennsylvania reached the Mason-Dixon line, its colonel halted the regiment just long enough for his men to give three rousing cheers for the "Old Keystone State."[92] Six of the seven infantry regiments came from Pennsylvania, and naturally these boys were mighty glad to be back in their native state.

The reception given them was less than cordial, however. Colonel Wainwright noted in his diary:

> The Pennsylvanians do not give us an over-warm welcome; they are much more greedy than the Marylanders. Butter has gone up to fifty cents a pound, and skimmed milk to twenty-five cents a canteen. Yet they are running [to us] with complaints if a single fence rail is burned.[93]

As the 14th Brooklyn prepared to make camp in a certain field, the farmer who owned the land strode up to Colonel Edward B. Fowler and demanded he move his troops elsewhere.Fowler replied politely that he was sorry the man was so disturbed, but his men were *not* going to move.[94]

During the afternoon the regiments and batteries mustered for pay. The troops on picket duty marched off to their assigned positions. Unit commanders got busy filling out the usual month-end reports on personnel, payroll, stores, and ordnance.[95] Enlisted men wrote letters, read the Bible, reread letters from home, played cards, whittled, joked, and swapped stories. In the 14th Brooklyn they dined on fried chicken. Colonel Fowler, though curious how they got it, discreetly refrained from asking any questions.[96]

In the 150th Pennsylvania three infantrymen invited Harry Kieffer, a drummer boy, to share their feast. The *piece de resistance* was boiled beef heart. The lad, feeling honored to be asked, accepted at once. His hosts were in a jovial mood; during the meal one of them quipped: "We were going to have boiled lion heart for supper, Harry, but we couldn't catch any lions. They seem to be scarce in these parts."[97]

The Eleventh Corps moved that day into the same area that Wadsworth's and Rowley's divisions had occupied the night before. Reynolds, who ordered the move, had been impressed with this high ground outside Emmitsburg and, though circumstances would change his mind, at first he seriously considered moving the First Corps divisions back there if battle appeared imminent. From Marsh Creek he wrote to General Butterfield, Meade's Chief of Staff: "I think if the enemy advances in force on Gettysburg, and we are to fight a defensive battle in this vicinity, that the position to be occupied is just north of the town of Emmitsburg...." Surmising that the enemy would "endeavor to turn our left by way of Fairfield," he felt "an engineer officer ought to be sent up to reconnoiter this position."[98]

That morning Reynolds had notified his Eleventh Corps commander, Major General Oliver O. Howard, of First Corps' march to Marsh Creek. And he had alerted him to be ready to move to support those troops if the enemy should advance on the Fairfield road.[99] Later, Reynolds informed Howard that Buford's cavalry was in Gettysburg and that its timely arrival caused a regiment of Rebel infantry, which had been advancing on the town, to withdraw. He also informed him that his headquarters was in Moritz Tavern and, in a postscript, revealed how uncertain he was about Lee's intentions. "The enemy are evidently branching out into this Valley," he wrote, "but whether it is for the purpose of going to York [28 miles east of Gettysburg] or to give us battle [here], I cannot say."[100]

Apparently soon after receiving the earlier message, Howard dispatched a cavalry unit attached to his corps to reconnoiter the Fairfield area. He so informed Reynolds and added, "Please send me word as to where you want support, in case you do." He also expressed his frustration at not having a map of Adams County (which encompassed Fairfield and Gettysburg) and asked Reynolds to send him one, if possible.[101]

The Third Corps, meanwhile, was marching north from Taneytown. Its commander, Major General Daniel E. Sickles, was in a quandary: Should he follow the written order from his wing commander, Reynolds, or the verbal order from the army commander, Meade? When his lead division was within a mile or two of Emmitsburg—the destination specified by Meade—Sickles gave the order to halt. Hurriedly he scrawled a note to Meade's adjutant at army headquarters in Taneytown. In it he pointed out the conflict with Reynolds' order, which he enclosed, then asked, "Shall I move forward?" Within minutes an aide was riding at top speed to Taneytown for an answer.[102] In the end, Sickles followed Reynolds' order exactly as issued: the Third Corps to bivouac along Cat Tail Branch, face toward Gettysburg, and cover the roads leading to that town.[103] The oddly-named stream was located a few miles east of Emmitsburg, near Bridgeport, Maryland.

Messages passed back and forth between Reynolds and Buford all day. The wing commander knew he could count on the cavalry leader not only for timely reporting of his actions but for reliable intelligence concerning the enemy.[104]

Late in the afternoon, an officer rode up to Moritz Tavern, dismounted, and announced he had come from General Meade to speak with General Reynolds. He was taken at once to a first-floor room where he found the general huddled over a table heaped with maps and reports. Reynolds greeted his visitor warmly and invited him to sit down. Just then the officer noticed that the papers on the general's makeshift desk had been pushed aside to make room for a cup of tea and some crackers. "A very frugal repast," he glibly remarked, "considering the work we may have to do tomorrow."

On that light note, a serious discussion of the military situation began. Reynolds recounted for Meade's benefit what he knew about the enemy and what his immediate plans were for each of his three left wing corps.[105]

"...they will come booming — skirmishers three deep."

After the meeting with Meade's staff officer, Reynolds sent word to General Howard, in Emmitsburg, to join him at Moritz Tavern.[106]

The two-story building was unpretentious: simply four brick walls studded with windows and doors under a steeply-pitched tin roof. But, as a headquarters for Reynolds that last day of June 1863, it was perfect. His whole staff could be housed under one roof and, with the tavern conveniently situated one mile south of Marsh Creek, he could communicate very quickly with both Wadsworth's and Rowley's divisions. (The former tavern, still in good condition, is now a private residence.)

At dusk, Howard, accompanied by two aides, rode up the Emmitsburg road. The party arrived at Reynolds' headquarters just in time to have a late supper with the general and his staff. Afterward the two generals retired to Reynolds' room to talk privately. Howard noticed an abrupt change in Reynolds' mood once they were alone. At supper, in the presence of his staff, he had been cheerful; but now he seemed quite depressed. Together they went over all the communications Reynolds had received that day. Most enlightening—and surely the most disturbing—was the report Buford sent at 5:30 p.m. from Gettysburg.[107]

In it the cavalry division commander related the findings of the scouting parties he had sent out in every direction. At the outset he resolved the mystery of where Lee was concentrating his army: "The enemy has increased his forces considerably. His strong position is just behind Cashtown." But Buford's troopers had discovered Confederates north of Gettysburg as well as west of it. One party "met a superior force, strongly posted" in the vicinity of Mummasburg. Another, riding due north, encountered "a strong picket" only three miles outside Gettysburg.[108]

No doubt Reynolds and Howard discussed at length the momentous import of these developments. Around 10:00 Reynolds sent his senior aide, Major William Riddle, to Taneytown with messages for Meade.[109]

Since Reynolds momentarily expected general orders from the army commander for the next day, Howard tarried to see what they might contain for his Eleventh Corps. When no orders came by 11:00, he and his aides rode back to Emmitsburg.[110]

Possibly only minutes after Howard left, Reynolds received another report from the diligent Buford. This one, marked 10:30 p.m., provided a comprehensive account of enemy positions. It also alerted Reynolds to the trying conditions the cavalry leader had to contend with.

> I am satisfied [wrote Buford] that A. P. Hill's corps is massed just back of Cashtown, about nine miles from this place. Pender's division of this (Hill's) corps came up today....The enemy's pickets (infantry and artillery) are within four miles of this place, on the Cashtown road....Near Heidlersburg today, one of my parties captured a courier of Lee's. Nothing [meaning no official document] was found on him. He says Ewell's corps is crossing the mountains from Carlisle, Rodes' division being at Petersburg [now York Springs] in advance. Longstreet, from all I can learn, is still behind Hill. I have many rumors and reports of the enemy advancing upon me from York. I have to pay attention to some of them, which causes me to overwork my horses and men. I can get no forage nor rations; am out of both. The people give and sell the men something to eat, but I can't stand that way of subsisting; it causes dreadful struggling. Should I have to fall back advise me by what route.[111]

While Reynolds would have regretted Buford's plight, the hardships would simply have to be endured. Continued reconnaissance was imperative. What the enemy's next move would be was uncertain. If the Rebels were to advance on Gettysburg, Reynolds intended to oppose them.[112] But, until he could bring up infantry, he would have to depend on Buford and his troopers to hold the town.

It had been a long day; by midnight Reynolds had to be exhausted. He might have used an upstairs bedroom (his first-floor room contained only table and chairs).[113] But, apparently, he was too weary even to undress. He wrapped himself in a blanket, laid down on the floor, and went to sleep.[114]

As soon as General Pettigrew felt the danger of attack by pursuing Federals was past, he set out for Heth's headquarters at Cashtown. Captain Louis G. Young of his staff rode with him. Pettigrew was in the midst of explaining to Heth why he had failed in his quest for shoes when A. P. Hill rode up. Heth then asked Pettigrew to repeat for the corps commander's benefit all he had just told him. Pettigrew again related his brigade's experience and stated his conviction that part of the Army of the Potomac now occupied Gettysburg and other Federal units were nearby. Both Heth and Hill were skeptical. "The only force at Gettysburg," said Hill, "is cavalry, probably a detachment of observation. I am just from General Lee, and the information he has from his scouts corroborates that [which] I have received from mine—that is, the enemy are still at Middleburg [Maryland], and have not yet struck their tents."

Heth, seizing the moment, then said, "If there is no objection, I will take my division tomorrow and go to Gettysburg and get those shoes!"

Hill replied, "None in the world."[115]

Pettigrew felt strongly that they were making a mistake. He therefore called upon Captain Young to support his testimony. While Pettigrew's troops were pulling back from Gettysburg, Young and another officer had stayed behind to make a full reconnaisance. The captain stated that the approaching enemy troops he saw were, unquestionably, trained soldiers, not home guard.

Hill replied, "I still cannot believe that any portion of the Army of the Potomac is up." Obviously Young had also failed to convince the corps commander. However, Hill did allow: "I hope that it is, for this is the place I want it to be."[116] He would soon know—unless Lee refused permission for Heth's march.

In his dispatch to Lee, Hill reported Pettigrew's near-encounter at Gettysburg, then proposed that Heth's full division march there in the morning to find out what enemy force actually was in his front. Although Lee emphatically did not want to bring on a general engagement, he had no objections to the march.[117] In contrast to the depressed Reynolds, Lee apparently was in fine spirits, confident, optimistic. Colonel E. P. Alexander, who visited him in his Greenwood headquarters that night, remembered that everyone there was relaxed and the conversation was "unusually careless and jolly. Certainly there was no premonition that the next morning was to open the great battle of the campaign."[118]

Lee wrote to Ewell at Heidlersburg, telling him that his order of June 29—to move the Second Corps to "Cashtown or Gettysburg, as circumstances might require"—was still in effect. Ewell discussed the choice of destination and its implications during a meeting with Generals Early, Rodes, and Trimble. Early, resorting to profanity, deplored the awkward position Lee had put them in.[119]

Meanwhile, Colonel White's "Comanches"—the cavalry battalion that had created such a stir at Gettysburg four days earlier—were patrolling roads as far south as Mummasburg and Hunterstown.[120] And when Ewell learned that a Yankee patrol had fired on Rodes' pickets, he sent out more cavalrymen to investigate.[121]

In Heth's camps outside Cashtown, the troops were told they would be marching early next morning. Thus any hope of a few days rest after the grueling marches of the past two weeks was shattered. For a number of them, however, there was at least the compensation of a good, home-cooked supper before they moved on. At farms close to their camps, they feasted on such unaccustomed treats as fried ham, stewed chicken, buckwheat cakes, preserves, and cold milk. Their enjoyment of the meal, one assumes, was only slightly diminished by the fact that, in many cases, they were asked to pay for it.[122]

The Seventh Tennessee men who were sent to find straw, reported back to Colonel John Fite that they had found plenty in a barn some distance from their camp. Then, as he related it:

> I took some fellows up there, told the lady of the house that I wanted to get some of the straw to make beds for the men, that the ground was wet and I didn't want them to get sick. She refused to let me have any of it and I told her then that I was going to take it anyhow. She said I'd better not.

Of course, Colonel Fite and his men began to help themselves. They soon discovered why the woman had been so adamant: Hidden under the straw were a great many huge slabs of bacon. Fite reported the discovery to division headquarters and "they sent wagons there and hauled the last bit of it away." The victimized woman, undoubtedly, was furious.[123]

Another incident about this time evoked a far different reponse from the two women involved. Even before they reached him, Lieutenant Colonel John Lane of the 26th North Carolina could see they were greatly distressed. Nervously, they explained that they were cut off from their homes by his picket line. With perhaps a hint of a smile, he assured them that Confederate soldiers did not make war on women and children. Furthermore, he told them he would advance his line beyond their homes so that they could come and go at will. The women continued on their way, duly grateful for his kind consideration.[124]

James J. Pettigrew went to see his fellow brigadier in Heth's Division, James J. Archer. Archer's Brigade, by normal rotation, would lead the division in the morning, and Pettigrew, though his superiors had rejected his warning, felt Archer should be told what to expect. The briefing was thorough. Pettigrew assured Archer he would encounter Federal troops, not militia. He acquainted him with the topography of the country between Cashtown and Gettysburg. And he warned him about a certain road intersection where he thought the enemy might attack his flank. Archer listened attentively, but, like Hill and Heth, probably discounted Pettigrew's advice.

Captain Young, who had corroborated Pettigrew's testimony to his superiors, later wrote: "This spirit of unbelief had taken such hold that I doubt if any of the commanders of brigades, except General Pettigrew, believed that we were marching to battle, a weakness on their part which rendered them unprepared for what was about to happen."[125]

In his latest dispatch to Reynolds, John Buford had voiced his grievances—no rations, no forage—and had even asked what route to take in the event he had to withdraw from Gettysburg. In light of all he then knew about the enemy, he had every reason to be worried. Nevertheless, for Buford, withdrawal would be a last resort; if at all possible, he and his troopers would hold the town until Reynolds and the First Corps arrived.[126]

At 10:40 p.m., having just finished the dispatch to Reynolds, he wrote to his cavalry chief, Pleasonton. Basically, he repeated the intelligence about Hill's and Ewell's corps. The roads north of Gettysburg, he added, were "terribly infested with roving detachments of cavalry." Also he inquired when his reserve brigade (Merritt's), then guarding supply wagons at Mechanicstown, would be relieved.[127]

Although he had sent out pickets and patrols in every direction, Buford took yet another precaution. Summoning his signal officer, Lieutenant A. B. Jerome, he told him to find the best vantage points and there, with the aid of field glasses, "to look out for campfires, and in the morning for dust." Buford, the lieutenant recalled, "seemed anxious, more so than I ever saw him."[128]

The fatigue of his men and horses coupled with the lack of food and forage was bad enough. But even more troubling was the growing evidence that his command was in peril of Confederate attack from three sides. Gamble's scouts had discovered the enemy's picket line four miles west of Gettysburg.[129] Devin's pickets had captured a number of Rebels both north and east of the town.[130] One of them turned out to be a courier from Major General Jubal Early. The dispatch found on this prisoner contained instructions to post pickets at Mummasburg and Hunterstown and to make a reconnaissance around Gettysburg. Finally, this: "A small body of Yankee cavalry has made its appearance between Gettysburg and Heidlersburg. See what it is."[131]

Early may have been referring to an incident involving a company of 17th Pennsylvania Cavalry. Three miles north of Gettysburg, on the Harrisburg road (which passes through Heidlersburg), Company A of that regiment came upon two Confederate soldiers and captured one of them. Suspecting an enemy force might be nearby, the troopers rode ahead to investigate. They had gone about a half mile, according to Sergeant Joseph McCabe, when they saw "Rebs forming into a column and getting [a] position to await an attack from us." But there would be no attack. The Pennsylvanians rushed back to Gettysburg to report the enemy's position and strength. Prudence dictated that the picket force on the Harrisburg road be augmented. Accordingly, Company B of the 17th Pennsylvania was ordered to support Company A.[132]

A 9th New York patrol of eighteen men, while riding out the Hunterstown road, became aware of hoofbeats behind them. Looking back, they saw horsemen in gray. Immediately the New Yorkers charged. The Rebels—probably a scouting party—fled. One was captured.[133]

Sometime before dark Lieutenant John Calef and his Battery A, 2nd United States Artillery, arrived in Gettysburg. (As they were passing through the town, a young girl stepped up to the lieutenant and handed him a large bouquet.) The battery turned off the Chambersburg Pike shortly after crossing Seminary Ridge and the artillerymen unlimbered their six 3-inch ordnance guns. Thus, if the need arose, they could be put into action quickly. But, as that precaution had been taken many times before, "we of the artillery," Calef distinctly remembered, "were not imbued with the idea that a great battle was pending."[134]

John Buford thought otherwise. Indeed, he was convinced that a battle was not only pending but imminent. During a discussion with Colonel Devin about the reports just in from various patrols and picket posts, he averred that a battle would be fought at this place, and he was afraid it would begin in the morning before the infantry arrived. Devin disagreed. Not that soon, he said, in effect. Rashly he declared he could take care of any force that attacked him in the next twenty-four hours.

"No you won't," Buford shot back. "They will attack you in the morning and they will come *booming*—skirmishers three deep. You will have to fight like the devil to hold your own until supports arrive. The enemy must know the importance of this position and will strain every nerve to secure it, and if we are able to hold we will do well."[135]

Chapter III

THE FATEFUL MORNING BEGINS

"...to get shoes, not to fight."

Darkness enfolded the sprawling Confederate bivouac beside Cashtown. It was a half hour before dawn (at 4:36) this fateful morning, July 1, 1863.[1] The privates of Heth's Division grumbled, as privates in every army have always done when roused from blissful sleep to begin an early morning march. They drank coffee and munched corn pone, or whatever else they had managed to forage in this rich farming country.

Colonel John A. Fite and some 7th Tennessee pickets fared better than that. When the colonel rode out to check on them, he found the group at a farmhouse enjoying a home-cooked breakfast, and he gladly accepted the invitation to join them. During the meal he struck up a conversation with the farmer's daughter, who talked about her sweetheart who had been killed in the battles around Richmond. Their tête-à-tête ended abruptly, however, when a messenger arrived, announcing that all pickets were ordered back to their regiment at once.[2]

By then the sun had peeped over the horizon. Clouds floated overhead and a delicious breeze wafted over the faces of the returning pickets.[3] Was there any presentiment among them of what a momentous day this would be? Perhaps; but most, if not all, simply anticipated another day's march, grateful for the prospect of fair weather.

Henry Heth was anxious to get his division moving. Under orders from A. P. Hill to start for Gettysburg at 5:00, he was making every effort to do so.[4] The stated purpose of the march was reconnaissance, or, as Heth put it, "feeling the enemy."[5] General Lee's wishes in the matter were perfectly clear. As reported by Lieutenant Colonel W. H. Taylor of Lee's staff, they were "to ascertain what force was at Gettysburg, and, if he [Heth] found infantry opposed to him, to report the fact immediately, without forcing an engagement."[6] Hill, in relaying these instructions to Heth, emphasized that, above all, he was not to bring on a battle.[7]

Despite Pettigrew's warnings the day before, neither Heth nor Hill expected any trouble at Gettysburg. Heth expected to confront nothing more daunting than local militia. "I knew they [the militia] would run as soon as we appeared," he told a Union officer after the war. Revealing an astonishing ignorance of the tactical situation, he added, "I did not know that any of your people were north of the Potomac. I was so confident of this that I was careless and marched with my batteries in advance."[8] Hill thought Heth might encounter a scouting party at most—nothing to be alarmed about.[9]

Whenever Hill expected heavy fighting he donned a flaming red shirt and a black felt slouch hat, but he expected none this day.[10] Furthermore, he was ill—too ill even to mount his horse.[11] He had no choice but to remain at Cashtown and hope he would feel better by the time Anderson's Division arrived from Fayetteville.[12] Colonel Fremantle, the British Army observer, noticed he looked "very delicate."[13]

For a general, Hill was uncharacteristically prone to illness. (It had taken him an additional year to graduate from West Point for that reason.)[14] While it is not known what ailed him this particular morning, one can assume it was stress related,[15] since he had only recently been promoted to corps command.

Likewise, Heth was new to division command and Joe Davis to brigade command. All three promotions had come in the wake of "Stonewall" Jackson's tragic death on May 10, eight days after being shot at Chancellorsville by one of his own soldiers. Thus, at Gettysburg three of the four Confederate generals most directly involved in the fighting on the morning of July 1 were new to their respective commands. By further coincidence all three were or within a few months would be 38 years old.[16] General Archer, who had commanded his brigade for slightly more than a year, was 46.[17]

Heth's efforts notwithstanding, his division was probably late in getting started, or else its rate of march was extremely slow.[18] At first, Major William J. Pegram's artillery battalion—five batteries with twenty guns and 400 men—marched ahead of the infantry.[19] Hardly a wise arrangement, which Heth himself later admitted, saying he had been "careless."[20] Archer's Brigade came next—1,250 infantrymen comprising four regiments and one independent battalion. Davis' 11th Mississippi regiment remained in Cashtown to guard the division wagons.[21] The 1,800 officers and men in his other three regiments fell in behind Archer's troops.[22]

On command, Archer's and Davis' men shouldered their Enfield muskets[23] and took the first step on the Chambersburg Pike toward Gettysburg. Before long they would be eating dust from the caissons up ahead. It had drizzled earlier—one private called it "misty rain"[24]—but its dampening effect would soon be lost in the bright sunshine. To Captain Edward A. Marye, riding with his Fredericksburg Battery at the head of the long column, the march seemed as idyllic as any march could be. He recalled: "The morning was lovely, a soft, fresh breeze, rippled over ripe wheat fields stretching away on either side of us. And we moved forward leisurely smoking and chatting as we rode along, not dreaming of the proximity of an enemy."[25] An officer in Pettigrew's Brigade declared: "I never saw troops in better spirits, everybody seemed lively."[26]

When Pettigrew's Brigade countermarched from Gettysburg the day before, it had not returned to Cashtown, electing instead to bivouac along the Chambersburg Pike about two miles west of Marsh Creek. This morning the four North Carolina regiments awaited their turn to join the procession. As Davis' regiments marched past, several officers stopped to ask questions of Pettigrew's officers. They were told they would encounter only militia.[27]

With Davis' Brigade disappearing from view, Pettigrew's 2,700 officers and men filed onto the road and took up the march. About this time, back at Cashtown, Brockenbrough's Virginia Brigade was preparing to move out. With a total of 1,000 officers and men in three regiments and one battalion, it was Heth's smallest brigade. When it started for Gettysburg—Chaplain J. M. Meredith of the 47th Virginia reported it "proceeded very slowly"[28]—a total of approximately 7,150 unsuspecting Confederate troops, infantry and artillery, were on their way to keep a date with destiny.

Heth, after riding a few miles, received an astonishing message from General Lee. The courier handed him a dispatch, "ordering me to get the shoes even if I encountered some resistance."[29] This complete reversal on Lee's part is so unfathomable one might think Heth misread the message or, in retrospect, distorted it. But an incident, yet to be recounted, involving two of Heth's colonels, confirms that Heth did indeed receive such an order.

Although the word "shoes" never appears in Heth's after-action report, obtaining them in large quantity was, nonetheless, his most ardent hope as he set out for Gettysburg. For months the Southerners had been masking their desperate need by joking that the main reason for killing Yankees was to get their boots.[30] After the war, Heth himself stated that his purpose in going to Gettysburg was "to get shoes, not to fight." As to the battle he precipitated, he admitted he "stumbled into it."[31]

"...I feel at liberty to advance to Gettysburg...."

Major William Riddle, riding along a deserted road in the middle of the night, would not be sorry when the solitary journey was over. If his horse slackened its pace, no doubt he used his spurs. General Reynolds had sent him on the 12-mile ride to Meade's headquarters in Taneytown, Maryland. Now, with an order from the commanding general in his saddlebag, he retraced his route.

It was 4:00 a.m., July 1, when he arrived at Reynolds' headquarters in Moritz Tavern. There he found his chief, wrapped in a blanket, sound asleep on the floor. Riddle hesitated to disturb him, knowing he had had little solid rest in the past week. Was Meade's order sufficently urgent to justify waking his chief? He took the liberty of reading it and decided that it was.[32] The order, dated June 30, was directed to all corps commanders. Somewhat diffuse, it mingled fact with opinion and exhortation with instruction.[33] To thoroughly digest its six long paragraphs, Reynolds—still lying down—had Riddle read it through three times.[34]

The opening paragraph contained marching orders for the day. For Reynolds' left wing they were: First Corps to Gettysburg, Eleventh Corps to Gettysburg "or supporting distance," Third Corps to Emmitsburg. For Meade's own right wing: Second Corps to Taneytown, Fifth Corps to Hanover, Sixth Corps to Manchester, Twelfth Corps to Two Taverns.

In succeeding paragraphs there were specific instructions for the cavalry and the Signal Corps. The locations of the three Confederate corps, as then known, were cited. Then: "The general relies upon every commander to put his column in the lightest possible order." To that end, "all empty wagons, surplus baggage, useless animals, and impediments of every sort" were to be sent to the rear.[35] (Reynolds later informed Meade of his compliance.)[36]

In addition to the above, there was Meade's statement (already quoted) that he believed Harrisburg and Philadelphia had been relieved, a call for "vigilance, energy, and prompt response," and finally an admonition that "orders and movements from these headquarters must be carefully and confidentially preserved, that they do not fall into the enemy's hands."[37]

Reynolds may well have pondered all this for a few minutes before arising. When he got up he was, typically, fully alert and ready for action. As was his custom, he personally roused his staff.[38]

Meanwhile, the First Corps camps, from just north of Emmitsburg to the village of Greenmount, were coming to life. Certainly most, if not all, of the troops were up in time to witness the "blood red sunrise."[39] They had not been awakened by the strident notes of a bugle, however. Because of the proximity of the enemy, buglers had been ordered not to sound reveille. "The silence was ominous," one officer recalled.[40]

Breakfast for the 24th Michigan consisted of hardtack, pork, and coffee.[41] Some regiments presumably had salt beef in place of pork. In the 150th Pennsylvania, however, haversacks were empty, the regiment having lost contact with its commissary wagons several days earlier. Captain John Sigler of Company I had an idea how to feed his hungry men: buy and slaughter a sheep. But when he requested permission to do so, he was turned down. Not enough time for that, he was told.[42] In the 147th New York, Captain J. Volney Pierce had to be content with only two hardtack and a cup of black coffee.[43] In contrast, Captain F. B. Jones of the 149th Pennsylvania said he had a "hearty" breakfast.[44] What made it so, he neglected to say, but its source may have been a kind farmer.

It was in fact a farmer and his wife who provided a hearty breakfast for Reynolds and his staff that morning. The preceding afternoon Reynolds had handed sixteen-year-old Jacob Shriver a note and a pass to give to his parents. In the note Reynolds respectfully asked the couple to bring food in the morning for breakfast for him and his staff; the pass would allow them to come through Union lines. Before daylight Christian Shriver and his wife Alice set out in a wagon filled with food and all the implements needed to cook and serve it. Since Reynolds had requested only the delivery of provisions, making the meal was their considerate decision. Close to Moritz Tavern, they turned off the Emmitsburg road into a clearing known locally as "The Commons." Hurriedly, they unloaded everything and got down to work.

Soon Reynolds and his staff—their appetites surely whetted by the aroma of Mrs. Shriver's cooking—sat down to a huge breakfast of meat, eggs, potatoes, and fresh bread. After everyone had eaten his fill, Reynolds offered Mrs. Shriver five dollars, which she politely refused. "Take it," he insisted, "for I may not live to come back this way and reimburse you for your great kindness."[45]

About this time Reynolds had an unexpected visitor. Captain James Hall, commander of Battery B, 2nd Maine Light Artillery, reported the meeting. It was "quite early," he said, when General John Buford, accompanied by several troopers, rode up to Reynolds and his staff, who were "dismounted and sitting near my guns before we hitched up for marching."

Hall overheard Buford say to Reynolds: "I have run upon a couple of regiments of infantry near Gettysburg, which owing to their being in the woods, I am unable to dislodge, and I think you had better move up and feel them." During the night Buford's patrols, ranging a mile or so west of Marsh Creek, had discovered Pettigrew's camp. Hall listened closely as Reynolds immediately dictated a message to General Meade. As the battery commander remembered it, Reynolds said:

> Buford just now reports that he finds a small force of the enemy's infantry [actually it was four regiments] in a point of woods near Gettysburg, which he is unable to dislodge; and while I am aware that it is not your desire to force an engagement at that point, still, from the scope of instructions I have all the time had from you since commanding this wing of the army, I feel at liberty to advance to Gettysburg and develop the strength of the enemy at that point.[46]

To Reynolds, the Confederate occupation of his own state was an abomination no more to be tolerated than a pig in the parlor. Thus the development reported by Buford was, in one sense, good news: It offered an opportunity to take the first step in ousting the despised intruder. Anxious to close with the enemy, Reynolds changed the marching order.

In normal rotation Wadsworth's division, which had led the First Corps march on June 30, should have marched last this day. But, since it was the nearest of the three divisions to Gettysburg, Reynolds had it march first again.[47] He personally notified Wadsworth of the change, whereupon Wadsworth sent orderlies to inform the regimental commanders. (The 14th Brooklyn's Colonel Fowler noted that he received the message about 7:00.)[48]

Before the march began, Reynolds heard from General Howard in Emmitsburg. After acknowledging Meade's order "to move within supporting distance of you," he proposed that two of his Eleventh Corps divisions take an alternate route to avoid congestion on the Emmitsburg road. "Unless you desire otherwise," he continued, he would reassemble his command "near the cross-roads, about two miles this side of Gettysburg."[49]

Reynolds agreed to the proposal. In reply, he merely added that Howard should proceed with all possible speed.[50] Major Riddle was assigned to relay the message. Only recently returned from Taneytown, he now rode to Emmitsburg.[51] Reynolds dispatched another aide to General Sickles, in the vicinity of Bridgeport, with instructions for the Third Corps' march to Emmitsburg.[52]

Reynolds also sent a message to Meade, assuring him that all horses and wagons not immediately needed were being sent to the rear. "The First and Eleventh Corps," he added, "will occupy the road from here to Gettysburg today, but they [the wagon trains] may be able to come up some time this evening."[53]

Abner Doubleday, having been summoned by Reynolds, arrived at Moritz Tavern at 7:30. By then, Reynolds (like Heth at Cashtown a few hours earlier) was extremely anxious to get his troops moving. But that had to be delayed until he had briefed his First Corps commander. Reynolds began by reading him the latest dispatches, so that Doubleday would be aware of the overall tactical situation. Next, he informed him that Wadsworth's division and Hall's Battery had already been ordered to move out, and he, Reynolds, would ride with them. Then he gave Doubleday his orders: Call in the pickets; assemble the remaining artillery; bring up the Second and Third Divisions plus the artillery. Lastly, he told Doubleday to join him when all these orders had been fulfilled. Without further ado, Reynolds mounted his horse and rode off. Doubleday never saw him again."[54]

The sun had reappeared after a brief interval of drizzling rain. It was quite pleasant then, but the foot soldiers forming in column on the Emmitsburg road could tell it would soon be hot and humid.[55]

While most regiments had mustered for pay the previous day, the 19th Indiana's enlisted men lined up for theirs this morning.[56] In the 24th Michigan, the troops gathered for a prayer service. Even as Chaplain William Way invoked God's blessing, sergeants were busily passing out ammunition to every soldier.[57] Colonel Charles S. Wainwright, meanwhile, was engrossed in paperwork for his artillery brigade. He was still working on status reports when he received Doubleday's order to prepare to march.[58]

Sometime before the march began, a sergeant of Cooper's 1st Pennsylvania Battery was sent to Stewart's 4th United States Battery. After accomplishing his mission, he stopped to talk with a group of Stewart's men, who saw at once that he was deeply troubled. His home was nearby, he said—which accounted for his obvious distress. "You are Wisconsin, Indiana, Michigan and New York boys," he continued, "and maybe you don't know how a Pennsylvanian feels when he may have to fight tomorrow in his mother's dooryard!"

The artillerymen allowed that maybe they didn't, but they swore they would stand by him "until hell froze over."[59]

"...a great battle was impending."

West of Willoughby Run, Gamble's pickets were alert for any enemy movement eastward. On both sides of the Chambersburg Pike a mile and a half beyond the run, a squadron of 8th Illinois cavalry stood guard on Whisler's Ridge. Several of their number manned an advance post some 300 yards ahead of the main force. Pickets from the 3rd Indiana and 12th Illinois Regiments extended the 8th Illinois' line northward. The 8th New York sent out patrols to scout the area south of the Chambersburg Pike in the direction of Fairfield.[60]

East of Willoughby Run and north of Gettysburg, Devin's pickets were alert for any enemy movement southward. Colonel William Sackett of the 9th New York had overall control of the line[61]—actually an enormous loop extending from the Chambersburg Pike at Willoughby Run to the York road on the opposite side of Gettysburg. Over its course the loop intersected the Mummasburg, Carlisle, Harrisburg, and Hunterstown roads, all of which offered the enemy access to Gettysburg.[62] Sackett had posted a squadron from his own regiment on high ground astride the Harrisburg road and a dozen more troopers on the Hunterstown road.[63] Three miles north of Gettysburg, a 17th Pennsylvania battalion under Major J. Q. Anderson guarded the Carlisle road.[64] Troopers of the 6th New York blanketed the sector between the Mummasburg road and the Chambersburg Pike. And vedettes from every regiment provided liaison between the picket posts.[65]

All these men had been vigilant but had seen no sign of the enemy for many long hours. Then, shortly after daybreak, Major Anderson's pickets spotted a contingent of Rebel skirmishers coming down the Carlisle road. In quick succession Anderson ordered his men to fall back, called for reinforcements, and sent word to division headquarters that an advance element of Ewell's Corps was headed toward Gettysburg. When his men had retreated about two miles and the reserves had joined them, they all dismounted, sent their horses to the rear, and took cover behind a stone wall. As soon as the enemy came within range, the Union cavalrymen opened fire. A brisk exchange ensued, with both sides holding their ground.

About this time a civilian walked up to the commander of the 17th Pennsylvania Cavalry. Colonel Josiah Kellogg noted the man was well up in years, wore a Quaker hat, and carried a cornstalk cane. He asked him his business. The old man replied that he had a message for him and, forthwith, drew a spindled piece of paper from the end of his hollow cane. Opening the paper, Kellogg read the note scrawled on one side. It stated that Ewell's Corps was within a short day's march of Gettysburg, and all indications were that it would march there this very morning. Was this bit of gratuitous intelligence reliable? Kellogg had confirmation that it was even as he was questioning the old man. Just then the trooper sent by Major Anderson rode up and reported the brush with Rebel skirmishers. Most alarming was his report of a large body of enemy troops—Ewell's!—advancing on the 17th Pennsylvania's front and right.[66]

About this same time, two troopers of the 9th New York had a close call. Entering Hunterstown, Tom Smith and Marcus Hall spied four Rebels lounging in their saddles outside a hotel. Not liking the odds, they instantly swung their horses around and left the town faster than they had come. They could only hope they had not been spotted. After putting what they thought was a safe distance between themselves and the enemy, they stopped at a farmhouse to inquire how many Confederates were in the vicinity. Told there were about three hundred, they rode on. A little later one of them looked

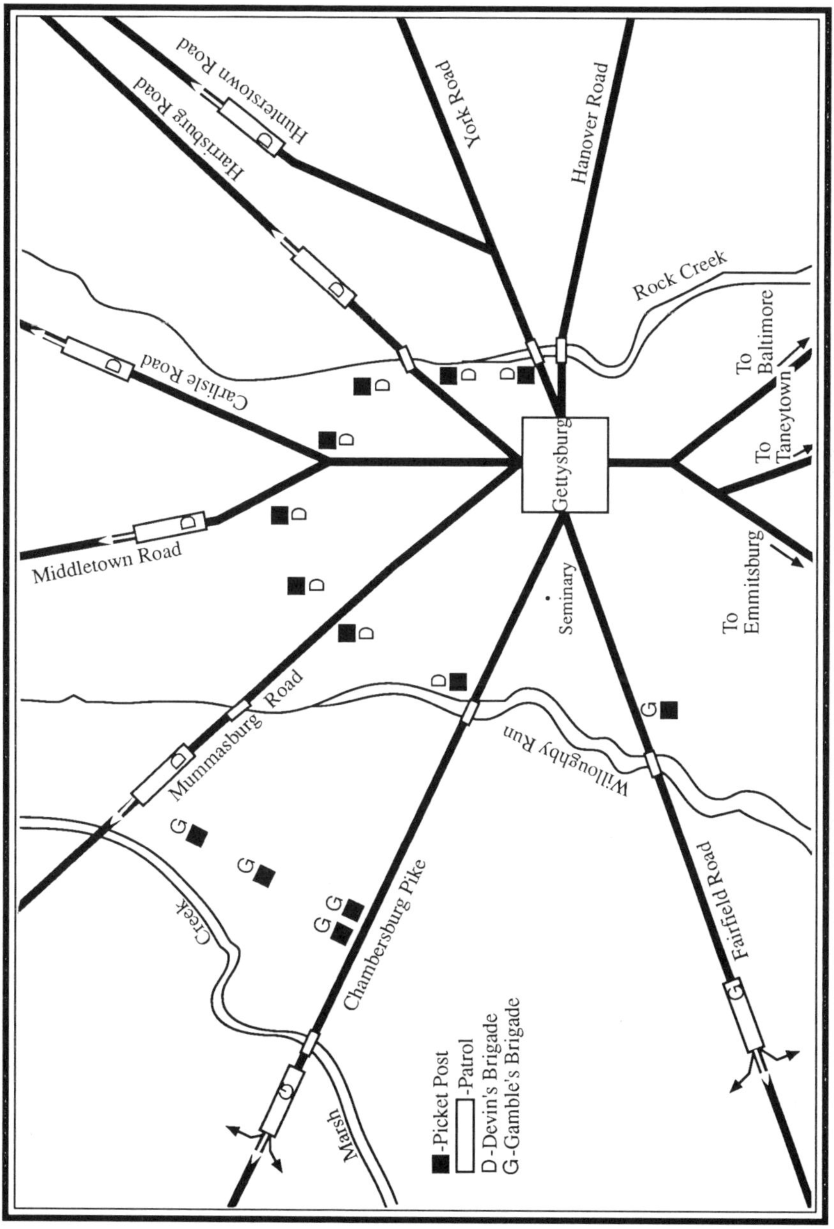

Buford's pickets and patrols, June 30 - July 1, 1863

back...and his heart skipped a beat. They were being pursued by the same Johnny Rebs they had seen outside the hotel! Digging in their spurs, they raced up a hill and—with rare good luck—just as they reached the crest, they saw a sizable Union patrol coming up the other side. Alerted to the approaching Rebels, these horsemen swooped down the hill and captured all four.[67] Other Union patrols on the Harrisburg road also reported seeing Confederates approaching from the north, but apparently none of these sightings resulted in a hair-raising experience such as befell Smith and Hall.[68]

When Colonel Sackett got word that Major Anderson's battalion was under fire from enemy skirmishers, he ordered all 6th and 9th New York units not otherwise engaged to rush to Anderson's aid.[69] Some troopers in Captain Timothy Hanley's 9th New York squadron were in the midst of watering their horses when the order came. Even so, Hanley's men were the first reinforcements to reach the scene. The squadron did not ride pell-mell into the fray, however. Before committing his men, Hanley sent Lieutenant A. C. Robertson with twenty men to determine the enemy's position and strength.

Finding the Rebels strongly posted on the Hoffman farm, north of the Mummasburg road, Robertson and his men pulled back across the road to the Forney farm. But the enemy was there too, as shots coming from behind the Forney farmhouse rudely informed them. Vaulting from their horses, Robertson's men crept up on the Rebels and with a few shots of their own succeeded in driving them off. That accomplished, they returned to the squadron, which in the meantime had dismounted and formed a line behind a stone wall.

Presently Hanley's troopers became aware of a rustling sound in their front. Looking closely, they could make out graybacks crawling through the wheat toward them. Daniel Cornish, squinting along the barrel of his carbine, waited for a clear shot. When that moment came, he squeezed the trigger—and one Southerner would never fight again. The perfect shot brought cheers from Cornish's comrades. The Confederate infantrymen—perhaps surmising the sudden outburst signalled a concerted charge—withdrew rapidly. When one of them got winded and paused behind a tree, Perry Nichols of Company F made a dash and took him prisoner.[70]

Nichols has been credited with taking the first Confederate prisoner in the three-day battle. But, if an 8th New York cavalryman's recollection of the time was accurate, there was an earlier capture. Alfred W. Davies, writing in 1889, said it was "just after daylight" when he and William Rollinson went on picket duty at a crossroads southwest of Gettysburg. There was a stream close by and the two Company F troopers they replaced paused there to let their horses have a drink before setting out for camp. Just then, two shots whistled by their heads and they skedaddled. Davies, however, spurred his horse in the direction of the firing and came upon two Rebels in the act of reloading. He described what happened next with a concision rare for his day: "I ordered them to surrender, which they did." Shortly, all 8th New York pickets were called in by the strident blare of a distant bugle. With two unhappy Rebels in tow, Davies and Rollinson returned to camp. Amid the ensuing confusion Davies soon lost track of his prisoners.[71] If he knew their unit affiliation, he failed to mention it.

Who were they? Hardly Ewell's men that far south, unless they were stragglers from Early's division, which had passed through Gettysburg five days before. More likely they belonged to Hill's Corps, possibly scouts.

In the skirmish north of town the 9th New York suffered its first fatality. Some Company G troopers, under a Sergeant Holcomb, had just closed a gap in the dismounted cavalry line when Rebels, who had been crouching behind a fence, suddenly rose up and opened fire, killing Corporal Cyrus W. James. Whether he was the first Union fatality in the battle, as has been claimed, is debatable.[72]

A 17th Pennsylvania surgeon, J. Wilson De Witt, reported that he was treating wounded soldiers before seven o'clock. The firing, he added, had begun two hours earlier.[73] Even if De Witt erred on the starting time by as much an hour, the skirmish north of Gettysburg began no later than 6:00 a.m. Admittedly, the fighting there had no bearing on the subsequent main action west of Gettysburg; but it was, nonetheless, the start of the three-day battle. As to which Union cavalry regiment fired the first shots, quite possibly it was the 17th Pennsylvania, whose pickets on the Carlisle road were furtherest north. Lieutenant Theodore Bean of that regiment later wrote: "It has always been asserted by the officers and men of [Major J. Q.] Anderson's command that they met the enemy in actual conflict on the Carlisle Road before the advance of Hill's Corps was struck by [Gamble's] First Brigade."[74]

Indeed, it could have been one of Major Anderson's men (his name lost to history) who fired the first shot in the Battle of Gettysburg. Over the years a number of claims for this distinction were made, each naming a certain Union cavalryman. (Not surprisingly, no Confederate ever sought credit for firing the first shot in a battle his side lost.) Only two claims merit serious consideration, and both involve Heth's advance on the Chambersburg Pike. Since Heth's Division started out at 5:00 a.m., at the earliest, and had to march at least five miles to be within firing range of Union pickets, the incidents related in these claims necessarily occured after the skirmish north of Gettysburg.

By the time Buford returned from his conference with Reynolds, the thick mist that blanketed the Gettysburg area at daybreak had completely disappeared. The sun now shone brightly and banks of cumulo-stratus clouds drifted overhead. The temperature at 7:00 a.m was 72 degrees; it would become hotter, and more humid, as the morning advanced.[75]

The action north of town had come as no surprise to the cavalry commander. Having "positive information of the enemy's position and movements," Buford had prepared even before his meeting with Reynolds to "entertain" the enemy until the First Corps arrived.[76] In fact, his cavalrymen not assigned to picket duty were "saddled and standing to horse by sunrise."[77] And his battery of horse artillery, under Lieutenant John H. Calef, had been alerted at its camp between Seminary and McPherson Ridges to limber up at a moment's notice.[78]

An incident that occurred early this morning further attests to Buford's conviction that engagement with the enemy was imminent. In the 9th New York, trooper A. R.

Mix was itching to get to town—to get those boots a resident had promised him the day before. But when he asked permission, he was turned down.

"Mix, I can't give you a pass," his company commander told him, "we are liable to move any minute. You go up and see General Buford and maybe he will give you a pass."

Buford listened sympathetically to the trooper's request. Then, turning to his adjutant, he told him to write out a pass. As that officer did so, Buford imparted a bit of advice: "Mix, you take all your belongings with you, for we'll be in line when you come back."

"Yes, sir," Mix replied. Clutching his pass, he hurried into town. As it turned out, the trip was a great success: He found the man who had made the offer and the boots fit perfectly.[79]

In the Confederate line of march Chaplain J. M. Meredith of the 47th Virginia rode with his brigade commander, Colonel John Brockenbrough, and his regimental commander, Colonel Robert Mayo. The trio had gone only a short distance when an aide rode up and announced excitedly, "General Heth is ordered to move on Gettysburg and fight or not, as he wishes." Thus Lee's order to Heth—simply to proceed with his mission even though he encountered some resistance—acquired a far more aggresive connotation in its translation to Heth's subordinates. After the aide rode ahead to relay the startling news to other unit commanders, Meredith overheard one colonel say to the other: "We must fight them; no division general will turn back with such orders."[80]

While Heth's top command had good reason to feel that a tussle with the enemy was more than likely, the men in the ranks had no such feeling. After marching three miles, Colonel Birkett D. Fry halted the 13th Alabama and ordered the regimental colors be uncased. According to Private E. T. Boland, this was the first intimation he and his comrades had that they might be going into battle.[81]

In contrast, at the Union advance picket post on the Chambersburg Pike, about 800 yards east of the Marsh Creek bridge, Privates George Sager and H. O. Dodge fully expected a fight. Through the night they had watched the enemy campfires flickering in the distance. "We felt sure," Dodge later wrote, "that a great battle was impending."[82] At 6:00 a.m. he and Sager were relieved by Privates James Hale and T. B. Kelley. Sergeant Levi Shafer was in charge of the post; he and his four men belonged to Company E, 8th Illinois. The rest of the company and its leader, Lieutenant Marcellus E. Jones, were positioned about 300 yards in their rear.[83]

Hale and Kelley had been on duty only about ten minutes when they noticed a small cloud of dust on the horizon. (Evidently the sun had completely dried the "misty rain" reported earlier.) The two men watched with mounting apprehension as the cloud grew larger and moved implacably toward them. By 7:00 they could discern a column of Confederate infantry with a flag flying out in front. (Heth apparently had come to his senses—perhaps on receiving Lee's order—and had pulled a body of infantry ahead of the artillery.) Since Sergeant Shafer was not in sight at that moment, Kelley dashed back to the main picket line to alert Lieutenant Jones. The 33-year-old officer, with a shout to his men to follow him, leaped on his horse and galloped off. Sergeant Shafer was anxiously waiting with his men when the lieutenant rode up. In the next few minutes the rest of Company E arrived. Jones was still forming his defensive line when George Sager exclaimed, "There they come!" Immediately Sager raised his carbine to fire.

"Hold on, George," snapped Jones. Jumping from his horse and handing the reins to Hale, he said, "Give me the honor of opening the battle." Then, grabbing Sergeant Shafer's carbine, he ran to a fence, steadied the weapon on a rail, and fired at the mounted officer halted beside the Marsh Creek bridge. As the range was 800 yards, predictably, Jones missed his target.[84] It was 7:30.[85]

While it was not the first shot of the battle, it was almost certainly the first shot fired against Heth's Division. The target was one W. Marion McCarty, six feet tall and an officer in Major Van de Graaf's 5th Alabama Battalion of Archer's Brigade. A colonel at war's end, he obviously held a lesser rank at Gettysburg, possibly that of captain. The erstwhile enemies, McCarty and Jones, met again, in 1890, at a veterans' reunion in Gettysburg. "It may be imagined," wrote H. O. Dodge, "that he [McCarty] and Lieut. Jones had a long and pleasant talk upon past events."[86]

"Tell the Johnnies we will be right along."

After briefing Doubleday at Moritz Tavern, Reynolds rode directly to Greenmount where Wadsworth was waiting for him.[87] By then the First Division was in a column of fours on the Emmitsburg road, ready to move out. The troops nearby watched as the two commanders dismounted, walked over to a bank along the road, sat down, spread out a map, and proceeded to study it. The impromptu conference soon ended and the march began.[88] It was 8:00.[89] With Federal troops now moving north toward Gettysburg and Heth's Confederates headed east toward the same place, a monumental collision was in the making.

Reynolds and Wadsworth, together with their staffs, rode out in front. Cutler's Second Brigade, Hall's Battery, and Meredith's First Brigade (the "Iron Brigade") followed, in that order. When all units were in motion, the column stretched nearly a mile on the Emmitsburg road.[90] Initially the pace was unhurried. In fact, one of Meredith's men wrote home that this morning the brigade marched "slowly."[91]

The Second brigade was minus one regiment, the 7th Indiana having remained in Emmitsburg to guard the division wagons. Thus Lysander Cutler had five regiments—a total of 1,650 officers and men—in line of march.[92] Front to rear, they were: 76th New York, 56th Pennsylvania, 147th New York, 95th New York, 14th Brooklyn. Cutler, accompanied by his staff and nineteen 147th New York men assigned to the headquarters guard, were in the van.[93]

The record is silent on whether the Brooklyn lads were wearing their red Zouave uniforms or the conventional blue ones on the march to Gettysburg. However, if their

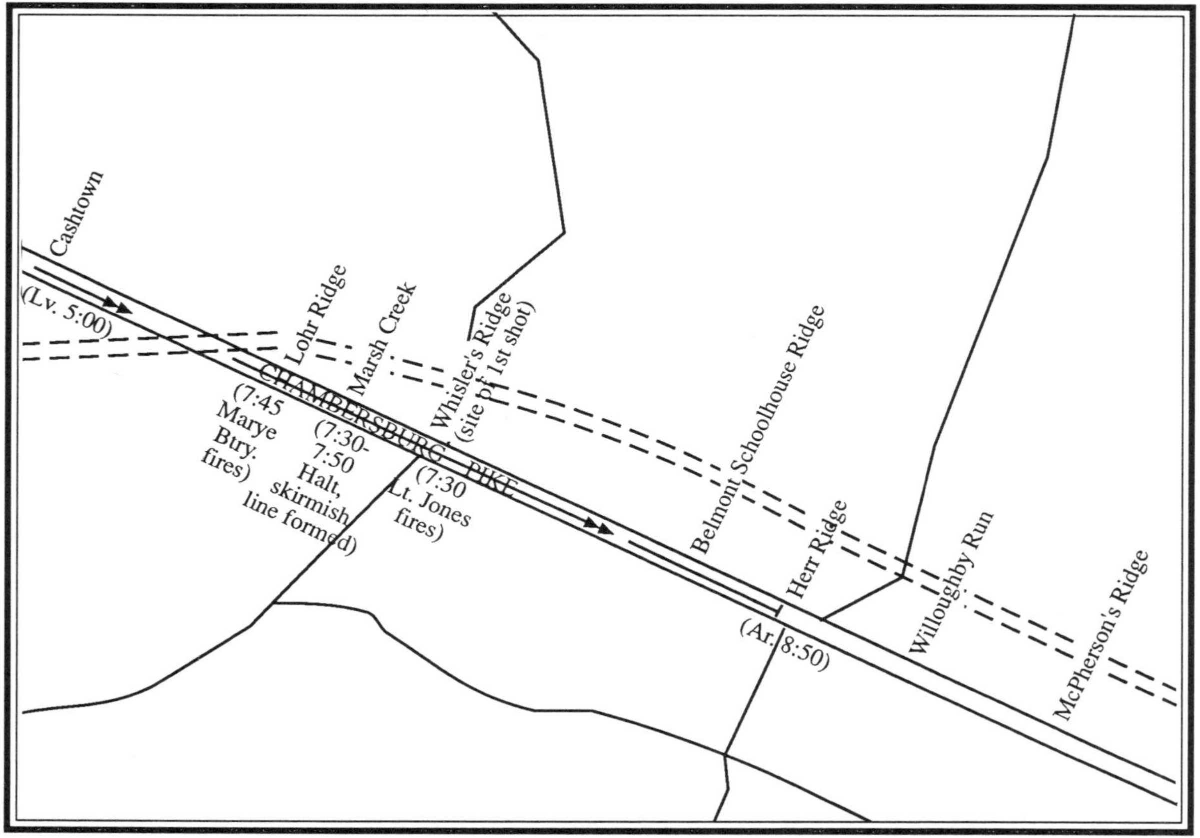

Heth's Division march — morning of July 1, 1863

commander, Colonel Edward B. Fowler, had any intimation they would see action this day, it would have been the billowy red trousers and the smart red caps. After a previous battle in which they had been caught in their blue uniform, he found out just how strongly they felt about the matter. As Fowler put it, in their view "if they were found dead they wanted to have the red breeches on." He had vowed then "never to take the regiment into action unless it wore its distinctive red uniform."[94]

Heading Solomon Meredith's First Brigade column was its most seasoned regiment—the 2nd Wisconsin, which had fought at First Bull Run in that long-ago summer of 1861. The 7th Wisconsin, 19th Indiana, 24th Michigan, and 6th Wisconsin followed, in that order. The brigade guard, comprising two officers and one hundred men (twenty from each regiment), brought up the rear.[95] Altogether, the brigade numbered 1,900 officers and men.

During the march, Colonel Wainwright rode forward to talk with General Reynolds.[96] The chief of the First Corps artillery wanted to find out Reynolds' opinion as to the likelihood of a fight this day. Wainwright personally did not expect one, and he learned that the wing commander was of the same mind. As Reynolds assessed the situation, the First Corps was "only moving up so as to be within supporting distance to Buford, who was to push out farther."[97]

According to Sergeant Cornelius Wheeler of the 2nd Wisconsin, the enlisted men of his regiment had no thoughts of imminent combat as they started out for Gettysburg.[98] Apparently this was true throughout the Iron Brigade. Lieutenant Colonel Dawes said of his 6th Wisconsin troops, "All were in the highest spirits." From time to time they burst into lusty song, though, as one of them grumped, "with about as much melody as a government mule."[99] Of the 24th Michigan soldiers, it was said they were positively "merry."[100]

To some extent, this feeling of well-being stemmed from a delectable rumor then making the rounds. It maintained that General George McClellan—ever the idol of the rank and file—was back in command. Surely some men were dubious, and indeed there was no truth to it. But the thought itself, the mere possibility, was enough to cheer them.[101]

The beautiful morning was certainly a factor. Many unit commanders commented on it, including Lieutenant Colonel Dawes (6th Wisconsin) and Major Alexander Biddle (121st Pennsylvania). A captain exulted that "Nature had put forth her loveliest colors." A drummer boy remembered how the air smelled "fresh and sweet with the scent of the new-mown hay."[102] One of Reynolds' aides, Captain Stephen Weld, complained that it was already "very muggy," but apparently for most men that negative aspect was overshadowed by all the favorable ones.[103] These were succinctly stated by Lieutenant Sidney G. Cooke of the 147th New York: "The road was excellent and unencumbered. Men were fresh from a day's rest and the influence of a perfect morning and a beautiful landscape inspirited them." Cooke added wistfully: "So accustomed to war had we become, that the incongruity of our martial display in such a scene was unnoticed."[104]

As Wadsworth's infantrymen marched past Stewart's battery, the foot soldiers took a good deal of heckling from the idle artillerymen. With mock solicitation, one cannoneer shouted, "Find a good place to camp." Another gibed, "Be sure and get near a good dry rail fence." Still another exclaimed, "Tell the Johnnies we will be right along." Such arrogance deserved to be put down—and it was. An infantryman snapped back: "Better stay here till we send for you; the climate up there may be unhealthy just now for such delicate creatures as you."[105]

But their high spirits were to dissolve in face of an anxiety that could no longer be dismissed. The Second Wisconsin's Sergeant Wheeler pinpointed its cause: "...we were all beginning to feel that we were getting near to Lee's army...that we were running a race with it, and that a battle could not be far off."[106]

Thus with apprehension mounting, Wadsworth's men pushed on, over the swells and troughs of the Emmitsburg road. Augustus Buell, a cannoneer in Stewart's battery, had a good view of the vast moving column and was struck by its resemblance to a surging sea. A quarter-century later, he recalled his vivid impression of "huge blue billows of men topped with a spray of shining steel." "The whole spectacle," he wrote, "was calculated to give nerve to a man who had none before."[107]

Abner Doubleday, meanwhile, was busy bringing up the Second Division and two brigades of the Third Division. (Stannard's Brigade of the latter division remained in Emmitsburg until late afternoon.) Robinson's two Second Division brigades and Stone's Brigade of Rowley's Third Division traveled the Emmitsburg road, while Biddle's Third Division Brigade followed a roughly parallel route on back roads. At 8:00, as Wadsworth's First Division began its march from Greenmount, Robinson's Second Division set out from its camp just north of Emmitsburg.[108] At that same hour Biddle's Third Division Brigade also got underway.

The preceding day, at Moritz Tavern, Biddle's Brigade and Cooper's Battery had turned onto Bullfrog road, marched a short distance, and then made camp. This morning they continued up Bullfrog road. After going about two miles, they turned onto a winding road that led across the covered bridge at Soch's mill and eventually connected with the Fairfield road near Willoughby Run. This longer route offered two advantages which more than compensated for the additional miles. Using it meant that the left flank of the other brigades was protected and the volume of traffic on the Emmitsburg road was thereby significantly reduced.[109]

Even so, Stone's Brigade, had to wait at its camp between Moritz Tavern and Marsh Creek, not only for its pickets to come in, but for all of Wadsworth's Division to move out. Therefore, most likely it was 9:00 before the road was clear and the brigade could get started.[110] Likewise, Robinson's Division, which in the meantime had come up behind Stone's Brigade, was also forced to wait. By the time Stone's rear regiment got underway and Robinson's troops could resume their march, it was probably 9:30.[111]

Once Doubleday had all 6,400 troops in four brigades of Second and Third Divisions moving forward, he rode ahead to check on the situation in First Division.[112]

It was around midnight when Major General Oliver Otis Howard got back to his Eleventh Corps headquarters in Emmitsburg after spending the evening at Moritz Tavern with General Reynolds. "It seemed I was hardly asleep," he recalled, when he was awakened at 3:30 to read a general order just in from Meade (the same one Reynolds received a half-hour later). Through a mix-up, this copy intended for Howard was addressed to Reynolds, but the corps commander did not hesitate to read it. As he explained, commanding officers read all dispatches, no matter to whom addressed, "lest they should fall into the hands of the enemy and be lost." He digested Meade's words, particularly noting that he was to move his corps to Gettysburg or within supporting distance of the First Corps. Then—unlike Reynolds, who got up after the order had been read to him—Howard went back to sleep for an hour or so.[113]

Upon arising, his primary concern was the inevitable congestion and consequent delay which would occur if all 8,000 of his troops were to follow the First Corps up the Emmitsburg road. This, he reasoned, could be largely avoided, if two of his three divisions took an alternate route east of the main one. He proposed doing so in a dispatch to Reynolds.

During the wait for Reynolds' reply, Howard instructed his division commanders to have their troops stand ready to march on a moment's notice. Also he sent a signal officer and several enlisted men to make a hasty reconnaissance of the Gettysburg area.[114] At about 8:00 Major Riddle arrived with Reynolds' approval of the alternate route. Soon the entire Eleventh Corps was moving forward, with Barlow's Division in the lead position. Schurz's and Steinwehr's Divisions marched about four miles on the Emmitsburg road, then turned right onto a country lane that met the Taneytown road at Horner's mills. At that junction they turned left and headed toward Gettysburg. Considering the unhampered passage on this route, the additional two miles it entailed were worth the extra effort.[115]

For two days, the Army of Northern Virginia had been concentrating its scattered forces. Reluctantly, Lee had recalled Ewell's Second Corps from their promising siege of Harrisburg, ordering it to proceed at once to "Cashtown or Gettysburg, as circumstances might require."[116] On the night of June 30 all three divisions were still north of either destination: Rodes' at Heidlersburg, Early's, three miles east of that town, Johnson's at Scotland.

At 7:30 this first morning of July, Rodes' Division, with Ewell and Rodes riding in front, started on the 14-mile trek to Cashtown. Whatever intelligence Ewell may have gained from his scouting parties between Heidlersburg and Gettysburg, it was not sufficiently compelling to dissuade him from going to Cashtown, which he knew to be Lee's preferred destination. However, about an hour into the march, a dispatch from General A. P. Hill changed his mind. When Ewell read that Hill had authorized Heth to go to Gettysburg, his first reaction may have been disbelief. Was Hill blind to the presence of Union cavalry there, and possibly infantry as well? Would Heth encounter more opposition than he bargained for? Would his division stumble into an ambush? Here, in Ewell's judgment, were "circumstances" (such as Lee foresaw might develop) that warranted changing course.

Having made up his mind, Ewell acted swiftly to insure that both Rodes' and Early's Divisions would swing southward at the first opportunity. Rodes' Division was then midway between Heidlersburg and Middletown (now Biglerville). Ewell ordered Rodes to continue on to Middletown, then take the Carlisle road to Gettysburg, seven miles away. He did not know where the head of Early's Division was, but he hoped to intercept it before it reached Heidlersburg and the intersection of the road linking Harrisburg with Gettysburg. The aide he sent racing to General Early arrived in time to divert the column onto the Harrisburg road. Several regiments in the rear of the column turned off onto a road east of Heidlersburg that also led to Gettysburg. Meanwhile, one of Ewell's aides, Major G. Campbell Brown, was riding at top speed to inform Lee of Rodes' and Early's altered course.[117]

With these 13,000 troops headed for Gettysburg, Lee's intention of coming to grips with Meade's army at Cashtown was doomed. Henry Heth, who, more than any other, was responsible for quashing that hope, acknowledged that Lee wanted to fight there, "with the [South] mountains at his back, so his flanks would be protected." Furthermore, as Heth himself believed, "There he could have whipped any army in the world."[118] Also lamenting Lee's thwarted intention was 15th Alabama's Colonel William C. Oates. In his view A. P. Hill was the culprit. "General Hill," he wrote, "inconsiderately blundered into the fight, and hence Ewell had to leave the road to Cashtown and go to his assistance, and after that day's terrible battle Lee thought it inexpedient to withdraw to Cashtown."[119] A Union officer, Jesse Bowman Young, concurred with the predominant Confederate view that Lee was right in seeking battle at Cashtown. From the perspective of fifty years, the former lieutenant in the 14th Brooklyn asserted: "He [Lee] could have fought here in a very strong position not easily flanked, with his back against the mountains, and with a clear road of retreat open in his rear...." In Young's opinion, a line facing east at Cashtown would have been "impregnable," and "had Lee simply planted himself here and waited a few hours, Meade would have been bound to attack him in that position."[120]

That Lee on July 1 still intended Cashtown as the hub of his operations is indicated in the order he wrote in Greenwood that morning to Brigadier General John D. Imboden in Mercersburg. Briefly stated, Imboden's cavalry was to proceed to Chambersburg that day, whereupon Pickett's Division would march to Greenwood. The next day Imboden's cavalry was to move to Greenwood and Pickett's infantry to Cashtown. In closing, Lee noted: "My headquarters for the present will be at Cashtown."[121]

As far as Lee knew at the time he wrote Imboden, the bulk of his army was converging on that obscure village: McLaws' and Hood's Divisions moving eastward from Fayetteville; Rodes' and Early's, westward from Heidlersburg; Johnson's, southeastward from Scotland; Anderson's, eastward from its bivouac between Greenwood and the Cashtown Pass. Pender's Division had reached South Mountain, just west of Cashtown, on June 30. This morning, instead of remaining at the center of the planned concentration, it was to follow Heth's Division to Gettysburg. The decision was made by General Hill, who may have had second thoughts about the possibility of enemy resistance to Heth's expedition. Pender's troops started down the mountain at about 8:00.[122]

Throughout the night of June 30, dispatches poured in to Union army headquarters in Taneytown, Maryland. From commanding officers, Meade received detailed reports of the day's operations combined with intelligence (both sound and questionable) about the enemy. Secretary of War Stanton apprised him of the latest information concerning Confederate activity that had come to his attention.[123] The conscientious commander of the Army of the Potomac was lucky if he got any sleep, for he would have read and pondered the significance of every communication.

Most alarming were the reports from Brigadier General Herman Haupt in Harrisburg. A masterful administrator of the military railroads, he also made it his business to ferret out what the Confederates were up to. At 10:30 p.m. and again at 12:45 a.m., he wired his latest findings to General in Chief Henry Halleck in Washington. Both times he sent a duplicate telegram to Major General Robert C. Schenck, Middle Department commander, in Baltimore. In the first message Haupt reported Confederate movements away from Harrisburg, Carlisle, and York, from which he deduced Lee's army was concentrating "at or near Chambersburg." The objective, he believed, was "a sudden movement against Meade, of which he should be advised immediately."

Schenck took it upon himself to notify Meade by courier. He then wired Halleck that he had done so and at the same time took the precaution of repeating Haupt's message in the event anything had prevented transmission of the original telegram. Later he sent his own assessment of the situation to Meade. It read: "Lee, I think, is either massing his troops, or making a general retreat toward Cumberland Valley. Most likely the former. They are so near that I shall not be surprised if a battle comes today."

Haupt, in the second telegram to Halleck, amended his earlier prediction. From information just received he was convinced that "the concentration of the forces of the enemy will be at Gettysburg rather than at Chambersburg. The movement on their part is very rapid and hurried. They returned from Carlisle in the direction of Gettysburg by way of the Petersburg pike." The reference was to Rodes' division, then en route to Heidlersburg. Haupt concluded: "Meade should, by all means, be informed, and be prepared for a sudden attack from Lee's whole army."

Once again Schenck forwarded the message to Meade. Although Meade would claim he received both of Haupt's messages at 3:00 a.m., it seems doubtful the second could have arrived that soon, even if (as Haupt suggested) the courier had traveled by Western Maryland Railroad from Baltimore to Westminster.

How did Meade react to the admonition, "be prepared for a sudden attack from Lee's whole army"? To judge from his subsequent orders, he was not nearly so convinced as Haupt. Yet eventually Meade did provide for a fall-back position in the event of that contingency. He disagreed with Haupt, however, on the point of concentration, believing it would be north of Gettysburg on a line between Chambersburg and York. As it turned out, both of Haupt's predictions proved accurate: The Confederates did concentrate at Gettysburg and did attack suddenly on July 1. Ironically, Lee intended neither.

At 6:00 a.m. the indefatigable Haupt sent a third telegram to Halleck. Longer than the earlier ones, it furnished details of enemy positions, movements, and strength. Haupt reiterated that Lee would suddenly concentrate and attack. It is not recorded that Meade received this message, but in any case it would have arrived too late to make any difference.[124]

At 7:00 a.m. Meade himself telegraphed Halleck. After informing him of the troop movements to be made this day and of Kilpatrick's "handsome fight" at Hanover the preceding day, he wrote:

> The point of Lee's concentration and the nature of the country, when ascertained, will determine whether I attack him or not. Shall advise you further today, when satisfied that the enemy are fully withdrawn from the Susquehanna. If General Couch has any reliable force, I shall call upon him to move it to aid me."[125]

(The reference is to Major General Darius N. Couch, commander of the Department of the Susquehanna, with headquarters in Harrisburg. His troops consisted largely of untrained, short-term militia.)

Evidently Meade was not yet committed to his defensive "Pipe Creek" plan when he sent the telegram; otherwise, he surely would have mentioned it to his superior. Thus it appears he composed the notorious "Pipe Creek" order sometime after 7:00. That such was the case is indicated in the context of the two documents. In the telegram he told Halleck he would advise him further "when satisfied that the enemy are fully withdrawn from the Susquehanna." The opening sentence of the "Pipe Creek" order discloses that this had been accomplished. He wrote: "From information received, the commanding general is satisfied that the object of the movement of the army in this direction has been accomplished, viz, the relief of Harrisburg, and the prevention of the enemy's intended invasion of Philadelphia, &c., beyond the Susquehanna."[126]

The tone of the entire order (even in third person) is far more positive than that of the telegram to Halleck. This is not to imply that Meade cast aside his habitual caution. Indeed the very next sentence exemplifies the trait: "It is no longer his intention to assume the offensive until the enemy's movements or position should render such an operation certain of success." Clearly, Meade was disposed to rest on his laurels for the present. But at the same time he realized that a sure plan of defense could be crucial. Accordingly, he proposed:

> If the enemy assume the offensive, and attack, it is his intention, after holding them in check sufficiently long to withdraw the trains and other impedimenta, to withdraw the army from its present position, and form line of battle [in Maryland] with the left resting in the neighborhood of Middleburg, and the right at Manchester, the general direction being that of Pipe Creek.

In addition, interspersed among specific instructions for the cavalry, artillery, quartermaster, chief signal officer, and corps commanders were these general exhortations:

> —[Commanders] should make themselves thoroughly familiar with the country indicated...so that no possible confusion can ensue, and that the movement, if made, be done with good order....
>
> —All the trains will keep to the right of the road...and, in case of any accident requiring a halt, the team must be hauled out of the line.
>
> —The commands must be prepared for a movement, and, in the event of the enemy attacking us on the ground indicated herein [the Pipe Creek line], to follow up any repulse.
>
> —All movements of troops should be concealed, and our dispositions kept from the enemy.

For years after the battle, Meade's critics—and there were many—continually harped on the "Pipe Creek" order, using it as evidence of weakness and vacillation, of a timorous predisposition to retreat from advanced positions in Pennsylvania to a defensive line in Maryland. Largely overlooked was one sentence in the nearly 1,000-word order that proves he had not totally closed his mind (as his critics alleged) to fighting on Pennsylvania soil. "Developments," he wrote, "may cause the commanding general *to assume the offensive from his present positions*"[127] (italics added). As it turned out, he took a defensive stance; he did not pull back any troops.

Meade deeply regretted the "Pipe Creek" order because of the furor it caused. Testifying before the Joint Committee on the Conduct of the War, he allowed that the order would have been different had he been aware of certain facts in Buford's messages to Reynolds and cavalry corps commander Alfred Pleasonton on the night of June 30. But this vital information, he told the Committee, did not reach him until "pretty late on the morning of the 1st of July."[128]

Sometime that morning Meade sent a lengthy message to his left wing commander. Since the dispatch was addressed to General Reynolds *at Gettysburg*, Meade obviously expected him to be there when his courier arrived after the two-hour ride from Taneytown. As he hardly expected Reynolds to arrive there before 9:00, most likely Meade composed the message after 7:00, and apparently before the "Pipe Creek" order. Indecisive, deferential, almost apologetic, it reflects the uncertainty that must have gnawed at the mind of the man entrusted with the fate of the Army of the Potomac. He wrote:

> GENERAL: The telegraphic intelligence received from General Couch, with the various movements reported from Buford, seem to indicate the concentration of the enemy either at Chambersburg or at a point situated somewhere on a line drawn between Chambersburg and York, through Mummasburg and to the north of Gettysburg.
>
> The commanding general cannot decide whether it is his best policy to move to attack until he learns something more definite of the point at which the enemy is concentrating.

This he hopes to do during the day. Meanwhile, he would like to have your views upon the subject, at least so far as concerns your position. If the enemy is concentrating to our right of Gettysburg, that point would not at first glance seem to be a proper strategic point of concentration for this army.

If the enemy is concentrating in front of Gettysburg or to the left of it, the general is not sufficiently well informed of the nature of the country to judge of its character for either an offensive or defensive position. The numbers of the enemy are estimated at about 92,000 infantry, with 270 pieces of artillery, and his cavalry from 6,000 to 8,000. Our numbers ought to equal it, and, with the arrival of General French's command, which should get up to-morrow, exceed it, if not too much weakened by straggling and fatigue.

The general having just assumed command, in obedience to orders, with the position of affairs leaving no time to learn the condition of the army as to *morale* and proportionate strength compared with its last return, would gladly receive from you any suggestions as to the points laid down in this note. He feels that you know more of the condition of the troops in your vicinity and the country than he does. General Humphreys, who is at Emmitsburg with the Third Corps, the general considers an excellent adviser as to the nature of the country for defensive or offensive operations. If near enough to call him to consultation with you, without interference with the responsibilities that devolve upon you both, please do so. You have all the information which the general has received, and the general would like to have your views.

The movement of your corps to Gettysburg was ordered before the positive knowledge of the enemy's withdrawal from Harrisburg and concentration was received.

Very respectfully, &c.,
S. WILLIAMS,
Assistant Adjutant General[129]

Was the battle, which so quickly mushroomed to cataclysmic proportions, unexpected? High-ranking Confederates said Yes. Colonel Edward P. Alexander, Longstreet's chief of artillery, stated: "In making this concentration [of the Army of Northern Virginia] Hill's corps unexpectedly came in collision with Reynolds' corps, and the thing began."[130] Brigade commander Cadmus M. Wilcox and Lee's aide Walter H. Taylor both agreed that chance had dictated the time and place of battle, and both blamed cavalry chief "Jeb" Stuart for it. The opposing forces, Wilcox contended, were "ignorant of the designs and proximity of each other. Had the cavalry been with the army Hill would have known the condition of affairs in his front and would have pushed Buford back and reached Gettysburg before the First and Eleventh corps moved from their camp at Emmettsburg [*sic*]."[131] Lieutenant Colonel Taylor asserted that, with Lee uninformed of the enemy's position and movements, a battle suddenly flared. In an oblique indictment of Stuart, he wrote: "An army without cavalry in a strange and hostile country is [like] a man deprived of his eyesight...."[132]

General Heth, though hardly contrite, did accept responsibility for the initial encounter. The battle, he admitted, "was the result purely of *an accident*, for which I am probably, more than any, accountable." Alluding to his mission to obtain sorely-needed shoes for his division, he continued: "Napoleon is said to have remarked that 'a dog fight might determine the result of a great battle.' Almost as trivial a circumstance determined the Battle of Gettysburg being fought at Gettysburg...." The action on July 1 was "without order or system," he contended, because "we accidentally *stumbled* into this fight."[133]

The British observer at Confederate Army headquarters, Colonel James A. L. Fremantle, stoutly affirmed: "I have the best reasons for supposing that the fight came off prematurely, and that neither Lee nor Longstreet intended that it should have been that day."[134]

Among those few who took exception to the predominant view was Union Lieutenant Walter Kempster. In a paper read October 1, 1913, the former 10th New York cavalryman maintained that the battle was *not* unexpected on either side. As to the Confederates, he cited Pettigrew's explicit warning to Hill, Heth, Archer, and Lee after his near-encounter on June 30. Further, he cited Hill's dispatch to Ewell on the morning of July 1, which prompted Ewell, anticipating enemy action, to march his corps to Gettysburg instead of Cashtown. As to the Federals, he argued: "Now, if the encounter of the armies was accidental, or entirely unexpected, why all the precaution on the part of Pleasonton and Buford?" Two days before the battle, Pleasonton had ordered Buford to move his division to Gettysburg, admonishing him to hold it "at all hazards." And Buford, on the night of June 30, had accurately predicted a fight in the morning and prepared for it accordingly.[135]

The jocose speculation that appeared in the *New York Times* on Sunday, June 28, also came true. It read: "The return game between the Army of the Potomac and the Army of [Northern] Virginia may be played this week."[136]

After being warned twice by General Haupt, Meade, though still doubtful, had to at least admit the possibility of a major battle that day. Until then he was not remotely expecting one—not that soon. Writing to his wife on the evening of June 30, he exulted, "All is going well. I think I have relieved Harrisburg and Philadelphia, and that Lee has now come to the conclusion that he must attend to other matters."[137] He knew of course that Lee would adopt some new strategy; but there is no indication in the letter that he thought a full-scale battle imminent. His son (also named George) theorized that his father's troop movements "compelled Lee to concentrate somewhere." And "somewhere" he went on to define as being within the rough parallelogram bounded by Chambersburg, Heidlersburg, Pipe Creek and Emmitsburg.[138]

The question remains: Why Gettysburg? To Civil War historian Bruce Catton, it was simply "because the roads led them there."[139] Lieutenant Colonel Henry C. Bankhead, who was brevetted for his actions at Gettysburg, declared flatly: "No one selected Gettysburg; the two armies met and immediately prepared for action."[140]

CHAPTER IV

BUFORD HANGS ON

"The Johnnies are coming!"

Initially, Heth's march from Cashtown was about as idyllic as an infantry march could be. Sunshine, light breeze, good road, unhurried pace, and a natural beauty to beguile every eye. Most impressive were the opulent Pennsylvania Dutch farms—the huge barns, cozy farmhouses, sleek cows, neat orchards, cool woodlots, and shimmering fields of wheat and corn. A contemporary visitor to this area remarked: "I have seen few views in Italy which exceed it in romantic beauty."[1] But, for the Southern wayfarers this morning, the crack of the single shot from Lieutenant Jones' carbine shattered their idyll.

Seconds later the command "Halt!" rippled from front to rear of Archer's column, continuing through Davis' column and Pegram's batteries. Henry Heth was fearful he "might be attacked in force before proper dispositions could be made. I thought we had struck a column of infantry, and was cautious." It took "some lively work," he recalled, "to get my artillery and advance troops in position."[2] In Archer's Brigade the 140 men of Major A. S. Van de Graaff's 5th Alabama Battalion dashed across the Marsh Creek bridge and deployed in a skirmish line south of the Chambersburg Pike. Lieutenant Will Crawford and about sixty men of the 13th Alabama Regiment followed them into line.[3] In Davis' brigade the 55th North Carolina threw out a skirmish line north of the pike. No sooner had all these troops deployed when they heard the boom of a cannon somewhere in their rear.[4] (Although no one then would have thought of that artillery shot as having any special significance, it was the very first of tens of thousands fired in the Battle of Gettysburg.)

Pegram's artillery battalion had halted just short of Lohr's Hill.[5] Major William Johnson Pegram (still pale from his recent illness) and the men around him had debated the identity of soldiers visible in their right front but too far off to discern the color of their uniforms. The prevailing opinion was that they belonged to Longstreet's corps, which they assumed to be advancing on a parallel road. But this view was dispelled by a sergeant who had returned to his battery the day before. He had passed that corps and could assert that it was still far behind them. That settled the matter for "Willie"

Pegram: The obscure figures must be Yankees! (They were in fact Buford's pickets.) Without further ado, he ordered Captain Edward Marye of the Fredericksburg Battery to run one of his 3-inch ordnance rifles up the hill and open fire.

As the gun was being unlimbered, a distraught farmer stormed out of his house. "My God!" he yelled, "you are not going to fire here, are you?" Seeing that that was precisely what they were going to do, he threw up his hands in despair and went back into his house. Captain Marye watched as the first shell burst high above the enemy on Whisler's Ridge. He was gratified to see the Yankees scramble for cover, but for good measure, he had the gun crew fire several more rounds.[6]

Besides scattering enemy pickets, the brief shelling had an unintended result: A non-combatant was literally frightened to death. Ephraim Whisler's home and blacksmith shop stood near Lieutenant Jones' advance picket post. This morning, with blue-coated troopers practically on his doorstep, it seems unlikely Whisler even started up his forge. In any case, he would have ceased whatever he was doing when he heard Jones' carbine shot. Then, when he heard cannon fire, he apparently decided to investigate. Just as he opened his gate and stepped onto the road, one of Marye's shells landed close by, plowing up the road and showering him with dirt. The shock was too much for him. As the *Gettysburg Compiler* put it some days later, "He took to his bed soon afterwards and never rose from it."[7]

By 8:00 on the morning of July 1 Heth's long skirmish line had begun to inch forward. The rest of Archer's and Davis' brigades, still in column on the Chambersburg Pike, followed at an interval of about one hundred paces.[8] The terrain now required greater effort from men and horses alike. The flat stretch east of Cashtown had given way to a series of steep north-south ridges that ran up to and beyond Gettysburg. Before noon the two brigades would climb no fewer than five of them.

Beyond the need for shoes, Heth's purpose in going to Gettysburg was (in his words) "to feel the enemy; to make a forced reconnaisance, and determine in what force the enemy were—whether or not he was massing his forces on Gettysburg."[9] As the march resumed, though a brush with the enemy now seemed both likely and imminent, he was not worried about fulfilling his mission.

Lieutenant Jones, on the other hand, had every reason to be worried. Without reinforcement, his situation was hopeless. He sent a message to Captain H. E. Dana, commander of the other company in the squadron, to bring up his troopers at the utmost speed. Although Dana responded at once, en route he received another urgent summons from Jones. When he arrived on the scene and saw the enemy's broad skirmish line and behind it masses of infantry moving into the woods, he fully comprehended Jones' anxiety.

Dana immediately dispatched a rider to apprise the squadron leader, Captain Daniel Buck, of their desperate plight. But until Buck arrived, it was his responsibility, as senior officer on the field, to lead the squadron. He certainly realized he had no chance of stopping the Rebels. Yet he had to try, and in the attempt delay them as long as possible.

Quickly scanning the terrain for the best place to form his line, Dana decided on a certain rail fence a short distance in the rear. Pointing to it, he ordered his company to ride there and deploy in a dismounted line. He ordered Jones' company to do likewise. The horses, accompanied by one trooper for every four steeds, were sent farther to the rear. With one-fourth of his men acting as horseholders, Dana had at most eighty men to put in line. With 30-foot gaps between them, he realized how precarious his position was. Would support come in time—or would his whole line be swallowed up?[10]

The Confederate brigades, meanwhile, were filing into the woods on either side of the Chambersburg Pike—Archer's to the right, Davis' to the left. Before the deployment was completed, the skirmishers out front opened fire.[11] Dana's Union cavalrymen, waiting expectantly with carbines steadied on fence rails, immediately unloosed a long-range volley. After that concerted outburst, they loaded and fired at will. According to Dana, they maintained such a rapid fire that they "induced the belief of four times the number of men actually present, as we learned from prisoners taken soon afterward."[12] Nevertheless, outnumbered as they were, it was simply a matter of time until they were forced to give way. When that moment came, they pulled back a couple hundred yards, hastily formed a line (taking advantage of any cover that offered), and resumed firing. Again and again, as the enemy drew close, the tactic was repeated.

At some point during the gradual withdrawal Dana's troopers were bolstered by the arrival of another 8th Illinois squadron. Captain Buck had relayed Dana's message to the regimental commander, Major John L. Beveridge, as well as to Colonel Gamble. Beveridge, unaware that Gamble had already been notified, had galloped off to inform that brigade commander and also General Buford of the skirmish then in progress and to urgently request reinforcements. Failing to find either commander quickly, Beveridge took decisive action himself. First, he sent one of his own squadrons flying to the aid of Dana's men. Second, he dispatched orderlies to spread the news throughout Buford's division of the approach of a strong Confederate force.[13]

While the 8th Illinois squadrons harrassed Archer's 5th and 13th Alabama skirmishers, to the north a 12th Illinois squadron was making it hot for Davis' 55th North Carolina skirmishers. In fact, the Carolinians had to call up reinforcements in a hurry.

Major Pegram, after firing one gun from Lohr's Hill, made two further attempts to scare the Federals into headlong flight. But neither the shelling from Whisler's Ridge nor the one from Belmont Schoolhouse Ridge succeeded. The Union cavalrymen were too tough to be routed that easily.[14]

Two civilians accidentally wandered into the midst of the conflict. Mrs. Joseph Bayly and her Uncle Robert had set out from the Bayly farm to learn what they could of the military situation. Coming upon Union troopers, they had begun to ply them with anxious questions when suddenly a cannon roared and a shell screamed over their heads. That shock was bad enough, but an even greater one was in store. As Mrs. Bayly recalled it, "As if by magic, thousands of men rose from the earth in the direction in which we had been going...." Her exaggeration is excusable; surely in that instant it seemed like thousands. The very next instant she and her uncle headed for home, "the roar of battle adding terror to our flight."

As luck would have it, they encountered Confederates on the way. Halted, they were told the man would be held prisoner. "You hurry home as fast as possible," Robert told his niece, "I am old and they won't keep me long." Reluctantly she left him, but had not gone far when, again, she met some of the enemy and was ordered to halt. *Where are the damn Yankees? How many are there?* they demanded. A flash of anger momentarily stifled Mrs. Bayly's fears. "Go on and you will soon find out," she snapped. "I did not stop to count them."

By then desperately hoping to avoid another confrontation, she took a short cut across familiar fields. But, a third time, Confederates blocked her path and this time she was taken prisoner. Apparently her captors reconsidered, however, as she was detained only a few minutes. When she finally got home, she found her two teen-age sons "in great distress" about her.[15]

It so happened the Bayly boys had just returned from a high adventure of their own. They and a cousin had been picking wild raspberries on Whisler's Ridge when they were startled by a loud boom. *Cannon! Must be fighting nearby!* they concluded. And, like all red-blooded boys, they were not going to miss out on any excitement. The possibility of danger to themselves never occurred to them. Bolting from the raspberry patch (where they could see nothing), they ran to a fence near Whisler's blacksmith shop and hopped up on it. Shortly—from front-row seats, as it were—they saw a grand spectacle. A grown Billy Bayly remembered it vividly:

> ...we noticed up the road, coming over the nearest hill great masses of troops and clouds of dust; how the first wave swelled into successive waves, gray masses with the glint of steel as the sun struck the gun barrels, filling the highway, spreading out into the fields, and still coming on and on, wave after wave, billow after billow."

With wide-eyed wonder the boys continued to watch until—with bullets flying and Rebels drawing closer by the second—they felt their situation had become "too hot for comfort." Even then, they were more sobered than scared. As Billy quaintly put it, they returned home "not riotously or in confusion, but decorously."[16]

Although the bold sparring of Gamble's pickets failed to stop Heth's advance, its contribution was invaluable. Precious time was gained by their dogged resistance—time for Buford to establish a defensive position on McPherson's Ridge and time for Wadsworth's infantry division to come up.

On the left of Devin's picket line, a 6th New York squadron barely escaped being outflanked and captured by an unidentified enemy force. "It was supposed we were gobbled up," said Captain William Heermance. Luckily, however, someone had had the "unusual foresight" to bring up the horses and "we left to care for ourselves as best we could." In short, they skedaddled.[17]

From the east bank of Willoughby Run, four 9th New York pickets spied dim figures nearly a mile ahead on the Chambersburg Pike. Corporal Alpheus Hodges was in charge, and neither he nor his companions could tell, at that distance, whether the men they saw were Rebels. But prudence dictated he assume they were and respond in strict compliance with his orders. Thus, instructed to alert all of Devin's pickets if the enemy was sighted, he sent one trooper to the right of the picket line, another to the left, and the third to the picket reserves. Then, Hodges rode up Herr Ridge, going just far enough to positively identify the approaching soldiers as Confederates. As he wheeled his horse around for the return trip, a couple of bullets whistled past his ears and he fairly flew back across Willoughby Run. Reining in just beyond the bridge, he jumped from his horse and grabbed his carbine. Rattled by his close call, the twenty-year-old corporal then quite forgot that he and his men had been ordered not to use their weapons under any circumstance. Crouching behind the stone bridge in the ravine of Willoughby Run, Hodges fired several shots in angry, but futile retaliation.[18]

A 3rd Indiana trooper had a similarly unnerving encounter. The incident would never have occurred had Tom Day's steed not been so persnickety. When the horse refused to drink from Willoughby Run, Day decided to look for water elsewhere. Riding west, he stopped at a farm with a convenient drinking trough. The trough water, it turned out, suited his horse just fine. But, before its thirst was assuaged, Day heard rifle fire on his right. The next moment, coming over the brow of a hill, he saw... graybacks! Instantly he jerked the animal's head out of the trough and applied his spurs. Horse and rider plunged down Herr Ridge and across Willoughby Run. As soon as Day came within hailing distance of his Company E comrades, he shouted, "The Johnnies are coming!"[19]

Indeed they were. As the Confederate skirmish line ascended Belmont Schoolhouse Ridge, an artillery officer rode up to General Heth and told him he saw what appeared to be mounted enemy troops in the woods about a half mile ahead. Drive them out! was Heth's testy reply. Marye's battery, being first in line, naturally got the assignment. Its two 3-inch rifles were rushed forward 400 hundred yards to the top of the next ridge. There, on Herr Ridge, the guns were unlimbered in the road, then dragged by hand a short distance into a field on the right. The skirmishers and the troops behind them had a brief rest while the two gun crews each lobbed four or five shells into the woods on McPherson's Ridge. (Later, a false rumor circulated among the Confederates that General Reynolds was killed in this barrage.) When there was no reply from the Federals, Heth's infantrymen resumed their slow advance.[20]

About this time a farmer in shirt sleeves and leather apron burst out of his cellar to find out why his dog was barking so persistently. Startled to find enemy soldiers in his own yard, he demanded an explanation. A 5th Alabama soldier told him General Hill had sent them to drive back the Yankees and warned him to expect heavy fighting.

"Tell General Hill to hold up a little," the farmer begged, explaining that his cow was out in the pasture and he wanted to bring her in before the fight began.[21]

After Tom Day's shrill warning, 3rd Indiana buglers sounded "Saddle and Mount." Since his Company E was alerted first, it was first to move out. Clattering over Willoughby Run bridge, these troopers rode to the farm where Day had seen the enemy while watering his horse. There they deployed. Soon their attention riveted on a lone figure riding down Herr Ridge. It was one of Buford's pickets, badly wounded and bleeding profusely. His horse, once white, had turned red![22]

As Buford's pickets were gradually pushed back to Willoughby Run, Heth's skirmish line moved to Herr Ridge (which overlooks the run) and halted at the crest. Archer's Brigade soon trudged up the slope and halted behind the skirmishers. Just ahead, in plain view, was a cluster of buildings dominated by an L-shaped, two-story, red brick tavern.

In 1863 Herr Tavern, with adjacent livery stable and blacksmith shop, had been acccomodating travelers for nearly half a century. Opened in 1815 by one Thomas Sweeney, the hostelry (then known as Sweeney Inn) became a popular stopover for settlers headed west. By 1826, however, Sweeney had serious financial problems. Before that year ended he declared bankruptcy and the inn closed. Two years later Frederick Herr bought the property and had operated it (evidently on a solvent basis) ever since.[23]

Shortly after Archer halted his brigade on the ridge named for the tavern keeper, Heth came up to his brigadier and brusquely ordered him to continue the advance. Archer demurred. Davis' Brigade had not yet reached Herr Ridge, and Archer—more wary than Heth—felt his brigade was too light to proceed unsupported against an

Major General Henry Heth launched a two-brigade attack on Buford's cavalry division on the morning of July 1, 1863, from the ridge on which the Herr Tavern stands.

Two post-Civil War views looking west along the Chambersburg Pike from McPherson's Ridge. In the top photo the Herr Tavern is visible in the distance. Below: Note the Toll House in the center.

enemy of unknown strength.[24] Acceding to Archer's view, Heth decided instead to shell the woods on his right front for thirty minutes and, meanwhile, to deploy both brigades in battle line, Archer's on the right of the Chambersburg Pike and Davis' on the left. These actions started at about 9:00.[25]

Pegram's artillerymen hopped to their tasks. Quickly they maneuvered ten Napoleons, five 3-inch rifles, and two 10-pound Parrotts into position at scattered sites on two ridges, Belmont Schoolhouse and Herr. (One 3-inch rifle had been disabled coming into position; the two 12-pound howitzers were brought into action later.) With their pieces trained on McPherson's Ridge, they rammed home powder charges followed by shot or shell. Crew chiefs yanked lanyards and deadly missiles hurtled through the air in rapid succession. Heth had ordered Pegram's batteries to "whale away," and so they did.[26]

Amid all the racket and smoke, Archer's men waited for Davis' Brigade to catch up. When it did, Archer ordered his four regiments and one battalion to cross over the crest, swing south, and deploy in line. The 1st Tennessee, in column of fours, led the march; it took the position closest to the Chambersburg Pike and the other units leapfrogged past it.[27] For Davis' regiments there was no rest; on reaching Herr Ridge, they were rushed into line north of the Pike. When all units were in place, the order of Heth's line from left to right was: 55th North Carolina, 2nd Mississippi, 42nd Mississippi, 1st Tennessee, 13th Alabama, 5th Alabama, 14th Tennessee, 7th Tennessee. With nearly 3,000 troops thus arrayed for battle, Heth felt reasonably confident, even though he was still in the dark as to the size and disposition of the enemy facing him.[28]

By this time Buford's retreating pickets had their backs to Willoughby Run.[29] With shells continually screaming over their heads, it must have dawned on some of them, at least, that this was going to be more than a mere skirmish. To this point they had done remarkably well; because of their dogged resistance, it had taken the enemy an hour and a half to advance approximately a mile and a half. Still, as G. W. Hosmer summarized the action in his dispatch to the *New York Herald Tribune*, for the Yankee cavalrymen it had been "a pretty sharp brush."[30]

Even as Archer's and Davis' Brigades were forming their battle lines, Heth's other brigades, under Pettigrew and Brockenbrough, were coming up in support. So, too, were Pender's infantry division and McIntosh's artillery battalion. As his guns rumbled down South Mountain and started for Gettysburg, Major David G. McIntosh, became sharply aware of a difference in the atmosphere, a difference in the mood of his men. "The smell of battle was already in the air," he remembered, "and the jocularity which always attends the early stages of a march was tempered by a secret feeling that serious business was ahead."[31]

The prediction Buford had made to Devin the night before was coming true. The enemy *had* come "booming," and Buford's troopers would have to "fight like the devil" to hold their position until the Union infantry arrived. Early this morning Reynolds had consented to "move up and feel" the enemy that the cavalry patrols had discovered in bivouac west of Marsh Creek. Buford knew he could count on a prompt response. Yet, there remained the niggling question: Would his cavalrymen be able to hold on long enough? Buford—never one to dwell on negative possibilities—plunged into organizing the defense of McPherson's Ridge.

Probably the earliest indication he had that the enemy had decamped and was moving in his direction came from his signal officer stationed in the cupola of the Lutheran Theological Seminary. Scanning the western horizon through field glasses, Lieutenant A. B. Jerome had seen what appeared to be a small group of mounted enemy troops on the Chambersburg Pike. As he recollected it, the sighting could have been "as early as seven A. M."[32]

The report Buford received around 8:00 was conclusive—an enemy force was definitely marching eastward. This time his informant was Colonel Gamble, who had heard the news from Captain Daniel Buck, the officer in charge of the pickets on Whisler's Ridge. Buck had informed Gamble that "infantry and artillery, in column, were approaching his pickets from the direction of Cashtown, with deployed skirmishers in strong force, about three miles distant." For Buford there was no need to deliberate. He fully expected this would occur and hence had already decided on the course of action he would take. Gamble was to form his brigade in a dismounted line on McPherson's Ridge. All details of the deployment, including the precise location of the defensive line, Buford left to Gamble's judgement.[33] As Major Beveridge, commander of the 8th Illinois, had sent orderlies to alert every one of Buford's regiments, there was no delay in executing Gamble's orders.[34]

They were: (1) proceed to the crest of McPherson's Ridge, (2) dismount and send the horses to the rear, (3) form a line on the western edge of the crest, with skirmishers well forward on the slope leading to Willoughby Run. With possibly 350 troopers already engaged west of Willoughby Run, Gamble had roughly 1,250 troopers at his disposal, of which one-quarter had to tend the horses. The remaining 900-plus troops he exhorted "to keep back the enemy as long as possible."

Gamble's line ran perpendicular to the Chambersburg Pike and an unfinished railroad cut. Almost parallel to the pike, the trackless cut lay about 150 yards north of it. The positions Gamble assigned his four regiments were: 3rd Indiana, just north of the railroad cut; 12th Illinois, between the cut and the pike; 8th Illinois, south of the pike and east of McPherson's barn; 8th New York, on the far left and slightly behind the rest of the line. Every regiment faced open fields except part of the 8th New York, which was behind Herbst's Woods.[35]

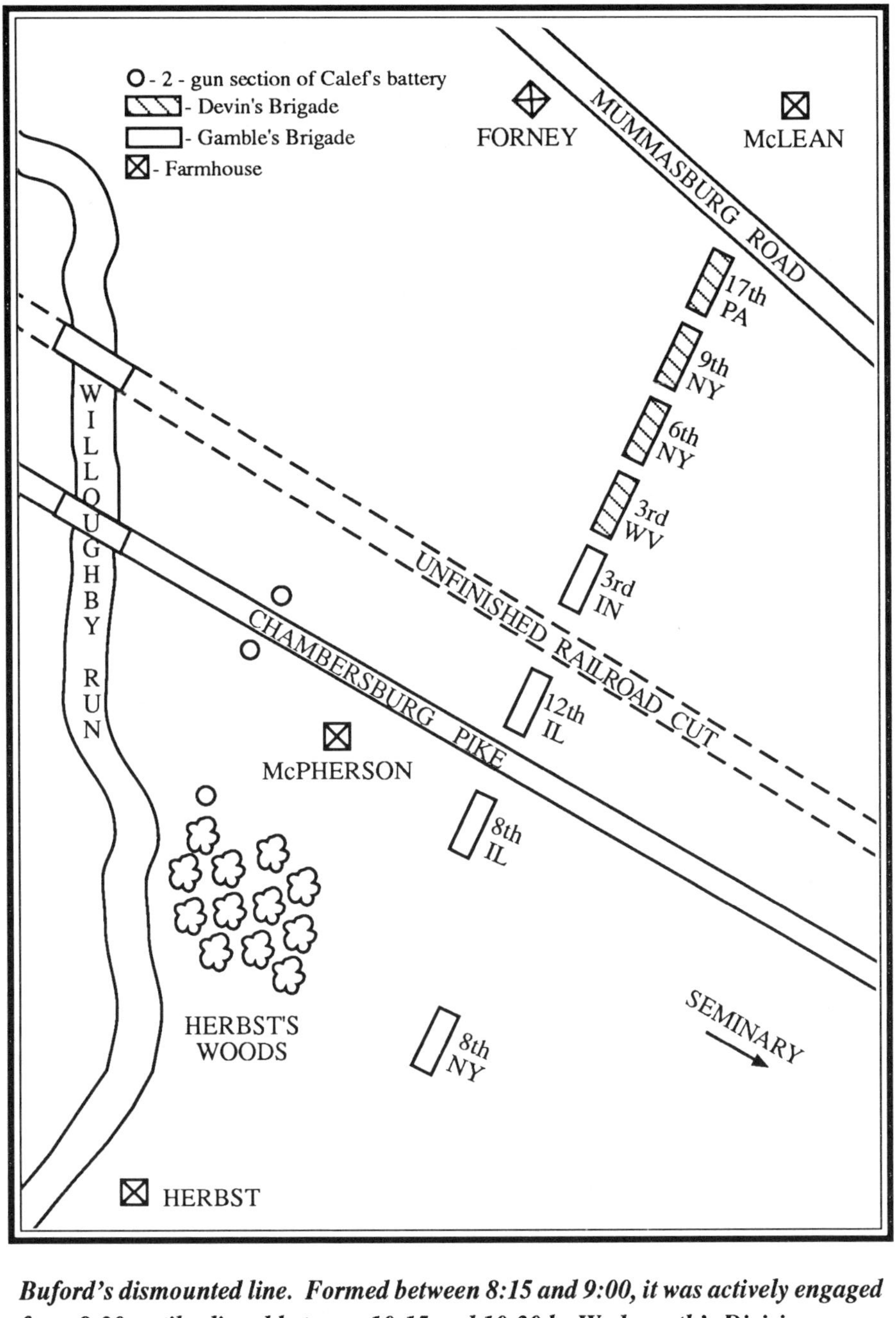

Buford's dismounted line. Formed between 8:15 and 9:00, it was actively engaged from 9:30 until relieved between 10:15 and 10:30 by Wadsworth's Division.

An 1863 panorama of Herbst's Woods as seen from the McPherson farm.

(For more than a century writers have referred to this 17-acre grove of oak and chestnut as McPherson's Woods.[36] Actually, the land it stood on belonged to McPherson's neighbor, John Herbst. The wide currency of the incorrect designation is hardly surprising, however, since the woods lay much closer to McPherson's house and barn than to Herbst's. Nevertheless, it seems high time to correct the misnomer.)[37]

Lieutenant John Calef, commander of Battery A, 2nd United States Artillery, had just finished breakfast at his camp near the Seminary and had called for his horse when he received word to report at once to General Buford and Colonel Gamble. He had intended to go to Gettysburg and "make some purchases for our mess." But, of course, there was no question of priority. He rode to his superiors. As Buford had delegated control of the battery to Gamble, it was the latter who gave the young lieutenant (one year out of West Point) his instructions. He was to select a good position on McPherson's Ridge and set up his six 3-inch rifles there as quickly as possible.

"In an incredibly short time," reported Calef, "our bivouac was broken and baggage and caissons sent to the rear." There was some delay en route, however, while ax-wielding soldiers leveled fences in the battery's path. After Calef had placed his guns in a close formation alongside the Chambersburg Pike, he saw Buford nearby and rode over to him. Although he had put Gamble in charge of the battery, Buford did not hesitate to express his displeasure with Calef's placement of the guns. He wanted them dispersed and went on to tell him exactly how: two guns on the right side of the pike, two on the left side, and two much farther to the left, on the fringe of Herbst's Woods. Overall, the battery line would then span 600 yards. With this disposition, Buford hoped to deceive the enemy into thinking they faced more artillery than were actually there.

Calef hustled his battery into the new positions. While observing Sergeant Charles Pergel's left section crew jostle their two guns into position between the 8th Illinois and 8th New York, he grew accustomed to the sound of skirmishing in his front and even to that of the enemy artillery. But when he heard a loud report directly on his right, he was startled. Realizing in a flash that it was almost certainly one of his own guns, he was at first relieved, then puzzled and probably perturbed. Why the single shot before he gave the order for concerted battery fire?

It turned out that Lieutenant John Roder, who was in charge of his right section, had seen a number of Confederates (part of Davis' brigade) coming onto the brow of Herr Ridge and found the urge to greet them irresistible. This—the first round fired by a Union gun in the battle—marked the beginning of an intense duel between Calef's battery and Pegram's five batteries.[38]

Trooper A. R. Mix, undoubtedly wearing the new boots he had just acquired in Gettysburg, returned to his 6th New York regiment. He found it in line of battle—just as Buford had told him he would. During his absence, Buford had directed Devin to form his brigade, dismounted, in a line which extended Gamble's line northward along McPherson's Ridge. Some of Devin's troopers had been released from picket duty north of Gettysburg to help meet the threat from the west. The majority, however, remained at their posts. Since Rebs in Ewell's Corps might return at any minute, constant surveillance of the roads leading north was imperative. Also unavailable at the time Devin formed his dismounted line was the 6th New York squadron that (as related earlier) narrowly escaped capture by a larger Confederate force. Thus, after allowing for this squadron, the pickets remaining at their posts, the horseholders, and the 17th Pennsylvania squadron assigned to defend Calef's Battery, Devin had only about 700 men to put in line. The 3rd West Virginia deployed north of the railroad cut on the right of Gamble's brigade line. The other regiments—6th New York, 9th New York, and 17th Pennsylvania, in that order—extended Devin's line to the Mummasburg road.

Buford ordered Devin to hold the position at all costs. Aware that he had considerably fewer men than Gamble, Buford repeated what he had told Devin the night before: "You will have to fight like the devil to do it."

At the outset Buford's line numbered about 1,650 officers and men. Later it was augmented by the return of the squadrons that had been skirmishing west of Willoughby Run. Buford then had approximately 2,000 cavalry opposing Heth's 2,900 infantry, or roughly two against three.[39]

The impressive performance of the Union cavalry under these odds has frequently been attributed to the seven-shot Spencer repeating carbine. But that is erroneous. Ordnance reports for the period in question reveal that Buford's division was equipped with an assortment of single-shot carbines—mostly Sharps, but also Smiths, Burnsides, Merrills, and Gallaghers. All were breech-loaders, and therefore could be fired much faster than the muzzle-loading muskets of Heth's infantry. They had another advantage: Unlike muskets, they could easily be loaded from either a crouching or a prone position, thus allowing the carbineer to remain behind cover while loading. Buford's horsemen, it may be noted, also carried the traditional pistol and saber. But, as it turned out, they had little use for either this day.[40]

When Buford was satisfied his line on McPherson's Ridge was as prepared to meet the enemy as it could be, he and his staff rode back to Seminary Ridge. Coming upon Lieutenant Colonel John A. Kress of Wadsworth's staff, he asked, "What are you doing here, sir?" Kress said he had been sent to get shoes for the division (not only the Confederates needed them). Buford advised, rather curtly, that he return to his division. The colonel naturally inquired, "Why, what is the matter, general?" At that moment, as though on cue, an enemy cannon boomed and Buford snapped, "That's the matter."[41]

After Calef's battery took up the gauntlet, eight of Pegram's guns concentrated frontal fire on Calef's four guns flanking the Chambersburg Pike and nine of Pegram's guns hammered away at Herbst's Woods and Calef's remaining two guns. Despite the disparity in firepower, the Union gunners worked their pieces with unflagging zeal. Their tenacity and skill were not lost on Buford. In his after-action report he paid tribute to the "wonderful effect" of their efforts.[42] Even those shells that sailed past Archer's and Davis' troops had a serendipitous effect. They quite unnerved troops in Pettigrew's Brigade, then approaching Herr Ridge. When shells began dropping close to the 26th

North Carolina Regiment, its commander, Colonel Henry Burgwyn, Jr., saw the instant apprehension in the faces of his men. To allay their fears, he rode up and down the column, calmly saying, over and over, "Steady boys, steady."[43]

Sallie Broadhead was baking bread in the kitchen of her Gettysburg home when she heard the ominous rumble of cannon fire. "What to do or where to go, I did not know," she wrote in her diary. "People were running here and there, screaming that the town would be shelled. My husband advised remaining where we were...." A dutiful wife, she acquiesced, however reluctantly.

At Pennsylvania College, a half mile northeast of the Lutheran Seminary, students attended classes as usual. Their concentration on such things as Latin or mathematics must have been minimal, and when the boom of not-too-distant cannon drifted through the open windows, it surely vanished altogether. With any further attempt at instruction absurd, classes were dismissed.[44]

From a vantage point behind the dismounted line of the 8th Illinois, Major Beveridge gazed across the ravine of Willoughby Run to Herr Ridge. Somewhere beyond it two of his squadrons were still contending with the enemy. Not knowing how they were faring weighed heavily on his mind. When he saw horses swarming over the top of Herr Ridge and the horseholders urging them on, he knew it could mean only one thing: Buford's skirmishers were rapidly being forced back. Beveridge noticed smoke rising above the ridge and heard the small arms fire that caused it. Only minutes later, he saw troopers (perhaps his own men!) running down the slope of Herr Ridge and Rebels pursuing them. Soon his attention riveted on the spectacle of a large Confederate force and many cannon inundating the ridge. He watched the infantry swing into line, the artillery prepare for action. Then the enemy guns erupted in a fierce cannonade. Beveridge and the whole Union line on McPherson's Ridge braced for the inevitable attack.[45]

After Pegram's guns had fired for a half hour, Heth ordered Archer and Davis to advance their brigades. This time Archer had no objection, since Davis' brigade had come abreast of his own.[46] The vast Confederate line, under fire from Calef's guns, began a slow descent of Herr Ridge. The slope was so gradual at first that Pegram's batteries had to withhold their fire lest they hit their own men. For a compulsive fighter like "Willie" Pegram, the constraint of inaction at this juncture must have been cruel torture. In any case, the moment the infantry was beneath the artillery's line of fire—when the foot soldiers were scarcely 150 yards from Willoughby Run—he gave the signal to reopen battery fire. To Private W. H. Moon in the 13th Alabama's color guard, that first volley was "the sweetest music I had ever heard," even though "the balls went whizzing just above our heads." On the second volley he and his companions saw one of Calef's guns topple, its axle shattered. They cheered the lucky hit.[47]

For Buford's troopers still holding on west of Willoughby Run, the time had clearly come to rejoin their respective regiments on the other side. Among the last to do so were Tom Day (whose horse refused to drink from the run) and his Company E comrades in the 3rd Indiana. "We held them a long time," he later wrote, "but finally we had to

Buford's dismounted troopers contest the advance of Heth's Brigades.

go, and when we came back across the bridge we found the artillery and men, dismounted, all in one long line."[48] Meanwhile, Heth's two brigades were drawing ever closer.

"The two lines soon became hotly engaged," reported Buford. The incessant clatter from muskets and carbines lent a treble voice to the deep bass of booming cannon. Before long the combatants were enveloped in smoke. An 8th Illinois trooper, with palpable understatement, described the action as "warm work." Actually, it was a fierce fight, and for Buford's Division a desperate one. The advantage of a good defensive position was being seriously eroded by the enemy's superior numbers. Buford had to face the fact that, despite the valiant efforts of his men, the advance of the enemy was not being checked; every minute brought them nearer.[49]

In the 8th New York Captain Albert Mills harbored gloomy presentiments. He expected momentarily "to hear the rebels yell and see the swift charge of superior numbers which would sweep us from our position. We held our line down there along Willoughby Run as best we could, hoping that reinforcements would come, fearing that they would not...."[50] An enticing alternative to standing fast occurred to 8th Illinois' Major Beveridge and was rejected. Watching Archer's regiments descend Herr Ridge, he thought, "We could easily fall back and elude pursuit; but we were not there to retreat, nor was it our habit to retreat."[51]

Buford certainly had no intention of doing so. According to his signal officer, "The general held on with as stubborn a fight as ever faced an enemy...."[52]

Confederates as well as Federals testified to Buford's determined stand. Captain J. B. Turney, for instance, reported that after his 1st Tennessee Regiment had advanced about 200 yards, "we met with stubborn resistance....For thirty minutes the firing was severe and the smoke of battle hovered near the ground, thus shutting out from view the movements of the Federal forces."[53]

Not long after Archer's battle line stepped off, the colorbearer in the 13th Alabama went berserk. He began screaming like a banshee and simultaneously waving the colors in a wildly erratic fashion. Even without such behavior Tom Grant would have been doubly conspicuous—not only because of carrying a flag, but because he was taller than everyone else. To W. H. Moon, who walked beside him, it was obvious his friend had drunk too much applejack. Moon was furious. "Tom, if you don't stop that, I will use my bayonet on you." Fortunately, there was no need to follow through on the drastic threat. Just then, a hail of minie balls came their way. And, while neither of them was hit, it had a very sobering effect on Grant.

Indeed Archer's whole brigade must have been sobered by the intensity of the Union resistance. More cautiously now, the Southerners continued their advance, continued to load and fire as they crossed the open field. At the far end there was a fence to hurdle and thick underbrush to plod through. The commander of the 7th Tennessee admitted that these were of "some disadvantage to our line." Actually, by the time the brigade reached Willoughby Run, every regiment's line was assuredly ragged. Halted on the west bank, Archer's men reloaded their muskets and reformed their lines. There, for a few precious moments, protected from enemy fire by an abrupt rise on the opposite bank, they had a chance to catch their breath and cool off a little. The order to advance soon rang out. Giving the Rebel yell, they rushed across the shallow stream to meet the enemy.[54]

Davis' Brigade, in the meantime, had encountered the same determined resistance from Devin's troopers that Archer received at the hands of Gamble. With the descent of Herr Ridge probably consuming a full half hour, both brigades would have splashed through Willoughby Run around 10:00, with Archer slightly ahead of Davis.[55]

By then Devin's line was entirely dismounted. Until heavy fire from Pegram's guns forced them to send their horses to the rear, some 17th Pennsylvania and 9th New York troopers had remained in their saddles.[56] As Devin's men blazed away at the enemy, Buford rode up to the brigade commander. In a voice suffused with gritty determination, he said, "Devin, this is the key to the army position. We must hold this if it costs every man in our command."[57]

From a vantage point behind Devin's line, Lieutenant James Stewart had been observing the hostilities. The battery commander happened to be there because a captain on Buford's staff had invited him "to come out and see the cavalry fight." Curious, he had set out with his bugler to "see what was going on" and "if there was any chance of a fight" for his Battery B, 4th U. S. Artillery. Once the Confederate assault on McPherson's Ridge was well underway, he realized that "our cavalry force was not equal to the enemies', although they were stubbornly holding every foot of ground." Colonel Devin told him his brigade was committed to fight until Reynolds and the First Corps arrived. Stewart returned to his battery, convinced that it would see action this day.[58]

Inevitably, casualties mounted when the skirmish escalated to a two-brigade attack. Buford's adjutant summed up his division's losses in the morning hours in one word—"severe."[59] One field-grade officer, Major Charles Lemon of the 3rd Indiana, was mortally wounded early in the engagement.[60] And at least fifteen enlisted men were killed before the division was relieved by Wadsworth's infantry. In addition, some eighty officers and men were wounded or missing.[61] A hospital was hastily set up at the Seminary and another at the railroad depot in Gettysburg. One of the first soldiers to arrive at the depot was a Private Williams of the 8th Illinois. The surgeon saw at a glance that Williams' arm, mangled by a minie ball, could not be saved. Amputation swiftly followed.[62]

As to Confederate casualties prior to the arrival of Union infantry, it can only be assumed that they approximated those of Buford's cavalry. The annals are silent in this regard, with one exception. Henry Raison (or Rison) of Company B, 7th Tennessee, was shot dead as he descended Herr Ridge. Reputedly, he was the first Confederate soldier killed in the battle.[63]

Besides human casualties, a large number of cavalry horses fell victim to Pegram's guns. While most of the horses, at some point, were taken to the rear, the problem was they were not taken nearly far enough. One hundred yards or so, which was customary, was still well within range of the enemy guns.[64]

Another casualty of sorts was the tenant family on the McPherson farm. When a Union officer warned Eliza Slentz of impending battle, she and her five young children had no choice but to leave. Her husband John had left earlier with the horses in an attempt to hide them before they were seized by predatory cavalry. (He did not succeed.) Eliza was putting bread in the oven when she heard the stunning news. What happened next is best told in her own words:

> Instantly, all was confusion, and before a moment had passed, myself and five children, driving our cows before us, were fleeing toward the town of Gettysburg. All we saved was the clothing we were attired in at the time, and, if I remember rightly, the children were bareheaded and without shoes or stockings.
>
> Before we reached the town our cattle were lost [seized, presumably] and we took refuge in the cellar of the "Seminary."[65]

As a measure of Buford's staunch resistance, it took the brigades of Archer and Davis two and one-half hours to cover the two miles from Marsh Creek to Willoughby Run. Yet, when Heth sat down to write his battle report, he became incredibly myopic, giving absolutely no indication of his engagement with Union cavalry! From that report it would appear he was totally ignorant of Buford's line when he ordered Archer and Davis to reconnoiter their front, whereupon (according to him) they immediately encountered Wadsworth's Division. Even more incredible is his blunt assertion in a letter written fifteen years later: "I did not have so much as a skirmish with General Buford's cavalry or with any other cavalry. The first force I struck was infantry." It was only when he got around to writing his memoirs that Heth finally set the record straight. Describing the march from Cashtown, he acknowledged that his leading brigades "soon became engaged with General Buford's dismounted cavalry."[66]

Under the circumstances, employing his cavalrymen as infantry was a smart move on Buford's part. It was not a brilliant innovation, however, as some writers have implied. While this may have been the only instance in the Civil War in which an entire cavalry division was employed in this manner, the tactic itself was not new. In fact, during the Indian Wars it was fairly common practice. No doubt Buford himself used it many times during his long service on the frontier. Although the 13th Alabama's Colonel Fry disparaged the efforts of the dismounted cavalry as "inconsiderable" and doing "no damage,"[67] Buford's effective use of the tactic at Gettysburg is affirmed by one indisputable fact: The Confederates, despite numerical superiority, were unable to rout the dismounted cavalrymen.

Buford's corps commander, Major General Alfred Pleasonton, had assigned a fall-back position this day to each of his three division leaders. Buford's was Taneytown, Maryland. In his dispatch Pleasonton explained that he was taking this precaution "in case the enemy should advance upon you and press you hard." All three leaders, he wrote, "will dispute every inch of ground, and fall back very slowly to the point designated." As if he not been emphatic enough, he added a postscript: "This movement is only to be made in case of great necessity."[68]

For Buford there would be no "great necessity," if only Reynolds and Wadsworth's First Corps division arrived in time.

"Hark! do you hear that rumbling sound?"

As Reynolds and Wadsworth began the march to Gettysburg, neither had any inkling that Buford's cavalry would be attacked in strength, nor that only the timely arrival of Union infantry could save it from precipitate retreat.

Consequently, Wadsworth's Division was under no pressure to hurry. In fact, one soldier wrote home that the column moved "slowly" until it drew near Gettysburg.[69] The sun was shining, the temperature in the mid-70s. The humidity, though rising, was not yet oppressive.[70] After a day's rest, the men were in good spirits and ready for whatever this day might bring.

There were exceptions, of course. Sergeant Cornelius Wheeler later described two striking cases in his own regiment, the 2nd Wisconsin. Sergeant Joseph O. Williams, Wheeler remembered, "had never missed a skirmish, a battle or a day's duty." But today, when Williams came up to him shortly after the march began, Wheeler saw at once that something was seriously wrong. Williams did not keep him in suspense. He did not feel "quite right," he said, "as though something was going to happen" and he would "not get through the day." Wheeler laughed at his fears, told him he was "foolish to feel so blue." Besides, Wheeler added, no fighting was expected, and even if there were, he would "come out all right," as he always had. But Wheeler could not shake

Williams' despondency. "Poor Joe did not have much more to say and soon fell back to his place." When the enemy opened fire on his regiment a few hours later, Williams was shot dead.

The other case was that of George H. Legate, 2nd Wisconsin's sergeant-major. He had the same premonition that afflicted Williams. And he, too, confided in Wheeler. "Corny," he said, his tone as matter-of-fact as if discussing the weather, "we are going to have a fight today, and I will not come out alive." Once again Wheeler laughed. He told Legate his words were "all nonsense," and twitted him further, saying that if he really felt that way, why didn't he drop out, since "a Sergeant-Major was not of much account in a fight, anyway." But Legate was in no mood to joke. "No," he said, utterly serious, "I will stay with the regiment whatever happens." He was also killed that afternoon.[71]

While there is no indication that General Reynolds shared the particular gloomy foreboding of Williams and Legate, he had been depressed nonetheless ever since Lee's army had invaded Pennsylvania. His concern for his home state and his relatives living there ran deep.[72] Whatever his thoughts were this morning, he was unusually taciturn, but his staff had grown accustomed to his frequent periods of silence on the march.[73] When he was informed that a band of Rebels had been sighted nearby, he merely voiced the opinion that they were foragers, "probably after cattle," and again fell silent.[74]

After the First Corps' artillery and Second and Third divisions were all underway on either of two routes, General Doubleday and his staff spurred ahead of the main body on the Emmitsburg road. Later he dispatched Lieutenant Jacob Slagle to check on the progress of General Robinson's Third Division, which was bringing up the rear. Slagle met the division commander near Marsh Creek and relayed Doubleday's injunction to hurry. Returning, Slagle found Doubleday in the rear of Wadsworth's First Division.[75]

Reynolds and his staff, meanwhile, were riding at the head of that division. Shortly before 9:00, when they were about two miles south of Gettysburg, they saw a horseman riding toward them at top speed. Reynolds halted his staff, then rode to meet him, possibly divining he bore important news from Buford. Breathlessly, the courier gasped out his message: A strong enemy force is approaching on the Chambersburg Pike. Buford is sharply engaged. He says he can hold on for awhile, if so ordered.[76]

Galvanized by the urgent message, Reynolds knew he must fly to Buford, assess the situation, decide whether the cavalry should stay put or pull back. But first he had to communicate with the army commander and with his subordinates. He sent an aide to inform Meade, another to urge Howard to press the advance of the Eleventh Corps, and still another to order Wadsworth to close up his division and hasten to Gettysburg. Captain James A. Hall, commander of Battery B, Maine Light Artillery, had joined the group of staff officers attending their chief. Turning to him, Reynolds said, "You ride forward and get between the enemy and the town; throw a few shells into them to keep them from plundering the town." Once all necessary contacts had been made, Reynolds, with his orderly and one staff officer, galloped off to meet Buford.[77]

About this time Reynolds heard cannon fire, which served to underscore the urgency of his mission. As he raced toward Gettysburg, he doubtless pondered what he might find there, what action he should take. Yet, though deep in thought, he did not fail to notice on his right the low ridge that culminated in a high hill just outside the crossroads town. He recognized at once its potential for defense. He would keep it in mind; it could prove invaluable.[78]

Before arriving in Gettysburg, Reynolds and his two companions came upon a civilian, on horseback, frantically waving his arms for them to stop. Reining in, they asked him what was the matter. The cavalry is being driven back! he wailed. Their attempts to elicit further information proved fruitless; totally unstrung, the man could only repeat that the cavalry was falling back. The trio rode on hurriedly. At the edge of town they paused only long enough to inquire how to get to the Lutheran Seminary. As they followed the directions through town, everywhere they saw people milling about, bewildered and afraid. At the corner of Chambersburg and Washington Streets, Reynolds noticed a civilian just sitting on his horse outside the Eagle Hotel and, to avoid any chance of a wrong turn, decided he would ask a favor of him. The local man, one Peter Culp, readily consented to lead Reynolds post haste to the Seminary.[79]

A mile and a half south of Gettysburg, Cutler's Brigade pulled off the Emmitsburg road to wait for Meredith's Brigade which had lagged behind. Some 76th New York troops happened to be halted beneath some cherry trees. The cherries were ripe, plentiful...and devilishly tempting. Major Andrew Grover saw his men staring upward, saw the acute longing on their faces. Going over to them, he said, "Boys, the General charges you to be very particular to keep strictly within the rules, and not meddle with those cherry *trees*! Be sure you don't break the trees down!" Well, they could take a hint—the cherries themselves were not forbidden. Needless to say, they enjoyed the luscious fruit while being reasonably careful how they plucked it.[80]

In Meredith's Brigade non-combatants and mules were left behind when the order was given to increase the pace from route step to quickstep.[81] The firing of Pegram's and Calef's guns was then faintly audible. A 24th Michigan private noted in his diary that he first heard it at 9:30.[82] Second Wisconsin's Captain R. K. Beecham recalled: "The shots sounded far away and we had no idea that we were coming almost immediately into the presence of the enemy."[83] In the 6th Wisconsin Lieutenant Colonel Dawes first became aware of artillery fire just as he ordered the regimental colors unfurled and the band began to play "The Campbells are Coming."[84] As Meredith's regiments advanced, the roar of cannon grew louder and more ominous.

Meanwhile, Cutler's resting troops had little to do but listen. One of them, Theodore Brokaw of the 14th Brooklyn, would evoke those moments in the opening lines of a long narrative poem.

Hark! do you hear that rumbling sound?
See the curling smoke? 'tis the opening dirge
Preceding the fearful scenes at and around
the grand, historic battle of Gettysburg.[85]

While most civilians cowered in their parlors or nervously walked the streets, others, hearing "that rumbling sound," took more decisive action. Abandoning their homes, they fled south on the Emmitsburg road. Wadsworth's troops, marching in the opposite direction, witnessed the exodus of "gray-haired old men tottering along; women carrying their children, and children leading each other, while on the faces of all were depicted the indices of the terror and despair which had taken possession of them."[86]

In contrast, two brave Gettysburg ladies stood by their front gate, calmly dispensing dippers of water to the passing Yankees. Those who took advantage of the offer had to gulp their drink and run to regain their places in the still-moving column. Second Wisconsin men, as they marched on, showed their appreciation by giving their benefactors a hearty cheer.[87]

In the 6th Wisconsin, a rumor circulated that the division would soon be tangling with "Jeb" Stuart's cavalry. (Doubtless someone had learned of Stuart's fight the day before at Hanover and simply assumed Gettysburg would be his next stop.) Some men muttered that they would "snuff out" the famous Rebel cavalry leader.[88]

As the 24th Michigan drew near Gettysburg, the men of Company B were surprised to see four comrades who had dropped out earlier. Not malingerers, these men had all left the ranks with permission from the regimental surgeon. But, when Privates Arnold, Pinkney, Conners, and Rider heard cannon booming, they forgot about their physical ailments and hustled to catch up with their company. They had been in every action so far, and they were not going to miss out on this one![89]

Anson Culver played field drum in the 24th Michigan's band. His instrument presumably was of Civil War vintage, but the implements with which he played it—his drumsticks—had a long and memorable history. In the hands of a drummer in the British Army they had executed ruffles and rolls at Saratoga in 1777. He was killed in that battle and the drumsticks were retrieved by a Continental soldier. In the intervening years, used by a succession of military drummers, they had served the American cause in the Revolution, War of 1812, Mexican War, and now the War Between the States.[90]

When Lieutenant Slagle got back to Doubleday, having contacted General Robinson and given him the message to hurry up his division, the corps commander sent him out on another mission—this time to order General Rowley to do likewise. The Third Division commander, Doubleday explained, would be found on the alternate route, with Biddle's Brigade. As Slagle would be traveling cross-country and the enemy's whereabouts were uncertain, Doubleday stressed the need for caution. As it turned out, the aide located Rowley without difficulty and without mishap.[91]

Stone's Brigade of Rowley's Division, it will be recalled, marched up the Emmitsburg road between Wadsworth's and Robinson's Divisions. It maintained "as fast a pace as it was possible to go on such a sultry morning," one of its officers later commented.[92] These troops and the batteries that followed them were now close enough to hear not only the boom of cannon but the crack of carbine and musket. To Augustus Buell in

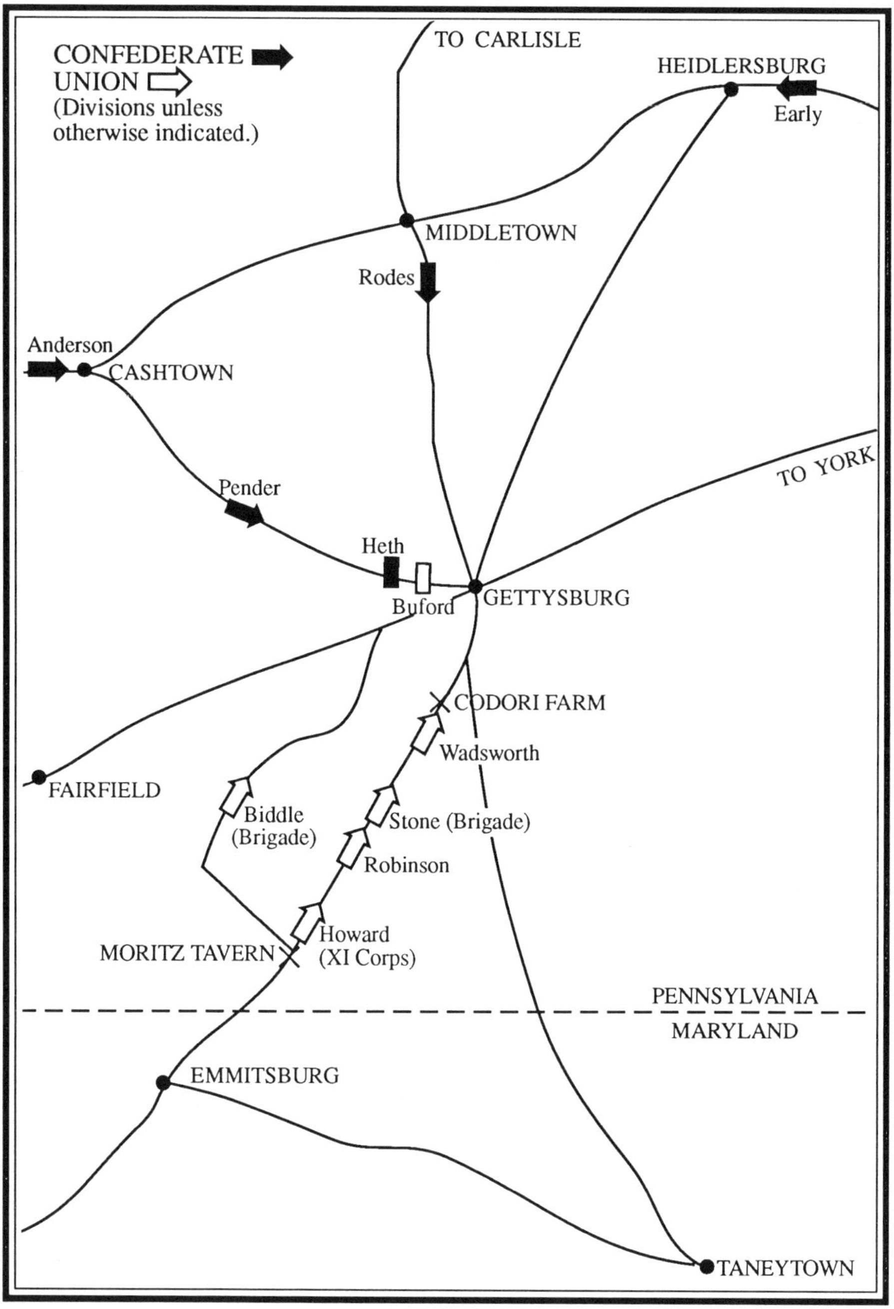

Situation at 9:30 a.m., July 1, 1863.

Stewart's battery the small arms fire sounded like "the snapping of a dry brush-heap when you first set it on fire."[93]

Several miles farther north on the Emmitsburg road, with the sounds of conflict dinning loudly on his ears, General Wadsworth anxiously awaited word from Reynolds. Presently he spied a mounted figure streaking across the fields of the Codori farm. Feeling certain the rider was from Reynolds, Wadsworth, with some of his staff, rode out to a rail fence. The horseman stopped short on the opposite side, sending up a cloud of dust. Saluting Wadsworth, he said, "General Reynolds desires you to turn your leading brigade [Cutler's] into this field following along the ridge at the double toward the woods yonder [pointing to Seminary Ridge]. Hall's battery will strike across to relieve Calef's guns, which are overmatched and have suffered severely. The General will meet the column and himself place the troops and guns. He wishes you, General, to hasten forward the other brigade."[94]

By this time, however, the "other brigade"—Meredith's—had come up to Cutler's Brigade. The rush into battle could begin.

"Now we can hold the place!"

In the meantime, Buford had sent a terse note to General Meade.

> The enemy's force [he wrote] are advancing on me at this point and driving my pickets and skirmishers *very* rapidly. There is also a large force at Heidlersburg, that is driving my pickets at that point from that direction. General Reynolds is advancing, and is within three miles of this point, with his leading division. I am positive that the whole of A. P. Hill's force is advancing.[95]

This note has been a stumbling block for a number of writers, deluding them into a false chronology. The problem lies not in the text but in the notation above it: "10:10 a.m." Purportedly, that was when the note was written. However, to correspond with the circumstances presented therein, it had to be written at least an hour earlier.

Three times this morning Buford climbed the porch steps, two flights of stairs, and lastly a ladder to join his signal officer in the cupola atop the Lutheran Seminary. The first time was in response to Lieutenant Jerome's sighting of some men on horseback, presumably Rebels, far to the west on the Chambersburg Pike. That was around 7:00.[96] The second time was not long after his division had formed a defensive line on McPherson's Ridge.

Jerome had been watching the seemingly endless stream of Rebels pour onto Herr Ridge. A mere five or six hundred yards separated them from Buford's thin line of dismounted troopers. To Jerome, the rout of the cavalrymen seemed inevitable. But then, swinging his fieldglasses to the south, he saw something that made his heart leap. Was that red speck a flag...a Union flag? It was definitely moving in his direction. After some minutes of intense watching, he was able to distinguish a white disc on a red field—the emblem of the First Corps. Even better, he could see a column of infantry in blue uniforms tramping along behind it. Immediately he sent one of his men racing to Buford with the exhilarating news. He felt certain the cavalry commander would come at once to see for himself.

He was not mistaken; in short order, Buford was at his side. Jerome offered his fieldglasses. Buford took them, peered at the approaching infantry, and declared: "Now we can hold the place."

Shortly after Buford left, Jerome spotted General Reynolds and his party galloping toward the Seminary. Again he sent word to Buford, this time to inform him that Reynolds should arrive there in about five minutes. Again Buford dashed up into the cupola. He had just noted with immense satisfaction that Wadsworth's troops were now within a mile of the Seminary when he was hailed from below.

"What's the matter, John?"

Looking down, Buford saw Reynolds standing at the foot of the Seminary steps. "The devil's to pay!" Buford shouted back. He clattered down the ladder as Reynolds rushed up the Seminary steps to meet him. After Buford had described the tactical situation in his usual laconic manner, Reynolds said, "I hope you can hold out until my corps comes up."

Lutheran Seminary building as it appeared in 1863.

"I reckon I can," Buford replied.

And Reynolds said, "Let's ride out and see all about it."[97]

A revisionist view holds that this episode, as reported by Lieutenant Jerome, never occurred—that Reynolds met Buford on McPherson's Ridge, not at the Seminary. Apparently the sole basis for the assertion is a sentence in a letter written nine months after the battle by Reynolds' orderly, Charles H. Veil. However, when Veil wrote his memoirs, he essentially corroborated Jerome's account. Thus, unless Jerome was a blatant liar and Veil and several officers close to Reynolds were completely deluded, the meeting of Reynolds and Buford did in fact take place at the Seminary. On the other hand, the romantic depiction in some accounts of Reynolds standing tall in the cupola and cooly surveying the scene through fieldglasses is almost certainly fictitious.

Before Reynolds and Buford started for the front, Major E. P. Halstead of Doubleday's staff rode up. The major reported on the progress of Robinson's and Rowley's Divisions. Reynolds' reply: Tell General Doubleday to hurry his troops forward.[98]

Also before leaving the Seminary, Reynolds sent Captain Stephen Weld, the youngest of his aides, on an important mission. "Ride at once at your utmost speed to General Meade," he told him. After giving instructions how to find the army commander, he said, "Tell him the enemy is advancing in strong force, and I fear he will get to the heights beyond the town before I can. I will fight him inch by inch, and if driven into the town I will barricade the streets, and hold him back as long as possible."

Reynolds had a parting admonition for Weld: Don't spare your horse![99]

"General, do not expose yourself so much."

On Herr Ridge Heth's battle line had started down the slope and Pegram's five batteries were spewing ball and shell all along McPherson's Ridge. One gun crew spotted a small band of Federal horsemen galloping over the opposite crest and immediately directed their fire on it.[100]

It was Reynolds and Buford, no less, accompanied by a few staff officers. The half-mile ride from the Seminary had taken only minutes; it was then probably a little past 9:30.[101] Although Reynolds had slowed his horse after the "shower of balls," he continued to press forward, oblivious to the danger.[102] Buford was much concerned. Turning to the wing commander, he said, "General, do not expose yourself so much." Reynolds grinned slightly and kept on going.[103]

Far more serious matters than his personal safety pre-empted his attention. For one, he certainly knew that a decision to contest every inch of ground could have far-reaching effects for the whole Army of the Potomac. For another, he certainly realized that for Buford's cavalrymen, valiant as they were, time was running out. Instinctively, he had taken in the surrounding terrain features as he rode to McPherson's Ridge. And he surely still bore in mind the commanding heights east of Gettysburg. If forced to withdraw.... But apparently he believed that could be avoided if the First Corps, particularly Wadsworth's Division, reached McPherson's Ridge soon enough.

Buford's line had been raked with artillery fire for a good half hour. Even Devin's pickets, two miles away on the Harrisburg road, had heard the noise and seen the "little puffs of smoke from the bursting shells."[104] Gamble's skirmishers had fallen back on the brigade line and joined in the steady fire against the oncoming Confederates. It proved effective. Although Archer's men fired back with cool deliberation and were never completely stalled, their progress was slow and very cautious. The stout resistance of Gamble's dismounted cavalry may have fooled them into thinking they faced veteran infantry.[105]

On the right of Buford's line Devin's troopers harried Davis' Brigade. "For a short time they got the better of us," a 9th New York trooper recalled, "but pretty soon we rallied and started to drive them back." (The last part seems dubious; if true, it was short-lived.) Devin, worried that he might be outflanked on the right, sent out scouts to give timely warning of any such attempt. Sixth New York trooper A. R. Mix was among them. Riding north of the Mummasburg road, he discovered the woods "full of Johnnies." It was in fact a rude volley in his direction that alerted him to their presence. Swinging low in his saddle, so that as much of his body as possible was shielded by his horse, he raced back to his company. It was only after he made his report that he noticed that two musket balls had whipped through his horse's mane. He considered it a "miracle" that he had come through the ordeal unharmed.[106]

Lieutenant Calef, by shuttling from one to another of his battery's three positions, kept in close contact with all six gun crews as they hammered away at the enemy guns. He was with his middle section, just south of the Chambersburg Pike, when he saw Reynolds and Buford conferring in the road. He rode over to inquire if there were any further orders for him. The generals were so engrossed that some minutes passed before they became aware of his presence. Calef, meanwhile, could not help but overhear their conversation on "military points of pressing interest."[107] One of these was the town of Gettysburg itself, its vulnerability, the safety of its residents. Reynolds had witnessed the ferment on the streets, townspeople milling everywhere, and had sent Lieutenant Joseph G. Rosengarten of his staff to persuade them to stay indoors.[108] Another point of discussion was the necessity to preserve the heights beyond Gettysburg for Union occupation. Calef heard Reynolds charge Buford, above all, to keep the enemy from getting through town and seizing the high ground. And Calef remembered the essence of Reynolds' parting words to the cavalry leader: Hold them in check from this position as long as you can. The First Corps will soon come to your relief.

Reynolds must have wondered whether one corps would be sufficient. There can be little doubt that Buford told him about what he had written to Meade—that he believed all of A. P. Hill's huge corps was headed for Gettysburg. In any case, Reynolds again called on Major William Riddle to deliver a message to General Howard. It was simply this: Bring up the Eleventh Corps with all possible speed, encamp along the Emmitsburg road just outside Gettysburg, and await further orders.[109]

Once the decision was made to confront the enemy from McPherson's Ridge, Reynolds was impatient to get back to Wadsworth, to exhort him to bring up his division on the double-quick. Leaving Buford, Reynolds and his aides rode furiously across fields and over fences to the Emmitsburg Road where Wadsworth was waiting. Although jumping fences posed no problem for an expert horseman like Reynolds, he nonetheless realized these obstacles would significantly retard an infantry advance. Accordingly, he sent out Wadsworth's pioneers (as army engineers were then called) to level them.[110]

After Reynolds' departure, Buford lit his pipe and called for his bugler. Together they rode down Gamble's line. Time and again, Buford called out to his men, encouraging them to stand firm. He paused briefly to speak with Lieutenant Calef. "Our men are in a pretty hot pocket," he admitted, "but, my boy, we must hold this position until the infantry come up; then you withdraw your guns in each section by piece, fill up your limber chests from the caissons and await my orders." Just then a shell burst so near that their horses reared in fright. By sheer luck neither they nor their horses were hit.[111]

After the meeting with Reynolds at the Seminary, Major Halstead started riding back to Doubleday. He had scarcely gotten underway when he saw something so bizarre, so incongruous that he could hardly believe his eyes. Walking westward, toward Buford's line, was a wiry old man in a blue swallow-tail coat and black silk hat, toting an ancient musket and powder horn. To look at him, no one would have suspected that his actions this day would earn him enduring fame. He was John Burns, Gettysburg's constable. The major, though in a hurry to deliver Reynolds' message to Doubleday, pulled up beside him. "Which way are the Rebels? Where are our troops?" Burns demanded, a truculent urgency in his voice. Halstead told him the enemy was only a short distance ahead and he would soon overtake them. "I know how to fight," Burns declared, "I have fit before."

A week earlier, Rebel foragers had driven away his cows, and he was still angry. Before the morning ended the grizzled veteran of the War of 1812 would have his chance to retaliate.[112]

"...the wise and soldierly-like move..."

In effect, Buford determined the site of the first day's battle when he posted his dismounted cavalry on McPherson's Ridge. But it might have been otherwise. Reynolds could have withdrawn the cavalry and deployed the First Corps on Seminary Ridge, just west of Gettysburg. Or on Cemetery Ridge, which, from a tactical standpoint, had greatly impressed him as he rode up the Emmitsburg road. The decision was up to Reynolds. There was no need (and obviously no time) to consult Meade. Before coming to Gettysburg, he had written the army commander: "...while I am aware that it is not your desire to force an engagement at that point [Gettysburg], still, from the scope of instructions I have all the time had from you since commanding this wing of the army, I feel at liberty to advance to Gettysburg and develop the strength of the enemy at that point."[113]

What he apparently did not know was that this very morning Meade had proposed a general withdrawal to Pipe Creek, in Maryland, and had assigned every corps commander a specific destination. There is no evidence that Reynolds ever received either the "Pipe Creek" order or a dispatch in which Meade sought his advice.[114] Had he received the latter, he would have been further reassured of his authority to act independently. Besides soliciting Reynolds' "views," Meade admitted he was "not sufficiently informed of the nature of the country to judge of its character for either an offensive or defensive position....He feels that you know more of the condition of the troops in your vicinity and the country than he does."[115]

Meade thought it "not improbable"—as he wrote to General Sedgwick of the Sixth Corps—that the enemy would reach Gettysburg ahead of Reynolds' First Corps. "Should such be the case and General Reynolds finds himself in the presence of a superior force, he is instructed to hold the enemy in check, and fall slowly back." Further: If Reynolds can do this, then the Pipe Creek line "will be occupied tonight"; on the other hand, if Reynolds runs into trouble, the other corps should support him. Thus Meade recognized the possibility of delay; but he still fully intended to follow through on his "Pipe Creek" plan.[116]

Before the day ended, however, Meade would scuttle the whole plan. His rejection of it has generally been attributed to Major General Winfield S. Hancock's report from the battlefield in the late afternoon. But Colonel P. Regis De Trobriand of the Third Corps had a different opinion. Not Hancock's report, he maintained, but Reynolds' actions convinced Meade that a Pipe Creek line was no longer a viable option.[117]

During the short visit to McPherson's Ridge with Buford, Reynolds made a quick decision but not a hasty one. He certainly reckoned with the likelihood of additional enemy troops coming up in support of the attack force and, in consequence, Wadsworth's Division being outnumbered until the rest of the First Corps arrived. The strong defensive position afforded by the heights on the opposite side of Gettyburg must have been a tempting alternative; he surely realized that in a prolonged engagement possession of them would be vital. Yet, if his troops invested Cemetery Hill at this juncture, the town would face heavy bombardment and possible destruction. As to Buford's position, he would have sized up its inherent weaknesses: exposure to artillery fire from the north and the inability to observe and fire upon an enemy flanking column coming up the railroad cut. But, on the other hand, that long ditch would serve as a buffer, impeding any enemy charge from the north. Moreover, Herbst's Woods offered a position from which enfilade fire could rake both the Chambersburg Pike on the right and the Fairfield road on the left, while at the same time providing cover for the troops.[118]

Reynolds' blood was up. The desire to fight, to whip the invaders, must have been irresistible. He accepted Buford's position "with that quickness of perception, which was one of his most marked characteristics." So wrote Colonel Chapman Biddle, adding that Reynolds "saw at a glance that here was the ground on which the great contest must be fought out."[119] Here was the opportunity he had wanted ever since Lee's army had crossed into his native state. At Poolesville, Maryland, on June 25, he had revealed his deep concern to Doubleday. It was necessary to attack the enemy at once, he had said even then, or else they would plunder the whole state.[120] He had waited nearly a week for this chance.

His intentions on McPherson's Ridge, as stated by Doubleday, were "to defend the [Chambersburg and Fairfield] roads, and to occupy and hold the woods between them."[121] Furthermore, as his staff officer Lieutenant Rosengarten attested, he was determined to hold on "at least until his other corps, the 11th and 3rd, could get up to the Cemetery Hill and the Ridge where the Battle was finally fought and won."[122]

The tactical decision to remain on McPherson's Ridge would be criticized by some analysts of the battle. Colonel Wainwright, the First Corps Artillery commander, felt that Reynolds should have (1) posted his troops on Seminary Ridge, (2) constructed breastworks, and (3) used the cavalry to extend the flanks.[123] Historian Cecil Battine concluded that Reynolds "would have done better to have occupied Cemetery Ridge at once...."[124] But perhaps his most severe critic was Colonel Thomas L. Livermore. In a speech before the Military Order of the Loyal Legion of the United States in 1912, he proclaimed:

> It was entirely possible for him [Reynolds] to have retired on the rest of the army in compliance with his instructions, drawing back Buford after him, without the risk of disaster, and there was no merit in the position which he took for a general battle. It was vulnerable to approach on the roads from the northeast by the enemy of whose presence in that direction he had been informed, and in it he was beyond possible support by any adequate force. His disregard of Meade's order must be laid to the ardor of a very martial soldier, and the revolt of a patriot against the delivery of an important town of his native State to the enemy.[125]

Historian Warren W. Hassler, Jr., writing in 1960, disagreed with Reynolds' critics. In his view, if Reynolds had fallen back immediately to Cemetery Ridge, the result "would, in all probability, have been disastrous." He argued:

> The Confederates, superior numerically to the Union troops present, and being augmented faster than the Federal forces, would have had the better part of the day to drive the Federals from the Cemetery heights, which would then have been occupied by the Southerners. In this position, the better-concentrated Army of Northern Virginia would be at the apex of the three converging roads to the south of the town upon which the more widely-scattered Union army was approaching Gettysburg. Additional hours of daylight would have been available for the Confederates, and defeat in detail of the Federal forces would have been quite likely.[126]

Did Meade himself approve of Reynolds' decision? Captain George Meade, the army commander's son and military aide, affirmed that he did. Reynolds acted, he wrote, "just as the commanding general contemplated he would act."[127]

CHAPTER V

REYNOLDS TO THE RESCUE

"...we saw the grand old 1st corps coming...."

At the Nicholas Codori farm, one mile south of Gettysburg, some 3,500 Union soldiers listened to the rumble of artillery fire off to the northwest and knew that it augured a fight—for them!

Meredith's Iron Brigade (as Reynolds directed before he rode to Buford) had closed the gap between it and Cutler's Brigade. Now both brigades comprising Wadsworth's Divison were halted either in or to the side of the Emmitsburg road. Just waiting, the troops grew restless and edgy; those kept standing in the road continually shifted their stance from one foot to the other. In the hot sun and high humidity every minute seemed longer than the last. As soldiers in the ranks have always done under stress, they griped and grumbled about everything from the weather and the seemingly interminable waiting to the hardships of army life and the alleged shortcomings of their immediate superiors.

Certainly Wadsworth was aware of their mood, and no doubt he frequently gazed across the Codori fields in hope of seeing General Reynolds returning from his conference with Buford. At last he spotted a dust cloud moving across the fields toward him. Confident it was his chief, he rode out to meet him.

Wadsworth was right—it was the wing commander. And Reynolds quickly made it plain that Buford's situation was critical, that speedy relief was an absolute necessity. Most urgent was his order for Wadsworth to get Cutler's Brigade moving, with pioneers well out in front tearing down the fences in its path. His instructions were precise: Cutler's column should wheel to the left, double-quick obliquely across fields to Seminary Ridge, cross the Fairfield road, proceed along the ridge, and halt near the Chambersburg Pike. He would be there to meet it and to give further instructions.[1]

For some reason Captain Hall had not yet advanced his 2nd Maine Battery, as Reynolds had directed him to do; therefore, he was now informed to take up the march behind Cutler's Brigade. Meredith's Brigade was to follow the battery.[2] In addition, Reynolds designated one of his aides, Captain Craig Wadsworth (the division commander's son), to serve as liaison between the two brigades.[3]

In some regiments non-combatants were permitted to drop out at this time; in others it was later. Likewise, in some regiments the order was given to load muskets before starting out; in others (as we shall see) the men ended up doing so literally on the run.[4]

Cutler's Brigade got underway probably a few minutes before 10:00.[5] With the blue New York State flag pointing the way, the troops moved across the Codori fields at the double-quick.[6] There were no fences to impede their progress; ambitious pioneers had not only taken down the rails but had chopped down the posts.[7] Far ahead of them, Cutler's men could see "circles of smoke" rise from exploding shells—an unwelcome reminder of what they were getting into.[8] By the time they reached the Fairfield road (over a mile from the departure point), they were all puffing from the dual effect of heat and exertion. A number of them decided right then that knapsacks were expendable and simply cast them aside. (Some of Meredith's men had done the same even before leaving the Emmitsburg road.)[9] As Cutler's troops jogged along the crest of Seminary Ridge, a mounted orderly approached from the opposite direction. Coming alongside the column, he warned that the Rebels were "thicker than blackberries."[10]

Wadsworth rode at the head of Cutler's Brigade; Reynolds stayed behind to spur on Hall's Battery and Meredith's Brigade. As he sat his horse in the angle where those units turned off the Emmitsburg road, Lieutenant Rosengarten rode up. The staff officer admitted he had had little success in convincing the townspeople to stay indoors. (Evidently they were more curious than frightened.) The general's countenance registered his displeasure. But then he noticed the lieutenant's glasses were covered with dust and his frown vanished. Smiling, he said with mock sympathy, "Oh, they have been throwing dirt in your eyes."[11]

With Reynolds looking on, Hall's drivers swung caissons and cannon off the road and started on the bumpy journey across field and meadow. Meanwhile, an Iron Brigade band swung into a brassy rendition of "The Girl I Left Behind Me."[12] Doubtless that and other familiar tunes bolstered the men waiting their turn to march into battle. Finally the brigade could go forward. As the column passed General Reynolds, the men had a good look at their leader. Captain Robert Beecham of the 2nd Wisconsin later wrote of that moment: "The General looked careworn, and we thought, very sad...."[13] Even so, no one doubted that he would be equal to the occasion, for they trusted him completely.

As soon as Reynolds was satisfied there would be no hitch in bringing up the Iron Brigade, he hastened to the scene of conflict. On the way he caught up with Wadsworth. Near McPherson's Ridge the two generals met Buford. Since the earlier meeting with Reynolds, the cavalry leader's situation had become critical. Heth's Division had crossed Willoughby Run and was pressing the dismounted cavalrymen hard. On the left Gamble's Brigade was in serious trouble. Nevertheless, according to Buford, the troopers "had to be literally dragged back to a position more secure and better sheltered." Having been forced back about 200 yards, it was then on a line with Calef's guns.[14] On the right Devin's Brigade still held its ground, but clearly it too would soon be forced back.[15] Both brigades were almost out of ammunition.[16] Calef's guns were still firing, but, like the cavalry, their ammunition supply would not last much longer.[17] Furthermore, cavalrymen and artillerymen alike verged on exhaustion. How much longer could they withstand the merciless hail of Confederate shells and bullets? To Lieutenant Colonel Theodore W. Bean of Buford's staff, it was "painfully evident" that their position "would have to be abandoned, unless support speedily reached us."[18]

Facing this crisis, Reynolds judged his first priority to be the replacement of Calef's nearly exhausted battery. Accordingly, he summoned Captain Hall. On receiving the message, the battery commander first directed his officers to press on at top speed, then rode to Reynolds, whom he met on the Chambersburg Pike near McPherson's barn. Reportedly, Reynolds simply told Hall: "Put your battery on this ridge to engage those guns of the enemy."[19] Even if Reynolds said nothing further, Hall would have understood he expected the fastest possible compliance.

Buford notified Calef to pull back his right and middle sections to Seminary Ridge and there refill the ammunition chests. The left section, however, was to keep on firing from Herbst's Woods until Meredith's Brigade arrived. The right section, just north of the Chambersburg Pike, apparently hitched up its two guns and got away without difficulty. Such was not the case for one of the guns in the middle section, just south of the pike. Four of its six horses had fallen victim to an exploding shell. Hence it required herculean effort on the part of the crew and the two remaining horses to drag the gun onto the pike and up the daunting incline of Seminary Ridge. Once there, the section leader, a Sergeant Newman, might have felt overwhelming relief that the gun had been saved; instead he felt terribly remiss for not having salvaged a single harness from the slain horses. Later, as it turned out, he and a few of his men were able to slip back to the vacated position and rectify the omission. With a lot of tugging and possibly some judicious cutting, they managed to free two sets of harness from the now-stiff carcasses. Thus Newman's sense of honor was fully restored.[20]

Cutler's Brigade double-quicked by the MacMillan and Shultz houses on Seminary Ridge, crossed the Fairfield road, and followed the narrow dirt road that led to the Seminary and the Chambersburg Pike.[21] Just before the lead regiment reached the pike, the long column was halted and the troops were allowed to rest. During that interval a number of stragglers rejoined their companies. Regimental and company officers soon began maneuvering their commands into line, facing west. Then, suddenly, those troops still standing in the road had to give way to plunging horses and careening vehicles.[22] They were "crowded out"—as one private put it—by Hall's Battery dashing to the front.[23] Captain J. V. Pierce of the 147th New York had a glimpse of the speeding battery horses, saw their nostrils flaring, their flanks "white with foam."[24] Hall's cannoneers obviously were determined that Reynolds would not be kept waiting.

When the infantry was realigned and ready, terse commands rang out—"Forward—double-quick—march!"—and the brigade began to spill over the brow of Seminary Ridge.[25] Ahead of them the road and the fields on either side teemed with diverse traffic. Hall's battery streaking toward McPherson's Ridge in a swirl of dust. Calef's Battery retiring by section to Seminary Ridge. Wounded cavalrymen moving to the rear—on foot, on horseback, on litters. Aides-de-camp galloping in every direction, each intent on relaying a message or a command from his superior. Private Francis M. Pease of the 147th New York wrote in his diary that the road was so crowded that "we could run but part of the way." Artillery fire added to the turmoil. "The reb cannon balls," Pease also noted in his diary, "soon began to hum over our heads, some pretty close."[26] And Captain Pierce remembered the air was "full of flying fragments of shells."[27]

A civilian obviously well up in years, carrying a musket and looking mad enough to bite nails, naturally caught the eye of every passing soldier. Some wiseacre in the 147th New York called out to him: "We are going to celebrate the Fourth for you, old fellow." The feisty reply came back: "It's a little early in the month, but I'll help you do it."[28] It was, of course, John Burns. The Gettysburg constable apparently had wandered around a great deal this morning. Earlier, somewhere between the Emmitsburg and Chambersburg roads he had watched the First Corps pioneers levelling fences. He was so impressed with their skill with an ax that, in later years, he often described the scene, "springing to his feet and swinging his arms as though handling one of those shining implements and laying low the fences before him."[29]

Cutler's regiments reached the McPherson farm in good time, considering they had had to contend with incoming shells and oncoming traffic. When they halted just east of the huge stone barn, the firefight between Gamble's and Archer's Brigades was scarcely more than a hundred yards in their front. The 76th New York and 56th Pennsylvania men had only minutes in which to catch their breath before they were off again, this time to engage the enemy. With a longer reprieve, the men in the other regiments (14th Brooklyn, 95th and 147th New York) had but one concern—to stay clear of the murderous enemy artillery fire. For the most part, these troops hugged the ground and hoped luck would be with them, but some prudently took refuge in the McPherson barn.[30]

Meredith's Brigade diverged from Cutler's route when it reached the Fairfield road. Instead of following the lane that led past the Seminary, these regiments "bore away to the left...along a hollow...between the Seminary Ridge and the ridge or elevation in front of it."[31] As the men rushed forward, "solid-shot tore through the treetops above our heads"—so wrote 2nd Wisconsin's Captain Beecham—"reminding us that the battle was on in earnest, and much nearer than we had supposed."[32] Staff officers scurried from regiment to regiment, excitedly informing commanders that the enemy was advancing up the far slope of the ridge in their front and they should prepare for a charge.[33] With McPherson's Ridge looming ahead, 2nd Wisconsin's Colonel Lucius Fairchild finally sent his non-combatants to the rear. At this time he also turned over his mount to his hostler, whereupon he set a "rapid gait" for his fighting men to follow. Since his regiment led the brigade and every minute counted, he evidently felt it inexpedient to take time to load muskets—every soldier would have to attend to it as best he could.[34] Colonel Henry A. Morrow did halt the 24th Michigan for the sole purpose of loading, but before his troops could do so, a staff officer rode up and admonished Morrow to keep them moving. So they too had to load on the run.[35]

The McPherson barn as it appears today.

This photo of the McPherson farm, taken sometime after the war, shows the house before it was destroyed.

Four of the five Iron Brigade regiments went into action *en echelon*; that is, in a series of staggered lines. In this instance, it was from right to left, with the 2nd Wisconsin in front, followed successively by the 7th Wisconsin, 19th Indiana, and 24th Michigan.[36] The remaining regiment, the 6th Wisconsin, was last in line of march this morning. Shortly after it crossed the Fairfield road, a Lieutenant Woodward of Meredith's staff galloped up to Lieutenant Colonel Rufus Dawes, saluted, and said: "Colonel, form your line and prepare for action." Dawes gave the necessary orders. "The evolution of the line," he later wrote, "was performed on the double quick, the men loading their muskets as they ran."[37] But confusion always exists in battle, indeed sometimes reigns supreme. The lieutenant's order was quickly countermanded; Dawes' regiment was halted and held in reserve. Before long, however, it would play a crucial role in the morning's battle.

Oddly enough, considering the need for haste, the knapsacks in certain Iron Brigade companies (those that had not casually discarded them earlier) were stacked in tidy piles and covered with ponchos. A lucky private in each company was assigned the easy, relatively safe job of guarding his comrades' personal gear.[38]

Meanwhile, for Buford's dismounted line atop McPherson's Ridge, the situation was becoming grim. The troopers could not avoid the alarming realization that, despite their brutal and incessant fire, the enemy was drawing ever closer. Lieutenant Calef, peering over the guns of his left section, saw Archer's double line "not over a thousand yards distant...their battle-flags looked redder and bloodier in the strong July sun than I had ever seen them before."[39] Time and again, Buford's men must have glanced toward Seminary Ridge for a sign of approaching relief. At last they were rewarded. The 8th Illinois' Major Beveridge exulted when he saw the First Division, "led by Reynolds and Wadsworth in person, coming across the meadow on the double-quick."[40] The 8th New York's Captain Mills — he who had hoped for reinforcements to come and had feared they would not — was likewise overjoyed when he saw the onrushing infantrymen and knew his hope would be fulfilled. Of that moment, he wrote: "How grateful and glad we battered troopers were then."[41] Even after a lapse of twenty years, Joel Swett, who had been a private in the 8th New York, vividly remembered how he felt: "There was a sense of relief on my own part which I shall never forget when we saw the grand old 1st corps coming...."[42] No one, and most especially Buford's grateful troopers, ever disputed that Wadsworth's Division arrived just in time.

Yet, now that the fear of being unsupported and overrun had been eliminated, the troopers seemed in no hurry to leave. In fact, some 3rd Indiana men decided to stay, arranged for horseholders, inveigled muskets and ammunition from the infantry, and fought with the Iron Brigade.[43] In the 8th Illinois one trooper either did not hear the command to withdraw or willfully defied it. At first he stood erect facing the enemy, as though daring them to try to hit him. Then he lay flat in the tall grass and waited. When the Rebels drew close, he suddenly jumped up and screamed, "Come on—we have them!" His actions were certainly quixotic, foolhardy. Still, his desperate ploy apparently deceived the enemy into thinking they had heard a Union officer exhorting his men to charge. As credible a witness as Buford attested that at that moment Heth's line faltered. He told regimental surgeon Abner Hard he had never seen anything quite as daring.[44]

The dismounted cavalrymen who chose to remain on McPherson's Ridge were the exception, however. The vast majority withdrew, though, according to Buford, they did so "most reluctantly."[45] Whether willing to admit it or not, every trooper had to be bone-tired. Those who contested the Confederate advance west of Willoughby Run had been engaged for well over two hours; those in the McPherson's Ridge line, after a long wait (which itself was enervating), had been fighting for more than an hour. The tension born of that fighting (and waiting) would dissipate once they were outside the combat zone. The Iron Brigade's Captain Beecham, who had observed Buford's cavalrymen just before they left the ridge, described them as a "thin line of horsemen dressed in faded blue with yellow trimmings, powder-begrimed and disordered by the heat of battle."[46] Bedraggled though they undoubtedly were, they had not lost their pugnacious spirit. One of them called out to the 95th New York as it came up the ridge: "Go in and give them hell!"[47]

Released from its infantry role, Buford's Division reverted to a normal cavalry function: protecting the infantry's flanks. Devin's Brigade guarded Wadsworth's right flank and two regiments of Gamble's Brigadeguarded his left. While the new positions largely eliminated the danger from enemy bullets, the cavalrymen were still exposed to errant enemy shells.[48]

Devin's squadrons on McPherson's Ridge returned to their mounts and rode off to join those squadrons still picketing the roads north of Gettysburg. Together they provided a formidable protective screen stretching eastward from the junction of the Carlisle and Newville roads to the Harrisburg road.

In Gamble's Brigade the 8th Illinois and 8th New York troopers, back in the saddle, rode south to the Fairfield road. The Illinois regiment halted in an orchard on the south side of the road, with one squadron advanced to open ground in its front. The New York regiment, after covering the withdrawal of Calef's left section guns, moved to a position directly across the road from the 8th Illinois.

The other half of Gamble's Brigade—the 3rd Indiana and the 12th Illinois Regiments—rode east to Gettysburg, where they were held in reserve.[49] En route, the cavalrymen had a curious experience. Amid the cacophony of battle they thought they heard singing...sweet voices from on high. Baffled, they must have thought: *Am I dreaming? Am I losing my mind?* Or, even, *Am I in Heaven!* Looking up, they had their answer: The comely students of a women's college which they were then passing had gathered on the roof and were at that moment serenading them with "Rally Round the Flag, Boys."[50]

For Buford's men, though they could not have known it at the time, the heavy fighting in this battle was over. Even though their effective strength had been drastically reduced by the necessity of providing horseholders, the two cavalry brigades plus a single battery had succeeded in holding two larger Confederate infantry brigades and an entire artillery battalion at bay until relief arrived. Their mettle had been sorely tested and not found wanting. They had played a vital role in the Army of the Potomac's eventual triumph at Gettysburg. When Major General Alfred Pleasonton wrote his after-action report for the cavalry corps, he appropriately singled out Buford's Division for special praise. Its officers and men were to be commended, he said, for their "splendid courage and skill" and for "displaying great obstinacy in holding all their positions."[51]

"Tell Doubleday I will hold on to this road...."

That John Reynolds was highly competent in the use of artillery is beyond cavil. It was, after all, the branch of service he entered upon graduation from West Point and the one in which he served with distinction during the Mexican War. After the battle at Monterey and again after the battle at Buena Vista he was brevetted for his skill and valor.[52] Thus, manifestly, it was not through ignorance that he now ordered Hall's 2nd Maine battery to an exposed position far in advance of the infantry. Exigent circumstances had forced him to take a calculated risk.

The intense shelling from Pegram's five Confederate batteries could cripple Cutler's Brigade before it ever got in line. Diverting their fire was Reynolds' best hope. Aggressive action by Hall's battery would surely draw the enemy fire upon itself. So Reynolds instructed Hall: "I desire you to damage the artillery to the greatest possible extent, and keep their fire from our infantry until they are deployed, when I will retire you somewhat as you are too far advanced for the general line."[53]

Hall's six guns turned off the Chambersburg Pike, went north a short distance, then west to a knoll on McPherson's Ridge. As soon as the guns came into view of Pegram's batteries a half mile away on Herr Ridge, the Southerners retrained their pieces and let them have it. Feverishly, Hall's three sections—under lieutenants William Ulmer, Albert Thomas, and Frank Carr—set up and soon replied in kind. Their line stretched one hundred yards from just north of the pike to a point about twenty yards from an embankment that dropped sharply to the unfinished railroad bed.[54]

Meanwhile, Reynolds conferred with Wadsworth and Hall. The artillery officer had to be worried about his battery's precarious position and therefore was much relieved when he heard Reynolds say to Wadsworth: "General, move a strong infantry support immediately to Hall's relief for he is my defender until I can get the troops now coming into line."[55] In due course a number of regiments buttressed Hall's position—principally the 147th New York on the right and the 95th New York on the left. Even so, the position would ultimately prove untenable.

Devin's dismounted troopers held their ground with amazing tenacity, considering their position was too exposed and their number too few. Nevertheless, their line almost certainly would have crumbled if the 76th New York and 56th Pennsylvania had not come to their relief when they did. During the approach to Devin's position, both regiments of Cutler's Brigade took some casualties from enemy artillery. The New Yorkers were on the right, the Pennsylvanians on the left. Hastily, they now formed a battle line within the half-mile expanse of fields between the railroad cut and the Mummasburg road.[56] After Sergeant Hubbard and his 18-man provost guard rushed into position on the far right, that end of the line was anchored on the road.[57] For a short while the other end hung in the air, with a wide gap looming between the 56th Pennsylvania and Hall's guns at the railroad cut.

Wadsworth intended that the 147th New York move into this space at the same time the other two regiments were forming their lines. But something went wrong and the 147th did not get the order. This did not prove serious, however, because the regimental commander, Lieutenant Colonel Francis Miller, waited only minutes after arriving at the McPherson farm before going himself to find out what was expected of his troops.[58] Apparently he obtained the answer fairly quickly. According to one officer in the 147th, his men had rested along McPherson's fence only five minutes when the order came to move out.[59] No doubt the respite seemed that short, but probably was a bit longer. Private John Bartlett gave a good account of what happened next, though he neglected to mention that the whole action was performed on the double-quick,[60] perhaps assuming that that could be taken for granted. Spelling and punctuation were obviously not his forte. He wrote:

> Very soon we mooved from the rear of the barn crossing the road and mooving to the right on low ground just in rear of the battery, I plainly saw the caisons horses (etc) of the battery as we went to the right As soon as we had crossed an old R. R. bed we were faced to front and mooved to the west up a gentle slope toward the crest of the ridge upon which the battery was at work.[61]

Reaching the crest, the troops fanned out, forming a line that was some thirty yards behind Hall's guns, on the left, and two hundred yards ahead of the 76th New York and 56th Pennsylvania, on the right.[62]

Reynolds notified Wadsworth that he would have full charge of the three regiments north of the railroad cut, the right of the Union line. He added: "I will look out for the left."[63] Thus Reynolds reserved to himself exclusive control of Meredith's Brigade—then rushing toward McPherson's Ridge—and the two remaining regiments of Cutler's Brigade.[64] The latter he posted south of the Chambersburg Pike in support of Hall's Battery. The right of the 95th New York rested on the pike; the left of the 14th Brooklyn reached to Herbst's Woods.[65] As the 14th Brooklyn was taking its position, some of Gamble's retiring troopers ran by crying, "They are coming, give it to them!"[66]

About the time the First Division of the First Corps took over for the cavalry, Lieutenant Benjamin Marten rode up to Reynolds with an inquiry from General Doubleday. What role should the Second and Third Divisions play in the current action, the First Corps commander wanted to know.[67] Reynolds' reply: "Tell Doubleday I will hold on to this road and he must hold on to that one."[68] By "that one" he meant the Fairfield Road, which was vitally important because of its proximity to the left flank of Wadsworth's Division. But there was an additional reason. Reynolds believed that

Confederate troops would arrive via the Fairfield Road since Buford's cavalry had had a brush with the enemy near Fairfield the day before.[69]

Meanwhile, Abner Doubleday hurried to the battlefield. By the time he arrived, the fight, which had been simmering for three hours, had reached the boiling point.

"Forward for God's sake...!"

Swaths of grayish-white smoke from the intense artillery fire hung in the hot, still air. Visibility was poor, but General Lysander Cutler, with the aid of fieldglasses, was able to trace a line of enemy infantry approaching from the west. He and his staff had halted midway between the Chambersburg Pike and the Mummasburg Road. In their immediate front the 56th Pennsylvania was sprinting into line. Its commander, Colonel John W. Hofmann, noticed Cutler looking through fieldglasses and called out: "Is that the enemy?"

Assured by his superior that it was, Hofmann turned toward his troops and bellowed: "Ready...right oblique... aim...fire!" The sudden outburst startled Cutler. He thought it premature—the men were not yet organized, not ready to fire. Furthermore, he doubted that firing at this moment would produce any beneficial result. So he shouted back to Hofmann, urging restraint until the enemy was within musket range. But Hofmann never heard him, and another ragged volley ensued. The Rebels replied with a shower of bullets that toppled a number of Pennsylvanians.[70]

Hofmann said it was 10:20 when he gave his precipitous command.[71] In the 76th New York, which fought alongside Hofmann's regiment, Captain John E. Cook reported that his men were fired upon at about 10:30.[72] These and other statements by participants agree that the fight between Davis' and Cutler's Brigades began at or shortly before 10:30. Later, the Iron Brigade would claim the honor of opening the infantry battle. Some fervent testimony was advanced for the 2nd Wisconsin, the first of its regiments to be engaged; but it is unconvincing.

Although the 56th Pennsylvania came up McPherson's Ridge behind the 76th New York, it was first to fire. This was so, Cutler explained, because these troops reached their sector "a moment sooner" than the lead troops reached theirs.[73] But there was another reason: The Pennsylvanians could see the enemy whereas the New Yorkers could not. For the latter, a ripple in the field ahead of them effectively hid the advancing troops. Major Andrew J. Grover, commander of the 76th New York, ordered his men to hold their fire until they had something to aim at. Very soon they did. The Rebels were then only 200 yards away, striding through a wheatfield, firing as they came. Grover's men, though still forming their line, managed a prompt return fire.[74]

On the receiving end was the 55th North Carolina—the same troops the 56th Pennsylvania had fired upon only minutes earlier.[75] The Carolinians were on the 56th Pennsylvania's right but directly in front of Grover's 76th New York. The Pennsylvania regiment, in the meantime, had diverted its fire to the 2nd Mississippi when that regiment suddenly appeared in its front. Just north of the railroad cut, the 42nd Mississippi came over the ridge and poured a savage fire into the 142nd New York. The New Yorkers were ill-prepared, as they were still maneuvering into position; nevertheless, they immediately took up the gauntlet.[76]

The din of six infantry regiments firing simultaneously had to be ear-splitting. Adding to the racket was the near-constant, deep-throated roar of cannon on both sides. The cannoneers of Hall's Battery persevered in the unequal match with Pegram's five batteries. They actually made it so hot for one Confederate section that it had to relocate its guns.[77]

General Oliver Howard, in the meantime, had dispatched Captain Daniel Hall to report to Reynolds on the progress of the Eleventh Corps and to obtain any further orders. Hall was surprised to find the commander of the army's left wing "nearly out to the extreme advance of our troops where the skirmishers and some regiments were already hotly engaged." Reynolds absorbed the news of the Eleventh Corps and replied crisply to Hall's inquiry about orders. Tell Howard, he said, that the enemy has been encountered "apparently in force"; that he should bring his corps to the assistance of the First Corps "as rapidly as possible"; and that he should "join him at the scene of action."[78]

Also about this time, Reynolds heard from the Third Corps. Major Henry E. Tremain, Dan Sickles' senior aide, rode up, reported the corps' arrival in Emmitsburg, and asked for further orders. Reynolds replied, "Tell General Sickles I think he had better come up."

Doubtless Reynolds often glanced to the rear to check on the progress of Meredith's Iron Brigade. If those troops did not occupy McPherson's Ridge soon, the Confederates south of the Chambersburg Pike would overrun the position. And that, conceivably, could lead to a rout of Wadsworth's whole division. The mere thought of such a thing would have been reprehensible to Reynolds, but he had to reckon with one inescapable fact: The enemy was already dangerously close and Gamble's dismounted cavalry could not hold out much longer. Calef had finally ordered his left section guns at Herbst's Woods to pull back. With the enemy drawing nearer every minute, he had deemed it "unadvisable to wait till they arrived within canister range."[79]

The "double-quick" mentioned in after-action reports was frequently a euphemism for "ran." Such was undoubtedly the case for the Iron Brigade's movement from the Fairfield Road to McPherson's Ridge. The staggered lines of the 2nd and 7th Wisconsin, 19th Indiana, and 24th Michigan blanketed an area five hundred yards wide. Their propulsive forward motion was arrested only when some units paused just long enough to load muskets or to attach bayonets.[80] The imminent prospect of a fight hardly daunted these seasoned veterans; rather it was a kind of fulfillment, something that lent meaning and purpose to the 85 miles of forced marches they had endured over the past week.[81] They went forward confidently, perhaps even arrogantly, for they were mindful of their past glories, their reputation for valor. This was, in their view, a chance for renewed, or even greater, glory.

Just as they were about to ascend McPherson's Ridge, the fight between Cutler's and Davis' Brigades erupted on their right.[82] The abrupt surge in the noise level gave clear notice that they, too, would soon be in combat.

Reynolds, in the meantime, had been informed of a sizeable enemy force racing ahead of the main Confederate line. Despite strong protests from his staff, he rode into Herbst's Woods to investigate. What he and the trio who rode with him saw was cause for alarm. If the Confederate horde coming up the western slope were to reach the crest at the northern end of the woods, it would gravely imperil the left flank of the two Cutler regiments he had just brought into position. There was no time to lose.[83]

Reynolds, followed by his orderly and Captains Mitchell and Baird, hastily threaded their way back through the woods. Once clear of the trees, they galloped to the line of the 2nd Wisconsin.[84] When Reynolds came within hailing distance, he implored the approaching troops to press on. With that, he wheeled his horse around and led the regiment up McPherson's Ridge.[85] As the 300 Badger State men, all nearly winded, were about to enter Herbst's Woods, he cried: "Forward, men! Forward for God's sake, and drive those fellows out of the woods!"[86]

Reynolds at this moment presented a clear target to the enemy. He, however, was completely oblivious to danger—to everything in fact except getting the Iron Brigade into action. After the battle one of Doubleday's aides, Lieutenant Henry T. Lee, talked with members of Reynolds' staff. It was their belief, he later wrote, that Reynolds' rash exposure of himself "was owing to his earnestness to occupy and hold the ridge."[87]

When the 2nd Wisconsin came over the crest of McPherson's Ridge shortly after 10:30, it ran head-on into Archer's 1st Tennessee regiment.[88] The Tennesseans reacted swiftly. Whipping musket to shoulder, they unleashed a tremendous volley into the Yankee line scarcely fifty yards away.[89] Many 2nd Wisconsin soldiers fell, leaving big holes in the plunging line.[90] The regiment's second-in-command, 28-year-old Lieutenant Colonel George H. Stevens, was among the first to be killed.[91] The men still on their feet, though shaken by the fearsome blast, recovered quickly. Uttering a shrill battle cry, they commenced a sharp return fire.[92]

How close to the enemy was Reynolds at this moment? His orderly, who was constantly at his side this morning, recalled that the Rebels were "not much more than sixty paces from where the Gen'l was."[93] Did such proximity denote folly or bravery? Major Riddle—he who had awakened Reynolds at 4:00 a.m.—gave this answer: "Here was again exhibited that brilliant daring by the gen[eral] which excites men to emulation always. He threw himself into the very front...but at what a sacrifice."[94]

"No man died on that field with more glory...."

On McPherson's Ridge General Reynolds nobly exemplified his firm belief that troops should be led, not driven. His energy and sheer determination were fueled by his obsessive desire to rid his home state of the Confederate invaders.[95]

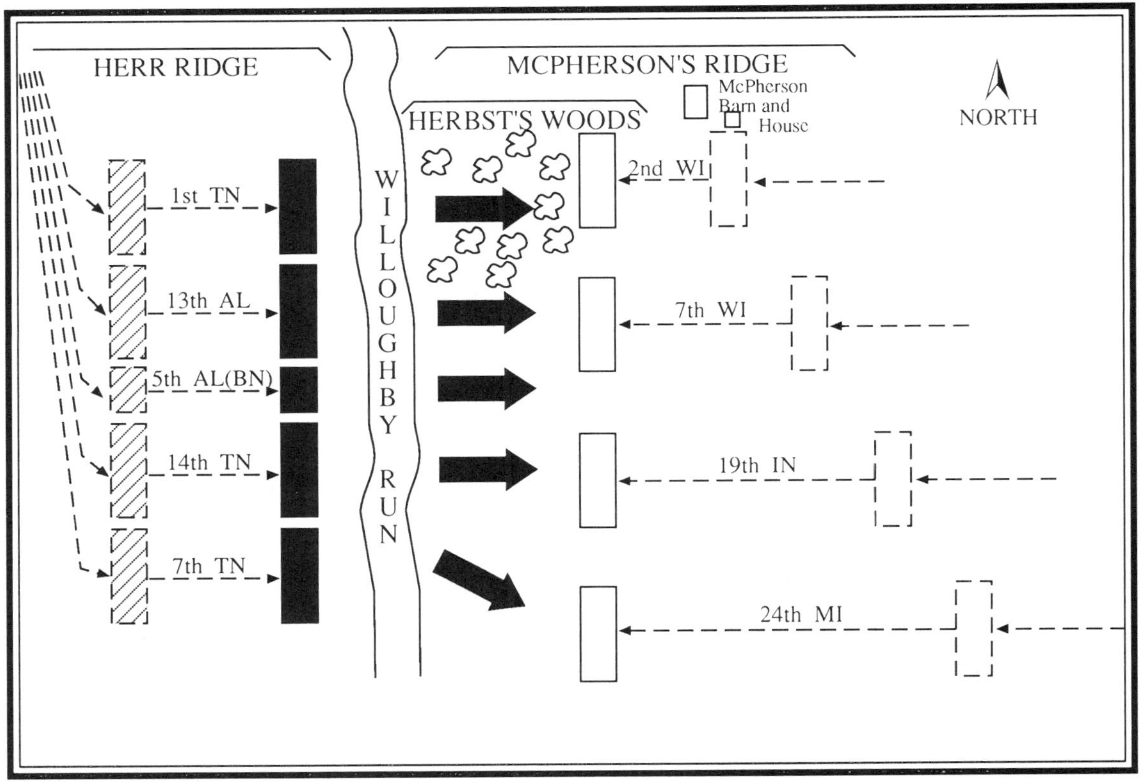

Confederate attack south of the Chambersburg Pike. About 10:35 Archer's 1st Tennessee regiment fired on Meredith's 2nd Wisconsin regiment, then just coming into position on McPherson's Ridge. Within minutes Union General Reynolds was felled by a Confederate bullet.

But these aspects of his behavior were far from his mind. He had just seen the 2nd Wisconsin men reel from the enemy's sudden fusillade, the impact causing them to veer to the right. He rode along the line, rallying them, fearing they would be overrun.[96] *They must have support!* The need was overpowering, supreme. And he surely agonized: *Where are the other regiments? They should be up by now!* The thick woods prevented him from seeing how close they were. So Reynolds went to find out, and when he was nearly out of the woods, he turned in his saddle to scan the open fields just ahead. In that instant the minie ball struck.[97]

The general's strapping black horse maintained its gait as Reynolds slumped in the saddle, swayed, and toppled to the ground. He fell face downward, arms outstretched, one foot caught in the stirrup. Before it came free, his body had been dragged at least ten feet.[98]

After being shot Reynolds never spoke again. In all probability death was instantaneous, though he may have lingered briefly in a deep coma. "I have seen many killed in action," his orderly Charles Veil later commented, "but never saw a ball do its work so instantly as did the ball which struck General Reynolds, a man who knew not what fear or danger was."[99]

For the Army of the Potomac, it was a tragedy of incalculable magnitude. But there can be no wonder that it happened. Reason dictates that a general officer facing the same risks as a private is equally vulnerable—and just as mortal. While on McPherson's Ridge Reynolds was at maximum risk. As Veil described the situation during that period and other witnesses confirmed, "Minie balls were flying thick."[100] Although Reynolds was riding back through the woods and had nearly reached its eastern edge when the ball struck him, he was still very close to the enemy—only one hundred yards, according to staff officers at the scene.[101] His position in relation to the 2nd Wisconsin was noted by a sergeant in Company I. After the first volley Cornelius Wheeler turned to see who had fallen in his company, and "glancing down the slope to the rear saw General Reynolds fall from his horse." Reynolds, he recalled, was then one hundred feet from the right rear of the 2nd Wisconsin.[102] Ironically, though Reynolds commanded three corps—almost half of the Army of the Potomac—he died leading a regiment.[103]

Usually surrounded by staff members, he was at that moment unattended except for his orderly.[104] Sergeant Veil, horrified on seeing his commander fall, sprang from his horse and ran to his side. "As I saw no sign of wound or blood when I turned him I thought he was only stunned by a spent ball....I took hold under his arms and pulled him...as fast as I could until [he was] over the brow of the rise out of range of the fire, where I found some of our men."[105] These included Captains Baird, Mitchell, and Wilcox of Reynolds' staff and Captain John P. Carson of his headquarters company.[106] (Just minutes earlier, both Wilcox and Carson had had their horses shot from under them; they themselves were uninjured.)[107]

It was a shocked, incredulous group that looked down on the still figure of their leader. Like Veil, the officers thought him only stunned; they saw no blood, only a bruise above his left eye. Captain Mitchell directed a question to Reynolds: General,

Alfred Waud sketch of Reynolds at the instant of his death.

are you in pain? There was no reply, but some thought they heard him gasp and noticed he seemed to smile slightly.[108] Captain Baird, seeking an explanation for Reynolds' fall, loosened the general's clothing. The coat collar, he discovered, had been pushed up over the wound, which had bled only slightly. But when Baird saw the hole made by the minie ball, he felt "there was no hope for his recovery." Nevertheless, he dashed over to an infantryman, borrowed his canteen, dashed back, raised Reynolds' head, and tried to get him to drink. To no avail, for Reynolds' eyes were already glazed.[109]

The ball had struck Reynolds behind the right ear, almost at the juncture of the spine and the skull.[110] It was a perfect shot, but whether it occurred by chance or by deliberate aim of a super marksman cannot be known. Many stories circulated of a sharpshooter in a tree, but it seems far more likely that Reynolds' killer was one of Archer's infantrymen stalking through Herbst's Woods. When the ball struck Reynolds, it was deflected downward, passing around the skull and lodging in the chest.[111]

The time of Reynolds' death has been variously stated, from 10:00 a.m. through 11:15 a.m. In view of the relationship of this occurrence to coincident events on McPherson's Ridge, both extremes are patently in error. While an exact determination is not possible, it can be averred that, give or take ten minutes, Reynolds died at 10:45.[112]

In fairly rapid succession the 7th Wisconsin, 19th Indiana, and 24th Michigan joined the 2nd Wisconsin in the vicious melee south of the Chambersburg Pike. These troops swarmed past the cluster of staff officers, unaware that in the center lay their revered leader.

It is probably true, as Lieutenant Rosengarten believed, that Reynolds saw the oncoming Iron Brigade regiments just before the fatal moment.[113] But the assertion by some writers that he was actually leading the 19th Indiana into battle when he was hit must be considered spurious.

Meredith's Iron Brigade, incidentally, would claim the honor of opening the infantry battle. Over the years much fervent testimony was advanced by and for its 2nd Wisconsin regiment; but it is unconvincing. As noted earlier, its sister brigade, under Lysander Cutler, preceded it into battle by a few minutes. Thus, Cutler's Brigade—to be precise, its 56th Pennsylvania regiment—earned the distinction of firing the first shots by Union infantry.

Enlisted men were recruited to assist Veil in carrying Reynolds' body to the rear. After placing the mute figure on a litter improvised with a blanket and two muskets, they lifted the heavy burden to their shoulders and started back at a slow walk toward Seminary Ridge.[114] The identity of the litter bearers is uncertain, since both the 14th Brooklyn and the 76th New York claimed they performed the service.[115]

It fell to Captain Carson to convey the sad news to the next-in-command. Having lost his own horse, he appropriated another and galloped off to find General Doubleday.[116]

With regard to Reynolds' conduct in battle, one of Doubleday's staff officers ruefully remarked that "it was always a fault of his to be right on the front when there was any fighting."[117] Paradoxically, it was this trait, as much as any other, that endeared him to his men. Lieutenant Rosengarten of his staff considered him "the best type of military leader," but allowed that his actions in battle created a "shining mark" for the enemy.[118] On this hot July morning the "shining mark" attracted the enemy ball that killed him. What Sir William Napier wrote in eulogy of a Crimean War hero can, with singular aptness, also be said of Reynolds: "No man died on that field with more glory than he. Yet many died and there was much glory."[119]

Residence of George George on the Emmitsburg Road circa 1863, where the body of General Reynolds was taken.

CHAPTER VI

REBELS FLANK YANKEES

"...a stubborn resistance...."

While the Iron Brigade rushed into battle on the left and a stunned group of officers looked down upon the mute figure of General Reynolds, the unanchored right of the Union line faced potential disaster.

When Rebels confronted Yankees there, the tactical advantage decidedly rested with the Southerners. Their line, as was immediately apparent to both sides, greatly overlapped the Union line. More precisely, it was the 55th North Carolina which overlapped the 76th New York.

Colonel John Connally, leader of the Carolina regiment, had his men attach bayonets at some point during the advance. When he saw he could flank the enemy, he ordered the left of his line to wheel sharply right. As his men swooped down on the hapless New Yorkers, they gave the fearsome Rebel yell.[1] Even to the most hardened Union troops, it was demoralizing. "There is nothing like it this side of the infernal region," one Yankee soldier declared, "and the peculiar corkscrew sensation it sends down your backbone under these circumstances can never be told."[2]

For the men of the 76th New York, the baleful effect of the blood-curdling cry was compounded by the sudden appearance of the enemy in strong force, not only on their front, but already starting to swing around their right flank.[3] The Rebels had been hidden from Union view until they came over a rise. As one New Yorker remembered it, they "seemed to spring up as it were out of the ground."[4] In the Union rear, Buford's signal officer, A. B. Jerome (still posted in the Seminary cupola), saw them through his fieldglasses and was aghast. The Confederates, he later wrote, "were advancing on the right flank in numbers as large as our whole front."[5] He can be forgiven the exaggeration, for so it must have seemed to him at that crucial moment.

The flanking movement was executed in "magnificent style," according to the North Carolinians.[6] Their enfilade fire, at close range, took a heavy toll.[7] The New Yorkers returned the fire as best they could, but unless some defensive maneuver was undertaken at once, their line would be rolled up and their escape route to the rear cut off.

Their commander, Major Andrew J. Grover, was alert to the grave danger. In the tenuous hope of resisting the onslaught, he refused his right, pulling back five

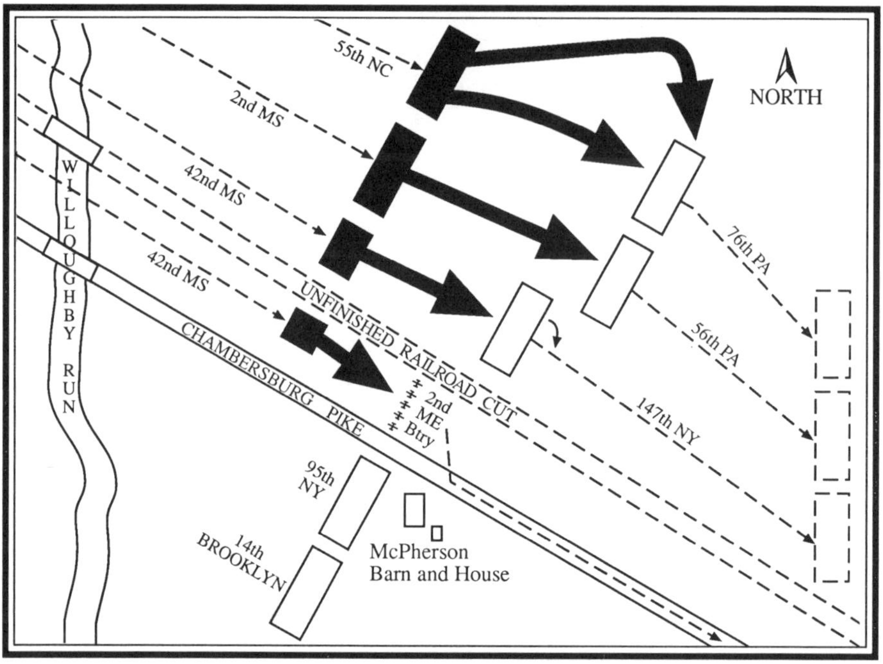

Confederate attack north of the Chambersburg Pike. The opposing brigades of Davis and Cutler opened fire at or shortly before 10:30.

companies to form a 90-degree angle with the rest of the line. A tricky maneuver, fiendishly difficult under fire. Yet Grover's battle-wise troops managed it. Before the movement was completed, however, the 32-year-old leader lay dead and his senior captain, John E. Cook, had taken his place.[8]

The 55th North Carolina also lost its leader early in the fight. Impulsively, Colonel Connally had grabbed the regimental flag, ran ahead of his men, and waved it vigorously to and fro. Such bravado inevitably had drawn enemy fire and he went down, shot in arm and hip. Major Alfred H. Belo, seeing him fall, dashed to his side and asked if he was badly injured. The colonel grimaced in pain. "Yes," he admitted, "but the litter bearers are here." Even at such a moment the fallen leader could not countenance the thought of his men being outshone by any other regiment. "Go on," he gasped, "and don't let the Mississippians get ahead of you."

Although Connally would lose his arm, he survived his wounds. Lieutenant Colonel Maurice T. Smith, his second-in-command, was not so fortunate. He also was struck down shortly after the battle opened, but his wound was fatal. With Connally and Smith *hors de combat*, command of the 55th North Carolina passed to Major Belo. If he still wondered whether his men were up against militia or regular army, he soon had his answer. A Yankee prisoner informed him: "We are Joe Hooker's men, and have marched five miles this morning."[9] (In the stress of combat, the soldier apparently forgot that Meade had replaced Hooker as commander of the Army of the Potomac three days before.)

The 76th New York doggedly fought on in spite of the brutal Confederate fire. Rifles grew hot with repeated firing; comrades fell on all sides; screams of the wounded sliced through the horrific noise. The perfectly still body of a Company A soldier lay beside a stone fence; presumably death had been instantaneous. But his company commander became suspicious when he noticed how neatly the man was wrapped in a blanket, his head completely covered. Going over to him, Captain Herschel Pierce whipped off the blanket, and seeing the man was very much alive, ordered him to get up.

"I can't," the man whined, "I am awfully wounded."

"Where?" Pierce demanded. The man pointed to his side. The captain took a look, found no trace of a wound there or anywhere else. "Get up you coward!" he bellowed. Thereafter, for the remainder of the day, the malingerer was made to fight in the front rank of his company.[10]

The 56th Pennsylvania, buffered by Federal troops on both flanks, was not quite as imperilled as the 76th New York. Still, subjected to a merciless frontal fire, they too were hard pressed. Casualties were mounting, and a savage charge by Mississippi troops had cost them their colors. In that bloody melee they had shot the lieutenant who led the charge as well as a number of enlisted men.[11] But that was small compensation for their own casualties and the humiliation of losing their colors.

General Davis noted in his battle report: "The enemy made a stubborn resistance, and stood until our men were within a few yards, and then gave way...."[12] Not exactly. Union General Wadsworth had been observing the action north of the pike and realized his troops there would soon be forced back. Before that moment came, he directed General Cutler to order a withdrawal.[13] The hard-pressed Yankees in the 76th New York and the 56th Pennsylvania were not in the least reluctant to leave.

In fact, the order to withdraw precipitated an uncontrolled dash to the rear. The Rebels, seeing the mass of blue coats high-tailing it toward a distant woods, had good reason to believe them "completely routed," as Major Belo claimed.[14] General Doubleday, who witnessed the flight of the two regiments just as he came on the field, admitted that it was "somewhat disorderly."[15] The 6th Wisconsin's Colonel Dawes, who also witnessed the retreat, was less generous. He flatly declared that Cutler's troops fled the field "in disorder."[16]

Cutler himself had a close call during the retreat. He was unhorsed but escaped serious injury when a bullet struck his mount. At the same time two members of his staff also had their mounts shot from under them. A 2nd Mississippi soldier, W. B. Murphy, told how it happened.

As the Yankees were falling back, Murphy spotted a party on horseback in their midst. By pointing and exclamation, he directed the attention of the men around him to the group. They opened fire and were gratified to see several horses fall, spilling their riders. Sometime afterward Murphy learned that their target was none other than General Cutler and his staff.[17]

Brigadier General Joseph R. Davis

Brigadier General Lysander Cutler

When the fleeing Federals reached the relative safety of the woods on Oak Ridge (the northern extension of Seminary Ridge), they paused to catch their breath. Officers immediately got busy rounding up their commands. The enemy, meanwhile, moved into the fields the Federals had just vacated. Although the Rebels had halted there, at any moment they might mount another assault. Consequently, it was decided to move Cutler's two regiments farther south, to the railroad cut. Arriving there, the 76th New York and 56th Pennsylvania reorganized and, in the process, learned the full extent of their losses.[18]

It was staggering. In less than thirty minutes the two regiments together with the provost guard had suffered more than 250 casualties.[19]

In the 76th New York a forlorn Captain Cook surveyed the pathetic remnant of his command. Besides Major Grover, two captains and two lieutenants had been killed. Thirteen more officers were wounded. Also missing were 151 enlisted men (27 killed, 124 wounded). Of the approximately 380 officers and men who went into battle, barely 200 could respond to the muster in the railroad cut.[20]

The 56th Pennsylvania also had fared badly, though less so than the 76th New York. "In twenty minutes," reported Colonel J. W. Hofmann, "our losses in killed and wounded was over seventy."[21] Thus, of some 250 officers and men engaged, fewer than 180 remained. Of the 18-man provost guard posted on the far right of Cutler's line, only six escaped unharmed.[22]

A reckoning of Confederate casualties for the same period is simply not possible. As there was no respite for the Southerners, obviously no one stopped to calculate the losses to that point. However, when Davis reported that enemy resistance in the opening stage of the infantry battle had been "stubborn," he tacitly implied the likelihood of substantial Confederate losses.

But Union losses, in all probability, were much higher. Confederate Major Belo recalled that when Cutler's regiments retreated, the line they had just vacated "was well marked by their dead and wounded."[23]

"It was a hot place, and no mistake."

Wadsworth's retreat order embraced all three of Cutler's regiments north of the Chambersburg Pike. But the 147th New York, on the north side of the unfinished railroad cut and some 250 yards in advance of the other two regiments, never received it until it was almost too late.

The 380 officers and men, on leaving the shelter of McPherson's farm buildings, had marched across the pike, through a field, and down into the cut. When they had scrambled up the far bank and entered a wheatfield, Lieutenant Colonel Francis C. Miller gave the command "By the left flank, guide center!"[24] North of them the infantry battle had been raging for several minutes.[25] As if to make amends for their late arrival, the New Yorkers rushed toward the western crest of McPherson's Ridge, trampling the tall wheat as they went. Their mission: to support and protect Hall's 2nd Maine Battery, which had already begun its uneven struggle against Pegram's five batteries.[26]

The regiment was about to receive its baptism of fire at the hands of the 42nd Mississippi, lying in wait for them along the western edge of the wheatfield.[27] For Lieutenant J. Volney Pierce, commander of Company G, it had to be supremely unnerving to see "innumerable heads of rebels bobbing up and down," knowing that combat—with its gruesome harvest of injury and death—would follow. And shortly it did, in a staggering blast of Confederate musketry. Many 147th New York men were hit before they could get off their first shot. A corporal and a private marching side by side were struck down at the same instant, their lifeless bodies falling one on top of the other. The wounded who were not totally incapacitated trudged to the rear.[28]

No sooner had the 42nd Mississippi opened fire than the 147th New York men heard the order "Lie down! fire through the wheat close to the ground!"[29] With Rebels scarcely sixty yards away, they obeyed instantly, commencing a brisk counterfire.[30] "Give them hell!" shouted Captain Than Wright, as he pounded the ground in utter rage.[31]

Rebel bullets sliced through the standing grain, strewing heads and stems all over the Yankees. Brushing these bits from their eyes and faces, they rose up, fired, and immediately dropped behind their undulating cover to reload.[32] Again and again they fired, "as fast as we could," one soldier said.[33] Another soldier wrote shortly after the battle that "balls whistled round our heads like hail. The men soon began to fall very fast and many wounded."[34] (As only the upper part of their bodies was exposed when they stood up, most of the wounds were to the chest, arms, and head.)[35] B. E. Parkhurst of Company F really spoke for every man in the regiment when he said: "It was a hot place, and no mistake."[36]

The firing of nearly a thousand muskets in the two opposing regiments, not to mention that of the artillery, produced a deafening roar and a thick pall of smoke. It was next to impossible for troops on either side to see the enemy. Harried officers, trying to direct and encourage their men, shouted in vain, their words swallowed up in the terrible din.[37]

The men of the 147th New York felt isolated, alone. The ubiquitous smoke and the thick brush that ran along a rail fence effectively screened the two Cutler regiments on their right flank from view.[38] John Bartlett of Company C remembered: "I saw nothing of troops on our right or left except the battery mentioned [Hall's], which I did see distinctly before the smoke of musketry obscured the view."[39] Thus, when the 76th New York and the 56th Pennsylvania withdrew, the 147th was unaware of it.

Bartlett was out of the fight after firing only a few rounds. The head wound he sustained was evidently superficial, since he was able to walk to the rear to get treatment.[40] In contrast, his regimental commander, Lieutenant Colonel Miller, had to receive medical attention fast—survival depended on it. Shot in the throat and bleeding profusely, he spun his horse around and galloped off the field.[41]

On Miller's departure, command of the regiment fell to Major George Harney. From the moment he took over, he was in the deepest trouble. His troops were within the enemy's noose, which was growing tighter every minute. Clearly, they faced decimation or capture en masse, with hasty retreat their only hope.

How did the 147th New York happen to be left stranded? According to Cutler, in his after-action report for the brigade, Miller received the withdrawal order but his untimely wound precluded his relaying it to his subordinates.[42] Doubleday apparently accepted Cutler's explanation, as he repeated it, almost verbatim, in his own report.[43] Although both officers affirmed that the withdrawal order was delivered to Miller, it seems almost too coincidental that he was shot just as he received it. While that might in fact have been the case, there is another possibility. The courier entrusted with the message had to brave the enemy's enfilade fire as he rode across the wide expanse separating the 147th New York from the other regiments. Perhaps he never made it. In any event, Major Harney never got the message.

About fifteen minutes into the fight, Harney's troops nearest the rail fence sounded a shrill alarm: "They are flanking us on the right!"[44] Having put two Union regiments to flight, Davis' Brigade was indeed preparing to pounce on the battery and the single regiment north of the Chambersburg Pike on McPherson's Ridge. To this end the 2nd Mississippi swung south and the 55th North Carolina continued the flanking movement that had just undone the 76th New York and 56th Pennsylvania. Some 42nd Mississippi troops remained directly in front of Hall's Battery; the majority crossed the railroad cut, heading north. This movement led the 147th's Lieutenant Pierce to think the Confederates were retreating. But he was soon disabused of that appealing notion. After a brief lull, he recalled, the fighting resumed with "redoubled fury."[45]

With Rebels swarming on their right flank and menacing their rear, Harney ordered several companies on that end of the line to fall back so that they faced north, while the rest of the regiment continued to face west.[46] The countermeasure afforded only slight benefit, for the New Yorkers were badly outnumbered—easily three to one.

As casualties mounted all along the bent line, corporals were elevated to sergeants; sergeants, to lieutenants. And one company commander, the aforementioned Lieutenant J. Volney Pierce, ended up directing the action of Company C as well as his own Company G.[47]

> I moved my men forward with the men of Company C [Pierce wrote], and discovered a line of Confederate skirmishers on our front advancing from a valley up a slope toward a rail fence, firing as they advanced into Hall's battery, while the battery was fighting for dear life. A detachment of Confederates gathered in a fence corner a short distance from the [railroad] cut. I immediately ordered, 'Left oblique, fire.' The order was responded to by the two left companies, G and C. Several shots were fired into the skirmish lines. It became too hot, and I saw them return down the hill with several of their number stretched on the hillside.[48]

While this action reduced the pressure on Hall's 2nd Maine Battery, its situation remained precarious. Reynolds was aware when he posted the guns in the forefront of the infantry that it would be risky. But the high ground on McPherson's Ridge between the pike and the railroad cut offered an excellent field of fire, and he had decided to take the gamble.

No sooner had Hall's six guns arrived on the scene than six of Pegram's guns diverted their fire to the 100-yard strip where the Yankee artillerymen were rushing their 3-inch ordnance guns into position.[49] Later on, Hall counted ten guns bombarding his battery.[50] Major Pegram probably had seventeen guns in action at this time; those not engaged in the duel with Hall continued to harass the Union infantry on both sides of the Chambersburg Pike. As one of Pegram's officers quaintly put it, they "played upon" the enemy lines "with telling effect."[51] That effect evoked the sympathy of one Rebel gunner. Martin Douglas was Irish and a devout Catholic. Every time just before he pulled the lanyard he muttered, "Lord, be marsiful to their souls."[52]

Hall's cannoneers, peering through the dense smoke, saw some Rebel guns—the two Napoleons and two Parrotts of the Richmond Battery—being moved forward 500 yards and readied to fire again.[53] What they could not see was part of the 42nd Mississippi forming in the railroad cut, then stealthily moving toward them. By the time Hall's men spied the Rebel column, it was perilously close. "I had no idea," Hall later confessed, "of the enemy's infantry being so near, till they rose up on my front and right, at a distance of not more than fifty yards."[54] He said this startling development occurred within thirty minutes after his battery opened fire; probably it was not quite eleven o'clock.[55]

Hall saw at once that he was most vulnerable on the right. He therefore had Lieutenant William Ulmer point his two right section guns in that direction. This involved rotating each 820-pound gun manually, but it was swiftly accomplished. Also at this time Hall ordered the right and center sections to switch to double-shotted

Hall's Battery in action on McPherson's Ridge.

canister and to keep firing as fast as they could. The left section was to continue shelling Pegram's batteries on Herr Ridge.[56]

Just as the Rebels came into view, a curious incident occurred. Two of them suddenly dashed ahead of their comrades and took cover behind an apple tree. They were oddly attired, each wearing a gum blanket over his uniform. (With a slit cut for the head, this article frequently doubled as a raincoat.) Perhaps they had put them on during an early morning shower and, absent-mindedly (though they surely sweltered in the oppressive heat), never got around to taking them off. Simultaneously, they poked their heads out from behind the tree and shouted to the Yankee gunners to cease fire, implying it would be folly to continue.[57]

But Hall's men had no intention of capitulating without a fight. Swiftly complying with their commander's order, they blasted the 42nd Mississippi troops with canister. A myriad of flying metal particles dealt maiming injury and untidy death to the attackers. Cries of pain mingled with the bellicose Rebel yell. All the while the Mississippians were giving Hall's battery a heavy dose of musket fire. Smoke enveloped everyone and everything. The battery horses whinied in terror, shrieked when shot down. Splinters flew as minie balls whacked into gun carriages. Inevitably, some artillerymen were struck down as they worked their pieces. At the height of the struggle Lieutenant Frank Carr informed Hall that the enemy was within twenty yards of Lieutenant Ulmer's right section guns. The battery commander thought Carr exaggerated but rode over to investigate for himself and found the report to be alarmingly accurate.[58]

Yet it was Hall's men who prevailed—initially—over five times as many infantry. Canister had totally quashed the Confederate attempt to take the battery by massed assault.

Although the Mississippians had fallen back in disorder, they quickly returned to try a different tactic: harassment by widely dispersed skirmishers. This nearly succeeded where the charge had failed. Insidiously, the Rebels picked off an artilleryman here and a battery horse there.[59] Meanwhile, Hall's canonneers kept up a steady fire, but artillery was ineffective against such a scattered enemy—"like shooting mosquitoes with a rifle," one officer remarked.[60] It was at this time that Lieutenant Pierce (as related earlier) saw enemy skirmishers advancing, perceived the dire threat to the battery, and ordered his two companies to give them a taste of lead, with the result that the skirmishers were driven off.

Hall, in his various writings, never acknowledged the contribution made by the 147th New York to the welfare of his battery. Amid the general confusion and his growing concerns—dwindling ammunition, mounting casualties, fear of being cut off—he might have been unaware of it. Furthermore, he had reason to believe his battery was totally without infantry support.

Earlier, on glancing to the rear, he had been shocked to see a mass of Union infantry streaming from the field. His reaction had to be one of indignation, if not downright anger. He must have thought: *Why haven't I been informed? How can I be expected to hold on without support!* Although Hall actually saw only the 76th New York and 56th Pennsylvania in retreat, he naturally assumed *all* regiments on the right of his battery were pulling back.[61] Nevertheless, he had felt duty-bound to hold his position until ordered to do otherwise.

He soon changed his mind, however. With the appearance of the enemy on his front and right, he reasoned: If the situation has already proven too hot for our infantry, it is certainly too hot for artillery. He therefore ordered his battery to withdraw, realizing he would be held accountable for his action.[62] Time was running out and getting his guns to safety would not be easy. Some enemy skirmishers had already reached the railroad cut at a point in his rear, thus endangering his escape route. He ordered Lieutenant Ulmer to pull back his right section about 75 yards to meet this latest threat.[63]

"My idea," Hall wrote after the battle, "was to set those two guns into safety, if no more, and perhaps by their aid save the other four." But it did not work out as he had hoped. By the time Ulmer's guns unlimbered in the new position, four horses of one team had been killed. Worse yet, "a raking fire swept over his guns so that he did not fire a shot." When Hall realized he would get no help from Ulmer's section, his top priority was "to get the other four guns away, if possible." He rode down a slope to the parked limbers and had them turned around to face Seminary Ridge, a measure he hoped would save precious minutes. Returning to his guns, he ordered them brought down, by hand, to the limbers.[64]

The "raking fire" Hall referred to undoubtedly came not only from the 42nd Mississippi but from the 2nd Mississippi and 55th North Carolina, which were then bearing down on the 147th New York. Through occasional rifts in the smoke, soldiers on the 147th's left saw Hall's battery preparing to withdraw.[65] To say they were dismayed is to put it mildly.

Outnumbered and outflanked, the New Yorkers were nearly surrounded and "very much cut up."[66] Still they fought on, heedless of the outcome. Lieutenant Pierce succinctly summed up their plight:

> The fight was fierce and hot; the boys on the right were falling like autumn leaves; the air was full of lead. Men fell all along the line.[67]

Men were dropping in the Confederate ranks as well. General Davis described the fighting in this phase as "desperate" and the losses on both sides as "heavy."[68] The difference between aggressor and defender, however, was that the former could tolerate a high casualty rate and keep on fighting; the latter could not. With retreat highly problematic, the 147th New York faced consummate disaster.[69]

The heroic stand made by these gallant men would be long remembered. Twenty-five years after the battle, veterans of the 147th held a reunion at Gettysburg. There, gathered together in the same field north of the railroad cut where they had so bravely fought, they listened to a great deal of florid oratory. The main address was given by their own J. Volney Pierce, and surely their hearts swelled with pride when they heard him declaim...

> You may point to Thermopylae and its Spartans, but a greater Thermopylae was here, and more than Spartan heroism stood within the dead angle on this ground. Never was a grander fight made against triple odds; never greater readiness to do and die on duty's line; never greater results hung trembling in the balance than swayed in the battle front of the 147th New York.[70]

"To do and die on duty's line" was not just pompous rhetoric on Pierce's part. It was truly the case for the embattled 147th New York that hot July morning as the enemy drew ever closer. With Hall's Battery out of action, desperately striving to save its guns, the New York regiment was the only buffer between Davis' rampaging Confederates and the Union regiments south of the Chambersburg Pike. And it could not hold out much longer.

Still, the outlook for the Union was by no means wholly bleak. While Rebels were whipping Yankees north of the pike, the reverse was true south of it—a case of quid pro quo on a monumental scale.

Chapter VII

YANKEES FLANK REBELS

"Thar comes them old black hats!"

John Reynolds' concern in his last moments was for the 2nd Wisconsin Volunteers. The commander of the left wing of the Army of the Potomac had just witnessed their violent clash with Archer's Tennessee Brigade. And he was endeavoring to bring up the other Iron Brigade regiments when the fatal bullet struck him.

Barely a half hour had elapsed since Solomon Meredith had deployed his five regiments to advance, *en echelon*, from Seminary Ridge to McPherson's Ridge. As if relieving Gamble's troopers and holding back the enemy were not enough, the front echelon—Colonel Lucius Fairchild's 2nd Wisconsin—had an added responsibility.[1] Division commander Wadsworth, uneasy about the exposed position of Hall's Battery, had ordered Fairchild to repulse any Confederate force swinging north to take those guns.[2]

Under a hot sun the 2nd Wisconsin had double-quicked across the fields separating the two ridges. As the 280 infantrymen drew near McPherson's Ridge, they saw some of Gamble's dismounted cavalrymen scurrying in the opposite direction and realized there was no time to spare; unless they got to the summit first, the enemy would likely gain control of the ridge. Briefly their momentum was forfeited when they had to clamber over a rail fence; but it was quickly regained. Directly in their front lay Herbst's Woods, which stretched from the ridgeline to Willoughby Run. During the advance some battle-wise veterans had stopped to load their Austrian rifled muskets, then sprinted ahead to their respective places in line. The rest, since no general order to load had ever been given, were woefully unprepared for what followed.[3]

The murderous volley that tore great gaps in the 2nd Wisconsin's line has already been mentioned in connection with Reynolds' death. Only the prudent few of Fairchild's men who had not waited for an order to load could retaliate at once. The rest had to go through the multi-step loading process before they could effectively respond. It was yet another handicap on top of the severe loss of manpower just incurred. Nonetheless, as Captain William Harries later reported, the 2nd Wisconsin "pulled itself together and with a cheer dashed forward."[4] The ensuing fight in the woods was at close quarters—under forty yards.[5] Fairchild described the action as "most desperate."[6]

The hot, humid air, trapped by overarching branches, quickly became insufferable, smoke-filled and foul-smelling from spent powder. The flight of countless bullets, varying in shape and caliber, produced an incessant, high-pitched whine—a shrill counterpoint to the raucous cries of the combatants. And all the while, the fiendish missiles thudded into trees, ripped through fragile flesh and bone.

One of the victims was Fairchild himself. Shortly after he entered the woods, a bullet shattered his left arm above the elbow. With Lieutenant Colonel George Stevens also *hors de combat*, mortally wounded in the opening volley, command of the 2nd Wisconsin passed to Major John Mansfield.[7]

From that point on the major led the regiment in the sense of making decisions and issuing orders. Physically, however, it was led through Herbst's Woods by a most unlikely private. Prior to the Gettysburg campaign R. E. Davidson had declared he would not enter another battle if he could possibly avoid it. He had already fought at Antietam, Chancellorsville, and in both battles at Bull Run, and had come through all of them unscathed. How long, he must have asked himself, could he expect his phenomenal luck to hold? But, alas, at Gettysburg no honorable alternative to fighting presented itself, neither sickness, guard duty, nor any kind of detached service. So it happened that Davidson, against his will, once again found himself running into battle with his company.

Whatever possessed him in those first few minutes, he probably could not have said. But obviously something had snapped in his mind, something that instantaneously transformed his avowed aim of self-preservation into reckless abandon. When the 2nd Wisconsin's color-bearer was hit and the cherished banner fell to the ground, he snatched it up and ran some ten or fifteen yards ahead of the line. Defying the storm of bullets, he maintained this interval as the regiment followed him through the woods. Incredibly, his luck held. While the attrition in his Company H was fearsome, not only did he escape being killed, wounded, or captured, he emerged from the day's fighting a sergeant.[8]

Another soldier in Davidson's regiment, Corporal Robert Beecham, gave this vivid account of the action from Seminary Ridge to McPherson's Ridge:

> [The 2nd Wisconsin] surged forward like a wave of the sea, and a dark line of worn and ragged blue swept on toward the wooded crest. Behind that line the cavalry retired, and on the crest of the hill we were confronted by a heavy line of ragged butternut, firing steadily as they advanced up the slope. Before us was the far-extending line of Archer's brigade; behind us were three regiments of our own brigade, which, wave after wave, surged forward to extend our line...as we moved steadily down the slope receiving a galling fire from Archer's men. It was, as in thousands of other instances, just the unadorned, long-drawn-out line of ragged, dirty blue against the long-drawn-out line of dirty, ragged butternut, with no 'pomp of war' about it, and no show of style except our old black hats. Archer's men recognized them at once, and shouted to each other, 'Thar comes them old black hats! It's the Army of the Potomac, sure!'[9]

Thus were Archer's Confederates disabused of any lingering notion that they faced militia. They had crossed Willoughby Run and driven back the thin line of Gamble's Brigade. When the fire from the dismounted cavalrymen abated, they assumed Union resistance had crumbled. But Captain J. B. Turney of the 1st Tennessee, on the left of the line, took the precaution of getting down on his knees to peer under the low-lying smoke. What he dimly saw, not far ahead, were trousers and boots, a great many of them. He felt certain they were not Confederate and went to inform General Archer. When he did, Archer only scoffed, "I guess not, Captain." Either the brigade commander's thinking was muddled or he completely misunderstood Turney, for he added: "General Joe Davis is to occupy that timber to our left."[10] The "timber" in question was still part of Herbst's Woods, and as Archer should have known, Davis' Brigade was much farther north on the opposite side of the Chambersburg Pike. As some of his men noticed, James Jay Archer was not his usual self this day—the customary vigor, the quick perception were missing. The symptoms indicated a deep fatigue.[11]

What Turney had seen was the front echelon of the approaching Iron Brigade, and because his warning went unheeded, the 13th Alabama and 1st Tennessee both ran pell mell into the 2nd Wisconsin. Farther down the line, in the 14th Tennessee, Sergeant June Kimble waded across Willoughby Run and started up McPherson's Ridge under the impression that the task ahead was merely to "brush away" a few skirmishers. It was a shock, therefore, "when suddenly a heavy line of battle confronted the brigade at close quarters and delivered a deadly volley into our very faces." The result, he added, was "instant confusion."[12]

The 1st Tennessee had gotten into the fight later than the 13th Alabama on its right, because, on the approach, it had to bypass swampy ground.[13] Nevertheless, by the time Captain Turney got back to his company after his fruitless mission to warn Archer, he found the whole regiment committed and already extremely hard pressed.[14] Its 23-year-old commander, Lieutenant Colonel Newton J. George, rode to the right to get help. Behind the 13th Alabama's line he found Archer and Lieutenant Colonel James Aiken of that regiment. Hastily he informed them of his precarious situation, and then asked that the Alabamans initiate a crossfire at once. The request was approved and the order given for those troops to wheel left. When the maneuver was completed, the right of the 13th Alabama's line was just below the crest of the ridge and barely 75 yards from the oncoming Federals. A gap had been opened in the middle of Archer's line, but the ensuing crossfire, alarming and diverting the enemy, did succeed for a short period in reducing the pressure on the 1st Tennessee.[15]

North of this action, the 14th Brooklyn and 95th New York—both posted by Reynolds himself between the Chambersburg Pike and Herbst's Woods—were still unengaged. That is, except for ducking incoming shells from Pegram's Batteries. Colonel Edward B. Fowler, with overall responsibility for both regiments (he was senior to the 95th New York's Colonel Biddle), was puzzled and, needless to say, greatly concerned. A battle had been raging on both flanks for what seemed eons, and he was in the dark as to how it was progressing. Not knowing whether the other regiments of Wadsworth's Division were winning or losing, and wondering why his own had not been attacked, had to be acute torment. On his right, thick smoke north of the railroad cut had precluded his seeing the retreat of the 76th New York and 56th Pennsylvania. And he was unaware of the plight of the 147th New York for the same reason. Hall's Battery, however, was fairly close—on the near side of the cut—and he may have been aware of its peril.[16]

On his left, the tactical situation was equally obscure. Fowler had watched Archer's troops veer across his front toward Herbst's Woods and disappear into it. He had heard the Confederates' first volley and the slightly delayed Union response, followed by general fire. But, until one side or the other emerged from the woods, he could not tell which had gained the upper hand.[17]

Earlier, the 14th Brooklyn and 95th New York had scuffled with enemy skirmishers, driving them back at a cost of several of their own men. Fowler at that time had lost his mount—shot through the head—but had himself suffered only a contusion when a spent ball plowed through his coat and hit him in the thigh.[18] Now, not knowing what was transpiring on his flanks or what to expect on his front, the colonel had good cause to be worried. Ignorance, under such circumstances, was anything but bliss.

Meanwhile, reinforcements for the embattled 2nd Wisconsin were charging up McPherson's Ridge. The first echelon to arrive on that regiment's left flank was the 7th Wisconsin. Immediately on entering Herbst's Woods, it was hit by a withering fire, comparable to that which had greeted the 2nd Wisconsin. The 7th Wisconsin men were in no better position to reply than the 2nd Wisconsin troops had been, for they too had rushed into combat with empty muskets. Lieutenant Colonel John B. Callis, 7th Wisconsin's second-in-command, "not feeling like standing under that gallant fire," ordered the companies around him to fix bayonets and advance. Just as they started out, "depending on cold steel," Captain Craig Wadsworth of Reynolds' staff galloped toward them crying, "Halt!...Halt!" But Callis had no intention of stopping. With obvious irritation, he shouted back, "Halt, halt—it is now too late to halt!"[19]

In another part of the 7th Wisconsin's line, the regimental commander, Colonel William W. Robinson, faced a terrible uncertainty. The smoke was so thick and the opposing lines so close together that he could not tell which murky figures were Confederates, which Federals. The very real possibility that he might inadvertently order fire on his own men or those of the 2nd Wisconsin haunted him. As he agonized over what to do, Captain Wadsworth rode up. Perhaps detecting the commanding officer's indecision, Wadsworth implored him to drive the enemy back. Robinson then confided his dilemma. Wadsworth surveyed the scene with eyes apparently sharper than the colonel's. Spotting a Rebel battle flag off to the left, he pointed it out to a grateful Robinson.[20]

The 19th Indiana, the third Iron Brigade regiment to engage the enemy, had a distinct advantage over its predecessors. Having been on picket duty the night before, these troops went into battle with their muskets loaded. Hence, when the 7th and 14th Tennessee opened fire on them, they could respond immediately with a "well directed volley." Their commander, Lieutenant Colonel William W. Dudley, would later commend them for their "celerity" and "great spirit."[21] (An enlisted man in the 6th Wisconsin had a simple explanation for the marvelous elan of the entire Iron Brigade this day. To C. B. Auberry, known as "Doc," it was because every soldier was "mad clear through.")[22]

The 19th Indiana had recently acquired new regimental colors. Even so, the order not to uncase them in battle was illogical and counterproductive. However, when color-bearer Burlington Cunningham saw his fellow soldiers double-quick up McPherson's Ridge, muskets at the ready, obedience to orders went glimmering. Pointing the staff toward Abraham Buckles who marched beside him, he said, "Abe, pull the shuck." The next moment the flag floated in the air and thus could fulfill its cardinal function—to inspire the men who served under it.[23] Before long its pristine beauty was sullied by Rebel musket balls that left ragged holes in the fabric. One member of the regiment averred that more than a dozen balls sailed through their colors that morning.[24] Cunningham had advanced only a short distance when he was shot down. Buckles, seeing him fall, dropped his musket, grabbed the flag, lofted it, and sprinted to a position well in front of the line. In fact he stayed so far ahead that Lieutenant Colonel Dudley rebuked him for taking such a risk.[25]

With the arrival of the 24th Michigan on the extreme left, the Iron Brigade's line was complete. For these men of the newest regiment in the renowned brigade, this day held special significance: It was the first time they wore their prized black hats in battle.[26] Their entry into the fight was less traumatic, less costly, than that of the other Iron Brigade regiments because there was no enemy directly in their front. But, as they swung toward the 7th Tennessee on their right flank, they began to reap casualties. The first 24th Michigan officer to be killed was Gilbert A. Dickey, a recently-commissioned second lieutenant who had come up through the ranks. In his battle report Colonel Henry A. Morrow sadly noted that Dickey had shown "great promise for future usefulness and distinction."[27]

While the vast majority of Buford's cavalrymen were not in the least reluctant to leave McPherson's Ridge and take up less hazardous positions on Seminary Ridge, on the Fairfield Road, and on the roads north of Gettysburg,[28] some 3rd Indiana troopers elected to stay and fight with the Iron Brigade. Quickly trading their carbines for longer range muskets, they fell in line with the 2nd Wisconsin.[29] As black slouch hats were standard attire in the 3rd Indiana as well as in the Iron Brigade, they were virtually indistinguishable from the infantrymen alongside them.[30]

Among the group of devil-may-care troopers who stayed on were Will Rea and Matt Glenber. The latter, a belligerent "Dutchman," was so eager to tussle with the Rebs he could hardly contain himself. He fumed about the delay, cursed the enemy, and harangued the soldiers around him to charge at once. With his thick German accent, the key word became a hiss—"S-s-s-scharge."

What motivated the 3rd Indiana cavalrymen to risk their lives unnecessarily? For some it may have been an irresistible thirst for glory; for others, simply anger. For Rea and Glenber it was neither. After the war Rea admitted that both of them had been driven by the selfish hope of capturing a Confederate horse, saddle, or pistol. Whether either was successful on any count, he did not say.[31]

Although explicit documentation is lacking, some 8th New York troopers may also have fought with the Iron Brigade. In 1889, one Henry Norton, a veteran of that regiment, wrote that a Captain Follett and a private were killed "in a charge in which the rebels were severely repulsed and a large number of them taken prisoners."[32] The only episode in 8th New York's proximity that matched those circumstances was the fight between Archer's and Meredith's Brigades.

Minutes dragged by for the privates guarding the piles of knapsacks in the Union rear. After each of them had covered his company's pile with ponchos, there was nothing to do but wait...and wonder how comrades on the front line were faring. When bullets began whistling round their heads, they either ducked behind a pile or crawled under a poncho.[33]

The 6th Wisconsin was also in the rear, still unengaged. It was certainly not what Lieutenant Colonel Rufus Dawes had been led to expect. No sooner had the regiment arrived on Seminary Ridge than he had been ordered to prepare for action. As the rear echelon, his 320 officers and men were to follow the other four Iron Brigade regiments to McPherson's Ridge. He formed his men in battle line, and in due course they moved out on the double-quick like the other regiments. They had gone only a short distance, however, when they were ordered to halt. Dawes was informed that his regiment would be held in reserve until further notice. Who issued the halt order is uncertain. Brigade commander Meredith may have reconsidered, deciding not to commit his entire force at once. Or it might have been Wadsworth, foreseeing a possibly urgent need for a reserve force. (The Confederates, incidentally, were well served in this regard, having two large brigades, Pettigrew's and Brockenbrough's, at their beck and call.)

Meredith's Brigade guard comprised two lieutenants and 100 enlisted men (twenty drawn from each regiment). During the halt of the 6th Wisconsin, it was placed under Dawes' command. Dividing the unit into two companies, he posted one on the right of his regimental line, the other on the left. After that it was simply a matter of waiting for further orders. His troops—now 420 strong—stood in the blazing sun, leaning on their muskets and repeatedly mopping sweat from their faces. Even so, it was infinitely better than dodging bullets and cannonballs.

But the respite turned out to be brief. The ferocity of the fighting on McPherson's Ridge and the growing number of casualties soon impelled Meredith to call up the reserves. Dawes' regiment and the brigade guard moved forward.[34]

At this time other reinforcements from the First Corps were drawing near the battlefield, though they would all arrive too late to affect the outcome of the separate contests then in progress on each side of the Chambersburg Pike. Biddle's Brigade of the Third Division emerged from a woods onto the Fairfield Road at a point near Willoughby Run. Directly ahead, barely a half mile away, Meredith's troops were battling the enemy. The other Third Division brigade, under Colonel Stone, was still marching up the Emmitsburg Road, but was now within two miles of the fighting. Trailing Stone's Brigade were the two Second Division brigades, Paul's and Baxter's, accompanied by three batteries of Wainwright's Artillery Brigade.

Early in the march, Colonel Wainwright's horse Billy had cast two shoes. It was a bit of tough luck; but, having no suspicion then of a battle brewing, he had had no misgivings about stopping at a farm and waiting for the brigade forge to come up so that Billy could be reshod. By the time that was done, a light rain was falling, and Wainwright, still feeling no compulsion to get back to his batteries, tarried until the shower passed. Finally he set out to rejoin them and, on the way, met Doubleday who immediately struck up a conversation. A perceived injustice still rankled the general and apparently he welcomed the chance to air his grievance. A few days before, George Sykes had been given command of the Fifth Corps, and he, Doubleday, was miffed that the plum had not fallen to him. After all, he told Wainwright, though he and Sykes both held the rank of major general, he had more seniority.[35]

The rumble of distant cannon banished all thoughts of the affront to Doubleday's pride. Just then, as though on cue, a staff officer rode up and announced that a battle was in progress, with Wadsworth's Division heavily engaged. By order of General Reynolds, Doubleday was to bring up the Second and Third Divisions at the greatest possible speed. Message complete, the staff officer saluted and rode off. Turning to Wainwright, Doubleday told him to take his batteries to Seminary Ridge, park them in the vicinity of the Seminary building, and await further orders. Then he galloped off to spur the infantry forward.[36]

Only minutes later, Captain Craig Wadsworth (who seemed to be everywhere this morning) rode up to Wainwright. His message was as blunt as it was tragic: "The General is killed; Reynolds is dead."[37] Wainwright was deeply shocked. The general's words to him only a few hours before—Reynolds saying he did not expect an engagement this day—may have flashed, with exquisite irony, through his mind. And surely the full implication of Wadsworth's message was not lost on the artillery commander: Doubleday was then in charge of all Union forces on the field. But Doubleday himself would not learn of his elevation to top command until much later, during a lull in the fighting south of the Chambersburg Pike.[38]

Colonel Roy Stone, on receiving Doubleday's order to make all possible haste, realized that to do so meant his men would have to leapfrog Battery B, 4th U. S. Artillery. He therefore ordered Lieutenant Stewart to pull his six Napoleons off the road.

Once the road was clear and until all three of Stone's regiments had passed by, the artillerymen were free to relax. Cannoneer Augustus Buell would vividly remember what he saw and heard during this interval.

> ...the musketry [he later wrote] had grown from the crackling sound of the skirmishing we had heard early in the morning to an almost incessant crash....We could hear every sound, even the yells of the troops fighting up on the ridge beyond Gettysburg, and we could see the smoke mount up and float away lazily to the northeastward; but we could not see the combatants.[39]

That would change soon after the battery got rolling again. As Buell related it, when Stewart's men came over a rise, "the whole scene burst upon us like the lifting of the curtain in a great play." They gazed upon a vast panorama of blue, gray, and butternut figures locked in furious combat. "The spectacle," said Buell, "was simply stupendous."[40]

"The old slouch hats have got them, you bet!"

With the arrival of three regiments in support of the badly mauled 2nd Wisconsin, the complection of the fight south of the Chambersburg Pike changed dramatically. As it turned out, the 24th Michigan and probably some companies of the 19th Indiana overlapped the enemy's right. It was an unexpected boon, and the two regiments were quick to take advantage of it. The 2nd Wisconsin, now supported on its left by the 7th Wisconsin, fought with redoubled fury, determined to rectify its initial setback. Before long the Western regiments had the enemy on the run—"skedaddling," as one sergeant gleefully put it.[41]

To Archer's Southerners, who had started up McPherson's Ridge so confidently, the sudden reversal in their expectations came as a rude shock. "We were rather enjoying the fray," wrote one of the 13th Alabama's color guards, "when an order was given to 'fall back on Willoughby Run.' We could see no reason for this order, as the Tennesseans were keeping the 'blue boys' busy, and things seemed going pretty well for us...."[42] The 7th Tennessee's Colonel John Fite was likewise chagrined: "We turned the Yankees [Gamble's cavalry] back some distance and the first thing I knew the Federals had attacked our right wing and turned it back and we fell back...."[43] What neither the colonel nor the members of the color guard realized at first was that the thin line of dismounted cavalry had been supplanted by a crack infantry brigade. But within minutes it must have dawned on everyone in Archer's line that they now faced a larger, more powerful enemy force. A 13th Alabama private ruefully admitted: "We discovered that we had tackled a hard proposition."[44]

Back on Seminary Ridge, the men of Stewart's Battery B, 4th U. S. Artillery, listened attentively to the sound of firing in their front. Cannoneer John Holland had previously served in the 2nd Wisconsin and consequently felt a fraternal bond with the Iron Brigade. When the cacophony swelled to fortissimo, he said to Gus Buell beside him, "Hear that, my son! That's the talk! The old slouch hats have got them, you bet!"[45]

He was right. But it was not the pushover Bonaparte implied in his dispatch to the *New York World*. The correspondent with the grandiose nom de plume wrote that "without firing a shot, but with a tremendous cheer, they [the Iron Brigade] dashed forward with such swiftness as to surround nearly six hundred of the foe, who were taken prisoner."[46] No doubt the Westerners did yell like demons—virtually all accounts mentioned it.[47] But Bonaparte was dead wrong about them not firing; literally thousands of shots were fired on both sides. And, although Archer's Brigade was fairly hemmed in on two sides, it was hardly surrounded, as the correspondent stated. Nor

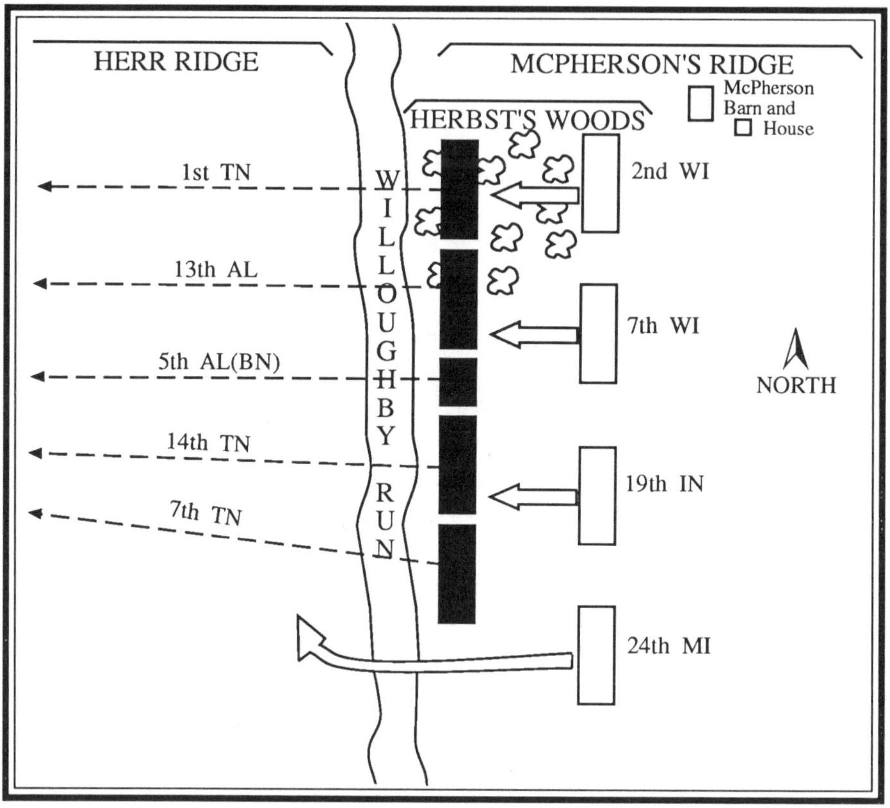

Repulse of Confederate attack south of the Chambersburg Pike. By 10:50 Meredith's Iron Brigade had Archer's Brigade streaming back across Willoughby Run.

was he correct about the number of prisoners. (More on that later.) He was not off the mark, however, with regard to the Iron Brigade's rapid movement. Colonel Morrow reported that his 24th Michigan "dashed up and over the hill and down into the ravine."[48] Similarly, the 19th Indiana was reported to have chased the enemy "pretty lively."[49] Both regiments, as well as the 7th Wisconsin, had open fields to cross. The 2nd Wisconsin, on the other hand, had to cope with Herbst's Woods; hence its progress was necessarily slower. Corporal Robert Beecham of that regiment recalled: "Archer's line gave way, retreating slowly and stubbornly through the woods....We followed closely upon their heels."[50]

The 19th Indiana's Lieutenant Colonel Dudley summarized the overall action thus: "The engagement, which seemed to be raging along the whole of the brigade line, soon ceased and we found the rebel brigade in our front in full retreat."[51] Nevertheless, it was not a complete rout. When forced to fall back, Archer's men, taking advantage of whatever cover offered and firing at will, continued to inflict casualties on the Federals.[52]

The two Tennessee regiments on the right gave way first. The 24th Michigan, swinging around their flank, had poured a merciless enfilade fire into the 7th Tennessee, pushing it into the 14th Tennessee, causing mass confusion. Even more critical was the threat to the Confederate rear. If the 24th Michigan along with the 19th Indiana (which had also begun a flanking movement) were to get completely behind the Tennessee regiments, the whole brigade would be in dire straits. Not Union pressure alone, then, but sound tactics and common sense dictated a speedy withdrawal. With the collapse of Archer's right, hope vanished that the troops on the left could stem the Union advance.[53] Presently, the 1st Tennessee and 13th Alabama regiments and the 5th Alabama Battalion retreated, by stages, to the east bank of Willoughby Run.[54]

There, amid trees and brush, 13th Alabama officers hastily formed their commands in a defensive line, with the men in prone position. Like his comrades, W. H. Moon lay there, numb with fear, looking up the slope they had just descended, eyes riveted on the host of blue coats coming ever closer. He would recall his fervent thought in those anxious minutes: "Our only hope now was that a supporting line would come up...." (One can only speculate that if Henry Heth had been another "Stonewall" Jackson, a detachment from either Pettigrew's or Brockenbrough's Brigade would have been rushed to their aid.) "But, alas!" Moon added, "our support did not materialize."[55]

Recrossing Willoughby Run was therefore inevitable. But, for the Confederates, getting their feet wet again was the least of their worries. With the Federals in hot pursuit, they fled across the shallow stream and up Herr Ridge. The 7th Tennessee troops kept on for a hundred yards before they finally stopped running.[56]

Willoughby Run, just south of the Chambersburg Pike, taken by Brady's crew shortly after the battle.

Even so, Archer's Brigade had not entirely given up the fight. Like a cornered tiger, it would turn to menace its foe. With what must have been lightning speed, some Rebels even managed to erect crude breastworks.[57] Yet, despite such rugged determination, the brigade's resistance in this last stand was to be short-lived.[58] At one point, then another, Southern lads simply decided they had had enough, dropped their muskets, and ran. Unless a minie ball found them, they made good their escape. Of those who kept on fighting, many ended up marching to the Union rear as prisoners.[59]

A number of Rebels had taken cover behind a sizeable stand of willows. With a rank undergrowth rendering their position virtually impenetrable, they had fired with impunity. But the supposed haven soon proved to be a trap. When the 2nd Wisconsin came up to that natural barrier, it split in two, one half circling around to the right, the other to the left. The 1st Tennessee and 13th Alabama troops caught in the pincers movement had no choice but to surrender.[60] Captain J. B. Turney of the Tennessee regiment acknowledged that "a portion of the left" was captured, including some of his own Company K men. He hastened to add that he and "the major part" of his company escaped.[61]

In the 7th Wisconsin Lieutenant Colonel Callis was now on foot, his horse having been shot from under him. He himself had been hit by buck shot, in the hip and right side "but not serious." These mishaps paled, however, beside the unnerving experience that followed.

As Callis described it, "an [enemy] officer hurriedly advanced toward me with saber drawn and coming point first saying 'I surrender' but still rushing toward me." Callis was taking no chances. Drawing his saber, he screamed, "That is no way to surrender!" The next instant he knocked the Rebel officer's saber from his hand and stabbed at his throat, but missed. "If you surrender," Callis rasped, "order your men to cease firing, pick up your saber and order your men to go to the rear as prisoners." The officer, by then totally subdued, did exactly as he was told.[62]

To the left of the Wisconsin regiments the 19th Indiana and 24th Michigan also took prisoners. In the latter regiment, it was a "large number," according to its colonel.[63] Doubtless that was true, considering that the Michigan troops had quickly flanked the 7th and 14th Tennessee on the right of Archer's line. But Lieutenant Colonel Dudley's boast that his 19th Indiana captured "most of the officers and men" of a Tennessee regiment must be regarded as gross exaggeration.[64]

After the battle everyone seemed to have a different opinion as to the total number of Archer's troops captured on the morning of July 1. The figures given ranged from 60 to 1,000! The actual number was probably around 200.

The biggest fish caught in the Iron Brigade's net was none other than the opposing brigade commander, James J. Archer. Throughout the action he had chosen to remain on foot. From his central position, behind the 13th Alabama, he had weighed all communications from staff officers and unit commanders, made decisions, and issued orders. Although not in top form this day, he nonetheless had capably led his troops in an increasingly difficult situation. Finally forced to retreat, he had recrossed

Brigadier General James J. Archer

Willoughby Run and halted about thirty paces west of it.[65] He was in the midst of rallying his brigade when, suddenly, he felt steely fingers clutching his throat. Instinctively he resisted, but in that moment he knew his adversary was the stronger and not about to let go until he surrendered.[66]

His nemesis was an impulsive Irishman named Patrick Maloney. A private in 2nd Wisconsin's Company K, he had been in the contingent led by a Captain Dow that had swung to the left around the impenetrable clump of willows and underbrush. Then, noticing a Confederate officer practically unattended, he had seen his chance for glory. A short dash, a momentary struggle, and the prize was his. He had caught himself a general—a brigade commander, no less.[67]

Yet Maloney was not sufficiently awed by his prisoner's high rank to extend him any preferential treatment. In fact he treated Archer roughly, no less so than if he had been an ordinary private. After cautioning the general in no uncertain terms to keep his hands raised, Maloney jostled him along ahead of him until they found Captain Dow. There can be no doubt the Irishman was elated, and probably that exultant feeling showed in his voice as he handed over his illustrious prisoner. Archer immediately offered his sword to Dow, though he might have exercised his perogative of surrendering it only to an officer of at least equal rank. The captain (with a chivalry unknown to Maloney) said, "Keep your sword, General, and go to the rear; one sword is all I need."[68]

As James Archer—the first of Lee's generals to be captured—started walking to the rear under guard, he was met by Lieutenant D. B. Dailey. Dailey was in charge of all prisoners taken by the 2nd Wisconsin. "I'll relieve you of that sword," he said coldly.

Archer refused, protesting that Captain Dow had allowed him to keep it. Dailey not only did not relent, he went on to demand his revolver as well. Archer, now furious, retorted that it was common courtesy for a general officer to be permitted to retain his side arms. But Dailey was adamant, and Archer, thoroughly disgusted, turned over both weapons. With that, Dailey told the guards to move on.[69]

Before the group was out of sight, Dailey unbuckled his own sword and tried on Archer's. Finding it lighter (not to mention more prestigious) than his own, he decided he would wear it.[70] Another 2nd Wisconsin officer, Captain William Harries, saw Archer before Dailey divested him of his sword. Years afterward he still remembered the Confederate general's "splendid gray uniform" and "beautiful steel-scabbard sword."[71]

Archer and Abner Doubleday had known each other in the "Old Army." Thus, when the Union general rode up to his former colleague, he greeted him warmly. "Good morning, Archer! How are you? I am glad to see you!"

Archer replied with choleric ill temper, "Well, I am *not* glad to see *you*, by a damn sight!"[72]

No doubt Doubleday bristled, stung by the rebuff. But he held his tongue. Then, turning to Archer's guards, he said, "Take him to the rear." Perhaps rattled by Archer's outburst, he repeated, "Take him to the rear."[73] Major E. P. Halstead, who witnessed the incident, noted Archer's deportment, which he later described as his "disappointed manner."[74] Certainly what the humiliated Confederate leader felt at that time far exceeded mere disappointment!

With the capture of Archer and many in his brigade, the battle south of the Chambersburg Pike reached its climax. The sporadic fire that followed was clearly a denouement. The Westerners of the Iron Brigade had scored a decisive victory—but also a costly one.

Among 2nd Wisconsin officers, Lieutenant Colonel Stevens and Lieutenant Winegar were killed; Colonel Fairchild, Lieutenant Jameson, and Captains Perry, Parsons, and Spoerri were wounded.[75] Company H suffered the heaviest loss: one officer killed (Winegar) and eighteen enlisted men killed or wounded out of a total of 27 engaged.[76] Overall, the regiment lost 116 of its 302 officers and men.[77]

Peter Arndt, a First Corps surgeon and close friend of William Winegar, tried several times to find the lieutenant's body but without success. Afterward, he wrote to Winegar's sister and her husband, telling them about his futile search. He regretted he could give no details of William's death except that he fell within thirty minutes of entering combat. He added: "I did not see your brother William after the regt. had formed their lines of battle and passed over the crest of a hill near where I had temporarily located my hospital depot....Within a few minutes the wounded came in so fast that I was ordered by the Col. to remove my location nearer the town...."[78]

The 7th Wisconsin, like the 2nd Wisconsin, suffered heavy losses, particularly in the enemy's opening volley.[79] Casualties in the 19th Indiana and 24th Michigan were lighter, in comparison, but still high. In the 19th Indiana one colorbearer after another was shot down.[80] In the 24th Michigan, within minutes of entering combat, Lieutenant Gilbert Dickey and Color Sergeant Abel Peck were killed. When Sergeant Peck fell, Corporal Charles Bellore seized the flag before it touched the ground and bore it into the fray.[81] Among the wounded in this regiment were all four Company B soldiers who had dropped out early in the march but, on hearing the repeated boom of cannon, had felt impelled to rejoin their company. Three of them eventually recovered, but John Rider died of his wound.[82]

Of the approximately 1,470 Iron Brigade officers and men engaged on McPherson's Ridge, some 300 were killed or wounded in the space of thirty minutes.[83]

As to Confederate losses, General Heth stated that both Archer's and Meredith's Brigades suffered "most severely."[84] That, of course, begs the question of numbers. Obtaining a quantitative answer for Archer's Brigade is complicated by two factors. First, casualty figures, where available, cover the entire 3-day battle. Second, the brigade sustained high (but, alas, not precisely determined) casualties in Pettigrew's charge on July 3. Nevertheless, through judicious assumption and careful analysis, it appears that total casualties (killed, wounded, and captured) in Archer's Brigade during the morning of July 1 were approximately 400, or one-third of the 1,200 engaged.[85]

Heth blamed the debacle on Archer's Brigade being "almost surrounded by overwhelming forces."[86] Actually, the disparity was not that great—roughly four Confederates to every five Federals. Doubleday, on the other hand, believed the Confederate brigade was whipped so badly because its officers underrated their opponents and therefore were careless.[87] The 19th Indiana's Lieutenant Colonel Dudley (tacitly paying tribute to the prowess of the Iron Brigade) said it was due to the Rebels becoming "demoralized."[88] With Archer languishing in a Federal prison, the after-action report for his brigade was written by Lieutenant Colonel Samuel Shepard. He cited crossfire and "obstructions" as the causes of its defeat. The former, he said, rendered its position untenable, forcing the troops to fall back; the latter (the stream, the thicket of willow and brush) accounted for the high number of prisoners.[89] Underlying Shepard's explanations was one inescapable fact: The brigade was simply outmaneuvered.

This came about as much by chance as by design. It was, after all, pure accident that the Iron Brigade overlapped Archer's right. Fortuitous, too, was the fact that that end of the line was weakened when the 1st Tennessee, on the left, ran into trouble and the 13th Alabama wheeled left to support it. Nevertheless, Meredith's Westerners deserve full credit for making the most of their good fortune. What puzzled the Confederates (as one of them stated) was where all those Federals had come from so suddenly.[90] "I cannot say how many were taken prisoner," wrote 13th Alabama's Private Boland, "but all who had not grasped time by the forelock and left when they realized what a deadly trap they were in surrendered." For Boland himself that realization came too late.[91]

As the dispirited Confederate prisoners straggled onto the Chambersburg Pike, an officer among them was moved to restore a semblance of order and discipline. In doing so, he shouted a command not to be found in Hardee's *Tactics*: "By twos, into fours, right smart—git!"[92] Better aligned, thanks to the gratuitous shepherding of their own officer, the prisoners of war marched to Gettysburg. They were detained there for several hours, then marched to Westminster, Maryland (and ultimately to Fort Delaware).[93] Before their departure G. W. Hosmer of the *New York Herald* approached a Confederate officer and began to ply him with questions. The officer, it turned out, was Lieutenant Colonel James Aiken of the 13th Alabama. When Hosmer asked the whereabouts of his regiment, Aiken replied bitterly, "Gone to Hell, sir."[94]

While the Confederate prisoners were moving eastward on the Chambersburg Pike, the Union soldiers carrying General Reynolds were plodding in the same direction on a parallel course.[95] Colonel Wainwright saw the party coming toward him and immediately recognized the still figure on the litter. (It was reported that the general's face appeared unchanged in death.) As the party passed him, Wainwright removed his hat in silent tribute to the fallen leader.[96] Lieutenant Colonel Dawes and his 6th Wisconsin troops also saw the party moving to the rear but were unaware that the soldier on the litter was the revered Reynolds.[97] Lieutenant Stewart got word of the tragedy as he was returning to his battery after observing the action north of the Chambersburg Pike.[98] The wounded Colonel Fairchild was being eased onto a stretcher when a staff officer galloped by, shouting that Reynolds had been killed.[99] The shocking news traveled swiftly; soon it was generally known not only in the Federal regiments but in the Confederate as well.[100]

Perhaps most deeply affected was Reynolds' devoted orderly, Charles Veil. The journey to the rear had scarcely begun when he thought he heard the general gasp. Gently, the litter was set down, and he tried to get his chief to drink from his canteen, without success. The litter bearers picked up their burden and resumed their slow but steady pace.[101] They halted again when Dr. J. T. Stillman rode up (the First Corps surgeon had been summoned after Reynolds fell). If Veil then clung to a faint hope that the general was still alive and might yet survive, it was totally dispelled when Stillman completed his brief examination and pronounced Reynolds dead. In the doctor's opinion death had occurred within fifteen minutes of the fatal shot.[102]

Near the Seminary the party angled off to the right, heading toward the Emmitsburg road. At some point, Lieutenant Rosengarten (the aide who at Reynolds' behest had urged Gettysburg residents to stay indoors) joined the group.[103] It was a long trek for the litter bearers. Before it was over every muscle in their arms and legs must have ached. Veil and Rosengarten had a much easier lot, with no weight to carry and horses to ride. Veil, incidentally, was astride Reynolds' horse, his own having been hit about the time the general fell.[104]

Mrs. John Sheads, at her Washington Street home, happened to see the group of soldiers approaching and went to meet it. Pity welled within her as she gazed at the ashen-faced soldier on the litter. Can I do anything for him? she asked. Whether she was told that the soldier was General Reynolds and that he was dead or simply that there was nothing she could do is not clear. In either case, whether moved by compassion or grief, she snatched the shawl from her shoulders, bundled it into a pillow, and gently placed it under Reynolds' head. Although the thought would then have been fartherest from her mind, her gesture entailed no small sacrifice. Both she and her mother had worn that beautiful white shawl on their weddding days.[105]

Moving on, the party came to the Emmitsburg road and halted in front of a small stone home, the residence of one George George. He or someone in his family answered the knock at the door and admitted the unexpected vistors. Reynolds' body was carried into the parlor. Presently Veil and Rosengarten left on a doleful mission. Mounting their horses, they rode into Gettysburg to procure a casket for their leader.[106]

The scene there was one of excitement, confusion, turmoil, and what one observer termed "painful expectation."[107] The combined efforts of Lieutenant Rosengarten, town burgesses, and sundry pastors to keep people indoors had met with scant success.[108] In large number they milled about the square and the streets radiating from it, restless, apprehensive, downright scared many of them, yet all strangely titillated by the surging panorama: sullen Rebels in motley dress herded along by shouting Yankee guards; couriers on lathered horses racing in all directions; high-wheeled army wagons driven by leather-voiced teamsters threading their way through town; sweating stretcher bearers carrying the seriously wounded into churches hastily converted into hospitals; blue-coated lads, with less serious injury, lining the sidewalks, leaning against hitching posts or sitting on the pavement, all looking rather dazed.

Adding to the congestion were all those people, young and old, who had left their homes on the west side of town because the fighting was too close for comfort, the shelling from Pegram's guns too unnerving. As if of one accord, they had gravitated to the center of town. Some sought temporary refuge in the homes of relatives; some were invited into the homes of acquaintances or even of sympathetic strangers. But the majority remained on the streets, drifting here and there, drawing comfort from the proximity of so many others enduring the same trial. When friends chanced to meet, they shared their feelings, of timorous hope or impending calamity, as the case might be. There was no hysteria; just stolid resignation. What everyone hoped for, prayed for, was some assurance that it was safe to return to their homes.[109]

Among those who had gathered in the town square were Mrs. Robert Horner and her children. Although her adult fears could not be so easily dismissed, the children no doubt reveled in all the excitement: milling townspeople; a military band playing martial airs; an occasional phalanx of sullen Rebel prisoners marching by. A Mrs. Carson, who lived nearby, noticed the Horners and invited them into her parlor. There, while the women discussed their mutual concerns, most likely the children huddled at a window, absorbed in the passing scene.[110]

Earlier—before rumbling cannon caused apprehensive citizens to leave their homes—C. J. Tyson noticed it was strangely quiet outside his photography studio on York Street. At first he had been busy taking "likenesses" of Union soldiers. Now, the awareness that the normal sounds of traffic outside his studio were missing reminded him that it had been a long time since anyone, soldier or civilian, had come through his front door. Wondering what was up, he stepped outside and found York Street deserted and all the neighboring stores already closed. Just then, Judge Russell came around a corner, heading in his direction. "What does this mean?" Tyson asked him. Apparently the judge had heard Lieutenant Rosengarten's admonition, for he now repeated it: "It means that all citizens are requested to retire into their houses as quietly and as quickly as possible."

So Tyson locked his studio and headed for his home, across town, on Chambersburg Street. In the meantime, his wife, growing more anxious by the minute, had left home to join him at his studio. Fortunately, as they both were crossing the town square, they spied each other going in opposite directions. When they arrived at their home, the thunder of artillery was "going on in good earnest." Neighbors, who themselves were preparing to go elsewhere, strongly advised them to do likewise. The Tysons needed no urging. Moreover, they could immediately comply with the advice, since Mrs. Tyson had taken the precaution of packing a small trunk against just such an emergency. Sentimental perhaps to a fault, she had seen fit to include their wedding clothes.

Within minutes the photographer and his wife were retracing their steps, he pushing a wheelbarrow containing the trunk and she walking beside him. They had gone only a short distance when a spring wagon with two occupants pulled up alongside them. They recognized Mr. Boyer, the driver, and his mother-in-law, seated behind him. Needless to say, his offer of a ride was gladly accepted. Tyson, abandoning the wheelbarrow, lifted the trunk onto the wagon bed. He and his wife climbed aboard, Boyer flicked the reins, and they all rode east, then south, finally stopping on Baltimore Street. After that it was a matter of waiting for some word or sign that it would be safe to return home. Hours would pass, with the sight of Rebel prisoners being marched south the only encouraging portent.[111]

Sallie Broadhead also lived in the section of town nearest the battle. Her husband advised her to remain at home, as he intended to do; but when shells began "to fly around quite thick," she disregarded his counsel. Taking their child with her, she went across town to stay with a friend. On the way she saw a number of wounded Union soldiers and became alarmed over "our fearful situation." Anxiously, she asked a passerby, "Will our army be whipped?" Just then some Confederate prisoners came into view. Pointing to them, the man assured her there was no danger of that yet.

Those prisoners made a deep impression on Sallie. In her diary she wrote: "Such a dirty, filthy set, no one ever saw. They were dressed in all kinds of clothes....Some were barefooted and a few wounded. Though enemies, I pitied them."[112]

"If we can't hold it, where will you find men who can?"

All of Archer's men who had escaped capture along Willoughby Run streaked up the slope of Herr Ridge. With Yankees dogging their heels, they kept on going until they reached the protective cover of the woods beyond the crest. At this critical juncture—with Archer a prisoner and complete rout a possibility—the 13th Alabama's Colonel Birkett D. Fry succeeded to command of the brigade. Confusion was rampant as he and his officers strove to sort out the survivors and to organize a makeshift defense.[113]

The pursuing Iron Brigade regiments halted at the crest, realigned, sent out skirmishers.[114] No sooner had they halted than someone in the 2nd Wisconsin, overcome by the heady feeling of victory, gave a loud cheer. Instantly soldiers all along the line joined in, whooping and waving their hats in the air. But for Sergeant Jonathan Bryan the euphoria was short-lived. A Confederate, perhaps seeing him wave his hat, took aim and shot him straight through the heart.[115]

While casualties were comparatively light in this final stage, the 24th Michigan had the double misfortune of losing its second-in-command, Lieutenant Colonel Mark Flanigan, and its adjutant, Captain William H. Rexford. Both were seriously wounded, Flanigan in the leg (later amputated), Rexford in the groin.[116]

It is not known exactly when General Doubleday arrived on the field of the Archer-Meredith battle, but most likely it was about the time many of Archer's troops were taken prisoner west of Willoughby Run.[117] As he had kept in contact with Reynolds through his aides, he felt no need to seek him out now. Furthermore, he was greatly disturbed because Meredith's men had pushed so far ahead. Having just witnessed the retreat of Cutler's 76th New York and 56th Pennsylvania, he realized how vulnerable Meredith's regiments were in their exposed position atop Herr Ridge. If the enemy then rampaging north of the Chambersburg Pike should cross that road and overwhelm Cutler's two regiments on the south side, Meredith's Iron Brigade regiments would be cut off.

Major General Abner Doubleday

For that reason, Doubleday—still unaware that Reynolds had been killed—ordered the Iron Brigade to pull back to McPherson's Ridge, then link up with Cutler's 14th Brooklyn and 95th New York to form a strong defensive line south of the pike.[118] Never one to shrink from taking full credit for himself, Doubleday nevertheless testified before the Committee on the Conduct of the War that he later learned that either Meredith or Wadsworth had given a like order at about the same time.[119] Apparently it was Meredith, as the 7th Wisconsin's colonel reported that he received the order from Captain Hollon Richardson of Meredith's staff. Further, according to J. H. Stine, the First Corps' official historian, Richardson also relayed the order to the 19th Indiana and 24th Michigan.[120]

How did Meredith's troops, in the flush of victory, react to the fall-back order? Undoubtedly they were puzzled. Certainly some were resentful; caught up in the terrible thrill of battle, they would have wanted to push on, to complete the rout of the Rebel brigade. Why retire now! they must have wondered. On the right of the line, however, there were 2nd Wisconsin troops who were not in the least reluctant to leave: They had glimpsed a large body of Rebels approaching. (These would have been some of Pettigrew's or Brockenbrough's men belatedly coming to Archer's rescue.) Private Sydney Mead of 2nd Wisconsin's Company F assumed this was the reason for their withdrawal. In his diary he wrote: "...it being evident that they [the Rebels] were advancing in strong force on the Cashtown road, we recrossed Willoughby Run and

Brigadier General Solomon Meredith

took up a line running nearly parallel to it."[121] Whatever their personal feelings toward the withdrawal, Meredith's men did an about-face and returned—"in perfect order," one of them said[122]—to the west slope of McPherson's Ridge.

Several things happened after the brigade recrossed Willoughby Run that were never fully explained. First, shortly after taking a position facing west, the 2nd Wisconsin manuevered so that it faced north. Was this due to the approach of Pettigrew's and Brockenbrough's Brigades on the Chambersburg Pike, or to a perceived threat by Davis' Brigade north of that road? In either case, the position was soon abandoned and the former west-facing position—in Herbst's Woods and midway between the run and the ridgeline — was resumed.[123] Second, this same regiment, which had entered battle on the far right, now switched positions with the 7th Wisconsin, which originally had been on its left. It was recorded only that Meredith rode to 7th Wisconsin's Colonel Robinson and ordered the change. Because the 2nd Wisconsin was so depleted, Meredith may well have deemed it advisable to put Robinson's regiment—which was larger and had sustained fewer casualties—on the extreme right. Its line lay partly in Herbst's Woods, partly in the open field north of it.[124] Third, the 19th Indiana and 24th Michigan also switched places. This, too, was undoubtedly Meredith's doing, but his reason remains a mystery. The 19th Indiana's Lieutenant Colonel Dudley merely stated that the 24th Michigan was "taken from our left and formed on our right." He went on to describe his regiment's position:

> ...the line of the 19th Indiana now extended from near the edge of the timber skirting Willoughby Run on the left...northward about two hundred and seventy five feet part way up the rising ground until it joined the 24th Michigan....[125]

The 24th Michigan's line curved up the ridge, through Herbst's Woods, to connect with the Wisconsin regiments.[126] Thus, the new disposition of the Iron Brigade regiments, from right to left, was: 7th Wisconsin, 2nd Wisconsin, 24th Michigan, 19th Indiana.

It was shortly after 11:00 when these troops formed their new line. The intense fight with the Tennesseeans and Alabamans had lasted only about thirty minutes.[127] Doubleday, aware of the enemy on the loose to the north and not knowing what other enemy force might attack from the west, believed it vital that McPherson's Ridge, particularly Herbst's Woods, be held. As troops moved into the woods, he exhorted them to hold it at all costs. One of them piped up: "If we can't hold it, where will you find men who can?"[128]

In his after-action report Doubleday explained why he considered Herbst's Woods so important.

> [It] possessed all the advantages of a redoubt, strengthening the center of our line, and enfilading the enemy's column should they advance in the open spaces on either side. I deemed the extremity of the woods, which extended to the summit of the ridge, to be the key of the position, and urged that portion of Meredith's brigade, the Western men assigned to its defense, to hold it to the last extremity.[129]

Before the 2nd Wisconsin deployed in line, company officers took roll call; with more than a third of its men missing, it had to be a wrenching experience. In every regiment skirmishers were assigned and sent forward to the east bank of Willoughby Run. The remaining troops, after filing into position, were instructed to lie down facing the stream—and be ready if their foes returned.[130]

Doubleday, while checking the left of the Iron Brigade line, finally learned of Reynolds' death.[131] Who was first to inform him cannot be positively stated since Doubleday never said. However, most likely it was Captain John Carson of Reynolds' headquarters company. Of the officers that gathered around the fallen Reynolds, Carson, it will be recalled, was delegated to notify Doubleday. It is recorded that he fulfilled his mission but details of time and place are lacking.[132]

Doubleday was stunned. Not only had he lost a friend and associate of many years, he had just inherited an enormous responsibility. "The whole business of the battle," he later wrote, "was thus suddenly thrown upon me."[133]

In the meantime the 6th Wisconsin had been summoned, presumably by Meredith, to reinforce its sister regiments. When Doubleday got wind of this, he sent Lieutenant Benjamin Martin flying to Lieutenant Colonel Dawes to countermand the order. Having inspected the McPherson Ridge line himself, Doubleday apparently considered it adequate to cope with the enemy in that sector. He would have been more concerned about the deteriorating situation north of the Chambersburg Pike. And he would have wanted his only reserves free to respond immediately if needed there, which seemed highly probable. The 6th Wisconsin along with the attached brigade guard had scarcely gotten underway when Dawes received the peremptory order to halt. Once again—but only for a short interval—his troops were reprieved from combat.[134]

After Meredith's Brigade withdrew from Herr Ridge, Confederate skirmishers crept down the slope and took a position along Willoughby Run, directly opposite the Union skirmishers. The ensuing musket fire was sporadic; with the men of both sides screened by thick brush, a clear shot was hard to come by.[135] Pegram's batteries, meanwhile, were raining ball and shell on McPherson's Ridge. Incredibly, no one was hit in the 24th Michigan (though the other regiments were surely less fortunate). Still, Colonel Morrow, the 24th's commander, was unhappy with his position. On the left his line dipped into a "deep hollow," which obscured visibility with the right, thus making control of the entire line difficult. Moreover, his left, like all of the 19th Indiana, was quite exposed. Three times Morrow sought permission to remedy the situation by moving both regiments to higher ground; three times he was refused. Their present position, he was told, must be held "at all hazards."[136]

On Herr Ridge an infusion of fresh Confederate troops was about to begin. Eventually the seven regiments plus one battalion of Pettigrew's and Brockenbrough's Brigades would line the crest, poised for battle. Throughout the long build-up, Archer's battered brigade was allowed to rest. Even so, it had been too badly cut up, too severely demoralized, to be of much use for the remainder of the day.

On the opposite ridge, the victors in the fight with Archer were also reinforced. Coming to their aid were the seven regiments comprising Biddle's and Stone's Brigades.[137]

After the rout of Archer's Brigade, the spotlight of battle shifted northward to the strip of open ground, some 150 yards wide, between the Chambersburg Pike and the unfinished railroad cut. There Captain Hall was struggling to save his six guns and Major Harney to extricate his 147th New York from an impending Confederate trap.

CHAPTER VIII

COUNTERATTACK!

"...our only chance was to charge them."

So far each side had scored a distinct but inconclusive victory. On the Confederate left Davis' Brigade had sent two of Cutler's regiments packing; on the Union left the Iron Brigade had trounced Archer's Brigade. But which side would ultimately prevail in this chance encounter remained an open question.

It would seem that the Federals held the upper hand when they stood triumphant on Herr Ridge. But that was not the case, for at that moment Davis' rampaging Missippians and Carolinians were about to overrun the 147th New York and the 2nd Maine battery. If they succeeded, the whole Union position would be in jeopardy.

Captain James Hall, though lacking an order to withdraw, had taken steps to extricate his endangered battery. With the aid of prolonges (towing ropes), his left and middle section guns had been pulled back to their limbers and hooked up. The two right section guns, meanwhile, had been moved back some 75 yards to cover the withdrawal. As it turned out, the crews were unable to fire a single round, so intense was the enemy's skirmish fire.

The prospects for the right section were grim, but Hall was determined to get the four guns in the other two sections out of danger. The instant one of them was attached to a limber, the driver cracked his whip and the flight to the rear began. Rebel skirmishers beyond the railroad cut had been sniping at the artillerymen for some time, and "the moment they saw we were getting away, rushed forward, and firing as fast as they could." The harrassment continued unabated as the guns rolled down the east slope of McPherson's Ridge and swung southward to the Chambersburg Pike. Although his attention was focused on these guns, Hall would not have forgotten his "terribly used up" right section. He could only hope that Lieutenant Frank Ulmer would somehow manage to effect its escape.

Even as the other two sections got underway, Ulmer and his two gun crews were feverishly preparing to follow in their wake. For them to reach the pike meant moving their guns across more than a hundred yards of open ground. To make matters worse, one gun had lost all of its horses and would have to be dragged by hand.

Several guns of the left and middle sections stacked up at the worm fence beside the Chambersburg Pike. Until a portion of it was leveled and each gun, in turn, could pass through the gap, men, horses, guns, limbers — all were sitting ducks. In those harrowing minutes more horses were lost, including Hall's own, shot through the rump. Hall reported the equine losses at the pike but made no mention of human casualties there. Nevertheless, in that morning's action Hall lost about twenty of his men, and most likely some of them were shot while waiting to go through the gap. A clue that this was probably the case lies in the battery commander's laconic summation of the flight from the limbering area to the point of exit onto the road. He said it was "hellish."

Even so, five guns — including the one dependent solely on manpower — made it to the Chambersburg Pike. Just as the sixth gun reached the gap, its whole team of horses collapsed. Every one had been shot! While horses were somewhat expendable, guns were not. Artillerymen were expected to make every effort, no matter how onerous, to save their guns. However, as Hall later explained, to stop at that moment, cut loose the horses, and try to pull the gun away by hand would have been "madness." The battery therefore had no choice but to continue on to Seminary Ridge without it.[1]

Brigadier General James S. Wadsworth

There Captain Hall met General Wadsworth. Still chafing at what he thought was gross neglect, Hall lashed out at his superior. Risking the serious charge of insubordination, he flatly told the division commander he considered it "cowardly" on his part to leave the battery stranded. No doubt Wadsworth's response to the accusation was equally heated. His excuse: Since General Reynolds had posted the battery in a hazardous position, he had assumed Reynolds would personally look after it.[2] (Neither officer had yet learned of Reynolds' death.) Wadsworth took no retaliatory action against Hall, probably realizing that his virulent outburst was due purely to the stress he had been under. Abruptly terminating the argument, Wadsworth told the battery commander, "Get your guns back to some point to cover the retreat of these troops."

Hall had the temerity to object: "This, General, is that place right here in the road."

"Oh no," Wadsworth countered, "go beyond the town for we cannot hold this line." He would have expected Hall to hop to it. Instead Hall brought up another matter — the gun he had been forced to leave behind. He asked permission to try and retrieve it. By then the general's patience had to be wearing thin; permission was denied. Signalling that the meeting was over, Wadsworth snapped, "Lose no time in getting your guns into position to cover the retreat."[3]

While Hall's Battery was escaping, the 147th New York troops were fighting for their lives. Across the pike, the 14th Brooklyn and 95th New York men were under fire from Rebel skirmishers north of the railroad cut. Once the 147th was out of the way — clearly it could not hold out much longer — Davis' Brigade would be free to swoop down on the rear of these two regiments and the Iron Brigade as well. "The moment," declared Doubleday, "was a critical one, involving the defeat, perhaps the utter rout of our forces." To prevent that from happening, he knew he had to act quickly. Thanks to his foresight he still had a reserve force — Lieutenant Colonel Rufus Dawes' 6th Wisconsin, "a gallant body of men who I knew could be relied upon."[4] He decided on a counterattack by these troops. Timely mounted and vigorously executed, it offered the best hope of averting disaster. Within minutes a Doubleday aide, Lieutenant Meredith Jones, was riding at top speed to Dawes with the attack order.

Wadsworth independently came to the same decision as Doubleday and, apparently, at almost the same time. Lieutenant C. E. Rogers delivered Wadsworth's order to Solomon Meredith. The Iron Brigade commander, in turn, dispatched one of his aides, Captain J. D. Wood, to inform Dawes.

Doubleday's aide reached Dawes first. Reining in his mount and saluting, Lieutenant Jones said, "General Doubleday directs that you move your regiment at once to the right" — that is, to the north. He then relayed Doubleday's instructions for the counterattack. No sooner had Dawes set his command in motion than he saw another officer galloping toward him. What now! he must have thought. It turned out to be Captain Wood bearing Wadsworth's attack order (transmitted through Meredith) for his command. Dawes was relieved to note that there was no conflict with Doubleday's order. Wood impressed on the regimental commander just how desperate the situation north of the Chambersburg Pike really was, adding, rather superfluously, that the Wisconsin lads should "go like hell."[5]

The 420 officers and men of the 6th Wisconsin and the brigade guard were only a short distance north of the Fairfield Road, in the swale between Seminary Ridge and McPherson's Ridge, when Dawes received Doubleday's halt order. Consequently they now had a half mile to cover before reaching the Chambersburg Pike, where the attack would begin. When Dawes came abreast of the Lutheran Seminary, he saw a large body of Rebels off to the right. Realizing at once that his command would be poorly positioned to strike them unless he changed course, he directed his troops to wheel right "by company into line on the right company." Realigned, they pushed northward to the pike. They needed no urging to proceed at the double-quick as the enemy had detected their approach and were peppering them with minie balls.[6]

> Dawes' horse suddenly reared, then plunged ahead. It did not occur to me [wrote Dawes] that she had been shot. I drew a tight rein and spurred her when she fell heavily on her haunches. I scrambled from the ground, where I had been thrown sprawling, in front of the regiment, and the men gave a hearty cheer. The gallant old mare also struggled to her feet and hobbled toward the rear on three legs. She had been struck in the breast by a minnie ball.... For the rest of the battle I was on foot.

(The plucky mare survived for years. But with the ball still lodged behind the right shoulder blade, she was inclined to be mean-tempered.)[7]

As Dawes' men raced to the post-and-rail fence on the south side of the pike, they must have been tempted to pause long enough to fire back at the Rebels. But discipline prevailed and they resisted the impulse. At last, when they all had reached the fence and the enemy was barely two hundred yards away, the expected command rippled up and down the line. Eagerly, with muskets steadied on fence rails, the Badger State troops unloosed a tremendous volley.

Those units of Davis' Brigade that had turned to face their new opponents took the blast head-on. For the rest — the majority still pushing eastward — it meant enfilade fire, which was ever more insidious, more unnerving. According to Dawes, the enemy lines "swayed and bent, and suddenly stopped firing." The next moment, as the Wisconsin troops looked on in amazement, the Rebels made a wild dash for the shelter of the railroad cut.[8]

In the meantime, on Dawes' left, the 14th Brooklyn and 95th New York had come up to the Chambersburg Pike. Thus was Dawes' line greatly extended, though he was unaware of it until sometime after his troops had opened fire. Colonel Edward Fowler, who ordered the move, was no less surprised to find that his regiments had strong support on their right.[9]

It had been a spur-of-the-moment decision on Fowler's part. As in the case of battery commander Hall, he had heard nothing from his superiors. Much to his relief, he had seen the enemy on his left fleeing from the Iron Brigade; but the enemy on his right continued to worry him. Although he had grown accustomed to the sniping from skirmishers north of the railroad cut, he was greatly shocked when he looked in that direction and saw Hall's guns pulling out. Even more ominous was a glimpse, through the smoky haze, of enemy troops approaching. With a tremor of fear, he realized that before long they would be behind his own troops. "I had no time for deliberation, my first impression was that we were lost," Fowler recalled. "Like lightning I reasoned that, if we attempted to retreat to the rear, every one of us would be shot, and that our only chance was to charge them."[10]

By his order, the 14th Brooklyn and 95th New York, with a combined strength of 560 officers and men, did an about-face and descended McPherson's Ridge. The retrograde movement, with the 95th New York in the lead, was strangely unhurried (Doubleday described it as "leisurely"). The 95th's Colonel George Biddle, who had been wounded earlier, still led his regiment. However, shortly before the charge, he realized his injury was more serious than he first thought and relinquished command to Major Edward Pye. When both regiments were opposite Davis' Brigade, they changed front ninety degrees to face the enemy. During the maneuver they came under a galling fire. And there was no letup as they advanced to the Chambersburg Pike.[11] Fowler reported: "...brave boys were dropping at every step...[I] shouted, cheered and urged our men on, making as much noise, excited as I was, as my lungs and throat were capable of."[12] At the fence the 14th Brooklyn deployed to the left of the 95th New York. With the 6th Wisconsin already in position on the 95th's right, nearly 1,000 Federals were perfectly aligned to charge Davis' 1,700 Confederates.[13]

Had a joint action by the three Union regiments been scrupulously planned, it could not have been executed any better.

"In retreat, double-quick, run!"

The lapse in communication with Hall's battery, Fowler's two regiments, and Harney's 147th New York had, in each instance, created grave problems. General Reynolds had been in closer proximity to all these units than either Wadsworth or Cutler; had he lived there might have been no lapse and the difficulties would have been avoided or at least mitigated. Nevertheless, Hall and his artillerymen had managed to escape with five of their six guns. And Fowler had resolved his predicament by electing to attack rather than risk trying to escape. But the plight of the 147th New York remained critical.

Actually, that regiment had been ordered to retire along with the 76th New York and 56th Pennsylvania. Its commander, Lieutenant Colonel Francis C. Miller, may have even received the order. If he did, he was prevented from relaying it to anyone by the inopportune bullet that sent him flying to the rear for medical attention. His successor, Major George Harney, naturally assumed his duty was to hold the position just north of the railroad cut. His right was soon refused, and after that, half of his line faced north and the other half, west. Hall's success in withdrawing his battery owed much to the

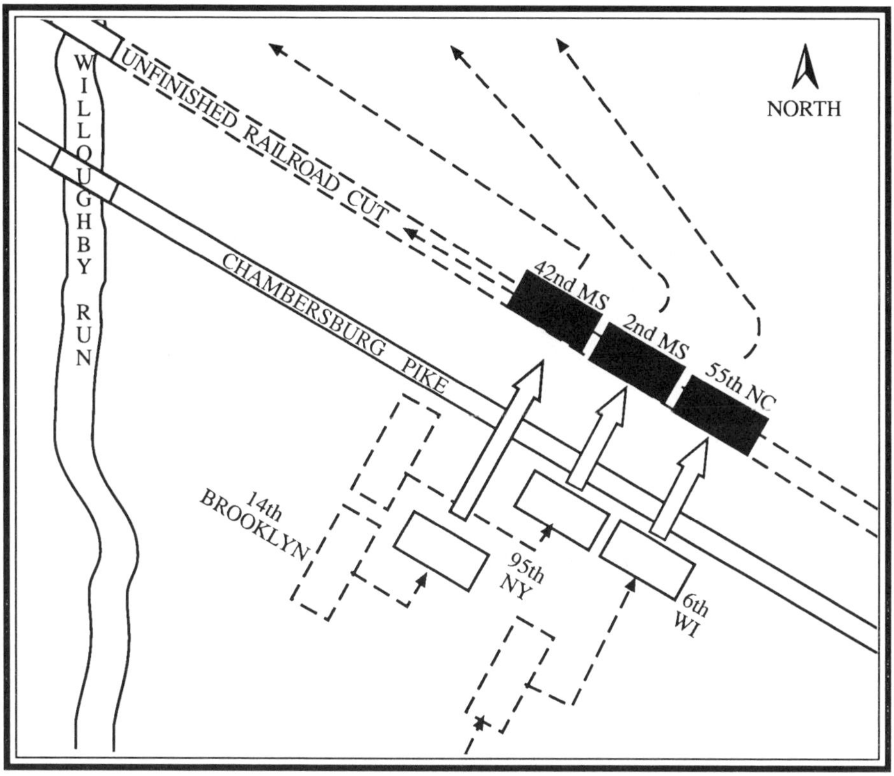

Union counterattack at the railroad cut. Shortly after 11:00 the three Union regiments crossed the Chambersburg Pike and charged the entrenched Confederates.

valiant stand of Harney's men. But in holding their ground they had sustained a great many casualties and were now completely isolated. It seemed inevitable that before long they would be hemmed in.

West of their position, part of the 42nd Mississippi had scrambled into the railroad cut. With Hall's Battery gone, these troops could move at any minute to block the New Yorkers from escaping to the south. The approach of the 55th North Carolina and 2nd Mississippi on a broad front from the north already precluded the 147th New York from escaping in that direction. And, if the enemy kept on at its present rate, very shortly the 147th's escape route to the east would also be blocked.[14] The only obstacle in the Confederates' path was a rail fence, which ran parallel to Harney's right wing.

As it was within comfortable musket range of the Federals, getting over it proved costly for the Confederate regiments. In the process, with men dropping everywhere, their lines disintegrated. Once over the fence, however, the Southerners showed their mettle under fire by cooly re-forming their lines. In the 55th North Carolina an officer strode out in front of his troops. Then, in full view of the amazed New Yorkers, he calmly proceeded to correct the alignment of his troops as if they were about to pass in review. The Confederate advance resumed.[15]

Major Harney, meanwhile, was asking a pointed question of his company commanders. Should the 147th keep on fighting or retreat? Withdrawal from battle without higher authority was not something to be undertaken lightly; but the situation was too critical to stand on formality. It so happened Harney was spared making a decision. Even as he solicited the opinion of his officers, a member of Wadsworth's staff rode up with the mandatory solution to his dilemma.[16]

When it became evident to the division commander that his withdrawal order for the 147th New York was not going to be carried out, he had dispatched his adjutant, Captain Timothy Ellsworth, to repeat it. Ellsworth had ridden down Seminary Ridge at breakneck speed, his "coal-black hair pressing his horse's mane."[17] On reaching Harney, he repeated Wadsworth's message: *Retreat at once!* Then Ellsworth raised his sword over his head and began rotating it in a rapid circular motion. All along the angled line the beleaguered troops saw the signal and understood it meant they were finally pulling out.[18] Before doing so, on Harney's order they abandoned everything except their muskets, ammunition, and cartridge boxes.[19] The prospect of nothing to eat for the rest of the day — even had it occurred to them — would have been supremely unimportant when they faced imminent capture, if not a worse fate.[20]

According to one officer, Harney gave the command "In retreat, march!"[21] According to another, he said: "In retreat, double-quick, run!"[22] In light of the urgency of their departure, the latter seems more likely. The New Yorkers did in fact run. Above all, they wanted to escape the galling Confederate fire. Yet it was not a complete rout. Harney's men, even as they were retreating, managed a scattered return fire. Some of them succeeded in slipping away north of the railroad cut, but most were forced to cross the ditch and continue south.[23]

The Rebels of course pressed their advantage, advancing steadily, firing furiously, and all the while yelling like savages.[24] It was reported that the 147th New York men fell "at every step."[25] Lieutenant J. Volney Pierce and Sergeant Peter Shuttz had just begun their perilous flight when they came upon Private Edwin Aylesworth, lying on the ground, mortally wounded but still conscious. They lifted him to his feet and tried to drag him along between them, but soon had to give it up. After they had eased him to the ground, he begged piteously, "Don't leave me, boys." But what could they do? To stay meant certain capture — if bullets did not cut them down first. They went on and shortly thereafter Shuttz was killed. Pierce got away safely. For the rest of his life he was haunted by Aylesworth's pathetic plea which cruel necessity had forced him to refuse.[26]

Color Sergeant John Hinchcliff presented a doubly conspicuous target. Not only did he attract attention merely by holding a flag, he towered over everyone around him. Yet the six-foot-two-inch Swede had lasted through the entire fight until the retreat order was given. Just then a bullet found its mark. As Hinchcliff slumped to the ground, shot through the heart, the colors wound around his body, and his blood began to seep into the fabric. Fifty feet away, Sergeant William Wyburn saw him fall and made a dash for the flag. He yanked it free, ripped it from the shattered staff, gathered it in his arms. Then, tightly clasping the precious bundle, he ran through the hail of bullets to the rim of the railroad cut and jumped in.[27]

Many of his comrades had preceded him there. The man-made ravine seemed to offer protection; instead, it proved to be a trap. West of their position, hidden behind some fence rails piled up at the base of the cut were a band of Rebels lying in wait. As soon as they spotted blue-clad soldiers they opened fire. This was bad enough, but far worse for the Yankee infantrymen was the prospect of the main enemy force looking down — and shooting — at them from the northern rim. Those who foresaw this development had no intention of waiting for it. Lieutenant Pierce's wry comment, "I did not stay to dispute possession," applied equally to all who left the railroad cut in the utmost haste. Pierce described his part in the exodus: "...I climbed up the rocky face of the cut, on the south side, and made my way with many of our men across the meadow between the railroad cut and the Chambersburg Pike...." Crossing the pike, they took refuge in McPherson's peach orchard.[28]

About sixty of their comrades were not so fortunate. Private Francis Pease confided to his diary:

> We got into an old railroad ravine, and was going along [eastward] as fast as we could, but not very, for the road was so crowded....Soon the Rebels came up each side of the bank in large numbers, and we had to throw down our arms and surrender....[29]

Prospects for the Confederates at this time seemed exceedingly bright. As yet unaware of the impending counterattack, they fought with a frenzied determination to destroy the 147th New York. Still yelling like furies, they fired with wild abandon.[30] In their haste, some forgot to remove their ramrods, which consequently took erratic but lethal flight into the Yankees' midst. A soldier on the receiving end later remarked: "Only those who have heard the sound [of flying ramrods] can realize the demoralizing effect they produce." Some Rebels even threw their camp hatchets at the enemy. Some hurled "vile and opprobrious taunts," hoping to induce the Yankees to surrender.[31] Many had already attached their bayonets, in anticipation of close combat.[32] Such was their zeal for total victory.

The New Yorkers who made it to McPherson's orchard were still not out of danger. Sergeant Wyburn was among those wounded there. A ball struck him in the back and he went down clutching the regimental colors he had retrieved just minutes earlier. Lieutenant Pierce, who had joined him only moments before, tried to relieve Wyburn of the colors, thinking him unable to carry on. But the sergeant held on "with true Irish grit." When Pierce ordered him to let go, he snapped, "Hold on, I will be up in a minute." As Pierce watched in amazement, Wyburn, grimacing with pain, struggled to his feet. Despite the severity of his injury, he brought the colors off the field. Subsequently, in recognition of his courageous action, he was brevetted first lieutenant.[33]

Back on Seminary Ridge, Captain Hall could not erase from his mind the ignominy of losing one gun. Believing there was a chance it could be recovered in all the turmoil and thus remove the blemish on his battery's reputation, he assigned a sergeant and five privates to the mission. Their efforts were unavailing, however: Not only did they fail to retrieve the gun, all six were either wounded or captured.[34]

According to one 147th New York infantryman, the regiment stood alone against the enemy "for fully 30 minutes."[35] The statement is not strictly correct, since Hall's Battery had remained on their flank until minutes before Captain Ellsworth arrived with the retreat order. But that does not diminish the New Yorkers' singular achievement—keeping Davis' whole brigade at bay long enough for a Federal force to mount a counterattack.[36]

Afterward it would be asserted that Dawes' and Fowler's Regiments "saved" the 147th New York. Certainly their combined attack prevented further pursuit of Harney's men, possibly even assured their escape. But for them to claim total credit for saving the New Yorkers loses sight of the fact that the 147th's retreat was well advanced by the time those regiments attacked.

Indeed, Harney's men were making good their escape when they heard a great commotion. It was the counterattack getting underway. The shouting sounded "so different from the rebel yell," one of them recalled, they knew it had to be Northerners at last coming to their aid; it "caused our hearts to beat fast with joy."[37]

With the enemy's attention diverted, the pressure on the 147th New York was greatly reduced. Animated by the single desire to escape, many of these troops became separated from their companies. Once out of danger, each had to set out looking for his own company. While the 147th was retreating, the two regiments that had retreated earlier—the 76th New York and 56th Pennsylvania—were getting reorganized north of the railroad cut on Oak Ridge (the extension of Seminary Ridge). All that remained of the 147th New York eventually joined them there, with Major Harney and the right wing men probably arriving slightly ahead of Wyburn, Pierce, and the other left wing men.[38]

As Harney came up Oak Ridge, a glowering General Cutler rode down to meet him. "You have lost your colors, sir!" he growled.

Harney rejected the rebuke, replying proudly, "General, the 147th never loses its colors." He then directed Cutler's gaze to a certain soldier still some distance off. It was the wounded Sergeant Wyburn, limping along, clasping the bundled-up flag against his chest. Seeing him, Cutler said, "I'll take it all back."[39]

The jumble of infantrymen, arriving singly and in small groups, finally got sorted out and each man took his place in formation. But what a shock — three-quarters of the regiment was missing! The survivors, fatiqued and in a kind of stupor, at first must have wondered, *Where is everyone?* But then they remembered...horrendous musket fire, comrades dropping right and left.

The approximately sixty men who were captured eventually escaped and returned to their regiment. But the loss in killed and wounded was permanent except in the case of minor injury. Out of the 380 who entered the fight, 207 officers and men were killed or wounded within a half hour, according to General Cutler. The 147th's monument near the railroad cut states "killed and wounded here — 212." And Lieutenant H. H. Lyman, adjutant of the regiment, reported a total of 220 killed or wounded in the engagement.[40] Regardless of the numerical differences, all three sources affirm that, in both number and percentage (54%-58%), the 147th New York suffered the greatest loss of any Union regiment in the morning's battle.

The 147th New York received many tributes for its valiant stand, but perhaps none more telling than this ingenuous compliment from the enemy: "I don't know what troops were fighting," wrote a 2nd Mississippi soldier, "but I do know they were hard fighters and retired only at the point of the bayonet after most of them were killed."[41]

After the survivors reached Oak Ridge, Cutler remarked, "It's just like cock-fighting today. We fight a little and run a little."[42] In a restricted sense that was true. But as a summation of the 147th's actions that morning, the jocular utterance is thoroughly inadequate, failing as it does to give due credit to the tenacity, valor, and sacrifice of those men. Few regiments, on either side, endured a more grueling, or more costly, baptism of fire.

"Throw down your muskets!"

Just when it seemed the Federals would be completely routed, Davis' Brigade had been rebuffed, its rosy expectation of undisputed possession of the field vanishing in the sudden volley from the 6th Wisconsin and the 100-man brigade guard. In that terrible outburst, Davis' troops had recognized the virtual certainty of imminent counterattack. They felt unprepared, vulnerable. Fear had taken hold and morale plummeted. In a spontaneous breach of discipline, they had bolted for the protection of the trackless railroad cut. Earlier, while chasing Cutler's regiments, there had been some intermingling of companies. But now, in the mindless dash for cover, all organization was lost. As one Mississippi officer admitted, by the time they poured into the railroad cut, "all the men were jumbled together without regard to regiment or company."[43] Joe Davis, directing his first battle, was in trouble.[44]

Upwards of one thousand Rebels blanketed the 18-foot-wide ditch and its steep shale banks. Amid mass confusion, company officers set about rounding up their men and restoring discipline.[45] While they made substantial progress, it seems unlikely that the sorting out process was completed by the time the counterattack began.

By and large, however, the troops were in their proper regimental positions: 42nd Mississippi on the right; 2nd Mississippi in the center; 55th North Carolina on the left. While Colonel Hugh R. Miller remained in charge of the 42nd Mississippi, the other two regiments had new commanders. In the 2nd Mississippi, with both Colonel Stone and Lieutenant Colonel Humphrey wounded, command devolved on Major John A. Blair. In the 55th North Carolina (as previously noted) Colonel Connally was wounded, Lieutenant Colonel Smith was killed, and, as a result, Major Alfred H. Belo assumed command of the regiment.[46]

From a tactical standpoint, the North Carolina troops were unquestionably in the best position. Half of them had halted just short of the railroad cut. The other half had dashed into the cut, but in a sector that was shallow enough to serve as a convenient trench.[47] This fortuitous disposition would weigh heavily in their favor when the time came to escape. The Mississippians, on the other hand, would find themselves trapped at the bottom of a twenty-foot ditch.[48]

That painful realization came later, however. Now, as the reorganization in the cut progressed, one Mississippi company after another scrambled up the forward bank, sighted the enemy two hundred yards off, and opened fire. About the same time, the better positioned 55th North Carolina troops also started firing.

Captain John A. Kellogg, acting adjutant to General Cutler, had to ride through the hail of bullets. Cutler had sent him flying to General Wadsworth with the news that the Rebels had taken possession of the railroad cut. Miraculously, he made it to Seminary Ridge unscathed, though his hat had been shot off, bullets had ripped through his uniform, and his horse had been hit twice, in the ear and rump.[49]

Although the Confederate firepower was truly formidable, 55th North Carolina's Major Belo was uneasy. A defensive stand, he felt, was wrong. In fact he was absolutely convinced that, in the present situation, the side that attacked first would emerge the victor. The 2nd Mississippi's Major Blair, to whom he expressed this view, concurred, and together they resolved to take offensive action. Before they could implement their plan, however, it was quashed by a peremptory order from brigade commander Davis.[50] (One can only conjecture what the outcome might have been had the Confederates rather than the Federals initiated the attack.)

Davis called for a general retreat through the cut, in the direction of Willoughby Run, with the 55th North Carolina covering the withdrawal of the Mississippi regiments. But, as it turned out, there was no general retreat. By the time the order reached the company level in all three regiments—some troops never did receive it—the entire brigade was simply too embroiled to disengage.[51]

Early on, the North Carolina men on the far left of Davis' line were plagued by artillery fire from one Union gun. General Buford, standing on Seminary Ridge, had seen them blazing away at the 6th Wisconsin and determined to do something about it. Going up to Lieutenant Roder's section of Calef's Battery, which was parked nearby, he ordered the lieutenant to take one of his guns into the cut and enfilade the Confederates. No sooner had the artillerymen dropped trail than a Rebel spotted them and exclaimed, "There is a piece—let's take it!" He and a handful of men around him rushed the gun, firing as they came. Corporal Robert Watrous took a minie ball in the leg as he was bringing up a round of canister. Before he fell, an alert private, Tom Slattery, snatched the round from his hands, ran to the gun, and rammed it down the muzzle. Seconds later a deadly spray of canister dispersed the would-be attackers.[52] According to Calef, some of them were so close "they were literally blown away from the muzzle."[53] Undoubtedly Slattery had saved the piece.

After this incident the gun crew apparently was able to fire with relative impunity. They kept on harassing the Carolineans until the approach of their own infantry rendered further fire too risky.

The leader of those Union troops on the right, Lieutenant Colonel Rufus Dawes, was unaware that a railroad cut stretched across his front until sometime after the charge began. When his command unleashed its first volley at the turnpike fence and the Confederates suddenly stopped firing and ran, then disappeared from view, he thought they were retreating under cover of a dip in the fields. Eager to press his (assumed) advantage, he ordered the 6th Wisconsin, together with the brigade guard on its right, to move out. Before the assault could begin in earnest, however, the rail fences on either side of the Chambersburg Pike had to be hurdled. As his men clambered over the first one, a sudden blast of frontal fire struck down a number of them. Thus was Dawes disabused of the notion of a Confederate retreat.[54]

More men fell at the second fence. Among them was Captain John Ticknor, commander of Company K, shot dead.[55] The troops who made it over both fences were totally disorganized. Before advancing another step, their line had to be restored. On their left, unknown to Dawes, the 95th New York had begun its advance northward at the same time as his troops, had suffered the same ordeal at the turnpike fences, and consequently had the same need of realignment. A Confederate officer, looking on, was impressed: "The Federal Regiments in front of us threw themselves into line of battle by a well-executed movement notwithstanding the heavy fire we were pouring into them...."[56]

It was only as his men were re-forming their line that Dawes became aware of Union troops on his left. "I did not then know or care where they came from, but was rejoiced to see them." They too, he noticed, were in the process of re-forming. Here was an unexpected opportunity for a concerted attack, which would greatly improve their chances of success. Dawes hurried over to the officer obviously in charge. The troops were, of course, the 95th New York of Cutler's Brigade and the commanding officer was Major Edward Pye. Dawes was blunt. "We must charge!" he said.

Equally terse was the major's instantaneous reply: "Charge it is!"[57] (Only later did Dawes learn that a third regiment, the 14th Brooklyn, also participated in the charge.)

The 6th Wisconsin commander rushed back to his troops. By then they were well aligned and the charge on the railroad cut could begin. Battle-hardened though they were, the prospects could hardly have been more daunting. The enemy facing them had already put three of Cutler's Regiments and Hall's Battery to flight and thus could give full attention to repelling a counterattack. Further, they had excellent cover, whereas Dawes troops charging across some 150 yards of fairly level meadow would have none. And, most assuredly, the Rebels would take full advantage of their unobstructed field of fire.

"Forward, charge!" Dawes bellowed, and his bluecoats plunged into the inferno of Confederate fire. As their objective was to close with the enemy as quickly as possible, they spent little time in firing back. Mostly they ran. And all the while they yelled at the top of their voices—which possibly did more to bolster their courage than to frighten the enemy. Whenever their alignment went askew, Dawes would sing out, "Align on the colors! Close up on the colors!" The sight of that flag flying out in front surely helped to keep them going when comrades began dropping on all sides. Not surprisingly, one color-bearer after another was struck down. Every time this occurred, a member of the color guard would spring into action, grab hold of the shaft, loft the banner, and go forward.[58]

One of Dawes' company commanders was called "Tall Sycamore." But Captain J. H. Marston claimed no Indian ancestry, as the picturesque nickname suggests. Rather, it stemmed from his great height, long limbs, and notably erect posture. Of all Dawes' memories of the charge on the railroad cut, none was more vivid than the image of "Tall Sycamore" extending his long arms "as if to gather his men together and push them forward."[59]

While Marston's physical appearance was exceptional, his exemplary handling of his men was not. Throughout the 6th Wisconsin Dawes' officers exhibited the same propulsive leadership and disregard of self. Always out in front and seemingly impervious to flying lead, they kept their men closed up and constantly moving ahead.

Meanwhile, the 95th New York and 14th Brooklyn were also pushing toward the railroad cut. Their experience was no different, no less harrowing, than that of the 6th Wisconsin. The 95th New York, as we have seen, had been alerted to coordinate its attack with the Wisconsin troops on its right. Hence, when Dawes ordered the 6th Wisconsin to advance, Major Pye followed with his command to the New Yorkers: "Forward, guide right!"[60]

The two regiments and the brigade guard, moving together on a broad front, had braved the enemy fire for some minutes before the 14th Brooklyn entered the fray.[61] In the interim Colonel Fowler had had to deal with a flagrant disregard of orders. Where the 14th Brooklyn crossed the Chambersburg Pike, a three-foot high embankment ran along the far side. It offered perfect refuge from the bullets buzzing thickly overhead, and the Brooklyners took advantage of it. Fowler shouted at them to get up and move out. But they did not get up. He knew he had to quickly overcome what he later could blandly dismiss as "a strong disposition...to halt at this point." Then, however, his reaction was far from benign. He unloosed an angry tirade that probably included pungent aspersions on their courage, loyalty, masculinity, and parentage.

Whatever he said, it worked. The men got up, went over the top—and received a fearsome blast of musketry. Soldiers crumpled to the ground; screams of pain sliced the air. For a few tremulous seconds, Fowler's whole line wavered. At that moment the temptation to return to the cover they had just abandoned must have been almost irresistible. But the will to fight instilled by their commander prevailed. They rallied, gave a cheer, and plunged ahead.[62]

Some 147th New Yorkers, then escaping eastward, caught a glimpse of their brothers-in-arms gallantly charging the enemy they had been forced to flee. To see "regiments with Union flags borne high and flying to the breeze," said one of them, "caused our hearts to beat fast with joy and thankfulness."[63]

After what must have seemed an eternity, those regiments—6th Wisconsin and 95th New York followed by the 14th Brooklyn—reached their objective. According to the measurement made by Lieutenant Colonel Dawes some years later, the Wisconsin men who made it to the rim of the railroad cut had come exactly 175 paces. Behind them, the meadow "streamed with men who had been shot, and who were struggling to the rear or sinking in death upon the ground."[64] Dawes' depiction of the terrible scene was underscored by one of his men. James Sullivan of Company K wrote: "All the while the enemy kept up a deadly fire, and our killed and wounded lay thick on the grass between the road and the cut."[65]

Just how many does "thick" connote? Dawes said it was about 180.[66] Other sources indicate he may have erred slightly on the high side. Perhaps the best estimate of total casualties in the 6th Wisconsin and the brigade guard would be 160.[67] As the combined force numbered 420 officers and men, this figure equates to a numbing 38% casualty rate.

As to casualties in the 95th New York and the 14th Brooklyn, it seems no one, participant or historian, ever ventured a figure for the charge on the railroad cut for either regiment. Nevertheless, there can be no doubt that in both cases the "butcher bill" was high, though probably a shade less sanguinary—in percent if not in number—than that for Dawes' command. Out of the 520 officers and men engaged in both regiments, the number killed and wounded can be confidently pegged at 150 to 175.

For the Confederates, it had been almost like picking off ducks in a shooting gallery. But, when the three attacking regiments finally reached the cut, the advantage shifted decisively to the Federals. Davis' Brigade, with a vengeful enemy looming above it, would have to fight its way out of a trap—if it could. To make matters worse, on their left flank some of Dawes' men had gotten astride the cut and, like Roder's cannoneers earlier, were pouring enfilade fire into their midst.[68]

Although Davis' troops must have sensed the hopelessness of their situation, they had not given up. Indeed, in the words of one 14th Brooklyn officer, they fought "with the ferocity of wild cats."[69] The Yankees were no less determined. A 6th Wisconsin officer, referring to that regiment's troops, remarked, "They were mad and fought with a desperation seldom witnessed."[70]

Firing at point-blank range, the combatants could hardly miss. The shoot-out was vicious, with no quarter given. Wounded Rebels sank to the railroad bed; Yankees hit at the edge of the cut pitched forward, rolled down the bank. Blood of both sides seeped into the loose gravel. With the fight going against them, desperate Rebels resorted to trickery. "Some of them," a 6th Wisconsin soldier stated, "would throw down their guns and cry 'I surrender,' and immediately pick them up and shoot some of our unsuspecting men."[71] In the same regiment Levi Tongue saw the lifeless body of his comrade, John Harland, topple into the ditch and land at the feet of the Rebel who killed him. Tongue raised his musket to retaliate. The instant the Rebel saw Tongue's musket pointed at him, he threw down his own empty musket and begged, "Don't shoot, don't kill me!" But Tongue was too angry to be dissuaded. "All hell can't save you now!" he screamed, then pressed the trigger. The Rebel fell dead across the body of Harland.[72]

An impetuous Union officer hurled his sword at a Confederate who at that moment was rallying his troops. "Kill that officer," he shouted to his men, "and we will capture that command." The officer at risk happened to be Major Belo, commander of the 55th North Carolina. Luck was with him, however. The sword sailed harmlessly over Belo's head. And, right then, one of his men shot the Union officer, thus diverting the Yankees from following through on their leader's command to kill him.[73]

Prominent on the 2nd Mississippi's colors were the names of the principal battles in which the regiment had fought thus far. In bold white letters on the red fields between the blue crossbars studded with white stars were the words "Manassas," "Seven Pines," "Gaines' Farm," "Malvern Hill." This day—exactly one year after Malvern Hill—the regiment would lose its colors early in the fight.[74]

After entering a deep part of the railroad cut, color-bearer W. B. Murphy was unhappy with his position. To ensure that every man in the 2nd Mississippi could see the colors, he and the rest of the color guard moved left to a point where the grading was only two feet deep.[75] He planted the colors atop the bank where all —including the approaching Yankees—could see it. In fact, before long Yankee bullets had torn ragged holes in it.[76]

As the 6th Wisconsin drew near the 2nd Mississippi's position, a handful of Union infantrymen made a spontaneous rush for the enemy flag. Out in front were William

Scene of the railroad cut where heavy fighting occurred and the 2nd Mississippi was captured. (The tracks were not laid until the 1880s.)

Remington, Lewis Eggleston, and Cornelius Okey. The air was so thick with lead, Private Okey recalled, that "it seemed impossible to breathe without inhaling a bullet." Lieutenant Remington went down, shot through the shoulder. The other two made it to the flag, but as they yanked it out of the ground, Corporal Eggleston was mortally wounded. Just then "Rocky Mountain" Anderson, another Wisconsin enlisted man, plunged into action. Running up to the Rebel who shot Eggleston, he lofted his musket and brought it crashing down on the poor man's head, splitting his skull. About this time, Okey became *hors de combat*, shot in the arm. With blood streaming from the wound, he took off at top speed, leaving the flag behind.[77]

It was probably at this moment that color-bearer Murphy recovered it. But, alas, without support—every one of his color guards had been shot[78]—the chances of keeping it were slim. As Murphy told it, before he could get away, "a large man made a rush for me and the flag. As I tore the flag from the staff he took hold of me and the color. The firing was still going on and kept up for several minutes after the flag was taken from me."[79]

The "large man" was Corporal Francis Asbury Waller (Company I, 6th Wisconsin). Clutching his prize, he sprinted to the spot where he had dropped his musket when he charged Murphy. Laying down the flag and standing on it, he picked up his musket and joined in the general firing. For his actions this morning Waller was awarded the Congressional Medal of Honor.[80]

At one point, then another, Union troops swept into the already congested railroad cut. Depending on how deep the chasm was at point of entry, the men either jumped in or raced down the bank. They were "black and grimy with powder and heat," one of them recalled, and "all unconscious to the terrible situation." Oblivious of the inherent danger, they had no fear for themselves.[81]

Hand-to-hand fighting ensued, each side battering the other with clubbed muskets.[82] The fury of the combatants knew no bounds and mayhem prevailed. Screams rent the air as heads and bodies were bashed and the victims doubled up in pain.

Yet it might have been even more ghastly. Despite some conflicting testimony, it seems the bayonet played only a minor role. Dawes disputed Doubleday's statement that the cut was carried "at the point of the bayonet," flatly declaring that none were used in his command.[83] Dawes' denial notwithstanding, one of his own men stated that they fought with clubbed muskets *and bayonets*. Another, in his present tense account, merely stated, "Bayonets are crossed," thereby indicating that the Confederates also used them.[84] However, no Confederate account substantiates that they did. Nor is there any mention of that weapon being used in the 95th New York or the 14th Brooklyn.

In any case, the fighting was so brutal it could not last long. And the outcome, once the Federals reached the railroad cut, was never really in doubt. Their superior position, their stout frontal and enfilade fire, their savage assault with clubbed muskets—all spelled doom for the Confederates.

They soon quit the fight in droves. This was not the orderly disengagement Davis had intended; poor transmission of his retreat order had banished any chance of that.

For every man in his brigade, it had become simply a matter of getting away if he could. On the right, the greater part of the 42nd Mississippi managed to escape westward through the railroad cut.[85] On the left, Major Belo and most of the 55th North Carolina "fell back to another position" (presumably to the north before retreating west).[86] But for the 2nd Mississippi troops in the center, where the cut was deepest, escape was a forlorn hope. Even so, some undoubtedly risked their lives in the attempt. If very lucky, they got over the rear bank without stopping an enemy bullet, then ran until they were well out of danger. The vast majority, however, remained to face the inevitable.

Cries of "Surrender!" and "Throw down your muskets!" pealed from Yankee throats. The Rebels were quick to comply, dropping their weapons and putting up their hands. The commotion brought Lieutenant Colonel Dawes to the edge of the cut. Looking down, he saw a throng of Confederates, all with hands raised over their heads. He could feel the tension in the air. If the tempers of his own sorely-tried men got out of hand, a massacre would surely follow.

The touchy situation demanded prompt action. Dawes called out at the top of his voice, "Where is the colonel of this regiment?"

The reply shot back, "Who are you?" The speaker was 2nd Mississippi's Major Blair.

Lieutenant Colonel Rufus R. Dawes

"I command this regiment," Dawes answered testily. "Surrender, or I will fire."

Blair then approached Dawes, holding out his sword in tacit submission. Dawes accepted it. Other Confederate officers followed suit, and the next thing Dawes knew, he had collected seven swords. Recalling the incident years later, he wrote, "It would have been the handsome thing to say, 'Keep your sword, sir,' but I was new to such occasions, and when six other officers came up and handed me their swords, I took them also. I held this awkward bundle in my arms until relieved by Adjutant Brooks."

Apart from this slight embarrassment, the surrender came off smoothly—without any more blood being spilled. Afterward, Dawes could boast: "The coolness, self-possession, and discipline which held back our men from pouring in a general volley saved a hundred lives of the enemy, and as my mind goes back to the fearful excitement of the moment, I marvel at it."[87]

At Dawes' behest, Major Blair formed the prisoners into ranks. Dawes assigned Major John F. Hauser the task of marching them to Gettysburg and placing them in the custody of the provost guard.[88] Among the universally despondent Southerners in the long column was the 2nd Mississippi's color-bearer, W. B. Murphy.[89] Disgraced by the loss of his colors, he was perhaps the gloomiest of all.

The total number of prisoners cannot be precisely stated because figures for the 95th New York and 14th Brooklyn are lacking. However, from Dawes' reckoning that 232 of the enemy were captured by the 6th Wisconsin and the brigade guard coupled with Colonel Fowler's admission that most of the prisoners were taken by Dawes' command, it can be concluded that, altogether, about 300 in Davis' Brigade surrendered in the railroad cut. In addition, an estimated 350 officers and men were killed or wounded.[90] Thus, with a total loss of more than one-third of his force, Joe Davis' first trial by combat was a palpable disaster.

Yet no one would have guessed it from reading the brigadier's battle report. Referring to the counterattack, Davis wrote: "In this critical condition, I gave the order to retire, which was done in good order, leaving some officers and men in the railroad cut, who were captured, although every effort was made to withdraw all commands."[91] Division commander Heth was more forthright, more honest. In Davis' Brigade, he noted in his after-action report, "every field officer save two were shot down and its ranks were terribly thinned." Moreover, Heth continued, because of "its shattered condition it was not deemed advisable to bring it again into action on that day."[92]

The counterattack, which had proved so costly for both sides, had lasted less than a half hour.[93] By 11:30 the Confederate prisoners were marching dejectedly toward Gettysburg.[94]

Adjutant Brooks, in the meantime, had disposed of the bundle of swords Dawes had handed him. He kept one for himself and unloaded the other six on a wounded soldier then headed for the rear.[95]

At some point Corporal Waller turned over the 2nd Mississippi's colors to Lieutenant Colonel Dawes. As it was a rule in battle that no one fit for duty should be allowed to leave the field, Dawes looked around for a disabled soldier to carry Waller's prize to safety. He saw an enlisted man hobbling toward the rear using two muskets as crutches. As the man drew closer, he recognized Sergeant William Evans of Company H, who had been wounded in both legs. Going up to him, Dawes said he wanted him to take the captured regimental colors off the field. Since Evans did not have a free hand, Dawes unbuttoned the sergeant's jacket, wrapped the flag around his waist, and closed the jacket over it. Evans then resumed his painful progress to the rear.[96]

When the fight in the cut was over and his troops had reassembled, Dawes called for volunteers to establish a skirmish line on McPherson's Ridge. He did not intend to be caught unawares if the enemy should return. In spite of the fatigue every one of his men must have felt, a sufficient number of them came forward. Lieutenant William Goltermann of Company F volunteered to head the group.[97]

Dawes need not have worried. The shattered Confederate regiments kept on going until they had put Willoughby Run between the Yankees and themselves. Clearly, Davis had no intention of renewing the fight.[98]

It was now feasible to recover the 3-inch ordnance gun Captain Hall had been forced to abandon north of the Chambersburg Pike. A party of 6th Wisconsin and 95th New York men dragged it to the road. Subsequently Hall was notified and (as recounted in detail in the next chapter) the gun was retrieved.[99] Having been exposed to the storm of musketry, it was almost certainly inoperable.

On Herr Ridge the Confederate batteries north of the Chambersburg Pike resumed firing as soon as the danger of hitting their own retreating troops was past. Not surprisingly, the nearest enemy troops—the 14th Brooklyn—took the brunt of their relentless bombardment. In that regiment tragedy befell four enlisted men who went to the aid of a wounded comrade.

Ever since he had been shot during the charge on the railroad cut, Corporal George Forrester had lain where he fell, powerless to move. Company C men realized his terrible plight when they noticed he did not move to a safer spot when lethal missiles began dropping around him. The 14th Brooklyn's regimental history tells what happened next:

> Although a veritable storm of shot and shell was sweeping the exposed situation in which he lay, four of his comrades volunteered to remove him. They took a piece of canvas, from a tent, and laying it upon the ground rolled him upon it. Then, one man holding to each corner, they lifted him up. Just as they raised the strip of canvas a Confederate shell exploded right among them. Forrester, and three of his would-be rescuers, were killed instantly. The leg of the fourth man was torn off, and his scream of agony was heard above the vast, pulsating roar of battle. He died while he was being taken to the hospital, from loss of blood.[100]

In comparison, the misfortune of an eighteen-year-old private in Company D of the same regiment was trivial. Yet, when Edward Riker discovered he had lost his diary during the action, he was heartsick. That small volume had been his constant companion ever since his enlistment ten months before. Now he expected never to see it again. But he did get it back—24 years later.

Six weeks after the battle, a young girl, crossing the fields where the 14th Brooklyn fought, spied a rectangular object lying on the ground. Curious, she picked it up, found it to be a soldier's diary, and from the flyleaf learned his name, rank, company, and regiment. She took it along home, wondering how she might return it to its owner. The girl grew up, married a local man named Weaver, and settled into the dawn-to-dusk routine of a nineteenth-century housewife. Years, indeed decades, passed; still she held on to the diary, though surely with waning hope that she would ever have an opportunity to return it. Then, in 1887, veterans of the 14th Brooklyn assembled in Gettysburg to dedicate their regiment's monument on the field. With rekindled hope, Mrs. Weaver and her husband went around asking veterans if they knew and had seen one Edward Riker. Eventually their efforts were rewarded, and, at long last, loser and finder met. For both it was a moment of pure joy when Mrs. Weaver placed the long-lost diary in Riker's hands. Who can say which one was the happier?[101]

After Union troops won the fight at the railroad cut, Doubleday directed Wadsworth to advance the three regiments of Cutler's Brigade that had retreated earlier to the positions they held at the start of the battle. Wadsworth's first thought was that they would need artillery support, and he proposed to get it. Hall's Battery, by his order, had gone "beyond the town" to cover a Union retreat, which the division commander then felt was a strong possibility. Now he dispatched a staff officer to bring the battery back to Seminary Ridge.[102] But that would take time, and he wanted artillery in place on McPherson's Ridge when the infantry got there. Colonel Wainwright had posted three of his five First Corps batteries (those under Captains Reynolds, Stevens, and Stewart) on Seminary Ridge. Knowing this, Wadsworth rode to the colonel and requested the use of all three. When he explained he wanted one of them to take up the position vacated earlier by Hall's battery, Wainwright bluntly refused. Too hazardous, the artillery chief said.[103]

Wadsworth rode off—in a huff, no doubt—to exercise his other option. Wainwright had no authority over Calef's Battery of horse artillery, which was nearby. Wadsworth was fully aware that it had seen hard service earlier in the morning, but that could not be helped—he needed those guns. Now!

Lieutenant Calef had the same negative view of the proposed move as Wainwright. In the first place, the position was too exposed; in the second, the number of enemy guns that could concentrate on his lone battery was simply too great. When he voiced these objections, Wadsworth exploded, no doubt thinking his judgment had been impugned. (Actually, as a politician turned general, he was hardly an expert in the proper deployment of artillery.) There was a brief but heated exchange. In the end Calef, resigned but not without trepidation, ordered four of his guns forward.[104]

It turned out he was right about the move. "As soon as the first gun was fired from my battery, three four-gun rebel batteries opened from the front and right of my position." Before long one of those batteries shifted farther to the right, thus setting up a deadly crossfire. Calef lost more men at this time than in the earlier action. Forced to withdraw, he had his guns limbered and drawn to "a position nearly on a line with my former one, but better covered by a corner of [Herbst's] woods."[105]

In the meantime Wadsworth's staff officer had found Captain Hall and his battery in the vicinity of Cemetery Hill. After repeating the order to proceed at once to Seminary Ridge, he told Hall he would lead the way through town to the "road" specified by his chief as the one by which the battery should approach the battlefield. The "road" turned out to be the unfinished railroad bed. When Hall's guns swung onto the grading and began their jolting passage over the rough surface, the staff officer departed. Almost immediately the battery came under heavy fire from a section of Pegram's guns on Herr Ridge. For Hall's men the next half mile was intensely nerve-wracking, though, by sheer good fortune, they made it without a single casualty. On reaching the deep cleft at Seminary Ridge, Hall ordered his battery to halt, as he expected that someone from Wadsworth's staff would be there to give him further instructions. No one appeared, however, so he parked his guns under cover of the ridge and rode ahead to find anyone who could tell him what his next move should be. As luck had it, he soon met a staff officer who knew precisely where his battery was to set up. The instructions were: Turn right at the nearest point where the guns could be pulled over the bank; proceed along a woods; pass over a crest; cross a ravine; and post the battery just beyond it.[106]

The 6th Wisconsin, 95th New York, and 14th Brooklyn pulled back to Seminary Ridge for a much-needed rest. Simultaneously, Cutler's three regiments that had been repulsed earlier—the 76th New York, 56th Pennsylvania, and 147th New York—returned to their original positions on McPherson's Ridge.[107] South of them, Meredith's 2nd and 7th Wisconsin, 19th Indiana, and 24th Michigan continued to maintain their defensive line.

In two distinct engagements, one north and one south of the Chambersburg Pike, Union forces had whipped the enemy. Although Doubleday exaggerated, his summation was essentially correct: "Wadsworth's little division of two brigades cleared its front and captured two brigades of the enemy."[108] But neither the Federals nor the Confederates were deceived. With that acute sense born of combat experience, they knew this day's fighting was not yet over.

When it resumed it would be on a much larger scale. Even as Wadsworth's and Heth's troops enjoyed a respite, vast contingents of Union and Confederate infantry were rapidly converging on the chance battleground.

Chapter IX

A LARGER BATTLE LOOMS

"General Longstreet, what is the meaning of this?"

Henry Heth's quest for shoes had ended in complete disaster: two brigades in shambles, one brigade commander captured. But that was not the worst of it. The accidental encounter quickly escalated into an epic battle that, in three bloody days, shattered the Army of Northern Virginia and forever crushed Lee's hopes of decisive victory in Pennsylvania.

Heth might have disengaged completely and headed back toward Cashtown as Pettigrew's Brigade had done the day before. But he probably knew that Pender's Division plus artillery were marching eastward on the Chambersburg Pike and, if he decided to retrace his route, his troops would soon collide with Pender's, causing mass confusion. To further complicate matters—though he may not have been aware of it—Anderson's Division was coming up the same road behind Pender's Division. In any case, Heth decided his best course was to stay put, apprise A. P. Hill of the situation, and await further orders. Meanwhile he could only trust that a steady fusillade from Pegram's artillery would keep the Yankees at bay.

Early this morning, in compliance with Lee's concentration plan, Ewell's Second Corps and two divisions of Longstreet's First Corps had resumed the march to Cashtown. McLaws' and Hood's First Corps Divisions were headed east from Fayetteville; Johnson's Second Corps Division, southeast from the village of Scotland. Rodes' and Early's Second Corps Divisions, as previously noted, had changed direction in mid-march. Instead of going west, then south to Cashtown, as originally intended, both were now proceeding almost due south to Gettysburg. As Ewell had Lee's approval to proceed to either Cashtown or Gettysburg "as circumstances might require," he had decided on the latter when he received Hill's message that Heth's Division was marching there.

Johnson's Division followed a dirt road that met the Chambersburg Pike at Greenwood. As Lee had moved his headquarters to that village the day before, he was on hand to prevent a collision between those troops marching south and Longstreet's, marching east. On realizing that the converging columns would reach the Greenwood junction at nearly the same time, he turned to Longstreet (who had ridden ahead to join the army commander) and ordered him to halt his column.[1] Longstreet later grumped about his divisions being "greatly delayed," not only by Johnson's troops and cannon but by the lumbering Second Corps supply wagons that followed them.[2]

At ten o'clock, as Johnson's Division was passing by, Lee dictated orders for Colonel J. B. Walton, commander of the First Corps artillery reserve.[3] Shortly thereafter Lee and Longstreet started for Cashtown. At first Lee seemed confident, relaxed, even cheerful.[4] But his sanguine mood evaporated when he heard the faint but unmistakeable rumble of cannon coming from the direction of Gettysburg. Instantly dismayed—he may have sensed it was sounding the knell to all his plans—he said, "General Longstreet, what is the meaning of this?"[5]

Somewhere in their front a confrontation was underway—that much was obvious. But "Old Pete" was at a loss to say what it augured. The muffled reports continued. Captain James P. Smith, a Second Corps liaison officer who rode with Lee's party, recalled that the sound of artillery fire was "a surprise and something spoken of with regret, that an engagement had been brought on."[6]

Driven by the urgent need to learn the details of that engagement, Lee rushed on to Cashtown. The ailing A. P. Hill was still there, and Lee went directly to him. But the Third Corps commander was unable to enlighten him, as he had heard nothing from Heth. Lee then summoned Major General Richard H. Anderson, whose Third Corps Division, after marching from its bivouac between Greenwood and South Mountain, had halted at Cashtown. Anderson, he discovered, was as uninformed as Hill.[7] With frustration overcoming his habitual reserve, Lee voiced his innermost feelings to the division commander:

> I cannot think what has become of Stuart. I ought to have heard from him long before now. He may have met with disaster, but I hope not. In the absence of reports from him I am in ignorance as to what we have in front of us here. It may be the whole Federal Army, or it may be only a detachment. If it is the whole Federal Army we must fight a battle here; if we do not gain a victory these defiles and gorges through which we are passing this morning will shelter us from disaster.[8]

Stuart's absence at this critical moment, the unknown scope and nature of the engagement now in progress, the near-certain demise of his plan to concentrate and give battle at Cashtown —all these troubled Lee greatly. Yet, while deploring these circumstances, he was not overwhelmed by them. Rather, he was impelled to action, immediately ordering "Dick" Anderson to hustle his division to Gettysburg in support of Heth and Pender.[9] About this time an officer from the Second Corps reined in his lathered mount in front of the army commander. General Ewell, he reported, had diverted Rodes' and Early's Divisions to Gettysburg and each had taken the first road south that offered. Since Lee had no idea how many enemy troops were opposing his own, it was encouraging news.

The officer was Ewell's aide and stepson, Major G. Campbell Brown. When he finished relaying Ewell's message, Lee asked him "with a peculiar searching, almost querulous, impatience...whether General Ewell had heard anything from General Jeb Stuart, and on my reply in the negative, said that he had heard nothing from or of him for three days—and that General Stuart had not complied with his instructions." Brown was quite amazed that the austere commander of the Army of Northern Virginia would thus reveal his perturbed state of mind to a mere aide-de-camp. Lee continued: "A scout [Harrison] reports Meade's whole army marching this way, but that is all I know about his position. Tell General Ewell to send out his left and try to open communications with General Stuart."[10]

Even more urgent was another message for Ewell. Lee instructed Brown to tell him that if the enemy force proved to be "very large, he did not want a general engagement brought on till the rest of the army came up."[11] With both messages firmly in mind, Brown galloped off to find his stepfather on the Carlisle road.

A. P. Hill, either during or soon after his conversation with Lee, apparently decided that, regardless of how badly he felt, he had to go to Henry Heth and find out exactly how things stood.[12] By the time he reached the glum division commander and heard the bad news, it was noon.[13]

Heth, in the meantime, had formed a three-brigade line south of the Chambersburg Pike on Herr Ridge. Archer's Brigade, now led by Colonel B. D. Fry, remained on the right, though its position had been shifted southward so that its right rested on the Fairfield road. North of the pike, Davis' survivors of the fight at the railroad cut had fallen back, across Willoughby Run, to a reserve position behind Herr Ridge. The brigade had been too badly mauled to be of much use the rest of the day. Heth brought up his two fresh brigades, Brockenbrough's and Pettigrew's, to form the left and center, respectively, of his new line.[14] As Pettigrew's North Carolina regiments came into position, they were harassed not only by enemy artillery but by Union sharpshooters firing from the second story windows of a "brick building" (undoubtedly the Herbst farmhouse).[15]

In the 26th North Carolina Regiment of Pettigrew's Brigade, Lieutenant Colonel John Lane was feeling perfectly miserable. He had been racked by nausea and vomiting after drinking water that was evidently contaminated. Compounding his discomfort, he had had no sleep the night before due to his being in charge of the picket detail. Going up to Colonel Henry K. Burgwyn, Jr., commander of the 26th, he requested permission to go to the rear. Taken aback, Burgwyn stuttered, "Oh, Colonel, I can't, I can't, I can't think of going into this battle without you." With that he whipped out a small flask and offered it to the sick officer. "Here is a little of the best French brandy which my parents gave me to take with me into battle. It may do you good."

After Lane took a few swallows of the fiery liquid, he did feel better. Thus encouraged, he said, "Colonel Burgwyn, I can go with you."

The 26th North Carolina's commander was himself much relieved; the brandy had been an inspired idea. "Thank you, Colonel, thank you," he said.[16]

Pender's Division consisted of four brigades under Colonel Abner Perrin and Brigadier Generals Edward L. Thomas, James H. Lane, and Alfred M. Scales. At

Whisler's Ridge the division paused to form a line athwart the Chambersburg Pike, Thomas' and Lane's Brigades filing to the left, Perrin's and Scales', to the right. With skirmishers out in front, the broad line advanced one mile and halted on Herr Ridge.[17] During the approach the men heard cannon booming, saw smoke drifting overhead, and knew they would soon have to face Billy Yank. If they needed any further reminder, there was the occasional glimpse of Yankee prisoners being marched to the rear, not to mention their own walking wounded.[18]

At some point after the division halted on Herr Ridge, Lane's Brigade was shifted to the far right, leaving only Thomas' Brigade north of the pike. The order of the brigades from left to right then was: Thomas, Scales, Perrin, Lane. Later on, Thomas' Brigade would stay put when the rest of the division advanced to engage the enemy. Its role: to watch for and swiftly counter any threat from enemy troops that might develop on the division's exposed left flank.[19]

When Pender's Division left South Mountain, the four batteries of Major David G. McIntosh's battalion were in the midst of the long column. Thus they were restricted to the pace of the foot soldiers who preceded them. But, at Whisler's Ridge, when all the infantrymen had cleared the road to form a battle line, the batteries were free to roll.

Lieutenant General A. P. Hill

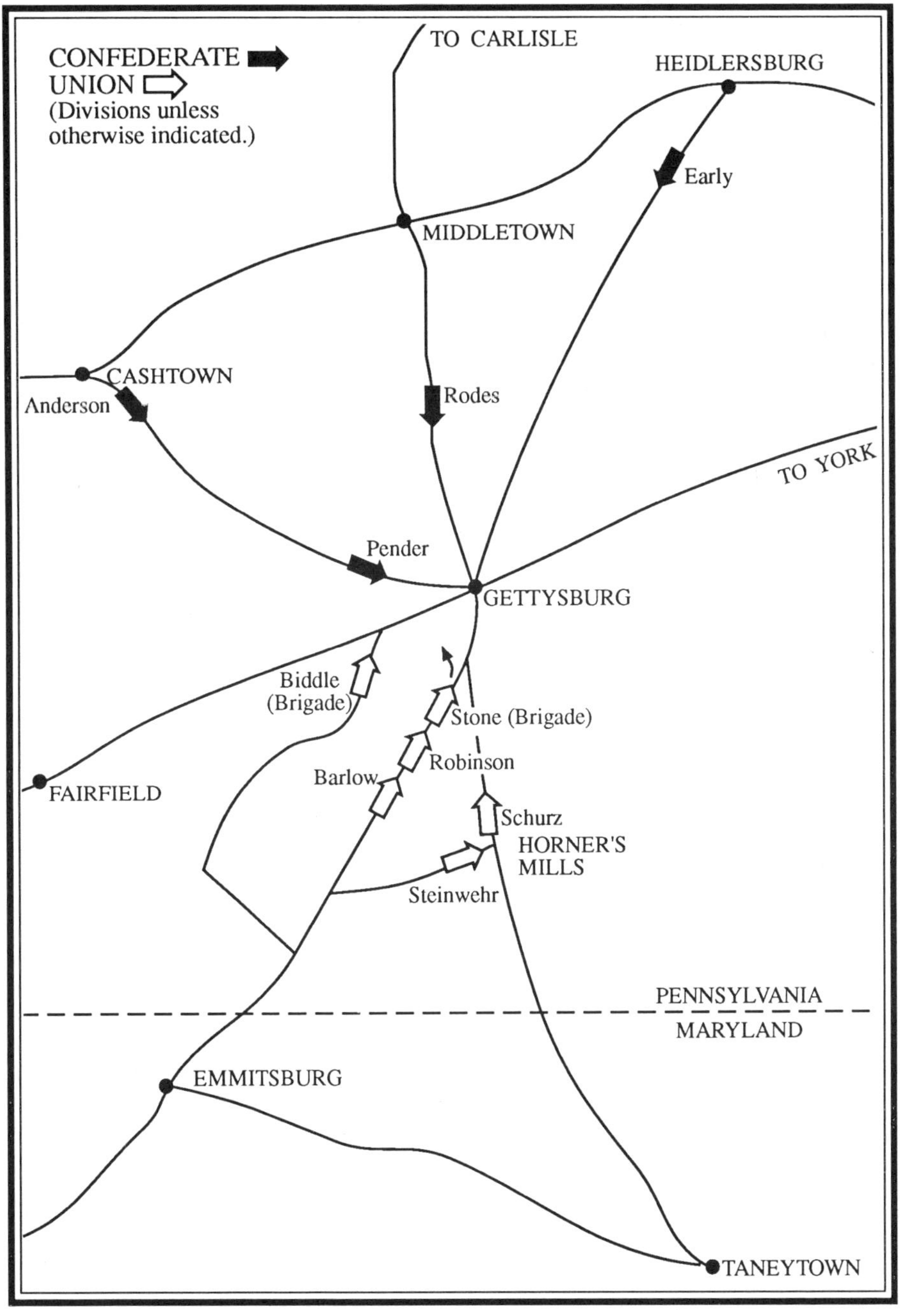

Position at 10:30 a.m. of Union and Confederate troops approaching Gettysburg

In total, McIntosh had eight 3-inch ordnance rifles, six Napoleons, and two Whitworths. With several of Pegram's twenty guns already disabled, the addition of these sixteen guns doubled Confederate firepower on Herr Ridge.

McIntosh deployed his batteries as follows: Virginia Battery plus one section of the Hardaway Artillery, just north of the Fairfield road; 2nd Rockbridge Artillery, a short distance north of the Chambersburg Pike; Danville Artillery and the Whitworth section of the Hardaway Artillery, a short distance south of the Pike. The breech-loading Whitworths (capable of firing up to five miles) soon were shelling distant Seminary Ridge. The eight guns flanking the Chambersburg Pike were slower to open fire, the cannoneers electing to wait until "considerable bodies of troops" came into view. The six guns near the Fairfield Road did not fire a single round. McIntosh reported there was no occasion to do so.[20]

All the while, reinforcements from the Second Corps were approaching the battlefield from the north. First to arrive, about noon, was Iverson's Brigade of Rodes' Division.[21] Around 11:00 its approach on the Carlisle Road had been observed by Devin's pickets on the high ground north of Rock Creek. Their pulses had quickened when they saw, scarcely more than a mile away, "long lines of Ewell's corps advancing over the hills and across the fields, followed by heavy columns of infantry." Captain James Dinnin had immediately dispatched one of his men to warn Colonel Devin.[22]

With Rodes' Division coming on the field, Early's and Anderson's Divisions drawing near, and Heth's and Pender's Divisions ready for action, Ambrose Powell Hill was moved to reopen the battle.[23] In so doing he contravened Lee's fervent desire (of which Hill was surely aware) that there be no general engagement until the concentration of the army was completed.[24]

Lee himself did not reach the field until about 2:00 p.m. His Chief of Artillery, Brigadier General W. N. Pendleton, noted that when they arrived "the battle was raging with considerable violence."[25] And Lee was forced to recognize and accept that the Army of Northern Virginia had been irrevocably committed.

"We have come to stay!"

The build-up of Union forces at Gettysburg late in the morning of July 1, 1863, rivaled that of the Confederates. By the time the fight at the railroad cut was over, most of Doubleday's First Corps was on the field. Augmenting Wadsworth's 1st Division were two brigades of Rowley's 3rd Division, those under Colonels Biddle and Stone. And Robinson's 2nd Division was then fast approaching the Lutheran Seminary. In addition, the three divisions of Howard's Eleventh Corps, en route to Gettysburg via the Emmitsburg and Taneytown roads, were then within a radius of four miles.

Biddle's Brigade arrived on the battlefield slightly ahead of Stone's Brigade, even though Biddle had followed a circuitous course on country roads while Stone had taken the main road north from Emmitsburg.[26] Prior to his recent elevation to division command, Brigadier General Thomas A. Rowley had commanded the brigade now under Colonel Chapman Biddle, and he had chosen to ride with his old outfit this morning. Before starting out, he instructed Biddle and the four regimental commanders "to promptly engage the enemy wherever met."[27] In the final lap of the 7-mile march, the brigade turned off the road and continued northward along the west bank of Willoughby Run.[28] Eventually debouching onto the Fairfield Road, Biddle's men were greeted by a tattoo of small arms fire. They had emerged into the sector held by Gamble's cavalry, where some 8th Illinois troopers were busily trading shots with Confederate skirmishers. Simultaneously they heard the bark of cannon somewhere off to the north.[29] But most alarming was the sight of Rebel infantry massed on Herr Ridge, barely a thousand yards away.[30]

Biddle's regiments—the 80th New York, 121st, 142nd, and 151st Pennsylvania—fell into line facing north on the Fairfield Road and at once moved into the fields of the Finnefrock farm. After advancing some 200 yards, the regiments wheeled right (away from the enemy), splashed across Willoughby Run, trudged up McPherson's Ridge and part way down the opposite slope.[31] Halted, the men were directed to drop their knapsacks, then retrace their steps to the crest.[32] It was then 11:00 or possibly a bit later.[33] Meredith's Iron Brigade had just returned to McPherson's Ridge following its victory over Archer's Brigade. The Union assault on the railroad cut had just begun.

Meredith's regiments were still getting organized in Herbst's Woods, when, in the fields south of those woods, three of Biddle's regiments began filing into line. From right to left they were: the 142nd Pennsylvania, 121st Pennsylvania, 80th New York (originally 20th New York State Militia). Cooper's 1st New York battery, which accompanied the brigade on the morning's march, unlimbered in the approximate center of the brigade line. In short order its four 3-inch rifles were sparring with the enemy guns on Herr Ridge. Biddle's remaining regiment, the 151st Pennsylvania, was detached, presumably by Rowley, to reinforce Stone's Brigade, then arriving on the north side of Herbst's Woods.[34]

Meanwhile, both the 80th New York and the 121st Pennsylvania were engaged in questionable maneuvers, possibly indicating impaired reasoning on the part of General Rowley. He drank heavily this day and ended up being courtmartialed for it.[35] While he probably started drinking early in the morning, whether he was noticeably intoxicated by midday is unclear.

In any case, only minutes after establishing its line on top of McPherson's Ridge, the 80th New York was ordered to descend the west slope. As the troops approached Willoughby Run across open fields, they were peppered by shots from Rebel sharpshooters hidden in the wheat on the opposite bank. The New Yorkers took to their heels, not stopping until they reached the far side of McPherson's Ridge. The regimental commander, Colonel Theodore B. Gates, was disgusted. In his opinion, the order had been foolhardy to begin with. As to why it was given, he later remarked sarcastically that "it is not probable that anyone knew." The next order he received—to return to their former position on the left of the brigade line—made better sense and was promptly executed.[36]

Initially the 121st Pennsylvania faced north in support of Cooper's Battery. Given the massing of enemy troops on its flank and the absence of a threat on its front, the position was a mistake. This was soon apparent, and the regiment was ordered to face west like all the others. Before long, however—with the men in the ranks probably wondering if their leaders had lost their minds—the Pennsylvanians were ordered to yet another position. This time they swung around the rear of the 80th New York, thus extending the line at least 200 yards but still short of the Fairfield Road.[37] With nothing on which to anchor it, the Union left hung in mid-air. It was not totally unguarded, however, as Gamble's troopers were posted along both sides of the Fairfield Road and only slightly in advance of the infantry.[38]

Even as Biddle's Brigade formed a defensive line south of Herbst's Woods, Stone's Brigade was streaming toward McPherson's Ridge to fill the gap north of those woods, from Meredith's right to the Chambersburg Pike. The three regiments—the 143rd, 149th, and 150th Pennsylvania—had been recruited the previous summer in the mountains of that state by Colonel Roy Stone himself. Collectively they were know as the "Bucktail Brigade."[39]

The mountain men had marched only a few miles up the Emmitsburg road when they heard cannon fire, muffled, obviously far off.[40] "Hear that!" exclaimed a private in the 149th Pennsylvania. It so happened that some of his Company C comrades had just sprinted over to a farmhouse to fill their canteens, and this activity served to delude their commanding officer, Captain John H. Bassler. It was only the sound of the pump handle slamming, he averred. But the soldiers who heard his disclaimer listened again and knew he was mistaken. "The pump handle is getting pretty lively, Cap," quipped one of them. Another called out, "That pump of yours, Captain, is in danger of being ruined."[41]

Bassler, realizing his error, accepted the joshing in good humor. He would recall the "excellent spirits" of his men that morning, "their buoyant steps and their pleasantries." He also recalled: "It seemed they were glad for a chance to fight the enemy on our own ground."[42] General Doubleday's impression of the morale throughout Rowley's Division was no less favorable. "The men were in fine spirits," he wrote, "and were elated to the highest degree."[43]

Stone's Brigade stepped up its pace after hearing cannon fire.[44] Now and again the "Bucktails" saw a farmer, obviously worried, driving his horses and cattle in the opposite direction. But this indication that there could be serious trouble ahead seems not to have affected their halcyon mood. After all, it was a beautiful day and the countryside was lovely—green meadows contrasting with "long stretches of golden grain and luxuriant growths of corn." Still, their high morale must have slipped a notch or two as the sun grew hotter and they began to perspire "as they had rarely perspired before."[45]

At a certain crossroads, troops of the 149th Pennsylvania witnessed a poignant scene: two children, no doubt brother and sister, astride the broad back of a plow horse, just waiting there, bewildered and afraid. The boy was possibly ten years old. The girl, who kept her arms tightly clasped around his waist, was even younger. Their piteous faces, Bassler noted, "would have made a fine study for an artist." Someone asked where they were going, and the boy replied pathetically, "I don't know. They are fighting on our place over yonder."[46]

The children were still there when the next regiment, the 150th Pennsylvania, passed by. By then both had dissolved in tears. The sight surely evoked pity in even the most callous soldier, for the youngsters were (as one officer remarked) "crying as if their little hearts would break."[47]

Like Wadsworth's Division some ninety minutes earlier, Stone's Brigade turned off the Emmitsburg Road at the Codori farm and headed northwest in the direction of Seminary Ridge. Presently the troops were ordered to double-quick. On they went, in column of fours, over fields and up the ridge.[48] For many the pace was too fast, the heat too intense. In the 150th Pennsylvania alone, more than forty men dropped out, including the commander of Company D, Captain William Dougal. His case was hardly surprising, as he was reputed to be "the largest and most corpulent officer in the regiment." His request to leave his company was granted on one condition—that he round up and bring back as many of the victims of heat and overexertion as he could.[49]

In the grove in front of the Seminary, a group of mounted officers anxiously waited for the arrival of Stone's Brigade. Among them were Generals Doubleday and Rowley. As each regiment came abreast of the group, it was halted and General Doubleday rode out to deliver a brief but impassioned speech. Practically shouting (the recurring boom of artillery demanded it), he emphasized that every soldier would soon be defending his native state. It was a "fiery appeal to our patriotism and state pride," one officer recalled.[50]

To the still puffing troops, the import of Doubleday's words was underscored by their view of a strong enemy force on Herr Ridge barely a mile away. After dropping their knapsacks, they fell into line, facing west. About this time, the shocking news of Reynolds' death was spreading through every Union regiment on the field.[51]

With flags flying and battalion-length lines closely following one another, Stone's Brigade surged toward McPherson's Ridge.[52] In the 150th Pennsylvania there was a momentary delay getting started when its leader made a blunder. "Forward!" cried Colonel Langhorne Wister, forgetting one important consideration. Immediately someone piped up, "Colonel, we're not loaded yet!" There was a tittering in the ranks as the embarrassed leader corrected his omission.[53]

Ever since the 14th Brooklyn and 95th New York joined the 6th Wisconsin in the assault on the railroad cut, the area between Herbst's Woods and the Chambersburg Pike (which embraced the McPherson farm buildings) had been undefended. This potentially dangerous situation was remedied by the arrival of Stone's Brigade. The 143rd Pennsylvania and seven companies of the 149th Pennsylvania formed in McPherson's lane, which ran due south from the pike to the farmhouse. The McPherson barn stood directly in their front. At the north end of the lane, the brigade line angled eastward along the pike to accomodate the remaining three companies of the 149th Pennsylvania. Lastly, the 150th Pennsylvania went into line south of the two-story farmhouse. Its right rested in an orchard and its left in an open field, just short of the Iron Brigade's position in Herbst's Woods.[54]

Going into line, Stone's troops carefully skirted the bodies of Union soldiers killed in the earlier fighting. Firing from the Confederate batteries had slackened somewhat. Even so, it was persistent enough to keep the Yankees' nerves on edge. Equally unnerving was the fire from enemy skirmishers. They had infiltrated the sector recently vacated by the 14th Brooklyn and 95th New York and were now blithely sniping away at the newcomers.[55] "We were not allowed to fire," wrote Corporal Simon Hubler of the 143rd Pennsylvania, "for fear of injuring our own troops, although the minie-balls were falling among us with uncomfortable frequency."[56]

Amid all the harrassment one of Stone's men was moved to exclaim, "We have come to stay!" His cry was taken up by others and it echoed up and down the line.[57] As the hours wore on, the bravado disappeared, and for many—in a macabre perversion of their intent—the words proved all too true.

But that was in the future. Colonel Stone's immediate concern was the enemy skirmishers in his front. To deal with them, he ordered his own skirmishers sent out, one company from each regiment.[58] Captain George W. Jones, whose Company B drew the assignment in the 150th Pennsylvania, asked his regimental commander, "How far should I go?" Colonel Wister replied, "Go forward until you feel the enemy and engage him."[59]

The 149th Pennsylvania's Captain Bassler remembered that at this time every soldier was "reeking with perspiration" and those not assigned skirmish duty flung themselves on the ground for "a short spell of rest." One of Buford's troopers killed in the opening engagement lay in McPherson's lane, and Bassler's attention was drawn to his "calm and peaceful features...and the curious fact that no wound or blood was visible." Going over for a closer look, he saw the crown of the man's head had been crushed.[60]

Meanwhile, most Iron Brigade men, like the majority of Stone's Brigade, took advantage of the lull in the fighting to rest. The lull, it should be borne in mind, was relative, not absolute. There was no moratorium on the activity of sharpshooters, skirmishers, and cannoneers, blue or grey. Thus, for the recumbent Iron Brigade men—with the sporadic intrusion of enemy shells into their midst and the continual rattle of skirmish fire in their front—rest meant relaxation for aching muscles but no relief from tension.[61] For the men in the companies sent out as skirmishers, rest of any sort was only a dim hope. And those who had been wounded during the pursuit of Archer's Brigade but were still able to walk continued their slow progress to the rear. One 2nd Wisconsin soldier with a nasty leg wound managed to propel himself along using two muskets as crutches. (He survived, minus the leg.)[62]

When the last soldier in the brigades under Biddle, Meredith, and Stone had been posted, Doubleday could feel he had established the best possible defense south of the Chambersburg Pike. On the other hand, north of it he had none. The remnants of the

6th Wisconsin, 14th Brooklyn, and 95th New York were trudging back to Seminary Ridge following their victory at the railroad cut. And it was absolutely necessary they be given a chance to catch their breath and to reorganize.

Doubleday therefore had reason to be worried. Although the Confederate brigades had been driven off in total disarray, he could not lightly dismiss the possibility of them mounting a counterattack. Until he could get troops in battle line north of the pike on McPherson's Ridge, the troops south of it were in jeopardy of having their flank turned. If that happened, the outcome could be disastrous. Doubleday had alerted Wadsworth (as noted earlier) of his decision to reinstate Cutler's original battle line. The 76th New York and 56th Pennsylvania, hard pressed early in the fight and ordered back to Seminary Ridge, had had time to recover from the sharp rebuff. The 147th New York, after narrowly escaping capture, had joined them there. It, too, was sufficiently recovered to return to combat, though at half its former strength. On Wadsworth's command the three regiments retraced their steps to McPherson's Ridge. There they deployed in virtually the same positions they had held when the fighting commenced.[63]

This force was soon augmented by three more regiments, thus doubling its strength. Lieutenant Colonel Dawes reported that he had thirty minutes in which to reorganize his 6th Wisconsin before the order came to advance. Colonel Fowler, on the other hand, claimed his 14th Brooklyn was marching again after "about five minutes breathing spell."[64] Probably it was somewhat longer. In any event, the 14th Brooklyn and 95th New York were soon forming a second line north of the railroad cut and directly behind the three regiments that preceded them.[65] The 6th Wisconsin meanwhile took a position south of the cut, with the pike (and the brigades of Stone, Meredith, and Biddle) on its left.[66] It was then noon.

The First Corps Artillery commander, Colonel Charles S. Wainwright, had halted Reynolds', Stewart's, and Stevens' Batteries on the east slope of Seminary Ridge around 11:00.[67] It will be recalled that he had refused Wadsworth's request for a battery to move into the position on McPherson's Ridge just vacated, under extreme pressure, by Hall's Battery, and that Wadsworth then had prevailed on Lieutenant Calef to move his battery of horse artillery into the hot spot. Not long afterward, still feeling that McPherson's Ridge was inadequately defended, Wadsworth again approached the artillery commander, this time imploring that Hall's Battery be returned to its original position. Again Wainwright refused.[68] However, when Buford asked him for relief for Calef's exhausted gun crews, he consented. He would bring up a replacement, he said, but with one stipulation: that Buford stay close to Calef's Battery and not allow Wadsworth to press it into service again. When Captain Gilbert H. Reynolds and Battery L, 1st New York Light, went forward, Wainwright rode with them.[69]

When they arrived at the spot north of the pike where Calef's Battery was supposed to be, it seems likely that they looked for those guns in vain. (In all his writings, Calef never gave any indication that Reynolds' Battery arrived before his own battery was forced to flee southward.) Nevertheless, Reynolds' cannoneers began to prepare for action. But they had scarcely jostled their four guns into position when the same crossfire that had sent Calef's Battery packing caused them to do likewise. Feverishly they limbered up, crossed the pike, and continued on until they came in sight of Calef's Battery at the edge of Herbst's Woods.[70] One of Reynolds' sections dropped trail in McPherson's orchard; the other, beside the farmhouse. About this time Reynolds was struck in the right eye by a shell fragment. Although in great pain, he refused to leave the field. When finally he did, Lieutenant George Breck took his place.[71]

The arrival of Reynolds' fresh battery to support Stone's Brigade on the right and Meredith's Iron Brigade on the left spelled relief for Calef's haggard, powder-stained artillerymen. They were surely grateful, for they had been dueling with the enemy, on and off, since 9:00 and had lost a dozen men and as many horses.[72] At one point, Buford noted in his after-action report, the battery had been fired on by no fewer than twelve Rebel guns. But, he added, "Calef held his own gloriously."[73] Now the battery pulled back some 500 yards to the southeast and set up in a wheatfield.[74]

In the meantime Captain Hall's 2nd Maine Battery had failed to reach its intended destination on Seminary Ridge, beside a woods north of the railroad cut. En route, Hall had been warned by an orderly that the enemy was advancing in his direction. Halting the battery, Hall rode ahead to investigate and was promptly fired upon (possibly by the vanguard of Rodes' Division). Prudence dictated an about-face. Accordingly, Hall countermarched his battery to the vicinity of the Seminary. Colonel Wainwright met him there, told him he had refused Wadsworth's request for the battery to return to McPherson's Ridge, and advised him that the gun abandoned earlier, which some infantrymen had dragged to the Chambersburg Pike, could now be retrieved. Hall needed no urging to remove a blemish on the battery's record. In short order, with the aid of a few men, some horses, and a limber, he brought the gun back to Seminary Ridge. Once again the battery was happily in possession of all six of its guns. But the morning's engagement had taken a high toll—three of them were *hors de combat*. On Wainwright's order the crippled battery moved back through Gettysburg to Cemetery Ridge.[75]

Two full-strength batteries remained to defend Seminary Ridge. The six Napoleons of Stewart's Battery B, 4th United States, were first set up in a grove 200 yards south of the Seminary. When they were shifted, around noon, to a position that straddled the railroad cut, the six 3-inch rifles of Steven's 5th Maine Battery replaced them in the grove.[76] On McPherson's Ridge, Cooper's 1st Pennsylvania and Reynolds' 1st New York Batteries continued their support of the infantry line. Thus, by noon the Union's deficiency in artillery firepower had been largely corrected, with about thirty operable guns contending against a maximum of 36 for the Confederates.

With his five batteries scattered over three ridges and the clear prospect of a busy afternoon for all of them, Wainwright may have reflected on how very wrong he had been. He had expected no hostilities this day! In fact, he had been so certain he would be "comfortably in camp by noon" that he had thrown his saddlebag containing all his personal articles (chocolate, tobacco, comb, brush, etc.) into his wagon. Well aware of the exigencies of battle, he knew he would not see his wagon anytime soon.[77]

Doubleday had done a commendable job in establishing a four-brigade line on McPherson's Ridge. But could it withstand the storm to come?

After all, two of the brigades had already sustained heavy losses in the earlier fighting. The survivors, buoyed by success, were still in a fighting mood, but how long could their resolute spirit overcome their fatigue? Because of the many casualties and the necessity to defend such a wide front, the line was thin and, regrettably, not continuous. It was "but a skeleton, with noticeable gaps between the several brigades as well as between the regiments," recalled the 150th Pennsylvania's Major Thomas Chamberlin. The spectacle of Rebels massing on the next ridge only served to heighten the natural anxiety of the Yankees awaiting battle. As Chamberlin described it, "the enemy was formed in continuous double lines of battle, extending southward as far as the accidents of the ground permitted the eye to reach, with heavy supporting columns in the rear."[78] Had the end of the enemy line been visible to the major, he could have added the ominous fact that the gray line overlapped the blue. This was observed early on by Union troops on the far left and Doubleday was promptly informed.[79]

Another circumstance must have been equally worrisome to the Union commander. Until Robinson's 2nd Division arrived on the field, he had no reserves to fall back on.

John Cleveland Robinson, after being expelled from West Point in 1839, might have jettisoned his military career. Instead, swallowing his pride, that same year he joined the army as a second lieutenant in the 5th U. S. Infantry Regiment. He went on to fight in the Seminole and Mexican wars, but after more than two decades of service he had advanced only to the rank of captain. After war erupted between the States, promotions came rapidly for most regular army officers, and Robinson was no exception. Within five months after Fort Sumter surrendered, he was a full colonel and eight months after that, a brigadier general. On December 30, 1862, he was given command of 2nd Division, First Corps.[80]

At Gettysburg the division numbered 3,000 officers and men in its two brigades. The First Brigade, under Brigadier General Gabriel R. Paul, comprised three New York regiments (94th, 104th, and 107th), the 13th Massachusetts, and the 16th Maine. The Second Brigade, led by Brigadier General Henry Baxter, had three Pennsylvania regiments (11th, 88th, and 90th) and two New York regiments (83rd and 97th), plus the 12th Massachusetts.

As the history of the 13th Massachusetts quaintly put it, the troops were "under no pressure of haste" as Robinson's Division began the march from Marsh Creek to Gettysburg. They seemed positively carefree, indulging in lively banter, telling jokes, and taking in "the beauties of the landscape."[81]

But the euphoria vanished in a twinkling when they heard the muffled roar of distant cannon. Robinson's veteran troops knew only too well what that could, and probably would, mean for them personally—a forced march with combat in the offing.[82] In the classic understatement of the 13th Massachusetts' Sergeant Austin Stearns, "the firing had a nearness that betokened mischief."[83] About this time, when the division was several miles from Gettysburg, Lieutenant Jacob Slagle rode up with instructions from Doubleday. The Second Division was to proceed as rapidly as possible to the Lutheran Seminary. There it would remain in reserve pending further orders.[84]

Brisk commands filled the air, and soon the long column, with Baxter's Brigade in the lead, moved forward. The pace alternated between quick time and double-quick. It was "blistering hot," a soldier in the 88th Pennsylvania remembered, "and the stifling clouds of yellow dust, settling on the ranks like a blanket, filled the eyes, mouth, nostrils, and entire person of the soldier with an impalpable powder, while the perspiration, running down the skin, ploughed furrows through the dirt."[85] Like Wadsworth's Division and Stone's Brigade earlier that morning, Robinson's troops turned off the Emmitsburg road near the Codori farmhouse and headed northwest, marching through fields to Seminary Ridge.[86] Sergeant Stearns recalled that he learned of Reynolds' death about this time.[87] Possibly Lieutenant Slagle had mentioned it and word quickly spread through the ranks.

Before the last of Robinson's regiments reached the grove beside the Seminary, two of them had been hustled off to McPherson's Ridge. The hasty move was precipitated by intelligence just in from Devin's cavalry pickets.[88]

As related earlier, the 9th New York troopers north of Gettysburg had spied a large Confederate force (Iverson's Brigade) coming over the horizon, and their leader, Captain Dinnin, had dispatched one of them to alert Colonel Devin. Minutes later, apparently worried that the first trooper might not get through, Dinnin sent another on the same mission. When neither man returned within what he felt was ample time, he rode back to inform Devin himself. During his absence, Rebel skirmishers began firing on his men, soon forcing them to high-tail it back across Rock Creek. Just as Asa Comstock was crossing the stream, his horse was shot from under him. Despite the extreme urgency of the situation, Comstock carefully removed his saddle and tucked it under his arm before sprinting to safety.

Captain Dinnin's orderly, a black boy named Jim, was washing some troopers' clothes at a nearby farmhouse when he was notified that the Rebels were coming and the troop was pulling out. Frantically, Jim stuffed the clothing into his mount's nosebag, then fairly leaped into the saddle and gave a violent tug on the reins, sending the startled beast off at a gallop. "The enemy's bullets began to sing about him," wrote Lieutenant Newel Cheney, and as Jim "lay flat to his horse, the nosebag was flying and shirts, collars, drawers and stockings were scattered along the road and, no doubt these garments afterward did service for the Southern Confederacy."[89]

Colonel Devin, on receiving Dinnin's report of Confederates approaching from the north, notified Buford at once. Buford, in turn, saw to it that Doubleday, Wadsworth, and Robinson were alerted to the danger. Following what had to be a swift relay of orders down the chain of command, the 11th Pennsylvania and 97th New York troops suddenly found themselves racing to McPherson's Ridge. The two Baxter Brigade regiments finally halted some 500 yards north of the railroad cut. There, on the right flank of Cutler's Brigade, they went into battle line with skirmishers out in front.[90]

By order of General Doubleday, the four regiments of Baxter's Brigade remaining on Seminary Ridge together with Paul's entire brigade were put to work erecting crescent-shaped breastworks out of fence rails. Before many hours passed, thanks to Doubleday's foresight, retreating Federals had a refuge to fall back to.[91]

But as Baxter's and Paul's men labored to finish the task, they were too engrossed in the present to entertain any thought as to the possible future value of their handiwork. Certainly not when cannonballs, arcing in a mile-long trajectory from Herr Ridge, were crashing into their midst. On top of that they were also unnerved by intermittent screams coming from the direction of the Seminary.

There, with gruesome efficiency, army surgeons were amputating limbs that could not be saved. In all probability there was not enough morphine to meet the need; hence the most blood-curdling screams heard by Robinson's men. Antisepsis still lay in the future. A surgeon therefore had no compunction about wiping his bloody tools on his filthy apron.

On his successive trips to the makeshift hospital in the Seminary, stretcher-bearer Harry Kieffer could not help but notice that it was "rapidly filling with the wounded." He would have noticed, too, that just as many injured men waited outside its walls. Some were staggering around, some were sitting up, but by far the greater number were lying down. All hoped and prayed for someone to come quickly, to relieve their pain and bind up their wounds. When shells began dropping around the Seminary, Kieffer was appalled. Yet, with uncommon charity, he thought: "This the enemy surely cannot know, or they wouldn't shell the building so hard!"[92] Even if, by sheer good fortune, no one was actually hit, the strain on the already wounded had to be excruciating.

In the 13th Masssachusetts' line, not far from the Seminary, a soldier became a casualty through his own folly. When a cannonball landed nearby, he—either ignorant of its latent power or simply not thinking—stuck out his foot to stop it! Comrades, seeing what was about to happen, shrieked a warning—but too late. The cannonball severed his leg. He broke down in tears, wailing, "I shall always be ashamed to say how I lost it."[93]

The shelling of Seminary Ridge was bad enough, imperiling both the hale and the disabled. But it paled in comparison with the pounding given the Federals on McPherson's Ridge. The Union batteries under Cooper and Reynolds contended manfully with the Rebel guns, but they were greatly outnumbered.[94]

Of all the regiments strung along McPherson's Ridge, it appears that the three comprising Stone's Brigade, wedged between Herbst's Woods and the Chambersburg Pike, took the worst beating. Officers of the 143rd, 149th, and 150th Pennsylvania all testified to a brutal onslaught by the Confederate guns.[95] Yet, when the bombardment began, one 150th Pennsylvania soldier actually made light of it. Like the rest of Company F, Private John Weber had been lying on the ground. But, when the first shell whizzed overhead, "Dutchy" (as he was called) sprang to his feet and shouted loud enough for all to hear: "Come, boys, choose your partners! The ball is about to open! Don't you hear the music?"[96] They heard it all right, and found it less than appealing. Indeed, as the tempo increased (a sergeant reported the missiles soon came in "thick and fast")[97] and the "music" swelled to fortissimo, they surely found it downright sinister.

It was also lethal, as stretcher-bearer Kieffer, along with countless others, could attest. Returning from a trip to the Seminary hospital, he and his partner, Andrew Daney, came upon the mangled bodies of six soldiers, one lying across another. They all belonged to Company C, 150th Pennsylvania, and apparently all had been killed in the same shellburst. Not long afterward Kieffer barely escaped the same fate. When Daney called for help with "some poor fellow" whose arm had been blown off at the shoulder, Kieffer ran to his aid, leaving the stretcher behind. Seconds later an exploding shell reduced it to tatters.[98]

After being under fire for twenty minutes, Colonel Stone moved his three regiments into different positions, but not because of the shelling. With Rodes' Division approaching on his right flank, he had to be ready for a possible attack from that quarter. He shifted the angled line of the 149th Pennsylvania eastward so that all its troops faced north along the Chambersburg Pike. Simultaneously, he had the 143rd Pennsylvania execute an about face, march just beyond the right of the 149th, and then wheel left to form a continuous line with that regiment. When these regiments moved out of McPherson's lane, the 150th Pennsylvania moved in. Still facing west, it now enjoyed the protective cover of McPherson's barn.[99] The 151st Pennsylvania, which had been temporarily attached to Stone's Brigade, remained in reserve. Although posted some distance from the other regiments, it too felt the sting of Rebel artillery and had to change position several times.[100]

An officer in another brigade, Major St. Clair A. Mulholland, paid tribute to Stone's Brigade in the following succinct account:

> Although some two hours elapsed from the time the brigade arrived until the first serious attack of the Confederate infantry, it was anything but an interval of peace. Exposed and in full view of the enemy, the line was pounded by the batteries from the distant hills, both north and west, and many were the casualties....It required courage of a high order to quietly await the attack, but Stone's men were equal to the occasion.[101]

Only slightly less intense than the pounding given Stone's Brigade was that inflicted on the eight regiments north of the Chambersburg Pike. After one Confederate battery moved farther north, the 14th Brooklyn got caught in a crossfire that (in Colonel Fowler's words) "soon compelled a change of position." The 147th New York, possibly caught in the same fire, also found its position untenable and moved to a safer one.[102]

The two brigades south of Stone's Brigade (Biddle's and Meredith's) probably suffered least from the enemy batteries. Lieutenant Slagle of Doubleday's staff, writing to his brother, stated that at this time "there was little firing on our left."[103] While the 121st Pennsylvania and the 7th Wisconsin both reported enemy artillery fire as "heavy," significantly, neither was forced to change its position.[104]

Throughout this period of continual cannonading, there was a great deal of skirmishing going on as well. Stone's Brigade, it will be recalled, encountered sharp skirmish fire as it deployed on McPherson's Ridge, and Stone immediately called for one company from each regiment to drive off those Rebels who had dared to cross Willoughby Run. While the three Union companies were forming their skirmish line in the open fields that sloped down to Willoughby Run, the Confederate skirmishers pulled back behind a fence, where they had both cover and a clear field of fire. When the blue-coats began to advance, the Rebels opened fire. Stone's skirmishers, not stopping to return the fire, broke into a run toward them. For a short time the Rebels kept on firing, but when they realized the blue wave would surely roll over them, they raced back to Herr Ridge. The Federals kept up the pursuit until they reached the run. There, screened by the dense vegetation that lined the bank, they sniped at the enemy on Herr Ridge. Their purpose, of course, was to discourage the graybacks from any thoughts of another incursion beyond Willoughby Run.[105]

Skirmishers from the Iron Brigade added to the Confederates' discomfort. "We...moved forward to the creek," wrote a 19th Indiana soldier, "and kept up a sharpshooting for some time."[106] According to one skirmisher in the 24th Michigan's line, the sniping back and forth was "desultory."[107] But Sergeant Cornelius Wheeler, with the 2nd Wisconsin in Herbst's Woods, had a different impression. "We lay there probably about an hour and a half," he wrote to his parents, with "skirmishing being kept up lively in our front all the while."[108]

South of Herbst's Woods, Biddle's Brigade was plagued by Rebs firing from inside Emmanuel Harman's house and barn. They took full advantage of the ideal conditions: easy range (under 200 yards), unobstructed view, superior cover. General Wadsworth, as it happened, had been watching the brigade come into line, and as soon as he discovered where the shots that were picking off these troops came from, he ordered Colonel Biddle to seize those buildings. The brigade commander logically assigned the mission to Colonel Gates, whose 80th New York stood nearest the source of trouble and therefore was taking the most punishment. Gates, in turn, chose Captain Ambrose N. Baldwin and his Company K to actually accomplish the task. Dashing across Willoughby Run, they stormed the enemy stronghold. After a brief resistance, the outnumbered Rebel snipers ran for their lives.[109]

North of Herbst's Woods, two field officers of the 150th Pennsylvania were in the midst of a discussion when a gruff, petulant voice interrupted them.

"Can I fight with your regiment?"

Lieutenant Colonel Huidekoper and Major Chamberlin, turned to see who had asked such an unlikely question. They could hardly believe their eyes. Before them stood a wiry, grizzled old man holding a musket at trail arms. He looked fierce enough to bite nails. Most incongruous was his attire: high silk hat, baggy trousers, black swallowtail coat with shiny brass buttons.[110]

It was John Burns, then almost seventy years old.[111] Other officers and enlisted men had seen the peripatetic town constable at various points on the field earlier this morning: near the Seminary (asking the way to the front); between the Emmitsburg and Chambersburg roads (watching the army pioneers tear down fences); beside the latter road (exchanging sallies with the 147th New York troops). He had been observed in yet another location prior to his appearance on McPherson's Ridge. Near Pennsylvania (now Gettysburg) College, some 9th New York cavalrymen had seen him walk up to a wounded soldier and ask if he had any further use for his musket, which was propped against a nearby tree. "No," the man replied, "you can have it. I can't carry it any further." He also offered him his cartridge belt. Burns tried it on, but it did not suit him. He removed the cartridges, however, and stuffed them in his trouser pockets. Then, having discarded his own ancient smoothbore firearm, he strode off bearing the injured soldier's more effective rifled musket.[112]

John Burns, at home, after the battle.

What had caused Burns' unshakeable determination to fight the Rebels? A week earlier, Confederate foragers had milked his cows and had gotten them so stirred up that several had run off.[113] Two days later, while Early's Division was in town, he seems to have tussled with some of the Southern lads. And apparently his conduct was so obstreperous that they kept him prisoner for the next two days. No doubt that humiliation still rankled, though he should have been somewhat mollified when, shortly after his release, he apprehended a Confederate chaplain and another soldier and put them both in jail. He never divulged the nature of their offense, but whatever it was, Burns would have considered his act poetic justice.[114]

Unquestionably these recent events had kindled Burns' intense desire for revenge. But his implacable resolve stemmed in at least equal measure from his temperament and background. Armed combat held no nameless terrors for him, for he had "seen the elephant" in previous wars. As a young man, he had fought at Plattsburg, Queenston Heights, and Lundy's Lane in the War of 1812. In the Lundy's Lane battle his regiment, the 10th United States, captured a six-gun battery at bayonet point, turned the British guns around, and proceeded to blast their former owners. While in his forties, Burns fought in the Seminole Wars. During the Mexican War, though well past fifty, he joined a local volunteer company; but when it was mustered into the U. S. Army, he was rejected because of his age. Nevertheless, when war broke out between the States, he did not intend to miss out on all the action, even though he was in his late sixties. Soon after Fort Sumter fell, he walked to Hagerstown (nearly forty miles) to sign up as an army teamster. Perhaps he had to do some tall talking to convince the recruiting officer; but he was accepted. The story is told that one day as his wagon rolled along Burns heard the crack of musketry and responded as if it were a personal summons. "They may want me over there," he said to his companion. Handing over his whip, he jumped from the wagon and ran toward the sound of firing.

Evidently the life of a teamster proved too strenuous, for he was discharged in the winter of 1861-62. Returning to Gettysburg, he sought the position of constable and was elected the following spring. On June 21, 1863, he rode out with a local guerilla band intent on stirring up trouble with any Confederates they could find. Nothing came of it, however. Before he and the others had gone very far, Union scouts persuaded them to turn back.[115]

Clearly, then, John Burns was a warrior at heart. Coupled with his innate pugnacity were a testiness and irascibility which inevitably led to harsh words and violent action. One strongly suspects he enjoyed a good fight.

On McPherson's Ridge, just as Burns was asking Huidekoper and Chamberlin for permission to fight, the commander of the 150th Pennsylvania rode up. In his usual bluff manner Colonel Wister said, "Well, old man, what do *you* want?"

"I want a chance to fight with your regiment."

"You do? Can you shoot?"

"Oh, yes," replied Burns, and the colonel then asked: "I see you have a gun, but where is your ammunition?" In reply, Burns simply slapped his bulging trouser pocket.

Satisfied that the man was prepared and capable of doing what he proposed, Wister said, "Certainly you can fight with us and I wish there were more like you." However, since his line was so exposed and he was concerned for the old man's safety, he told him to go to the left and join the Iron Brigade in the shelter of Herbst's Woods.[116] When the soldiers who had been looking on saw the valiant old codger set out with purposeful stride toward the woods, they gave him three rousing cheers.[117]

Burns kept on walking until he met 7th Wisconsin's Lieutenant Colonel Callis. "Sir, are you in command of this regiment?" he asked. Callis allowed that he was, and Burns again asked permission to fight.

Unlike Colonel Wister, Callis was not amenable to Burns' offer. "Old man," he replied, "you had better go to the rear or you might get hurt. The Rebels are very careless about how they shoot and you are liable to get killed any moment. See, the bullets are flying pretty thick now."

"Tut!" scoffed Burns. "I've heard the whistle of bullets before."[118] The argument continued, Callis insisting he go to the rear and Burns protesting that he be allowed to fight. Finally the infantry leader relented. More than that, he presented him with a better rifled musket than the one given him by the wounded soldier—a superb firearm with silver mountings captured in the fight with Archer's Brigade.

Once Burns got into battle line alongside regular troops, one would have expected him to be content. But no, before long he grew restless—too little action. So, without a word to anyone, he simply ambled down the west slope of McPherson's ridge and joined the 7th Wisconsin's skirmishers along Willoughby Run.[119]

Sergeant George Eustice saw him coming. "It must have been about noon," he later wrote, "when I saw a little old man coming up in the rear of Company F." He and his comrades stared in disbelief at the oddly-dressed citizen toting a musket. "We boys began to poke fun at him as soon as he came amongst us," Eustice continued, "as we thought no civilian in his senses would show himself in such a place. Finding that he had really come to fight I wanted to put a cartridge-box on him to make him look like a soldier, telling him he could not fight without one. Slapping his pantaloons-pocket, he replied, 'I can get my hands in here quicker than in a box.'"

Burns told them he was going to get even with the Rebels for molesting his cows. About this time, Eustice recalled, "Bullets were flying thicker and faster, and we hugged the ground as close as we could. Burns got behind a tree and surprised us all by not taking a double-quick to the rear." The Wisconsin lads and the aged Pennsylvanian did not stay pinned down for long. Recovering their aplomb, they pelted their adversaries with as heavy a fire as they received. Eustice said Burns was "as calm and collected as any veteran on the field."[120] And Callis affirmed that he "fought nobly until I called the skirmishers in."[121]

The image of a truculent old man, in outlandish garb, volunteering to fight the invaders and then doing so with elan, courage, and tenacity was (and still is) irresistible. Is it any wonder that the John Burns story circulated rapidly, by word of mouth in the Army of the Potomac, by newspaper account to the public at large? Abraham

Lincoln—he who appreciated a good story as much as anyone—heard it. His reaction, one can assume, was a mixture of delight, astonishment, and deeply-felt gratitude.

Almost completely forgotten, on the other hand, are two civilians—both young enough to be Burns' grandsons—who also participated in the first day's battle. That morning a local boy named James Watson rode up to a small band of Devin's troopers north of Gettysburg and asked to join them. It turned out they belonged to Company A, 9th New York Cavalry. Having observed that the would-be trooper had come fully equipped, including carbine and saber, they readily consented. After a long stretch of picket duty, when companies A and H left the field to escort Confederate prisoners to Westminister, Maryland, Watson rode with them.[122]

The other young civilian fought with the infantry. He had tagged along behind the 12th Massachusetts when it marched out of Emmitsburg the preceding day. This morning, before the regiment got moving, the boy—he appeared to be about sixteen years old—mustered his courage, then strode up to the regimental commander and fervently asked that he be allowed to join the regiment. Colonel James L. Bates had his doubts but agreed to give him a trial for a day or two. The boy was overjoyed; it was the chance he wanted, and he was determined to make good. His high spirits and unflagging step throughout the exhausting march to Gettysburg did not go unnoticed. When the regiment halted on Seminary Ridge, he was rewarded with a uniform. He could not have been happier. But, alas, before the day ended the blue garments he so proudly donned would be stained with his blood, seeping from two wounds. The last the Massachusetts men saw of him he was being carried to the rear on a stretcher. Afterward no one could recall his name.[123]

While the east-west sparring match continued between Union and Confederate canonners and skirmishers on opposite sides of Willoughby Run, the troops in Stone's Brigade line atop McPherson's Ridge suddenly became aware of musket fire coming from the north. It was merely the calling card from skirmishers in the van of Rodes' Division. The hour, as Captain John Irvin of the 149th Pennsylvania recorded in his diary, was "about 12 o'clock."[124] Simon Hubler, the corporal in the 143rd Pennsylvania who earlier had lamented he could not fire for fear of hitting a Union soldier, now had his chance. But, on his very first shot, his musket misfired. In his eagerness, he had poured *two* powder charges down the barrel![125]

The eight regiments nearer to the approaching Confederate division than Stone's Brigade were, obviously, in greater, more immediate peril. Cutler's five regiments and Dawes' 6th Wisconsin of Meredith's Brigade had all been severely weakened in the earlier fighting. Although they had been bolstered by the arrival of two fresh regiments from Baxter's Brigade, they were still at risk of being overrun. Consequently, Baxter's other four regiments, on Seminary Ridge, were rushed to the scene.

When the order came, the 12th Massachusetts, 83rd New York, and 90th Pennsylvania were still constructing breastworks. In the 88th Pennsylvania the men had just started to make themselves some coffee, a luxury denied them earlier because of being on picket duty. Now, the long-awaited pleasure would have to be postponed indefinitely.[126]

Only Paul's Brigade remained in reserve on Seminary Ridge after the last of Baxter's regiments moved out.[127] On reaching McPherson's Ridge, the 83rd New York, 88th Pennsylvania, and 12th Massachusetts extended the Union line northward to the Mummasburg road. At that point the line doubled back (eastward), with the 90th Pennsylvania forming along that road.[128]

Before these troop movements were completed, Doubleday was superseded as senior commander on the field by Major General Oliver O. Howard. Although top authority actually passed to the Eleventh Corps commander the moment he arrived at Gettysburg, neither he nor Doubleday were aware of it for some time. Howard naturally assumed that Reynolds was in charge. When he was finally apprised of Reynolds' death, he resolutely took up the reins of supreme command. He was unaccountably derelict, however, in not notifying Doubleday at once of his presence on the field.

After the Battle of Gettysburg, Howard reaped lavish praise for his actions on the first day, whereas Doubleday was roundly criticized for his. Doubleday, understandably, was bitter. Referring to Howard at one point during his interrogation by the Joint Committee on the Conduct of the War, he sniffed, "The most prominent successes of the day occurred before he assumed command of the field."[129]

Which was undeniably true.

"God helping us, we will stay here...."

The Eleventh Corps, formed in September of 1862, apparently did not show much promise as a fighting unit. McClellan did not employ it in that capacity at Antietam Creek; nor did Burnside at Fredericksburg. In the Chancellorsville campaign Hooker assigned it to a sector where he least expected action. Hooker was wrong.

On May 2, 1863, "Stonewall" Jackson, with Lee's approval, led his Second Corps on a daring flank march around Hooker's whole Union army. Screened by dense woods, the movement escaped the enemy's notice and when completed, Jackson's force immediately pounced on the nearest Federals, which turned out to be the Eleventh Corps, then under its new commander, Oliver Otis Howard. Howard's men reeled from the sudden onslaught. In that instant they lost the will to resist and simply ran away.

The Eleventh Corps, after that, was derisively referred to either as "the flying Dutchmen" (stemming from the preponderance of German immigrants in its ranks) or, because its symbol was the crescent, "the flying half-moon."[130]

Howard had been assigned to these troops just one month before the Chancellorsville debacle. A wide-shouldered, heavily-built man, he had a square face, black hair, full beard, deep-set eyes. And, like his nemesis, Jackson, he was profoundly religious. When war broke out he was teaching mathematics at West Point (where he had graduated fourth in his class in 1854). Since then he had had more than his share of hard luck. In addition to the misfortune of being in just the wrong spot at Chancellorsville,

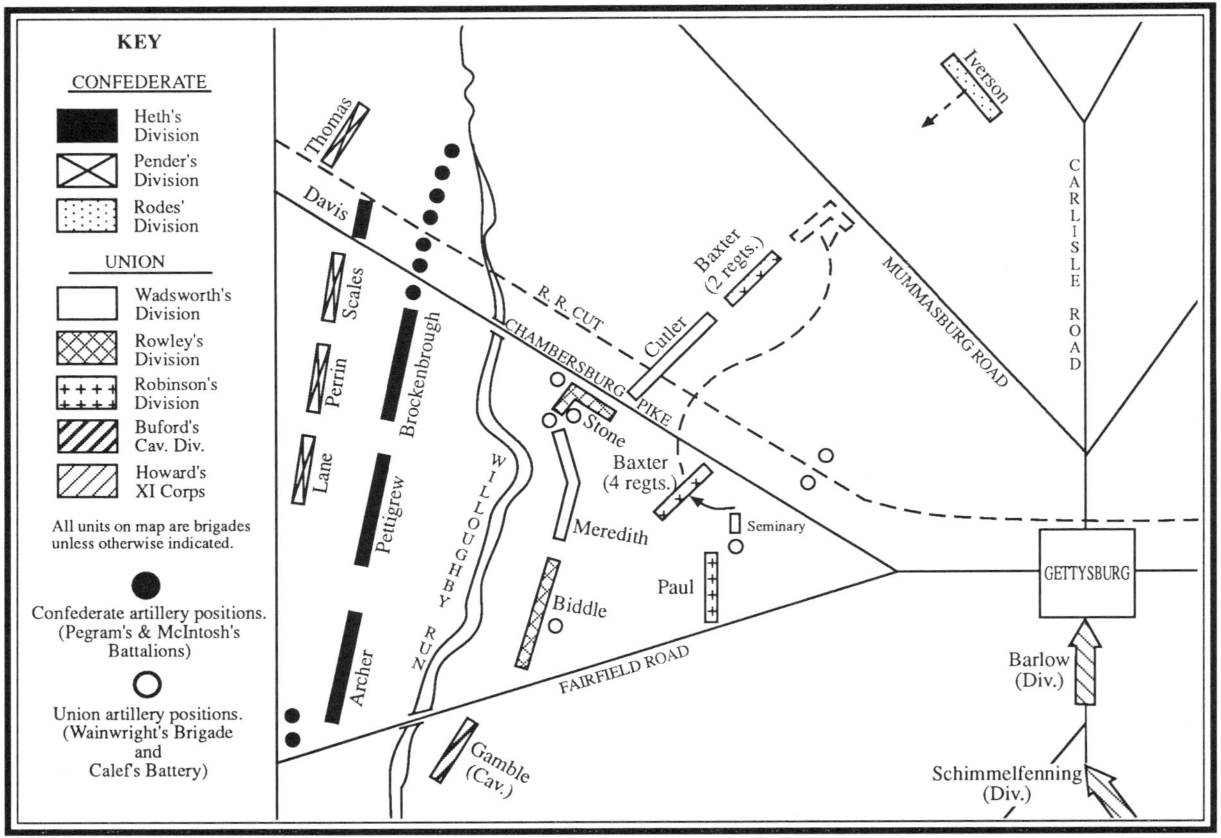

Situation at 12:30 p.m., July 1, 1863.

Major General Oliver O. Howard

he had lost his right arm in the battle at Fair Oaks the preceding May and, four months later, he had lost some 550 men of his Second Corps brigade in ten bloody minutes of the Antietam battle. As a leader, he was respected rather than liked; he had none of the charisma of a McClellan or a Reynolds. When displeased, he could be quite testy.[131]

This first morning of July 1863, Howard and Reynolds kept in close touch through their aides. On receiving Howard's proposal that two of his divisions follow an alternate route, Reynolds dispatched Major William Riddle to relay his approval. When Buford reported to Reynolds that during the night his cavalry pickets had spotted a large enemy force west of Gettysburg, the wing commander sent another aide to Howard, instructing him to bring up his troops quickly. Later, with skirmishing going on and battle imminent, Reynolds again sent Major Riddle galloping to Howard, this time with the message that the Eleventh Corps should assemble just outside Gettysburg and stand ready for action. Shortly, one of Howard's aides, Captain Daniel Hall, rode up to Reynolds with a report on the Eleventh Corps' progress. Reynolds told the captain to impress on General Howard the urgent need for his corps to come up and reinforce the First Corps. Further, Howard should meet him on the field.

In the meantime, Howard, accompanied by his staff and a small escort, had spurred ahead of his command. They had soon found it expedient to make their way in the fields and woods bordering the Emmitsburg road, since that thoroughfare was chock-a-block with First Corps troops, not to mention artillery and assorted wagons.[132] As Howard and his party approached Gettysburg, they heard firing on their left—enough to convince them that a battle was "warmly in progress."[133] They were within sight of the town when Major Riddle rode up with Reynolds' order for the Eleventh Corps to come "quite up to Gettysburg." Just where does he want my divisions placed? the corps commander asked, and Riddle replied, "Choose your ground anywhere near here." Howard then instructed his brother Charles, a major on his staff, to ride with Riddle and report back on Reynolds' whereabouts on the field, so that he would not lose time in trying to find him.[134]

Like Reynolds before him, Howard noted the long, wooded elevation on his right as he rode toward Gettysburg. Undoubtedly he, too, recognized its outstanding merit as a defensive position. In particular, his attention was drawn to a high point overlooking the town. This was Cemetery Hill, northern terminus of Cemetery Ridge. On impulse he rode over to it and continued up its slope. At the top he paused to survey "the broad expanse of country over and beyond the little town at my feet." Turning to his chief of staff, Lieutenant Colonel Theodore Meysenburg, who was among the party accompanying him, he said, "This seems to be a *good position*, colonel." Meysenburg agreed: "It is the only position, general."[135]

About this time Captain Hall returned with Reynolds' latest order: the Eleventh Corps is to proceed with all possible haste directly to the scene of action in support of the First Corps.[136] Accordingly, Howard at once sent word to his division commanders. Most likely one courier was dispatched to Barlow on the Emmitsburg Road and another to Schurz and Steinwehr on the Taneytown Road. Howard and the others with him descended Cemetery Hill. At the base Howard drew rein and pointed to the summit. As Hall recollected it, Howard then said, prophetically, "There's the place to fight this battle."[137]

As the mounted party swung onto Baltimore Street, Howard must have noticed the cupola atop a building a few blocks ahead and decided he would try to get a view of the surrounding countryside and the overall military situation from there. The building in question was the Adams County Court House, which had already been transformed into a military hospital. Coming alongside it, Howard raised his hand, signalling a halt. Dismounting, he strode into the Court House and was told there was no way up to the cupola. No steps led up to it nor was there a ladder handy.[138]

Frustrated, Howard left the building. At that moment a young lad came up to him and timorously offered to take him to a good observation post. He, Daniel Skelly, together with another teen-age boy named Bentley and a Mrs. Fahnestock, had been watching the battle from an "observatory" on the roof of the three-story building beside the Court House. The clatter of horses' hoofs had caused them to shift their gaze. They had watched the Union horsemen coming down Baltimore Street and halting almost directly beneath them. An officer in Howard's party had called up to them, asking how to get up there, and Skelly had said he would show the way. Racing down to the street, he made his offer to Howard, who readily accepted it. Surely bursting with pride and importance, Skelly led the two-star general and a captain through Fahnestock's clothing store on the first floor, up two flights of stairs, and onto the roof.[139]

Howard was at once "delighted with the open view."[140] He asked the aide for his field glasses and had just begun his reconnaisance when he was interrupted by a call from below. A mounted Union officer had come flying down Baltimore Street. Reining in abruptly at the Court House, he had inquired for General Howard and his attention was directed to the roof of the Fahnestock building. Seeing the corps commander there, he touched his hat and shouted, "General Reynolds is wounded, sir."

"I am very sorry," Howard shouted back. "I hope he will be able to keep the field."[141] This was indeed bad news, but he would hope for the best. As he resumed his reconnaisance, perhaps the memory of pleasant hours spent with Reynolds just the night before flashed through his mind.

Skelly's friend Bentley remembered the general peering "long and anxiously" through the field glasses.[142] Actually, Howard must have been heartened by what he saw. As he later described it, "I got glimpses of Wadsworth's division of infantry,

Fahnestock clothing store as it appeared at the time of the battle. General Howard viewed the progress of the battle from its rooftop "observatory."

fighting near the Oak Ridge railroad cut. Success was then attending him, and prisoners in gray were being conducted to the rear." In addition, he could see some of Rowley's men coming up "with considerable rapidity." Also visible, at various compass points, were elements of Buford's cavalry. These included Devin's pickets, up to two miles away, on roads which, from his elevation, appeared as "spokes from the hub of a wheel."[143]

Within ten minutes after Howard learned that Reynolds had been wounded, Major Riddle arrived to inform him of the whole truth. Howard had clung to the hope that the field commander's injury was slight, would not prove incapacitating; but in that moment he said he was "undeceived."[144] Reynolds was dead and he was in command! Of necessity he had to put personal grief aside. He resolved: "God helping us, we will stay here till the army comes."[145] It was then a few minutes after eleven o'clock.[146]

To young Bentley, General Howard appeared "profoundly agitated." He heard him say to his aide, "Captain, go immediately to General Steinwehr and tell him to stop his division on Cemetery Hill and put his men in position for defense." Mrs. E. G. Fahnestock, the woman in the observatory with the two boys, had remained silent in the presence of the two officers. But on hearing Howard's instruction to his subordinate, she pleaded, "Oh, sir, you are not going to let the rebels come into town, are you?"

Howard was hardly reassuring: "Madam, no one can tell what may happen in war."[147]

The two officers descended to the street, the general to attend to the urgent matter of communication, the captain to ride to Steinwehr. Howard quickly dispatched one aide to Schurz, another to Barlow. Both division commanders were to hurry up their troops, and Schurz was to ride at once to Howard. Still another aide was called upon to ride to General Sickles at Emmitsburg, then to General Meade at Taneytown, and finally to General Slocum somewhere in the vicinity of Two Taverns. All were to be informed of Reynolds' death and of Howard taking command of the field. In addition, the Third and Twelfth Corps commanders were enjoined to bring up their commands as rapidly as possible.[148]

After the battle Doubleday would repeatedly aver that the courier to Meade delivered a false and defamatory report from Howard. He claimed that Howard, informed that Union troops had retreated, but "without waiting to ascertain the extent of the disaster," had written the army commander that "First Corps had run away at the first contact with the enemy." (Actually it was only the 76th New York and 56th Pennsylvania regiments of Cutler's Brigade that were soon forced to retreat.) Doubleday said it was most regrettable that Meade had had to bear not only the grievous news of Reynolds' death but the slanderous assertion that "his corps had ingloriously fled the field." Doubleday added: "It is impossible to paint the distress caused by this false report."[149]

But did such a negative report really exist?

It seems highly unlikely.[150] Howard, as we have seen, gave an impression quite the opposite of that alleged by Doubleday. In his after-action report and in later writings, he spoke only of Union success prior to his assuming command. Moreover, Meade not only gave no indication of "distress" over a dispatch in which Howard denigrated the First Corps, he never mentioned receiving such a report. Lastly, the dispatch itself never came to light.

It seems the whole matter was a canard on Doubleday's part. One suspects it arose from his need to save face. On the second day of the battle Meade demoted him, placing Major General John Newton, a Sixth Corps division commander with less seniority, in charge of the First Corps. No doubt Doubleday was quite disturbed to be returned to his former command, and his not inconsiderable egotism would have insisted upon a scapegoat. Even assuming he heard some gossip that Howard had maligned the First Corps, he apparently twisted it to suit his own purpose.

Around 11:30 on the first morning of the Gettysburg battle, General Howard returned to Cemetery Hill where he and his staff hastily established their headquarters overlooking the Baltimore Pike. From his observations atop the Fahnestock building he had concluded that Cemetery Ridge, and this eminence in particular, offered "the only tenable position for my limited force."[151] After the battle Howard was widely acclaimed for recognizing the tactical importance of Cemetery Ridge (the shank of the famed "fish hook"), which became the site of total Union victory on July 3. There were those, however, who felt that the praise heaped on Howard was misplaced. The credit for first recognizing the merit of the position, they contended, was really due Reynolds, or possibly even Buford.

Shortly after Howard returned to Cemetery Hill, General Carl Schurz arrived with his staff. The two generals conferred near the cemetery gatehouse, a two-story brick structure with an arched gateway in the center.[152] Due to his overall responsibility, Howard put Schurz in charge of the Eleventh Corps. In consequence, Brigadier General Alexander Schimmelfennig and Colonel George von Amsberg moved up to division and brigade command, respectively.[153]

Howard left Schurz in no doubt as to what he expected of the Eleventh Corps. Steinwehr's Division was to occupy the ground on which they stood and had been so directed. "We must hold this hill," he added emphatically. Then this instruction: "Tell Osborn to put his artillery here."[154] (Major Thomas W. Osborn commanded the Eleventh Corps' artillery brigade.) Schurz' own division, now under Schimmelfennig, together with Barlow's Division were to "seize and hold" Oak Hill, on the right flank of the First Corps.[155] Howard certainly had no illusions that it would be an easy matter, especially after receiving an ominous report from Doubleday.

In close succession Howard was contacted twice by Doubleday and once by Buford. A signalman in the Seminary cupola had reported the approach of the Eleventh Corps to the cavalry leader. And Buford had sent Lieutenant A. B. Jerome to Howard to urge that his troops be brought up at the greatest possible speed. Presumably Howard had Jerome assure Buford that this was already being done. But Buford's concern apparently had one effect, for it was at this time that Howard ordered his batteries to rush forward ahead of the infantry.[156]

The first word from Doubleday came by way of Major Charles Howard. While seeking out Reynolds, at his brother's behest, he had met Doubleday, who promptly informed him of Reynolds' death. Doubleday told him to inform General Howard and also to convey his acknowledgement that the Eleventh Corps commander outranked him in seniority and therefore was in command of the field. By the time the major got back to Cemetery Hill, General Howard had already heard the tragic news about Reynolds.[157]

The second communication from Doubleday was delivered by one of his own aides. It could hardly have been more alarming. Lead elements of Ewell's corps were rapidly approaching Oak Hill! As Doubleday later testified before the Joint Committee on the Conduct of the War, he had then implored Howard "to keep Ewell off of my flank, as I had as much as I could do to attend to A. P. Hill."[158]

Howard—surely thankful he had acquired a familiarity with the surrounding terrain through his visit to Fahnestock's observatory—replied to Doubleday's aide with a confidence bolstered by that knowledge: "Tell Doubleday to fight on the left and I will fight on the right." Further, if he (Doubleday) should be driven back, he should hold Seminary Ridge "at all hazards."[159]

By this time Howard's three divisions, approaching on the Taneytown and Emmitsburg roads, were finally within sight of Gettysburg. The men, without exception, were puffing from the accelerated pace. During the past hour they had encountered a number of townspeople fleeing on foot in the opposite direction. General Schurz observed that they "seemed to be in great terror." One woman with a small child in tow exclaimed as he rode by, "Hard times at Gettysburg! They are shooting and killing! What will become of us!"[160]

Around 12:30 the first Eleventh Corps troops entered the crossroads town. It would be a full hour before the last of them had passed through it.[161]

Howard eventually confronted his second-in-command in person. Doubleday later said "it must have been about two o'clock" when Howard rode up, though one suspects it may in fact have been somewhat earlier.[162] Howard's brother Charles gave only this vague clue as to the hour: "Having established his headquarters on Cemetery Hill, Howard then went in person to see Doubleday and get a closer view of the field...."[163]

In Taneytown, Maryland, Captain Stephen Weld of Reynolds' staff threaded his way through a street thronged with soldiers and army vehicles of every description. Meade's headquarters—his destination—was in a tent set up in a field just beyond the town. When he arrived there, he had been in the saddle one hour and twenty minutes and had ridden thirteen miles. It was then nearly noon. Ushered into the presence of the army commander and his chief of staff, Dan Butterfield, Weld relayed Reynolds' electrifying message: A strong enemy force is advancing from the west, and General Reynolds fears they will seize the high ground south and east of Gettysburg before he can stop them.

"Good God!" exclaimed Meade, "if they get Gettysburg, we are lost!"

Weld quickly went on to repeat Reynolds' declaration that if his troops were driven into the town, he would barricade the streets and hold back the enemy as long as he could.

"Good!" said Meade, "that is just like Reynolds; he will hold on to the bitter end."

The army commander then asked Weld to repeat the whole message. When Weld had done so, Meade turned to General Butterfield and royally chewed him out for taking "so long to get the orders out that now it was all useless." The allusion was to his now-defunct Pipe Creek plan.

When the tirade was over, Meade got busy sending aides in all directions with new instructions for his corps commanders. Presently he received Buford's report that a battle was raging. About this same time he received the stunning news that Reynolds was out of action—killed or seriously wounded, according to this report. A little earlier Major General Winfield S. Hancock had come to see Meade to learn the latest developments; now Meade had reason to ride to Hancock. Although aware that both Howard and Sickles had more seniority, Meade knew that in the present crisis he wanted Hancock in command of the field in place of the fallen Reynolds. The Second Corps commander pointed out the irregularity of the promotion, but Meade had made up his mind. Hancock started for Gettysburg at 1:30.[164]

Upon arrival, he assumed command of the field, thus becoming the fourth in that role that day. Howard returned to corps command, disgruntled because Meade had seen fit to put Hancock in authority over him.

By then the tide had turned decisively against the Army of the Potomac and the Army of Northern Virginia was in control. Over the next two days Lee's army would remain the aggressor and Meade's the defender. Yet, the success of Union arms at Willoughby Run on the morning of July 1, 1863, proved a good omen, foreshadowing ultimate Union victory.

CHAPTER X

AN ASSESSMENT

To sum up the infantry battle at Willoughby Run in the fewest possible words: Two Confederate brigades assaulted two Union brigades and were repulsed. But it might have turned out differently that first morning of July 1863, for the Union troops arrived barely in time to stop the Confederate advance. In fact, on the Union right, two regiments were driven back almost immediately.

The outcome in favor of the Union stemmed, essentially, from three factors. First, the magnificent fight put up by the four Iron Brigade regiments on McPherson's Ridge, in which they turned the tables on the attackers and succeeded in driving them back across Willoughby Run. Second, the timely, well-coordinated counterattack on the railroad cut by the 6th Wisconsin, 95th New York, and 14th Brooklyn. Third, Union superiority in the overall number of troops engaged—3,400 as compared to the enemy's 2,900.

Casualties

The fighting was savage and casualties ran high on both sides. For the North, there were approximately 1,100 infantrymen killed, wounded, or captured—nearly one-third of the number engaged. For the South (including those lost in the opening skirmish with Buford's cavalry), the total was about 1,050, or slightly over one-third. However, the Confederates had only half as many killed or wounded, considering that some 500 of their total casualties were prisoners, whereas the number of Union prisoners was minimal.

The reason for the wide disparity becomes clear in light of the adverse events and circumstances borne by the Federals. Namely:

- The rout of the 76th New York and 56th Pennsylvania, which were outnumbered at the outset and quickly outflanked.
- The near-entrapment of the isolated 147th New York.
- The brutal assault on the 2nd Wisconsin just as it came into line ahead of the other Iron Brigade regiments.
- The exposure of the 6th Wisconsin, 14th Brooklyn, and 95th New York during the charge on the railroad cut.

- The preponderance of Confederate artillery fire.

Of the Union regiments on the field, the 147th New York sustained the highest casualty rate during the morning hours—almost 60%. On the Confederate side the dubious distinction fell to the 2nd Mississippi, which by noon had lost two-thirds of its men, many of them captured. (Percent of casualties for every unit is shown in Appendix 1 and Appendix 2.)

Compared to the infantry, casualties in Buford's Cavalry Division were light—about 100, the majority being in Gamble's Brigade.

Calef's and Hall's Union batteries sustained a combined loss of about thirty men and at least forty horses. Casualties in Pegram's five Confederate batteries are unknown but can be assumed to have been minimal.

Although Robinson's and Rowley's Union Divisions did no actual fighting before noon, they came under the intense enemy artillery fire and inevitably suffered casualties. While a precise determination is impossible, it can be safely assumed that the two divisions combined lost at least fifty men.

As was invariably the case throughout the Civil War, the officer class was hit hard. The North lost a wing commander in the fatal shooting of Reynolds. The South lost a brigadier in the capture of Archer. In addition to scores of captains and lieutenants on both sides, the following field-grade officers are known to have become casualties on the morning of July 1, 1863:

UNION	
Col. Lucius Fairchild (14th Brooklyn)	wounded
Col. Henry A. Morrow (24th Michigan)	wounded
Col. George H. Biddle (95th New York)	wounded
Lt. Col. George H. Stevens (2nd Wisconsin)	killed
Lt. Col. Willam W. Dudley (19th Indiana)	wounded
Lt. Col. Francis C. Miller (147th New York)	wounded
Maj. Andrew J. Grover (76th New York)	killed
Maj. Charles Lemon (3rd Indiana Cavalry)	killed

CONFEDERATE	
Col. J. M. Stone (2nd Mississippi)	wounded
Col. John K. Connally (55th North Carolina)	wounded
Lt. Col. James Aiken (13th Alabama)	captured
Maj. John A. Blair (2nd Mississippi)	captured

The number of officers and men of both sides killed or mortally wounded during the morning hours was at least 400 and probably closer to 450.

Confederate Leaders

There could be no dissembling on the part of the Southerners. As one Rebel officer referring to the situation at noon said: "...it must be admitted that so far at least the Confederates got the worst of it."[1] Heth's expedition to get shoes and at the same time to spy on the enemy had been a complete disaster. But this miscarriage of plans was hardly the worst of it, for it effectively cancelled Lee's hopes of giving battle at Cashtown. Pettigrew, after his aborted march to Gettysburg the day before, had counseled Henry Heth and A. P. Hill against a return mission. But they had ignored his warning. Nevertheless, Hill was surely aware of the chance of a confrontation with a considerable enemy force, and one suspects, given his aggressive bent, that he would have welcomed it.[2] Hence his sly notification to Ewell (whose corps was headed toward Cashtown) that Heth's Division was en route to Gettysburg.

Union General Doubleday maintained that the Confederates were "careless" because they "underrated us."[3] He may well have been right, for Hill himself admitted "the Yankees had fought with a determination unusual to them."[4]

Certainly Henry Heth must be faulted for not making every effort to bring up Pettigrew's and Brockenbrough's Brigades when he saw those of Archer and Davis in deep trouble. In short, he was guilty of committing half of his men, then not supporting them. Moreover, he hastily committed that half without the benefit of reconnaissance—which, along with the need for shoes, had been cited as justification for making the march. Athough he can be accused of being too eager to give battle, he can hardly be criticized for proceeding against an enemy he had reason to believe was inferior in strength to his own, especially when his superiors had given him the leeway to do so. Buford's hold on McPherson's Ridge was indeed tenuous, and Heth's two brigades, given a little more time, would have overrun the thin line of Union cavalry. But, with the appearance of a sizeable body of Union infantry (Wadsworth's Division) in their front, the Confederates were no longer in the catbird seat. Disengagement, which earlier would have been a simple matter, would then have been tricky and no doubt costly.

So Heth continued the attack.

In this test of every man's courage, when commanders needed to direct, control, and inspire their men, the performance of Heth's brigadiers was less than distinguished. This is hardly surprising in the case of Joseph R. Davis: The nephew of the Confederate President had never commanded troops in combat before. Nevertheless, he managed well enough until the Federals counterattacked. Then, at the first enemy volley, his men panicked and he found himself powerless to prevent the stampede that ensued. Not long after his men poured into the railroad cut, he realized they were in a trap and immediately ordered a retreat. The decision was undeniably prudent, and probably the wisest under the circumstances. Yet one must wonder what the result might have been if the bold plan of Majors Belo and Blair had been initiated before the retreat order reached them. Each had succeeded to command of his regiment when its colonel had been wounded; together they proposed to lead their men in a coordinated attack on the attackers. The desperate measure might well have failed utterly; on the other hand, if executed with total commitment, it just might have stopped the onrushing Federals.

While the lackluster performance of Davis can conveniently be attributed to inexperience, the same cannot be said of James J. Archer. Resigning his commission in the U. S. Army and joining the Confederacy in 1861, he had since fought numerous battles and in all had proved himself a skillful and dependable leader. This day, however, his junior officers noticed he acted strangely; he did not seem quite alert and his usual brisk efficiency was missing. While it is not definitely known, it is believed he suffered from extreme fatigue.

While it can be asserted that Davis and Archer should have provided better leadership, primary responsibility for the Confederate disaster must remain with Henry Heth, who brought on the battle, and his superior, A. P. Hill, who approved the risky expedition to Gettysburg.

Heth had all the makings of an outstanding general. He was well-trained, brave, aggressive, intelligent, even-tempered, and respected by inferiors and superiors alike. Yet he never lived up to expectations.[5] A dark cloud seemed always to hover over his head. Was he, as Douglas Southall Freeman summed up, simply "capable but unlucky"?[6] Not quite, for he had two glaring defects, both of which he exhibited at Gettysburg: the tendency to be impulsive and a complete lack of the ability to foresee what the enemy's response would be in a given situation.[7]

Afterward, Heth's attitude toward his role in the battle was ambivalent. In turn, he felt guilty or persecuted. He ruefully admitted, "...we stumbled in there." Again: "...that battle was fought by my going there after shoes for my division."[8] At other times he felt he had been made a scapegoat. Resentful of insinuations that he had been reckless, had used poor judgement, he tried to place the blame for the defeat at Gettysburg on "Jeb" Stuart, whose cavalry failed to arrive until the afternoon of the second day's battle. Still, the suspicion that he himself was culpable continued to nag at him. For that reason, he frequently sought reassurance from his fellow officers that his actions at Gettysburg were justified. Yet, in one sense, he could not possibly dodge the responsibility for what happened there. "After all," wrote James L. Morrison, editor of Heth's memoirs, "he personally had set in motion the chain of events which culminated in disaster."[9]

A. P. Hill, though fully aware of Lee's intention to fight at Cashtown, had consented to Heth's march on Gettysburg. But this was not his worst blunder. When Heth reported that two of his brigades had been forced to retreat, Hill—apparently without consulting Lee—ordered him to renew the fight employing his whole division. In so doing, Hill delivered the final blow to Lee's carefully laid plans. In effect, he sealed the fate of the Army of Northern Virginia; it was impossible then for Lee to avoid total engagement before his forces were fully concentrated. He had no choice but to accept immediate, all-out battle on ground not of his own choosing.

Buford

But Lee was not entirely without blame, either. Before the march began, he emphatically cautioned Hill that Heth should not bring on a battle. Then, during the march, in an inexplicable about-face, Lee sent word to Heth that he should proceed with his mission *even if he encountered resistance*. Well, Heth did meet with resistance...and the rest is history.

The Federals had three things going for them this hot July morning: good leadership, fierce determination, and luck. The combination enabled them to sweep the enemy from the field. The first two elements warrant substantial elaboration. As to the third, it need only be remarked that it was sheer good fortune that Wadsworth's Division arrived when it did. To say it was in the nick of time is no exaggeration. Even ten minutes later would probably have spelled disaster for the Union. Also, it was pure luck that the 6th Wisconsin, 95th New York, and 14th Brooklyn were in just the right position at the right moment to mount a unified counterattack.

While Reynolds exhibited his usual high standard of leadership and his role cannot be minimized, it can nonetheless be argued that John Buford deserves even greater praise. Undeniably he played the pivotal role. If he had been deficient—less alert, less prepared, less diligent in keeping his chief informed, less capable of inspiring his dismounted troopers to hold on—all of Reynolds' efforts and expertise would have come too late.

Meade, in his battle report, singled out Buford and his cavalrymen for special praise, commending them for the "gallant manner" in which they held the enemy in check.[10] Meade's cavalry chief, Major General Alfred Pleasonton, in his appearance before the Joint Committee on the Conduct of the War, said: "To the intrepidity, courage and fidelity of General Buford and his brave division the country and the army owe the battlefield of Gettysburg. His unequal fight...and his saving the field, made Buford the true hero of that battle."[11] Alike in its import, though posed as a rhetorical question, is the tribute of battery commander Lieutenant John H. Calef: "...is it too much to claim for Gen. John Buford that he saved to us the strong position of Cemetery Ridge by his bulldog tenacity in clinging to the line of Willoughby Run until the arrival of the infantry?"[12]

A statue of Buford stands on McPherson's Ridge today. The tablet below the bronze figure informs us he "selected this battlefield." And in effect, at least, this is true. But one of Reynolds' aides, Lieutenant Joseph G. Rosengarten, went beyond that, proclaiming that the cavalry leader actually caused the battle. A debatable view, certainly, but nonetheless provocative. Said Rosengarten: "It was his [Buford's] foresight and energy, his pluck and self-reliance in thrusting forward his force, and pushing the enemy [on June 30] and thus inviting, almost compelling their return, that brought on the engagement of the first of July."[13]

If Buford hadn't been at Gettysburg, hadn't held back Heth's Brigades, hadn't impressed Reynolds with the need to hurry, the whole scenario of the battle would have been vastly altered. So reasoned Lieutenant Walter Kempster of Gregg's Cavalry Division. He went on to project what might have happened:

> ...receiving notice that the Federals were approaching on the Emmitsburg Road, General Heth, or any other officer possessing command sense, would have occupied Culp's Hill, Cemetery Ridge, and adjacent points as a matter of course, and the advantage of position would have been with the Confederates, and instead of Pickett's charge, it might have been Reynolds's, or Howard's, or Sickles's charge.[14]

After the war, Buford's signal officer, Lieutenant A. B. Jerome, felt strongly that his former chief was not getting the recognition he deserved. Writing to Major General Winfield S. Hancock on October 18, 1865, he complained:

> Yet, General, in all the parade that has taken place since [the war] of names and incidents, memories oratorical and poetical from [Edward] Everett to General Howard, have you not noticed that your friend the heroic Buford has been nearly disregarded? I was a young Lt. and staff officer, and loved the General, and I am sure you will pardon me if I call your attention to the injustice.

In the same letter he asked Hancock to "endeavor to bring Gen. Buford's name more prominently forward." He added, "Everyone knows that he 'in his day' was first and foremost."[15]

In succeeding years not only Hancock but many others would publicly praise Buford—from the orator's platform and in the press. As the word spread and the cavalry leader's courageous stand at Gettysburg began to be widely acclaimed, Jerome was certainly pleased that his idol was finally receiving his just due. Even to this day, dissenting voices have been very rare. William F. Fox, indefatigable Civil War researcher and author, was one. "There is no acceptable evidence that Buford fought a cavalry action on the morning of July 1 that amounted to much," he sniffed. Moreover, in view of the fame accorded the cavalryman for deploying his troopers in a dismounted line, Fox apparently felt obliged to point out (correctly) that the tactic was neither new nor innovative. He did acknowledge that Buford's stand delayed the enemy long enough for the Union infantry to come up, but carped that it lasted only "a very limited time."[16] But is that really relevant? What was accomplished—not how long it took— is surely the overriding consideration. But even in point of time, if the skirmishing prior to forming a dismounted line on McPherson's Ridge is taken into account, Buford's troopers were heavily engaged for more than two hours. In the opinion of historian J. O. Buckeridge, these were "two of the most vital hours in our nation's history."[17]

Another detractor was a Boston newspaperman who wrote under the pseudonym "Miles." He contended (in 1912) that, when a large Confederate force was reported approaching, Buford should have immediately pulled back to Marsh Creek, joining Wadsworth's Division. Or if he tarried until the enemy drew near, he should at least have withdrawn to Cemetery Hill. In Miles' opinion, since he did neither, "he cannot be acquited of an error of judgment which proved most disastrous to the Union army."[18] Miles obviously alluded to the events of the afternoon of July 1, but his verdict against Buford was unjust. He overlooked two salient facts: Reynolds did not intend that Buford should run at first sight of the enemy and, second, that if the Union cavalry had retreated to Cemetery Hill, Heth could have occupied Gettysburg.

As Buford's fame grew, Joseph Hooker, former commander of the Army of the Potomac, felt terribly slighted because his one-time subordinate got all the glory. After all, he protested, it was he who had had the foresight, on June 27, 1863, to order cavalry sent out "in the direction of Gettysburg and Emmitsburg" with the express purpose of ascertaining "what they can of the movements of the enemy."[19] Cavalry corps commander Alfred Pleasonton, learning of Hooker's bid for recognition, was nettled. The credit for cavalry being at Gettysburg, he firmly believed, was rightfully his. So he took up his pen and wrote Hooker, attempting to set the record straight as he saw it. "I considered it [Gettysburg] would be a point...which Lee would seek to occupy. My authority [to post a cavalry division there] was my own good sense in the matter...."[20] (The latter statement is not strictly true, for it was Meade who authorized him to send out the cavalry corps to guard the army's flanks. And it was with Meade's approval that Pleasonton posted Gregg's and Kilpatrick's Divisions on the right and Buford's Division on the left, at Gettysburg.)

Hooker, unconvinced by Pleasonton's letter, conceded nothing. But this was mere squabbling; Buford's fame was not diminished in the least by it. Even some Southerners paid him grudging tribute. One of these, Daniel H. Hill, Jr., admitted that John Buford "practically neutralized Archer's gallant brigade."[21] Union veteran James K. P. Scott, in his detailed account of the battle, praised Buford and his troopers for their stubborn resistance, adding: "By all rules of war, Heth should have pushed his column through and past Buford's thin lines on the ridges north of town, through its streets to the heights beyond—and there would have been no further battles at Gettysburg."[22] Historian Matthew F. Steele, in his monumental *American Campaigns*, declared the performance of Buford and his division "the most valuable day's work done by the cavalry in the Civil War."[23]

In view of all the glowing tributes from soldiers, historians, and the general public, Buford's own words on the subject seem positively modest. He said: "...a heavy task was before us; we were equal to it, and shall all remember with pride, that at Gettysburg we did our country much service."[24]

Reynolds

The death of General Reynolds was the single most tragic event of the first day's battle. Its full effect is beyond reckoning. Meade felt he had lost his right arm,[25] just as Lee did when Jackson was mortally wounded at Chancellorsville.

To Meade, Reynolds was "the noblest as well as the bravest gentleman in the army."[26] To General George B. McClellan, under whom Reynolds had also served, he was "remarkably brave and intelligent, an honest true gentleman."[27] To Captain Stephen Weld of Reynolds' staff, he was simply "the best general we had."[28] In every action, said historian Samuel P. Bates, "he displayed unsurpassed devotion and bravery."

> If he had any fault [Bates continued], it was one which must excite the admiration and quicken the pulse of him who contemplates it—that of too much exposing himself in the hour of battle.... Little less than a miracle had thus far preserved him. But at Gettysburg he was in a more exalted position, having the command of nearly half of the army, and a due regard to its preservation and safety demanded that he should exercise care of his person. His own safety, however, was the least of his cares. He knew that the two armies

were rapidly approaching each other, and collision could not long be avoided. The choice of the field and the initiative of the battle was in his eyes all-important, and he determined to push to the front and decide everything from personal observation; and who will say that he did not do right?[29]

Almost inevitably, some did. The criticism of Reynolds by artillery officer Wainwright, author Battine, and infantry officer Livermore has already been given in an earlier chapter. Briefly restated, the first two believed the Union leader should have elected to defend a ridge other than McPherson's, but they disagreed on which one. Colonel Wainwright opted for Seminary Ridge; Cecil Battine for Cemetery Ridge.[30] The argument in either case is weak in light of the initial success of Reynolds' troops in the position he chose. Colonel Thomas Livermore, on the other hand, maintained that Reynolds should have "retired on the rest of the army" rather than risk disaster in a position that had "no merit." He did allow, however, that for Reynolds—being the dedicated soldier he was, and in addition a native Pennsylvanian—to abandon the town of Gettysburg to the enemy was unthinkable.[31]

In 1886 Reynolds' staff officer Joseph G. Rosengarten noted: "It has often been hinted, rather than asserted, that Reynolds was the victim of his own rashness, that he heedlessly and impetuously engaged the enemy in an overwhelming force, and was not ready to open battle nor right in doing so."[32] Given Rosengarten's known loyalty to his chief, it can be safely assumed he did not personally share this view. He mentioned no names of those who did, but Livermore (though his negative appraisal came later) is a case in point.

Another instance is that of "Miles," the newspaper columnist who criticized Buford. He also had disparaging words for both Reynolds and Meade. The army commander's ordering of the First Corps to Gettysburg he deemed "strategically unsound." But Reynolds, he said, was even more to blame for recklessly plunging into combat. This he attributed to the general's "ardor [which] may well have overcome his prudence."[33] These statements are hardly more than the facile conclusions of an armchair general and should be regarded as such.

By and large, commentators on the battle, both military and civilian, have had only praise for John Fulton Reynolds. "The very energy of Reynolds' attack deceived the Rebel general and made him cautious," wrote Major General Oliver Howard. He felt strongly that had Reynolds been less aggressive, Wadsworth's Division might have been crushed.[34] Colonel Wainwright, in his diary entry for July 1, 1863, said of the revered leader:

To his death much of our loss afterward was doubtless owing. Not that I think we would not have had to fall back here had he not been killed, for the enemy outnumbered us three to one; but it would have been done in better order, with half the loss to ourselves and much more to the enemy.[35]

Years later, Rosengarten echoed Wainwright's belief, affirming that if his chief had lived he would somehow have managed "an orderly withdrawal to Cemetery Ridge."[36]

Brigadier General John C. Robinson believed the fight on the first afternoon of the battle would have gone better for the Union had Reynolds been in charge. In that event, he declared, "there would have been a different history of that battle."[37]

A century later, Glenn Tucker, in his *Lee and Longstreet at Gettysburg*, mirrored the views of Wainwright, Rosengarten, and Robinson. He wrote:

> Had Reynolds survived, it is not likely the defeat of the Federal army on the first day at Gettysburg would have developed into such a violent debacle. He was competent and could have conducted an orderly withdrawal to Cemetery Hill without fighting the battle north of the town, where Howard's Eleventh Corps was broken by the arrival of Early's Division on its flank.[38]

In 1960 Warren W. Hassler, Jr. provided an incisive rebuttal to Cecil Battine and others who argued that Reynolds should have immediately fallen back on Cemetery Ridge. Such a move, he contended, would "in all probability, have been disastrous." The Confederates, he pointed out, were able to amass troops on the field faster than the Federals. And, if the Federals had invested Cemetery Ridge at the outset, the swelling Confederate force would have had the greater part of the day in which to drive them off and no doubt would have succeeded. Then, from those heights, the Southerners would have commanded the three roads from the south and the arrival of Union reinforcements from that direction would have been seriously compromised. Hassler concluded: "Reynold's decision to sacrifice, if necessary, Buford's cavalry division and the First Corps, and even the Eleventh Corps, while taking as heavy a toll as possible of Lee's soldiers, was the wise and soldierly-like move to make."[39]

One can only speculate what the result might have been if Reynolds had accepted Lincoln's offer to lead the Army of the Potomac. Certainly he would have prosecuted the battle with skill, sound judgement, and the utmost vigor. Most likely he would have come out of it alive. And, assuming the situation at the close of the battle was the same as Meade faced, it can be confidently asserted that his pursuit of Lee's bedraggled army would not have been dilatory or half-hearted, as Meade's was, but rather it would have been swift and relentless. (As Gus Buell of Stewart's battery put it, had Reynolds been in charge, "Lee would have had a much livelier time getting back into Virginia than he did.")[40] Conceivably, under Reynolds, the Army of the Potomac might have destroyed the Army of Northern Virginia, and with that the Confederacy would have collapsed.

In any case, the statement of Edwin B. Coddington concerning Reynolds seems incontestable: "If the fates had decreed other than they did, he might have gone down in history as one of the greatest generals of the Civil War."[41]

Other Union Leaders

For both Doubleday and Howard, elevation to field command during a battle was a new experience. How well did they cope?

Colonel Wainwright considered Doubleday "a weak reed to lean upon."[42] A friend of Meade's, Captain William Rawle, testified that the general had no confidence in Doubleday, which explains why he put Major General John Newton in charge of the

First Corps on July 2, with Doubleday reverting to his former division command.[43] Yet, after stripping away Doubleday's bombast and overweening self-justification, one is still left with a solid impression of competent leadership. He was alert to the threat developing on the right flank and sent the 6th Wisconsin racing to counteract it. Prudently he recalled the Iron Brigade to McPherson's Ridge after the rout of Archer's Brigade and reestablished a strong line of defense there. On the other hand, his claiming credit for organizing the attack that led to Archer's defeat is without basis.

Major R. L. Ashhurst, adjutant of the 150th Pennsylvania, lauded Abner Doubleday and his subordinate commanders for "the skill and boldness with which the command was handled after Reynolds' death."[44] Nevertheless, in his official report and again in his *Chancellorsville and Gettysburg*, Doubleday felt compelled to defend his actions. In the former, referring to the lull before the fight reopened, he wrote: "...it might seem, in view of the fact that we were finally forced to retreat, that this would have been a proper time to retire...." But, since Reynolds "had formed his lines to resist the entrance of the enemy into Gettysburg, I naturally supposed that it was the intention to defend the place." Furthermore, "A retreat without hard fighting has a tendency to demoralize the troops...and would...in my opinion, have dispirited the whole army...while it encouraged the enemy in the same proportion." Then, apparently in case he had not sufficiently vindicated himself, he passed the buck to his immediate superior, Major General Oliver Howard. Still referring to the option of withdrawing from the battleground west of Gettysburg, Doubleday stated that "if circumstances required it, it was his place, not mine, to issue the order."[45]

It was never a secret that Doubleday held Howard in low esteem. But despite his persistent denigration of the Eleventh Corps commander, the fact remains that Howard, too, gave a creditable performance in the morning of July 1. On learning of Reynolds' death, he was quick to grasp the reins of full command, quick to deploy the troops then at hand to confront Ewell's infantry sweeping down from the north, quick to realize the key importance of Cemetery Hill and to secure it for the Union. Although Doubleday thought him unpardonably remiss in not consulting him sooner, there is no evidence of dallying on Howard's part; more urgent matters simply intervened. To those who claimed he was slow in bringing up his corps, Howard responded with some asperity: "The men did not move too slowly for a hot July day."[46]

Wadsworth and his brigade leaders, Cutler and Meredith, served their commands well, each making a notable contribution to the total effort. Sixth Wisconsin's Rufus Dawes singled out Wadsworth for special praise, stating that he seemed to be everywhere and (like Reynolds) was "absolutely fearless in exposing himself to danger."[47] In general, officers at the regimental and company levels provided leadership of high quality. Of course they were not all equally efficient, equally inspiring. "All the officers, with one or two exceptions, behaved well," wrote Major Edward Pye in his after-action report for the 95th New York. Probably that was true of some other regiments as well.[48]

Valor

Luck and good leadership alone would not have turned the tide in favor of the Federals at Willoughby Run. Accomplishing that required a third element: determination, the true grit of the man on the firing line.

There was no better example of this in the first morning of the Battle of Gettysburg than the heroic stand of the 147th New York. Isolated, outnumbered, and nearly hemmed in, the regiment continued to fight, though its right had been refused and its commander wounded. All along the crooked line men were dropping, cut down in a murderous crossfire. "The smoke of carnage rose as an incense and wrapped the folds of the flag defended within its shortened lines," wrote Lieutenant J. V. Pierce. "Not a man flinched; none left the field except the wounded; the untouched living and the dead remained."[49] It was little short of a miracle that, at the very last minute, the all-too-few survivors were able to make good their retreat.

Doubleday, in his battle report, noted the "particularly distinguished" performance of the 2nd Wisconsin.[50] The commendation was well deserved. This regiment, it will be recalled, led the Iron Brigade's advance up McPherson's Ridge and immediately on crossing over the crest was hit by a massive volley from Archer's Brigade, then charging up the opposite slope. The Wisconsin regiment reeled from the stunning blow. Less-disciplined troops, in all likelihood, would have buckled right then and high-tailed it back down the slope. But not Colonel Fairchild's veterans. Although totally on their own in those critical first minutes of the engagement—three hundred infantrymen facing a whole brigade—the Badger State boys quickly recovered from the initial shock and plunged into the fray with grim determination. Before their sister regiments joined them, they had begun to drive the Rebels out of Herbst's Woods and back toward Willoughby Run. Such valor, not surprisingly, exacted a stiff penalty—casualties exceeding one-third of their number.

The contribution made by the two Union batteries cannot be overestimated. Without it, Buford's cavalry and Wadsworth's infantry would have been hard pressed to maintain their positions. The crews of Calef's and Hall's Batteries worked their guns with unflagging zeal, subjecting the Confederate force to constant harrassment. Since Hall's guns replaced Calef's, each battery in its turn had to contend singlehandedly with the five Confederate batteries of Pegram's Battalion.

With his three 2-gun sections widely separated and all firing intensely, Lieutenant Calef may have deceived Confederate General Heth (as the lieutenant later claimed) into thinking there was more Union artillery against him than really existed.[51] In any event, he certainly made him wary, causing him to proceed with caution, thus gaining precious time for Wadsworth's Division to come to Buford's relief. It seems no exaggeration on the part of Brigadier General Henry Hunt, Meade's chief of artillery, when he flatly declared it was the action of this battery that enabled Buford's cavalrymen to hold their line until the infantry arrived.[52] The cavalry leader himself described the effect Calef and his cannoneers had on the enemy as "wonderful."[53]

Calef, writing his after-action report, commended his men, particularly noting the "coolness and intrepidity" of his section chiefs "during the hottest of the firing."[54]

Reynolds was aware of the risk involved when he assigned Hall's Battery to a position on McPherson's Ridge ahead of the infantry; nevertheless, from a tactical standpoint, he felt it justified. From this precarious position, Hall's gun crews valiantly supported the infantry—as long as they could. Then, with time running out, they made a daring escape. Many years later, reflecting on how lucky he had been, Hall wrote: "If I should be asked if I could again take the Second Maine Battery as it was July 1, 1863, into that action, do what we then did, and get away with so little loss, I would answer, 'I do not think I could.'"[55]

Courage, tenacity, initiative, compassion, endurance, devotion to duty—all were abundantly displayed by the fighting men of both sides. Yet, although in retrospect they seem to have been paragons of soldierly conduct and virtue, at heart they were just civilians in military attire. An incident of the morning's fight, though trivial in itself, illustrates with engaging honesty what must have been the sentiment of most of them, regardless of rank.

A Union officer riding into battle happened to notice a rabbit running lickety-split to the rear. He was overheard to exclaim: "Molly Cotton-tail! If I had not a reputation at stake I would be with you."[56] But reputations—and loyalty to the Cause, whether Union or Confederate—*were* at stake. Except when compelled by injury or insuperable odds, Yankees and Rebels by and large resisted the natural impulse to leave, stood their ground, and fought on.

Envoy

In 1875 an ex-Confederate major, addressing veterans of Lee's Army of Northern Virginia, made this deft comparison: "Such is war—a game of skill and chance—a game of chess and 'blind man's buff' compounded together."[57] The analogy is apt, and strikingly so in relation to the events that took place on both sides of Willoughby Run on the first morning of July 1863.

Nor would all that followed be much different. After the midday pause in the hostilities, the desperate game resumed. Over the next two and a half days there would be more moves and countermoves calling upon the skill of the players, blue and gray. And there would be the same monumental groping in the dark for tactical advantage, for the means to final victory.

Chapter XI

CONTROVERSIES

Who fired the first shot in the Battle of Gettysburg?

AUTHOR'S CONCLUSION: An anonymous soldier of either side from a position *north* of Gettysburg. Thus it was either a skirmisher of Ewell's Corps or a picket of Devin's Brigade. If the latter, the most likely possibility seems to be a member of the 17th Pennsylvania picket battalion commanded by Major J. Q. Anderson. Posted three miles north of town, this was the first unit to confront Confederate skirmishers.

BASIS FOR CONCLUSION: Regimental histories of the 9th New York Cavalry (Cheney, pp. 107-108) and 17th Pennsylvania Cavalry (Moyer, pp. 61-62); *New York at Gettysburg* (Vol. III, p. 1153); *Pennsylvania at Gettysburg* (Vol II, pp. 885-887); *Battles and Leaders* (Vol. III, p. 275).

As Chapter III has shown, the action north of Gettysburg preceded the encounter west of town on the Chambersburg Pike. However, since this encounter between Gamble's advance pickets and Heth's Division led directly to, and in a sense actually precipitated, the major battle, it seems in order to rephrase the original question.

Who fired the first shot in the initial encounter west of Gettysburg?

AUTHOR'S CONCLUSION: Lieutenant Marcellus E. Jones, Company E, 8th Illinois Cavalry.

BASIS FOR CONCLUSION: Articles by H. O. Dodge (*National Tribune*, 9/24/1891) and Ezra B. Fuller (*Journal of U. S. Cavalry Association*, Vol. XXIV, p. 793); Major J. L. Beveridge's account included in *Gettysburg Papers* (Vol. I, pp.173-174); Vautier's history of the 88th Pennsylvania (p. 117).

A small monument stands today on the spot where Lieutenant Jones fired his historic shot. It was placed there by Jones himself and three comrades at their own expense. Their action was undeniably self-serving; but it is not unlikely they viewed it as a tangible way to establish the supremacy of Jones' claim over all others. To the extent that his was the first shot fired against *the principal enemy force* on the morning of July 1, they were justified.

Before taking up a discussion of conflicting claims, two points should be made. First, every claim placed the Union soldier involved in the vicinity of the Chambersburg Pike. Second, it is recognized that the matter of who fired the first shot — albeit a fascinating topic — has no tactical significance whatsoever.

The controversy has revolved primarily around Lieutenant Jones' claim versus that of Corporal Alpheus Hodges, Company F, 9th New York Cavalry. The latter has not lacked adherents over the years. Authors Vanderslice, Young, Catton, Bellah, and Stackpole all accepted the claim for Hodges and repeated the incident first described by Captain Newel Cheney in a paper written for New York State's Gettysburg Monument Commission. The claim gained wide currency when Cheney's account was quoted in 1887 in *Battles and Leaders* (Vol. III, p. 275). Cheney himself retold the story, adding a few details, in his history of the 9th New York Cavalry (p. 106), published in 1901. Substantially the same account appeared the following year in *New York at Gettysburg* (Volume III, p. 1153) and again in 1908, in Hall's *History of the 6th New York Cavalry* (p. 137).

There is no problem with the incident Cheney relates; the problem lies with *when* he says it occurred. Briefly stated, Corporal Hodges and three privates, on vedette duty east of Willoughby Run, spotted Rebels a mile ahead. Hodges rode toward them, was fired at, raced back across the bridge over the run, dismounted, and fired his carbine at the approaching enemy. According to Cheney, the incident occurred about 5:30 a.m., but he added the qualification "as near as Hodges can remember."

Corporal Hodges' recollection as to the hour was quite erroneous, since Heth's Division did not begin the march until 5:00, at the earliest, and the starting point was about seven miles west of Willoughby Run. Furthermore, the Confederates' first point of contact with the enemy had to be Gamble's westernmost outpost — the one commanded by Lieutenant Jones — and that did not occur until 7:30. When Jones fired, Heth's troops halted, reorganized, and then had to march a mile or so before Hodges and his companions could have spied their vanguard. Thus, Hodges' confrontation had to take place much later than it was claimed. Around 8:30, as a matter of fact. (The incident is related in detail in Chapter IV.)

Less well known is the claim of Private F. W. Whitney, Company B, 17th Pennsylvania Cavalry, who averred that it was he — not Jones or Hodges — who fired the first shot. Sparse in detail and totally lacking corroboration, the claim is unconvincing. According to Whitney, while he was on picket duty on the Chambersburg Pike, he saw the enemy approaching and opened fire. The time, he said, was shortly before 6:00 a.m.. If Whitney had been on one of the roads north of Gettysburg, where many in his regiment were stationed, his claim would at least be feasible. But he specifically stated he was on the Chambersburg Pike.

H. P. Moyer, who related the incident in his *History of the 17th Pennsylvania* (p. 373), evidently had reservations about it, for he commented "whether this be true or not."

Even more obscure is the claim of an unnamed trooper in the 6th New York. James L. McClean, Jr. mentions it in his comprehensive article, "The First Union Shot at

Gettysburg," (*Lincoln Herald*, Spring, 1980, pp. 318-323). He came across it in *Illinois Monuments at Gettysburg*, an 1891 Illinois State publication.

According to this anonymous source, the trooper fired the first shot at dawn. While on picket duty (presumably in the 6th New York's sector east of Willoughby Run between the Chambersburg Pike and the Mummasburg Road), he heard a noise, thought enemy cavalry were coming, and simply fired. The man must have had a bad case of jitters; there was no enemy cavalry within miles of him. Nonetheless, it must be admitted that he could have fired his carbine at the time he said. Indeed, there may have been other unreported instances of nervous, trigger-happy pickets firing at nothing. To qualify for the distinction of firing the first shot, however, a *sine qua non* would have to be that an enemy was at least in sight!

A number of authors in this century have claimed that the reason Buford's troopers performed so admirably against a larger enemy force can be attributed to their employment of seven-shot Spencer repeating firearms. They differ, however, on the degree to which Buford's Division was so armed (partial or total) and also as to type of weapon (carbine or rifle).

On the other hand, some authors have totally rejected the claim of enhanced performance due to Spencer firearms.

What role, if any, did Spencer repeating firearms play in the remarkable resistance of Buford's Division to the Confederate advance?

AUTHOR'S CONCLUSION: A very minor role. And the relatively few Spencers used would have been rifles, not carbines.

On June 3, 1863, the Spencer Repeating Rifle Company made application to U. S. Army Ordnance to manufacture 11,000 repeating carbines at a cost of $25 each. Six weeks passed before the application was approved and production could begin.[1] The Spencer carbine would prove so efficient that it would be adopted late in 1863 as the standard arm of the Union cavalry.[2] By war's end 64,685 had been sold to Mr. Lincoln's army.[3] But at the time of the Battle of Gettysburg, the first one had yet to be made.

The Spencer repeating *rifle*, however, was then available. Two of Custer's cavalry regiments definitely carried them at Gettysburg.[4] Buford's case is not so clear-cut. Officers who could be expected to report the use of a superior new firearm — one that fired five times faster than the ordinary musket — are silent on the subject. Captain Albert M. Mills (8th New York) stated only that both of Buford's Brigades were "armed with carbines."[5] And Captain H. E. Dana (8th Illinois) simply reported that "firing was rapid from our carbines."[6] Ordnance reports indicate they were single-shot breechloaders. Captain William L. Heermance (6th New York) mentioned the existence of Spencer repeating rifles in Custer's Brigade, but gave no hint of any in Buford's Division.[7]

Yet, at Manassas Junction fifteen days earlier, Buford had received an allotment of these rifles, and a "limited distribution" was made.[8] Just how many companies were involved is unknown, but the lucky troopers with the new improved rifles had the chance to break them in the next day, June 17, in the fighting at Aldie, Virginia. Sergeant Joseph A. McCabe of Company A, 17th Pennsylvania, left no doubt about their effectiveness and reliability: "The field was literally covered with dead and wounded — our Spencer rifles never failed us."[9]

Assuredly, then, this company fired Spencer rifles at Gettysburg. The "limited distribution" may have included one or two additional companies in the 17th Pennsylvania. As to the other regiments, all evidence points to their *not* having Spencers.

So, even though the Spencer repeating rifle played only a minor role, it made a vivid impression on at least one Rebel. Captured in the morning's battle, he remarked to his Yankee captors, "What you all do — load on Sunday and fire all week!"[10]

Who was the first Union soldier killed in the Battle of Gettysburg?

AUTHOR'S CONCLUSION: Impossible to determine. All claims are partisan, of course, and unfortunately too sketchy to pinpoint time of occurrence. However, the first Union fatality may have been Cyrus W. James, Company G, 9th New York Cavalry.

Corporal James was killed during a skirmish with Ewell's troops north of Gettysburg.[11] His death probably occurred before the onset of fighting west of Gettysburg, where all the other claimants are presumed to have been killed. Separate claims arose for two 12th Illinois troopers, Private Ferdinand Ushuer and Sergeant Gabriel B. Durham. Ushuer was killed by a shell from Marye's battery.[12] Nothing is known of the circumstances of Sergeant Durham's death, but his Company I comrades placed a "small shaft" on the spot where he fell. The shaft (most likely a crude wooden marker) has since vanished. But a member of Durham's company recalled the inscription on it. According to Homer Calkins, it consisted of the deceased's name, rank, unit, and these words: "The first soldier killed at Gettysburg fell here."[13] Among 3rd Indiana troopers it was claimed their own John E. Weaver was the first fatality in the battle.[14] In the same regiment — though no claim was ever lodged for him — Major Charles Lemon may have been the first officer, Union or Confederate, to be killed at Gettysburg.[15]

Who was the first Confederate soldier killed in the Battle of Gettysburg?

AUTHOR'S CONCLUSION: Again, impossible to determine. It may have been the skirmisher in Ewell's Corps who was shot dead by marksman Daniel Cornish of the 9th New York. Or it may have been another unknown soldier in Ewell's Corps.

It was not Henry Rison (or Raison), for whom the only Confederate claim has ever been made. He — a private in Company B, 7th Tennessee — was killed later in the morning, as Archer's Brigade descended Herr Ridge. The claim surfaced in the May 1885 issue of *The Southern Bivouac*. The author of the article, A. H. Moore, had served in Rison's company.[16] Moore's claim was repeated seven months later in an article by Colonel William H. Swallow in the same magazine.[17] In succeeding years other writers accepted and published it.[18]

Worthy of mention, though unrelated to this controversy, are two deaths that occurred prior to the battle.

On June 22, 1863, Corporal William H. Rihl of the 1st New York Cavalry was fatally wounded near Greencastle, Pennsylvania, shot in the jaw by one of Jenkins' Confederate cavalrymen. He is believed to be the first Union soldier killed on Union soil in the Gettysburg campaign.[19] The very first fatality at Gettysburg occurred on June 26, during the visit of Early's Division. That day two troopers of Company B, 21st Pennsylvania Cavalry, were riding near the Baltimore Pike when suddenly they encountered enemy pickets. The Rebels opened fire. One trooper got away safely. The other, George W. Sandoe—a local boy who had enlisted only six days before—was killed.[20]

Is the 10:10 a.m. heading on Buford's dispatch to Meade a reliable indication of the time of the events described therein?

AUTHOR'S CONCLUSION: No. It simply does not fit.[21] To be consonant with prior and subsequent events, the dispatch had to be written about 9:00.

Point 1: In the dispatch Buford informed Meade that the enemy were *then* advancing and "driving my pickets and skirmishers very rapidly." As he was certainly aware of that fact before 9:00, it is unlikely that he would have waited more than an hour to tell the army commander. Moreover, before 10:10 his skirmishers west of Willoughby Run had fallen back on the division's dismounted line.

Point 2: Buford also informed Meade that Reynolds and his leading division were *then* "within three miles of this point." Since Wadsworth's Division had started its march at 8:00, it would have reached the position Buford indicated about 9:00. At 10:10 these troops — as Wadsworth and others have confirmed — were deploying in battle line.

Point 3: In light of Buford's statement about Reynolds' whereabouts, the dispatch was obviously written before they met. Apart from this dispatch, all evidence points to that meeting taking place between 9:15 and 9:30.

Point 4: In the afternoon Buford informed General Pleasonton that "a tremendous battle has been raging since 9:30" [*OR* 43, pp. 924-925]. At what point would he have considered the engagement, which began with sporadic skirmish fire, a "raging" battle? Doubtless when Heth's Division launched a full-scale attack from Herr Ridge.[22] Therefore, if Buford had written to Meade after 9:30, his message would have been radically different.

In sum, the dispatch in question had to be written *while* Buford's skirmishers were being driven in, *when* Reynolds' troops were about three miles off, and *before* the Union generals met and the Confederate attack began. The time frame that best fits all conditions is 8:50 to 9:10.

Where did Reynolds and Buford meet — at the Lutheran Theological Seminary or on McPherson's Ridge?

AUTHOR'S CONCLUSION: At the Seminary.

BASIS FOR CONCLUSION: The testimony of Buford's signal officer, members of Reynolds' and Doubleday's staffs, and Doubleday himself. (Buford, in his battle report, was silent on the matter.)

At the heart of the controversy are the statements of signal Lieutenant A. B. Jerome and Reynolds' orderly, Charles H. Veil. Jerome, who was on duty in the Seminary cupola on July 1, gave a firsthand account of the meeting, even including the shouted salutations of Reynolds and Buford.[23] Veil, constantly at Reynolds' side this morning, was thus in as good a position as Jerome to know what really happened. In a letter written nine months after the battle, he gave the strong impression that Reynolds rode directly to McPherson's Ridge and met Buford there.

This letter to Gettysburg resident David McConaughy needs to be examined. Veil's exact words were: "When we got into town we saw that there was considerable excitement so the Genl rode to the front at once — found Genl Buford engaged on ridge in front of Seminary...."[24] At face value the statement seems conclusive. Yet another interpretation lies beyond the literal one. Veil could well have employed metonomy in referring to Buford being engaged, letting the commander's name stand for his whole division, which was in fact then engaged on McPherson's Ridge. Thus, the assumption of Buford himself being at the Seminary and meeting Reynolds there is not unreasonable. As to Reynolds riding at once to the front, the Seminary, which stood only about 800 yards behind Buford's dismounted line, would hardly be disqualified.

Historian Edwin B. Coddington argues that it seems "more logical" that Buford would have been on the front line "when the situation was getting tight" rather than at the Seminary[25]; and that is true. But, in any event, Buford actually did ride back to the Seminary during the fight, as a number of contemporary accounts attest.[26]

Veil himself would eventually set the record straight. In 1908, in his memoirs, he wrote: "Gen. Reynolds sent orders...wrote a note to Gen. Meade...then rode rapidly into Gettysburg and out to *Seminary Ridge* to Buford."[27] (Italics added.)

Like Veil in his 1864 letter, Captain Stephen Weld of Reynolds' staff made no reference to stopping at the Seminary. In his diary entry for July 1 he wrote that Reynolds rode through town "and a mile out on the other side, where he found General Buford and the cavalry engaging the enemy...." Again, it appears that Reynolds went directly to McPherson's Ridge. But Weld was grief-stricken over his chief when he wrote the entry ("I cannot realize that he is dead") and may have completely forgotten about the episode at the Seminary, which, after all, was brief.[28]

Another Reynolds' aide, Lieutenant Joseph Rosengarten, gave two versions of the meeting. In 1871 he wrote: "[Reynolds] went through the town and out on the Chambersburg pike, where he met General Buford, and with him made an examination of the ground in front of the town."[29] In 1885 he specifically stated that the meeting took place at the Seminary.[30] Writing for the *New York Times Magazine* in 1913, he repeated the later version.[31]

What can be said about Lieutenant Aaron Brainard Jerome, on whose testimony the meeting at the Seminary primarily depends? Did he fabricate a story, replete with dialogue, to add luster to his role in the battle? Or did he tell the truth? Buford spoke highly of his signal officer's services at Gettysburg, saying he "was ever on the alert, and through his intrepidity...kept me advised of the enemy's movements when no other means were available."[32] Later, with Admiral Porter in the Red River expedition and with Admiral Farragut at Mobile Bay, he served with distinction.[33] Nowhere in the record is there any indication of a lack of integrity, nor is there any evidence of a penchant for self-glorification. Major General Winfield S. Hancock believed in Jerome's veracity to the extent that he appended his written endorsement to the Jerome account that J. Watts DePeyster used in *The Decisive Conflicts of the Late Civil War*.[34]

As we have seen, the later testimony of Veil and Rosengarten both support the Jerome account. But there is more. George E. Jepson of Reynolds' headquarters company wrote: "The General galloped out to the Lutheran Seminary, where Buford was anxiously awaiting his chief."[35] Major E. P. Halstead corroborated Reynolds' presence at the Seminary. It was there, he said, that he "overtook" Reynolds and delivered a message from Doubleday.[36] And Doubleday, though not an eye-witness, was nonetheless convinced that Reynolds joined Buford at the Seminary and so reported it in 1875 and again in 1882.[37]

Reynolds reconnoitered the battlefield and environs from the cupola of the Lutheran Seminary — fact or myth?

AUTHOR'S CONCLUSION: Myth, almost certainly.

BASIS FOR CONCLUSION: The absence of any convincing evidence that Reynolds ever set foot in the cupola, and a strong argument — by virtue of omission — that he did not. Lieutenant Jerome, who was in the cupola the entire time and who later reported Buford's visits and the meeting of Reynolds and Buford in great detail, made no mention of a visit from Reynolds.

Nevertheless, the image of Reynolds standing tall and heroic in the cupola had undeniable romantic appeal. Not surprisingly, it was widely disseminated in both word and picture. The following example appeared in 1867: "...as Reynolds showed himself on the summit of the Seminary building, the glory of that midsummer day and the occasion seemed actually to invest him with an aureola." The author, J. Watts DePeyster, coyly declined to name his source but said his informant was "so earnest" that he believed him.[38] Earnest or not, the description has a most spurious ring to it. Imagine — nature conspiring to give Reynolds a halo!

Another writer who placed Reynolds in the cupola was none other than General Abner Doubleday. It can be argued that he had an ulterior purpose in doing so. In his long- running feud with General O. O. Howard after the war, he sought to nullify the acclaim accorded Howard for recognizing the tactical importance of Cemetery Hill. The credit, he contended, belonged to Reynolds. In his ardor to support his thesis, he may have gotten carried away. In any case, he envisaged Reynolds and Buford side by side in the cupola, with Buford "pointing out the different localities and explaining their advantages and disadvantages with reference to the coming battle and as he had time to make himself thoroughly acquainted with the country he could hardly have failed to call Reynolds' attention to the most prominent features of the landscape."[39] Reading this, one would think Reynolds had all the time in the world. Actually there was none to spare. A battle was about to erupt and both Reynolds and Buford knew it.

George E. Jepson of Reynolds' headquarters company and the First Corps historian, J. H. Stine, also stated that Reynolds and Buford surveyed the field from atop the Seminary.[40] But they, like DePeyster and Doubleday, were not eye-witnesses and therefore subject to misinformation.

Those who were on the scene and could have confirmed the event had it occurred, did not. This is especially significant in the case of Buford's signal officer, Lieutenant Jerome. Since he gave such a detailed account of the Reynolds-Buford meeting,[41] it is inconceivable that he would have failed to mention Reynolds' presence in the cupola.

Certainly the situation Reynolds faced when he arrived on the field militated against his going up into Jerome's observation post, however instructive the visit might have been. Time was of the essence. His outward composure must have belied an inner anxiety — first, to check on the immediate situation at McPherson's Ridge and, second, to get back to Wadsworth's Division and spur those troops forward. To spend even minutes in the cupola would have simply delayed the accomplishment of both objectives.

Who killed Reynolds?

AUTHOR'S CONCLUSION: An infantryman in Archer's front rank, not a sharpshooter concealed in a tree. Possibly it was Private Tom Hendrix of Company F, 13th Alabama; it was most assuredly not sharpshooter Ben Thorpe of the 55th North Carolina.

BASIS FOR CONCLUSIONS (principal sources): The accounts of Charles Veil (Reynold's orderly), Lt. J. G. Rosengarten (on Reynold's staff), Eleanor Reynolds (his sister), Lt. Col. W. W. Dudley (19th Indiana), Capt. W. H. Harries (2nd Wisconsin),

Capt. W. P. Tolley (1st Tennessee), and enlisted men W. H. Moon and E. T. Boland (13th Alabama).

Evidently word of Reynolds' death spread like wildfire. Lieutenant Francis Wiggin of Reynolds' headquarters company heard it from a passing orderly.[42] Captain James Stewart heard it as he rode back to his battery after talking with Colonel Devin.[43] Colonel Chapman Biddle heard it while leading his brigade to McPherson's Ridge.[44] Before long, newspaper correspondents got wind of the tragedy. Many of them repeated the hearsay then rife — that a Rebel sharpshooter fired the fatal shot.[45] Typically, their dispatches placed the marksman in the branches of a tree, but one had him concealed in a stone barn.[46] (Even a member of Reynolds' staff slipped up on this point. Lieutenant Rosengarten once remarked that the Confederate who shot his chief was "almost overhead." In other statements, however, both prior and subsequent to this one, he plainly indicated that Reynolds was killed by a soldier with both feet on the ground.)[47]

The sharpshooter story seems to have had little currency in the South until 1885, when ex-Confederate Colonel William H. Swallow wrote an account of the Gettysburg battle for the *Southern Bivouac*. In describing Reynolds' death he largely repeated the sharpshooter-in-tree accounts of Northern writers. However, he did add one dramatic, though fanciful, detail. Reynolds, he wrote, was "brandishing his sword and issuing orders" when the ball struck him.[48]

The most intriguing account surfaced, by pure chance, in 1902.

In the fall of that year a party of Yankee hunters stopped at a small farm near Satterwhite, North Carolina. Benjamin Thorpe (whose farm it was) got to talking to his unexpected visitors. He seemed friendly, eager to chat, but when they said they were from Lancaster County, in Pennsylvania, they noticed he appeared upset and somehow sad. The mention of "Lancaster" had triggered the change. John Reynolds, he remembered — could he ever forget? — was buried there. Thorpe apparently felt his obvious change in mood called for an explanation. He told them he had been a sharpshooter during the Civil War and for nearly forty years had been haunted by the certainty that he had killed the esteemed General Reynolds. "Not until long afterward," he continued, "did I learn who it was my bullet brought down, and when I did learn, when I heard and read of what a great and good man and splendid soldier I had brought to death, I was genuinely sorry. I have been sorry ever since...."[49] His visitors listened with rapt attention as Thorpe told his story in full detail. When he finished, they knew it was too good to keep to themselves.

Thus, on November 7, 1902, residents of Lancaster and surrounding communities belatedly learned how their distinguished native son, John Fulton Reynolds, happened to be killed back in '63. With consuming interest, they read the article that appeared that day in the *Lancaster Intelligencer*.

A Confederate sharpshooter named Ben Thorpe (they were informed) was perched in a cherry tree, his rifle cradled in his arms, when his superior, Captain Henry Webb, called up to him: "Look to your right, at the battery on the hill, there. There's a general; take him!" Webb peered through his fieldglasses, judged the range to be 1,100 yards, and told Thorpe to try that. But the lanky sixteen-year-old's first shot was much too high. He fired again, this time at 900 yards. "You are yet too high. Bring it down a trifle," Webb advised. Compensating for 800 yards, Thorpe took careful aim and fired a third time. Webb, seeing the distant figure fall, exclaimed: "Well done, Thorpe; you got him!"[50]

But did he really kill Reynolds? For one thing, as Veil himself pointed out four days after the article appeared, the general was not posting a battery when he was shot.[51] For another, Reynolds, who had not quite exited Herbst's Woods when the minie ball struck, would have been screened by innumerable trees. A sharpshooter 800 yards away could not possibly have seen him. Therefore, the answer must be a resounding No.

Thorpe's lifelong remorse was totally unfounded!

On the extreme left of the 13th Alabama, the men of Company F tramped through Herbst's Woods toward an enemy they could not see but knew were there. Then, suddenly, a great many Yankees materialized in their front. Private John Hendrix spied a mounted Union officer among them, took aim, and fired. He and the soldier beside him, Private E. T. Boland (who later recounted the incident), both saw the officer fall from his horse. Subsequently, the two privates — along with fifteen others of their company — were taken prisoner. As they were led under guard through Gettysburg, they overheard the news that the famous General Reynolds had been killed. An astounded Hendrix turned to Boland, still by his side. *That was the man I shot!* he exclaimed. Years later Boland returned to the battlefield and saw the monument marking the spot where Reynolds fell. "I inspected the ground," he wrote, "and I can truthfully say at that spot John Hendrix shot a man off his horse."[52]

Boland's account is reinforced by the testimony of another enlisted man in the 13th Alabama. W. H. Moon wrote:

> I had been under the impression that General Reynolds was shot by a Tennessean until I met Captain Simpson, of Company F, 13th Alabama, at Gettysburg in 1913, and we went to the Reynolds monument, when he pointed to the place where he and his men were standing when he ordered them to "shoot the man on the horse" (only about thirty yards distant), which was promptly done....I have no doubt of his statement being true.[53]

The 1st Tennessee, on the left flank of the Alabamans, also claimed credit for shooting the top Union commander on the field. It, too, fought in Herbst's Woods. According to Captain William Tolley of that regiment, Major Felix Buchanan led a detachment "which in its impetuous dash at the enemy killed Major General Reynolds."[54] Tolley was probably mistaken, since the 1st Tennessee had had to skirt swampy ground and therefore had joined the fight considerably later than the 13th Alabama.[55]

In his after-action report for the division, Major General Henry Heth attributed Reynolds' death to Pegram's guns. Major D. G. McIntosh, commander of another artillery unit, also believed this to be the case.[56] On the other hand, Edward A. Pollard, in 1865, in his *Southern History of the War*, expressed what was certainly the predominant view in the South. Namely: that Reynolds was killed in a volley by Archer's infantry.[57]

Among Union officers, Major General Abner Doubleday and Colonel Chapman Biddle subscribed to the sharpshooter theory.[58] Lieutenant Colonel W. W. Dudley (19th Indiana) and Captain W. H. Harries (2nd Wisconsin) disagreed, both asserting that Reynolds was killed by one of Archer's infantrymen.[59] Their view must take precedence, if only because they were on the scene and Doubleday and Biddle had not yet arrived.

One minor question remains. Was Reynolds hit accidentally, or was he the victim of a deliberate, well-aimed shot? His sister Eleanor and Captain E. C. Baird of his staff both thought it was an "accidental" or "chance" shot.[60] However, any soldier offered a tempting target — especially a high-ranking, mounted officer — would surely take aim at it. And therefore it seems more likely that some Johnny Reb drew a bead on General Reynolds and squeezed the trigger.

At what time on the morning of July 1, 1863, was Reynolds shot?

AUTHOR'S CONCLUSION: Between 10:35 and 10:45. He may have died instantly, or he may have lingered possibly as long as ten minutes. Hence his death would have occurred between 10:35 and 10:55.

This 20-minute period, it should be noted at the outset, does *not* represent the majority view. Nearly a dozen published accounts say Reynolds was shot at 10:15.[61] Brigadier General James S. Wadsworth, one suspects, is largely responsible for these misstatements. In his after-action report he coupled Reynolds' death with the opening of hostilities between Cutler's and Davis' Brigades, declaring that both events occurred at 10:15.[62] Cutler's opening volley probably occurred a bit later, between 10:20 and 10:30. The shooting of Reynolds — considering he led the 2nd Wisconsin into action *after* Cutler's troops started firing — had to be still later.

One account has Reynolds killed at "about 10:00;" another, "about 10:20;" and still another, at "almost 10:30."[63] But, as in Wadsworth's case, these are all too early. The time given by Major General O. O. Howard, on the other hand, is too late. During the afternoon of July 1, he informed Meade that Reynolds had been killed at 11:15.[64]

Reynolds' sisters were naturally curious about every aspect of their brother's death. As most of Reynolds' staff attended the funeral, the grieving women had ample opportunity to ply them with questions. As to the precise time of death, the officers probably were not in strict agreement. Even so, from their testimony, Reynolds' sisters could conclude that it had to be between 10:30 and 11:00. Eleanor Reynolds so informed their brother William in a letter written the day after the funeral.[65]

Support for this time frame, though comparatively sparse, is nonetheless persuasive. Its adherents include: Colonel Chapman Biddle (writing in 1880), Captain William W. Strong (in 1893), John Purifoy (in 1925), and Edwin B. Coddington (in 1968). Biddle and Strong stated the tragedy occured shortly before 11:00; Purifoy said about 10:45, Coddington, between 10:45 and 11:00.[66]

Although in the minority, their collective view can hardly be refuted.

What direct involvement with the 19th Indiana did Reynolds have just prior to his death?

AUTHOR'S CONCLUSION: None. The handful of writers who had him leading or urging forward that regiment were mistaken. Significantly, not a single member of this regiment ever claimed any direct involvement with Reynolds at the time he was fatally shot.

In 1867 J. Watt DePeyster (brevet major general in the National Guard and not present at the Gettysburg battle) wrote that Reynolds was killed while urging forward the 19th Indiana.[67] It appears he simply misidentified the regiment; the statement would have been true had he named the 2nd Wisconsin. Had Reynolds lived, he would have next turned his attention to the 7th Wisconsin. It was the second of Meredith's regiments to become engaged; the 19th Indiana was third.

Lieutenant J. G. Rosengarten of Reynolds' staff blundered even worse than DePeyster. In 1871 he wrote: "Reynolds took the Indiana 17th into the woods to drive them [the enemy] out, and then put in the whole of the Iron Brigade...."[68] Of course Rosengarten meant the *19th* Indiana. But he was also wrong in implying (1) that this regiment was the first to confront the enemy and (2) that Reynolds personally directed the rest of the brigade into battle.

Colonel Chapman Biddle, writing in 1880, had Reynolds actually leading the charge of the 19th Indiana.[69] Incredibly, the same assertion cropped up in Strong's history of the 121st Pennsylvania (1893) and also in the omnibus *New York at Gettysburg* (1902).[70]

Since writers at second hand—which was the case for all of the above—are more apt to err than eyewitnesses or particpants, what is needed to resolve the issue in question is a dependable first-hand account. Fortunately, there is one by no less an authority than a top officer of the 19th Indiana. In an undated letter to Colonel John B. Bachelder, Lieutenant Colonel William W. Dudley described exactly what happened. He wrote:

> ...Aides of Genl. Reynolds and Meredith hurrying down the line informed us that the enemy were advancing up the western slope of the hill [McPherson's Ridge] in front of us and that we should move on the right into line and charge them, and save the battery [Hall's], which was the object of the enemy's charge. Almost simultaneously we received the sad information of our beloved Genl. Reynolds having been fatally wounded, and the men set their faces resolutely to meet the foe and avenge his death.[71]

Which Union regiment fired the first infantry volley in the Battle of Gettysburg — 56th Pennsylvania or 2nd Wisconsin?

AUTHOR'S CONCLUSION: 56th Pennsylvania.

This controversy smoldered for years, each side persisting in its conviction. In the spring of 1884 the dispute flared into a brief but heated fight in the pages of the *National*

Tribune. The opening salvo, in the March 20th issue, consisted of a letter from the former commander of the 56th Pennsylvania and another from an ex-private of the 2nd Wisconsin. To cap his case, Colonel John W. Hofmann quoted his brigade commander's letter of November 5, 1863, to Andrew G. Curtin, then Governor of Pennsylvania. In it Brigadier General Lysander Cutler stated unequivocally that the 56th Pennsylvania was due the honor. Private E. R. Reed, on the other hand, relied solely on his own experience to persuade the readers of the *National Tribune* that the credit was due the 2nd Wisconsin. His regiment reached the battlefield before the 56th Pennsylvania, he contended, had gone into action at once, and consequently had fired the first Union volley. On the march that morning he had been able to see ahead "a mile or more," he said. And seeing no other troops, he was convinced the 2nd Wisconsin had led not only Meredith's Brigade but Wadsworth's Division. Cutler's men, he insisted, would have to explain how they "passed by us in our rear, and went into action far away on our right" ahead of his regiment.[72] But Reed was quite mistaken: Cutler's entire brigade did in fact precede Meredith's, and almost up to the time both brigades plunged into battle, the gap between them had been more than a mile, which explains why Reed had not seen any other troops. Indeed, Meredith's Iron Brigade lagged so far behind that Wadsworth had to dispatch an aide to hurry them up.[73]

J. V. Pierce, a captain in the 147th New York at Gettysburg, became incensed when he read Reed's letter. Although his regiment was not a contender for the distinction of firing first, Cutler's Brigade, to which his regiment belonged, was. Just two weeks after Reed's letter was published, Pierce's rebuttal appeared in the same magazine. In it he pointed out that Cutler's Brigade started out before Meredith's, was not passed en route, and, becoming engaged before Meredith's lead regiment, fired the first shots by Union infantry.[74]

But that was not yet the end of the battle of words. In short order Frederick L. Phillips (erstwhile private in the 2nd Wisconsin) brought up a battery of officers in support of his regiment. In his letter to the *National Tribune*, which appeared in the May 29th issue, he drew upon the testimony of a captain in Company I, a lieutenant in Company B, and one of Meredith's aides. All three were vehement in their rejection of 56th Pennsylvania's claim. Captain George H. Otis spluttered, "Nothing is further from the truth." (In his history of the 2nd Wisconsin, published four years earlier, he had endorsed his regiment's claim to opening the infantry battle.) Lieutenant D. B. Daily vowed, "I know as well as I know that I am living, that there was not a shot fired from a musket in the hands of an infantryman until our regiment took the place of Buford's cavalry, and we engaged General Archer's brigade of Heth's division." Aide G. M. Woodward was "prepared to swear that, unless I am insane and have forgotten everything I ever knew, there were no troops ahead of us."[75]

On June 19, 1884, the verbal duel in the pages of the *National Tribune* came to a close with a last thrust, as well as a rebuke, from the 56th Pennsylvania's Colonel Hofmann. To settle once and for all the matter of who marched onto the field ahead of whom, he cited division commander Wadsworth's official report, which gave the following order of march to McPherson's Ridge: Cutler's Brigade, Hall's Battery, Meredith's Brigade. Hofmann then went on to express his dismay at the furor. The 56th Pennsylvania, he wrote, "never dreamed that...there would rise up such a body of honorable men in the State of Wisconsin and attempt to rob the 56th Pennsylvania of the honors it had received...."[76]

In the meantime, the 2nd Wisconsin's commander at Gettysburg, Lucius Fairchild, had evidently been following the debate in the popular magazine. On April 11, 1884, he wrote to R. K. Beecham, who had been a captain in his regiment: "I am positive that the first infantry engaged at Gettysburg was the 2d Wis. Vols." (The assertion smacks of the invincible chauvinism endemic among unit commanders.) "I saw no troops in advance of us," he continued, "and heard no firing by others until after (a very short time) we were sharply engaged."[77] That the colonel saw no other troops is believable; that he had not heard the firing by Buford's men as well as Cutler's is not.

As late as 1893, 2nd Wisconsin's Cornelius Wheeler (a sergeant at Gettysburg; later, a lieutenant) tried to build a case for his regiment firing the first infantry volley. But his time statements are fallacious and hence his argument collapses.[78]

It can hardly escape notice that all the advocates for the 2nd Wisconsin belonged to that regiment, with the exception of Woodward, and he was in the same brigade. Of course, prejudice, or at least partiality, can also be imputed to those just cited on the opposing side. Hofmann, Pierce, and Cutler would naturally have been predisposed in favor of their own regiment in their own brigade. But supporters of the 56th Pennsylvania's claim also included corps commander Doubleday, division commander Wadsworth, brigade commander Chapman Biddle, and others of lesser rank, all of whom lacked a vested interest in either regiment.[79]

Incised in the 56th Pennsylvania's bronze monument on the battlefield are these words: "THE REGIMENT HERE DELIVERED THE OPENING FIRE OF THE INFANTRY IN THE BATTLE OF GETTYSBURG IN THE FORENOON OF JULY 1, 1863." No such claim appears on 2nd Wisconsin's monument. And that is as it should be.

Which regiment supplied litter bearers for Reynolds—14th Brooklyn or 76th New York?

AUTHOR'S CONCLUSION: Probably both, with men of the 14th Brooklyn carrying the general's body initially and men of the 76th New York relieving them somewhere along the route, most likely at Seminary Ridge.

BASIS FOR CONCLUSION: Address by Seth Low (*New York at Gettysburg*, Vol. 2, 688); statement by J. C. Rosengarten of Reynolds' staff (quoted in Stine, *History of the Army of the Potomac*, 455); news item in the [Gettysburg] *Star & Sentinel*, Apr. 10, 1888.

In the course of his address, on July 1, 1888, at the dedication of the 14th Brooklyn monument on the battlefield, the eminent orator Seth Low said: "The sad duty fell to them [14th Brooklyn enlisted men] of removing from the field the body of heroic Reynolds when he fell directly behind their lines." Although confirmation of Low's statement could not be found in any other source, it is logical to assume that when help was needed the nearest troops not then engaged would be called upon. Since the Iron Brigade at that moment was charging the enemy, that would have been the 14th Brooklyn.

According to Lieutenant Rosengarten of Reynolds' staff, however, the duty fell to four privates of the 76th New York (Milo Morgan, Melvin Reed, France Brace, and Benjamin Taylor). But it seems unlikely that these men carried the general's body the entire distance from McPherson's Ridge to Seminary Ridge and thence to a house on the Emmitsburg road. Furthermore, when Reynolds fell, the New Yorkers were not even close. They were, in fact, a half mile away, on the Union right, and already firing at the enemy. However, something transpired that would render it feasible for 76th New York men to carry Reynolds' litter in the latter stage of the long trip to the rear.

Hard pressed by Davis' Confederate Brigade, this regiment, together with the 56th Pennsylvania, was soon forced to retreat. These troops would have arrived at Seminary Ridge about the same time as the slow-moving cortege accompanying the fallen Reynolds. At this juncture, most likely, the original litter bearers were sent back to their regiment and replaced by 76th New York men.

Chance confirmation of Rosengarten's statement that the 76th New York furnished litter bearers for Reynolds appeared in the Gettysburg *Star & Sentinel* on April 10, 1888. In the "Battlefield Notes" column there was brief mention of Benjamin Taylor — one of the four privates named by Rosengarten. The news was that he, as President of the 76th New York Survivors' Association, had been in town during the preceding week making arrangements for the dedication of its regimental monument three months hence. He was further identified as "one of the detail that carried Reynolds' body from the field."

How many officers and men of Archer's Brigade were captured west of Willoughby Run?

AUTHOR'S CONCLUSION: About two hundred.

Contemporary estimates ranged from ridiculously high to ridiculously low. In the absence of any reliable physical count, Northerners naturally tended to maximize their achievement and Southerners to minimize their disgrace. This is best exemplified in the reports of the two major generals closest to the action, Doubleday and Heth. The former claimed nearly 1,000 Confederates captured, while the latter admitted only the loss of Archer and sixty to seventy men.[80] As the wide disparity suggests, both veered sharply from the truth.

Doubleday, it should be noted, later toned down his original extravagant claim. In his *Chancellorsville and Gettysburg*, published in 1882, he defined the number of prisoners simply as "a large part" of Archer's Brigade.[81] In the meantime the Comte de Paris, Samuel P. Bates, and other historians had accepted and published his inflated figure. Heth apparently never retracted his unrealistic assessment, and Southern writers (James D. Porter and John Purifoy among them), appropriated it as gospel.[82]

In the Northern press the *Cincinnati Gazette* reported 300 Confederate prisoners, the *New York World*, 600. The headline in the *Philadelphia Inquirer* must have cheered its readers: "CAPTURE OF THE REBEL GEN. ARCHER AND HIS WHOLE BRIGADE." Even more absurd was the figure given in the 80th New York's regimental history—"nearly 1,500."[83] Archer had only 1,200 troops!

Meade, Wadsworth, and the Iron Brigade commanders were more circumspect than all of the above. Rather than hazard a specific number (as Doubleday and the others did), they resorted to indefinite locutions, albeit invariably denoting a great many. According to Meade, the "greater part" of Archer's Brigade was taken prisoner; Wadsworth said "several hundred."[84] Colonel Morrow (24th Michigan) and Major Mansfield (2nd Wisconsin) both reported the Iron Brigade captured a "large number"; Colonel Dudley (19th Indiana) said "the larger portion"; Lieutenant Colonel Callis (7th Wisconsin), "the greater portion."[85]

With Colonel B. D. Fry captured on July 3, the task of writing the after-action report for Archer's Brigade fell to Lieutenant Colonel Samuel Shepard. His estimate of 75 men captured on July 1 was only slightly higher than Heth's.[86] Fry, however, was not deluded about the brigade's casualties on the first morning at Gettysburg. During those hours, he wrote after the war, a "considerable part" of the brigade was lost.[87] Although he referred to casualties of all types, the implication is there, nonetheless, that the number of men taken prisoner exceeded what Heth and Shepard reported. That this was indeed the case is confirmed in the accounts of two Confederate officers. The enemy, wrote Captain J. B. Turney of the 1st Tennessee, succeeded in "capturing General Archer, with quite a percentage of his brigade, including a portion of the left of the First Tennessee."[88] Colonel William H. Swallow could be completely objective. Having served with Early's Division, he had no partisan ties with Archer's Brigade, or even with Heth's Division. In 1885 he asserted that approximately two hundred of Archer's men were captured in the first day's battle.[89]

Returning to Colonel Fry's statement: Given two premises, his "considerable part" can be quantified, then reduced by the number killed or wounded, leaving the number captured. First premise: Fry meant at least one-quarter but less than half of the 1,200 troops engaged. If one-third is adopted as a fair compromise, Archer's total casualties in the morning's fight would have been 400. Since Confederate records are silent as to how many of Archer's men were killed or wounded in this phase of the battle, another assumption must be made. Hence the second premise: The percent killed/wounded in Archer's Brigade approximated the actual percent for the combined 7th Wisconsin, 19th Indiana, and 24th Michigan regiments. (The 2nd Wisconsin is excluded because of its exceptionally high loss in the enemy's opening volley.) The figure for the three Union regiments is 16%, which, applied to Archer's 1,200 men, yields 192 killed/

wounded. Thus, by subtraction, the number of men captured out of the estimated 400 casualties is 208.

The imprecision of the above method is of course recognized. Yet the end result is remarkably consonant with the statements of Turney and Swallow. Reduced to the round figure of 200, it coincides with Swallow's estimate. As to Turney's "quite a percentage," 200 equates to a substantial seventeen percent of Archer's total force.

Do any Union sources support a figure as low as 200? The answer is Yes, assuming two enlisted men in the 2nd Wisconsin referred to Meredith's Brigade and not to their regiment alone. Private Sydney Mead of Company F noted in his diary that "two or three hundred prisoners" were taken.[90] And Sergeant Cornelius Wheeler of Company I wrote his parents: "We followed them as far as [was] prudent capturing Brig Genl Archer and upwards of a hundred fifty prisoners."[91]

Did the 6th Wisconsin, 95th New York, and 14th Brooklyn "save" the 147th New York?

AUTHOR'S CONCLUSION: No, not really. If the three regiments had not counterattacked, the 147th New York would still have escaped, though almost certainly with heavier casualties.

According to J. H. Stine in his *History of the Army of the Potomac*, published in 1903, the 147th New York was "hemmed in" until the Union counterattack made it possible for that regiment to escape.[92] Four years earlier, another respected historian, John M. Vanderslice, made the same assertion in his book, *Gettysburg Then and Now*.[93] At the core of the long-standing belief that the attack force actually rescued the 147th New York were the statements of Doubleday and Cutler. Both conveyed the strong impression that had it not been for the efforts of the 6th Wisconsin, 95th New York, and 14th Brooklyn, Major Harney and his men would not have gotten away.[94]

Several weeks after the battle, the 14th Brooklyn's Colonel Edward B. Fowler penned his recollections of July 1. "I have since learned," he wrote, "that when we made the charge the 147th N. Y. was lying behind the R. R. cut, and that our charge enabled them to go to the rear, otherwise the entire Regiment would have been captured."[95] Nineteenth Indiana's Lieutenant Colonel William W. Dudley, on the other hand, felt that exclusive credit was due Lieutenant Colonel Rufus Dawes and the 6th Wisconsin for the "brilliant success" that "relieved them [the 147th New York] from their peril."[96] (Dudley's glowing appraisal may have owed something to the fact that Dawes' regiment and his own belonged to the same brigade, Meredith's, whereas the other two regiments in the attack were in Cutler's brigade.) E. B. Quiner, in *The Military History of Wisconsin*, published in 1866, also lauded the 6th Wisconsin, declaring that it "saved" the 147th New York.[97] Significantly, Dawes never made any such claim.

If a whiff of chauvinism is apparent in the statements of Fowler, Dudley, and Quiner, what did the men who were allegedly "saved" have to say on the matter? Three officers of the 147th can be quoted in this regard.

Lieutenant Sidney G. Cooke affirmed the role of the attacking regiments as put forth by Cutler, Doubleday, *et al.* Addressing a veterans group, he said: "It was only by the prompt and gallant action of other troops that the regiment, when it finally received the order to fall back, was saved from annihilation."[98]

At one point Lieutenant J. Volney Pierce expressed a view synonomous with Cooke's; at another, a view quite contrary to it. Writing to Colonel John B. Bachelder in 1882, he told how he and the two companies he then commanded climbed the steep bank of the railroad cut to escape from the enemy. "At this moment we were all liable to capture by the confederate brigade on our right rear, and but for the prompt action of Col. Dawes of the 6th Wisconsin, we would the whole forty of us [have] gone to the rear as prisoners of War."[99] From this it is reasonable to conclude that not only the troops under him but the entire regiment was in a hopeless situation. However, when Pierce wrote the account of his regiment for the omnibus *New York at Gettysburg*, he took pains to give the opposite impression. Disputing the assertions of Doubleday and all others that the 147th New York was surrounded and subsequently rescued, he maintained that the whole area in its rear, as well as the railroad cut (except at the western end), was "unobstructed" throughout the fight. He went on: "There was no other regiment in reach of us to assist while we were fighting on the right of this railroad cut; when we left the ground it was by order, and we carried our colors with us." Further, he insisted that his regiment started to retire *before* the three Union regiments attacked.[100]

This last point is critical to the resolution of the controversy. If the 147th New York (at least the major part of it) could disengage and retire on its own initiative, then obviously it was not saved by other troops. Pierce's claim of prior retirement is reinforced by a fellow officer in the 147th, James Coey. (At the time of the Gettysburg battle he was either a captain or a lieutenant.) It was *during* the retreat, Coey said, that he heard Union troops cheering "in our rear (our former front)," and, turning his head, saw them charging the enemy.[101]

Additional support for the thesis that the retreat was underway prior to the counterattack is found in the multi-volume *Confederate Military History*. D. H. Hill, Jr. (author of the North Carolina volume and son of the famous general) clearly defined the sequence of events: Davis' troops (1) pursued the retreating 147th New York, (2) discovered Union troops forming on their right, and (3) took cover in the railroad cut.[102]

There is no argument that the Union charge relieved the pressure on the retreating New Yorkers, but to assert that it saved them from capture *en masse* is to overstate the case. This, apparently, is what Cutler did; and Doubleday (possibly influenced by his brigadier's report) duplicated the overstatement. Lieutenant Cooke's unselfish tribute to the attacking force would have appealed to his audience, but his reference to the certain "annihilation" of his own regiment is perhaps best ascribed to an orator's penchant for hyperbole.

Colonel John W. Hofmann, whose 56th Pennsylvania had fought alongside the 147th New York, was nettled by the common perception that the latter regiment was completely cut off and escaped solely because of the action of the attacking regiments. That view, he contended, was all wrong. In 1884 he wrote: "...in fact, it was owing to the pertinacity of the 147th New York in holding on to their ground and their heroic fighting that kept this part of the enemy's forces in check for a time, and thus enabled the other troops of Cutler's brigade to arrive on this part of the field and make the capture [of Confederates at the railroad cut] possible."[103]

How many officers and men of Davis' Brigade were captured at the railroad cut?

AUTHOR'S CONCLUSION: About three hundred.

At least Abner Doubleday was consistent. He flagrantly overestimated the number of troops captured in Davis' Brigade just as he had done for Archer's Brigade. In the latter case he claimed 1,000 prisoners; in the former, without specifying a number, he boasted the capture of two whole regiments![104] Perhaps he got this impression from Wadsworth, who also reported two regiments captured.[105] After allowing for the killed and wounded, this would mean a minimum of 800 prisoners. Brigade commander Cutler, on the other hand, was more circumspect than his superiors. He merely stated that a "large body" of enemy troops surrendered.[106]

Oddly enough, after the war an ex-Confederate officer erred on the high side, though not as wildly as Doubleday and Wadsworth. William H. Swallow, formerly a colonel in Early's Division, stated that the number of prisoners taken at the railroad cut was about 600.[107] In stark contrast, Joseph R. Davis reported a mere eighty or ninety for his entire brigade.[108]

References by Confederates to the number captured in individual regiments are rare, and those few either lack authority or are vague. According to W. B. Murphy, 2nd Mississippi's color-bearer, Major Blair and 87 men were captured. Members of the other two regiments had also been captured, he said, but he did not venture a guess as to how many.[109] A 55th North Carolina captain, Samuel Ashe, recorded only that in his regiment "many were captured in the cut."[110] All that is known of the 42nd Mississippi troops in this regard is that a great many escaped through the western end of the cut. It follows that some did not.

Out of the farrago of vague and contradictory statements by participants on both sides, one emerges as being authoritative, credible, and probably reasonably accurate. Lieutenant Colonel Dawes, in his battle report and later in his *Service With the Sixth Wisconsin*, credited his command (which then included the 100-man brigade guard) with the capture of seven officers and about 225 men.[111] By far the greater number belonged to the 2nd Mississippi. It is interesting to note that Confederate writer John Purifoy, who fought at Gettysburg, accepted Dawes' total and used it in his account of the first day's battle.[112]

Evidently Purifoy was unaware of the fact that the 95th New York and 14th Brooklyn also took prisoners. Colonel Fowler seems to have provided the only clue—

nebulous as it is—as to how many. The 6th Wisconsin, he wrote, "from its position, made most of the captures."[113] In light of this admission vis-a-vis the number of captures by Dawes' command, it seems probable that the other two regiments combined captured some sixty to seventy of Davis' troops. Given this assumption, the total for the three regiments and the brigade guard would be approximately 300.

Finally, the conclusions of certain 20th-century historians may be noted. In 1960 Warren W. Hassler, Jr. pegged the total number of prisoners at 350. Ten years later he modified his view to "about 250" captured by the 6th Wisconsin plus an indeterminate number by the 95th New York and 14th Brooklyn.[114] Edwin B. Coddington determined that there were "two or three hundred" and Jesse Bowman Young, 300.[115]

Was Brigadier General Thomas A. Rowley drunk on duty, July 1, 1863?

AUTHOR'S CONCLUSION: Yes, as determined in his subsequent court-martial.

BASIS FOR CONCLUSION: Transcript of the court-martial proceedings, April 26-27, 1864, at Culpeper, Virginia.

During the trial a number of officers swore that General Rowley was not intoxicated on the day in question. But the singular thing about this group is that they were all his subordinates, and hence could hardly be considered unbiased. While the testimony of General Doubleday was equivocal, General Cutler and others who did not have to fear reprisal from the accused stated that, in their opinion, Rowley was drunk.

Especially damaging was the testimony of Captain Craig Wadsworth of Doubleday's staff. He said he had seen General Rowley "five or six times during the day," and on one of those occasions he saw him fall off his horse. The Judge Advocate then asked whether Rowley was or was not intoxicated at that time.

Wadsworth: He was intoxicated.

Judge Advocate: State why you believed General Rowley to be intoxicated.

Wadsworth: From his previous behavior: he rode up to me when I was standing in the Cashtown Road—in a very excited manner. There were only about twenty or thirty men of his command—of the provost guard—present. He wished to know why that Cavalry did not charge. I told him the Cavalry was under command of General Buford, besides that the horses there belonged to Cavalry who were dismounted and were behind the stone wall. He said: "By God I shall order them to charge" and rode away from me.

Judge Advocate: What was there in the conduct of General Rowley at the time he fell from his horse which led you to believe him intoxicated—if anything?

Wadsworth: From the peculiar manner in which he rode his horse swaying to and fro.[116]

The presiding general officers found Rowley quilty on three counts: drunkenness on duty, conduct prejudicial to military discipline, conduct unbecoming an officer. His sentence: dismissal from the army. As it turned out, he was spared that disgrace. Judge Advocate General Joseph Holt wrote to President Lincoln, recommending that, in view of the conflicting testimony, the sentence not be carried out.[117]

Rowley resigned his commission on December 29, 1864.[118]

Who deserves the credit for selecting Cemetery Ridge as the Union line of battle—Howard or Reynolds?

AUTHOR'S CONCLUSION: Howard. He not only recognized the tactical importance of this ridge (as Reynolds did), he actually secured the position when he posted Steinwehr's Division on Cemetery Hill.

The strongest advocate for Reynolds deserving the credit for the Cemetery Ridge position was Abner Doubleday (which is hardly surprising in light of his animosity toward Howard). He expressed his view privately, in 1875, in a letter to Samuel Bates and publicly, in 1882, in his *Chancellorsville and Gettysburg*. To quote from the book: "Reynolds, in reply [to the request for orders from Howard's aide], directed that General Howard bring his corps forward at once and *form them on Cemetery Hill* as a reserve."[119] In the letter to Bates, after making his case for Reynolds, Doubleday went on to speculate:

> If one could get at the whole truth, we would probably find that Buford was the first to suggest the importance of Cemetery Hill for he was up in the steeple of the Seminary with Reynolds pointing out the different localities and especially their advantages and disadvantages with reference to the coming battle and as he had time to make himself thoroughly acquainted with the country he could hardly have failed to call Reynolds' attention to the most prominent feature of the landscape.[120]

While it seems virtually certain that Reynolds did not join Buford in the cupola atop the Seminary, the cavalry leader might well have mentioned, even strongly endorsed, Cemetery Hill and the adjoining ridge as a fall-back position.

Lieutenant Joseph G. Rosengarten of Reynolds' staff also felt that his chief was responsible for the selection of the Union's winning position and therefore deserved full credit. However, he did allow that Howard may have acted independently. Writing in 1871, he recalled Reynolds' decision to hold Buford's position on McPherson's Ridge "at least until his other Corps, the 11th and 3rd, could get up to Cemetery Hill and the Ridge where the battle was finally fought and won." Then:

> His orders to the Staff Officer sent to hasten Howard's movements, included a direction to put a proper reserve of Infantry and Artillery on Cemetery Hill, and this was done by Howard, either in consequence of receiving these orders or from his own appreciation of the necessity and importance of that position.[121]

The controversy had begun to percolate within nine months after the battle. When Howard wrote to Major William Riddle on March 22, 1864, he was clearly on the defensive.

> It has been told me that a member of Gen. Reynold's staff says that he brought me an order to place a Division on Cemetery ridge at the battle of Gettysburg. I think there must be some mistake. I did not receive the impression from any written or verbal communication on that memorable day....I never thought your order to me contemplated or directed any subsequent disposition.[122]

Certainly Howard felt vindicated when he received Riddle's reply two weeks later.

> ...I did not carry to you any order to place any troops on Cemetery Hill, nor do I know that General Reynolds sent you such order by any of his staff at Gettysburg.[123]

Eighteen years later there was further vindication from one of his own aides at Gettysburg. Captain Daniel Hall had been sent by Howard to report the Eleventh Corps' progress to Reynolds and to ask for orders. He had returned with the message that Howard should bring up his troops as rapidly as possible. In 1882, after reading Doubleday's book on the Chancellorsville and Gettysburg battles, Hall was moved to write his former chief, to set the record straight on matters in which he had first-hand knowledge. After describing his brief interview with Reynolds, Hall made this flat statement: "Gen. Reynolds gave no order whatever in regard to occupying Cemetery Hill, nor did he make any allusion to it."[124]

Howard was surely not averse to the lavish praise accorded him for posting troops on Cemetery Hill. Yet he was not puffed up with pride about it, either, as though only he would have thought to do so. This is revealed in a letter he wrote in 1875: "General Reynolds did not designate Cemetery Hill at all. Had he lived he might have done so—would doubtless have done so."[125]

EPILOGUE

Up to the day he died, John Reynolds apparently told no one he was in love. He usually confided in his sisters, but even they were kept in the dark. The senior officer on his staff, Major William Riddle, was aware that his chief wore what appeared to be two religious charms; depending from a string around his neck, they were kept concealed beneath his uniform. No doubt his orderly, Charles Veil, had also seen them. And they as well as the rest of his staff would have noticed the gold ring on his little finger.[1] But these objects—even the clasped hands engraved on the ring[2]—did not necessarily point to a deep ongoing romance, and there is no evidence that anyone suspected that such was the case.

Almost all of Reynolds' staff—Riddle, Veil, Weld, Willcox, Mitchell, and Rosengarten—accompanied the body of their beloved leader from Gettysburg to Lancaster, Pennsylvania, where he was born. The journey began several hours after Reynolds died and ended three days later.[3] Veil and Rosengarten had tried to obtain a proper casket in Gettysburg. But the best they could find was a plain wooden box. When they got it back to the George house, it was found to be too short for the six-foot general. It would serve its purpose, however, after one end had been knocked out.[4]

In the meantime Major Riddle had commandeered an ambulance and arranged for a mounted escort. Once the makeshift casket had been placed inside the vehicle and Lieutenant Rosengarten had taken his seat beside the driver, the party (which also included orderly Veil and Captains Willcox and Mitchell) set out on the Taneytown road. After a brief pause at army headquarters just outside Taneytown—presumably to wire Reynolds' relatives in Baltimore—the party continued on to Westminster, Maryland.[5] After the casket had been deposited at the railroad station in that town, the ambulance and the mounted escort returned to Gettysburg. The four staff members made the necessary arrangements to board the next train to Baltimore. Sometime before the 5:00 a.m. departure they were joined by Major Riddle and Captain Weld, who had remained on the battlefield until dark.[6]

When the train pulled into the Baltimore station shortly before noon of July 2, Reynolds' brother, Major Sam Reynolds, and his brother-in-law, George Gildersleeve, were waiting on the platform. As the general had died some 24 hours earlier, it was imperative that his body be taken to a mortuary at once, and this was done.[7] Since jewelry would have been removed prior to embalming, it could have been then that Riddle got a close look at Reynolds' ring and the two charms. The latter, he noted, were Catholic medals (one bearing a heart, the other, a cross). Reynolds, as he knew, was Protestant. Even more intriguing was the inscription on the inner side of the ring. Just two words: Dear Kate.[8] Well, this was a startling development! It probably crossed Riddle's mind in that instant that this same person had given his chief the medals as well. Obviously she had meant a great deal to him. The central question—*Who is she?*—must have nagged at him and he wondered if he would ever know. The discovery of two letters in Reynolds' valise signed simply "Kate" only added to the mystery.[9]

With much else to attend to, Sam Reynolds and George Gildersleeve left the mortuary at the earliest opportunity. They returned several hours later, rejoining Reynolds' aides who had waited there. George's wife, Jennie, came with them, bringing flowers and two flags to adorn her brother's casket. (By then a metal casket painted to simulate rosewood had replaced the crude wooden box.) It was taken to the railroad station and subsequently loaded on the 8:30 train to Philadelphia. Aboard the same train were the three relatives of the deceased and the six staff members. When they got off at the Philadelphia station, around midnight, they were greeted by a Mr. Wilson and a Mr. Temple whom Reynolds' sisters, Kate, Eleanor, and Harriet, had asked to meet them. Reynolds' aides, who had had no solid sleep in two days, went directly to a hotel. The others went to Kate's home at 1829 Spruce Street. Her husband, Harry Landis, was off serving with a Union artillery battery, but she was bolstered in her grief by the presence of her two unmarried sisters. It was nearly 2:00 a.m. when the four men carried the casket into the Landis parlor and set it down on a sturdy table that had been moved in from the kitchen. Certainly Kate, Eleanor, and Harriet plied their Baltimore relatives with many tearful, anguished questions about their brother's last hours, and Sam, George, and Jennie would have answered them as best they could.[10]

Everyone, needless to say, was greatly perplexed by the ring and the Catholic medals John was wearing when he died. To William Reynolds, John's brother who commanded the Union naval forces in Port Royal, South Carolina, Jennie wrote: "We all thought a lady was the donor and must be prized and wished we could only know who and where she was." As it turned out, their curiosity was soon satisfied.

Eleanor and Harriet ("Ellie" and "Hal" to the family) were upstairs in the Landis home on the morning of July 3 when they heard a knock at the front door. There were two callers, they were informed, both wishing to see General Reynolds. One was a Mr. Ewing (presumably a friend of the family) and the other, a Miss Hewitt. "Is it Kate?" Ellie wondered aloud. Brimming with expectation, they hurried downstairs to find out.[11]

Opening the door, they were somewhat taken aback—the soberly-dressed, dark-haired woman before them was obviously much younger than their brother. Her face betrayed the deep, barely constrained grief she felt. It was indeed the mysterious Kate. Her full name: Catherine Mary Hewitt.[12]

Although she must have been nearly overcome by shock and grief when the terrible news reached her in Torresdale, Pennsylvania, on July 2, she nonetheless managed to leave for Philadelphia that same day. Now, ushered into the Landis parlor, she fell to her knees before the open casket and wept copiously. At last, summoning her strength, she stood up and gazed upon the face of the man she loved and had hoped to marry.[13]

She and John had met four years earlier in California, while he was stationed at the Presidio and she was in the employ of a wealthy San Francisco family as governess. She was then in her early twenties; he was approaching forty. That same year, 1859,

John was transferred to the U. S. Military Academy at West Point to serve as its commandant. The following year she came East, not primarily because of him but to fulfill her decision to convert to Catholicism. For that purpose she entered Eden Hall of the Academy of the Sacred Heart in Torresdale. Apparently they continued to correspond and their feelings toward each other ripened into love. How often they were able to meet in person is not known, but during one rendezvous, they exchanged rings in token of their mutual love and committment. Ever since he had worn the ring inscribed "Dear Kate" and she had worn his West Point class ring.[14]

"I promised when he put this ring on my finger, I would never take it off," Kate confided to Ellie. But now, with quiet resignation, she said she must give it up. Ellie protested, though with little hope of changing her mind.

Since Kate's arrival, Ellie and her sisters had learned many details of the romance that until then they never knew existed. Cruelly ironic was the fact that, under happier circumstances, within a week all this would have been revealed to them. Unless prohibited by the military situation, John had planned to bring her to this very house on the following Wednesday, July 8. They had planned to marry after the war and go to Europe on their honeymoon, Kate said. But, if he were to be killed, she had vowed she would enter a convent and he had given his consent.

On July 5 Jennie penned a long letter to William Reynolds. In it she related in detail the sad events of the preceding four days. She also informed him of their brother's secret romance, commenting, "I need not tell you what a thunderclap it was to us all." As to Kate Hewitt going into a convent, Jennie was convinced that "she intends to do it as the world has no interest for her now."

Even so, parting with the ring John had given her was very hard. On removing this most prized possession from her finger, she gazed at it for a moment, then kissed it tenderly and placed it on the casket, saying, "Never let it be tainted by a disloyal hand. He was too true for that."

It was only natural that Kate would elicit the sympathy of everyone present. But beyond that, she seems to have won their complete respect and affection as well. To Ellie she was "a most heroic mourner and most worthy of our dear one." To Jennie she was "a very superior person. We all regret that he had not told us about her...." And yet it can be readily understood why John had been so secretive. For one thing, there was the wide difference in their ages. For another, there was the difference in religion, she being a staunch Catholic whereas his family was wholly Protestant. Therefore, doubtless to avoid any prejudgments of Kate before his family could meet her in person, he elected to remain silent. The wisdom of this is hinted at in the letter Ellie wrote to brother William. To her account of Kate Hewitt's surprising visit, she added: "She made no mention of his religion nor in any way did anything that was in the least disagreeable."

Through the night Kate kept vigil beside the body of her beloved in the dimly-lit, flower-scented parlor. Ellie stayed with her but remained silent, not wishing to disturb her sorrowful meditation. Occasionally Kate would whisper the word "Dearest!" And, at least once, Ellie heard her say, in a voice filled with the utmost anguish, "Dearest, how can I give you up!"[15]

Early the next morning—July 4, the nation's birthday—Reynolds' staff members checked out of their hotel and went directly to the Landis home. Around 8:00 they, together with Reynolds family members and a number of close friends, boarded a train to Lancaster, where General Reynolds was to be buried in the family plot beside his father and mother.[16] Missing from the group were Kate Landis and Kate Hewitt.[17] Mrs. Landis was under doctor's orders not to travel.[18] The other Kate, thwarted in her expectation of ever becoming Mrs. Reynolds, may have declined because she felt she could not bear the emotional strain.

Sam Reynolds, Jennie Gildersleeve, and the staff members rode in the special car provided by the Pennsylvania Railroad to transport the general's casket. The train pulled into the Lancaster station around 11:30 a.m., where a large crowd had gathered to await the sad final homecoming of their most distinguished native son. Among the crowd were the eight soldiers of the Pennsylvania Reserves (which Reynolds once commanded) who would serve as pallbearers. The funeral cortege soon began its slow journey to the cemetery. A great many townspeople followed, on foot, behind the long string of carriages. All along the route flags were at half-mast and draped in black crepe. Throughout the city, church bells tolled.[19] At the cemetery, the graveside service was simple, moving, and—with kind consideration for those most deeply affected—brief.[20] The out-of-town mourners returned to the railroad station; by mid-afternoon they were on their way back to Philadelphia.[21]

Barely a week after the funeral Kate Hewitt applied for admission to the Sisters of Charity at St. Joseph's Provincial House in Emmitsburg, Maryland, and was accepted.[22] Soon after she embarked on her new life, Charles Veil paid her a visit. Kate had asked him to come because there was something she wanted him to have—an exquisitely embroidered handkerchief John had given her. Veil was deeply touched by her thoughtfulness and always cherished the memento.[23]

Some months later Kate was sent to Albany, New York, to teach in a school run by the sisterhood. Over the next few years she occasionally received a letter from one or another of Reynolds' sisters. On September 3, 1868, Kate resigned her teaching position, left the school, left the Sisters of Charity. Just why she did is not known, though there was some indication it might have been due to poor health. She left no forwarding address.

Subsequent attempts by the Reynolds family to find her proved futile.[24]

Despite his advanced age, John Burns was about as tough as they come. Three times during that first afternoon of July 1863 he was hit by enemy bullets; all that night he lay helpless on the battlefield. Yet he survived.[25] Truly—as a 7th Wisconsin sergeant who fought alongside him remarked—he was "grit to the backbone."[26]

Constantly in the midst of the action, Burns had fought with unquenchable fury. At one point, seeing a mounted Confederate officer approaching, he had taken quick aim and fired, knocking him out of the saddle.[27] How many others felt the sting of his bullets cannot be told. When an enemy bullet ricocheted off his belt, the impact left him momentarily speechless. If he was more affronted than hurt, as seems likely, he would have been more determined than ever to whip the hated Rebels. Later, a second bullet struck him in the arm. This seems not to have fazed him too much, for he kept on firing until a third bullet grazed his leg. While the wound itself was minor, it had paralyzed the limb. A Union surgeon subsequently attended to his various injuries, but because of the persisting numbness in his leg, Burns was unable to leave the field on his own.

The next morning he was carried to a home that had been converted into a hospital and given further treatment. Before the day ended he had recovered sufficiently so that he could be taken to his own home.[28]

He had fought mainly with the 7th Wisconsin but also, because he seemed to gravitate to where the action was hottest, with the 24th Michigan and the 150th Pennsylvania.[29] Through these troops and an avid press, the North soon learned about the pugnacious old man who had fought so valiantly beside men one-third his age.

When Lincoln came to Gettysburg in November of 1863 to deliver "a few remarks" at the dedication of a national cemetery, he sought out the famous civilian hero. Given Lincoln's innate affability and unpretentious manner, it seems certain the two men—in spite of the marked difference in temperament—got along splendidly. Some years later both the U. S. Congress and the State of Pennsylvania granted Burns a pension for his extraordinary military service.[30]

One can envision the old veteran taking his ease in the rocking chair on his porch and musing over his part in the fight out on McPherson's farm. More than once he averred that, if the battle were to be repeated, he believed he could do even better.

One summer day while tramping over the very ground on which he had fought, he saw a spectral figure. It was, he later said, "a man of immense proportions and the very image of the one whom I had seen on the day of the battle at the very spot, and in the exact attitude."

"Did you speak to it?" he was asked.

"No sir, I did not," Burns shot back. "It beckoned me to come toward him, but I turned and left the ground as rapidly as I could, and have never been on that field since. I could face them alive and respond to their challenge, but when the dead men come back, I am not in for that style of warfare."[31]

John Burns died on February 4, 1872, at age 78.[32] His statue on McPherson's Ridge depicts him as his comrades in arms saw him that memorable July day—baggy civilian attire, musket balanced in one hand, and a gleam of fierce determination in his eyes.

Curiosity prompts the question: What became of the top Union and Confederate leaders who survived the fighting at Willoughby Run? To summarize: (1) many, sad to say, did not live to see the end of the war; (2) some on the Union side elected to remain in the army; (3) the remainder—gladly or dejectedly depending on which side the individual was on—returned to civilian life.

Confederate Generals Pender, Pettigrew, Hill, and Archer all succumbed either to wounds or illness before the war ended. William D. Pender lingered for sixteen days after being wounded on the second day of the Battle of Gettysburg. James J. Pettigrew was mortally wounded on July 14, 1863, at Falling Waters, West Virginia, and died three days later. A. P. Hill was killed on April 2, 1865, at Petersburg, exactly one week before Lee surrendered to Grant at Appomattox. (The day before Hill's death, the intrepid Colonel "Willie" Pegram was killed in the fighting at Five Forks.)[33]

James J. Archer's death stemmed from the rigors of his long imprisonment. After his ignominious capture by a Yankee private, he was taken by way of Fort McHenry and Fort Delaware to the infamous Federal prison on Johnson's Island. With the onset of winter, the icy wind off Lake Erie exacerbated the already miserable lot of the Southern prisoners. As a general officer he would have received somewhat better treatment than those of lesser rank; still, so compelling was his desire to get away that he enticed a Yankee guard with an offer of $150 and a gold ring to help him escape. The guard took the bribe but reneged when the time came to keep his end of the bargain. Thereafter, Archer could only hope he would soon be exchanged for a Union prisoner of comparable rank. By the time this did occur—in August 1864, thirteen months after his capture—his health had been seriously undermined. Within two months of his return to his old command, he had to face the fact that he was simply too debilitated for active duty.

On October 16 Archer went on sick leave to the home of Brigadier General Joseph Anderson in Richmond. There, eight days later, he died.[34]

On the Union side, Generals Buford and Wadsworth both died before the Confederate surrender at Appomattox. Colonel William Sackett, commander of the 9th New York Cavalry, was killed at Trevilian Station, Virginia, on June 14, 1864.[35] Two months later, Brigadier General Lysander Cutler was so badly wounded at Globe Tavern that he would never again be fit for field command. He resigned his commission in June 1865, and died the following year.[36]

Two weeks after the Battle of Gettysburg, John Buford enjoyed signal success at Falling Waters, capturing hundreds of Rebels, not to mention two guns and three battle flags. In succeeding months he led his cavalrymen in skirmishes at Liberty Mills and Morton's Ford. But by mid-November he had to admit that the rigors of active campaigning were just too much for him. Physically exhausted, plagued by rheumatism, and possibly experiencing a flare-up of an old wound that never fully healed, he accepted the invitation of Major General George Stoneman to take a long rest in his home in Washington. Instead of recuperating, however, Buford grew weaker and pneumonia set in. He died on December 16, 1863, not long after receiving his commission as major general.[37]

On the second day of the Wilderness battle, May 6, 1864, James S. Wadsworth, while leading his division, was shot in the head. His blood splattered on the aide riding next to him. The aide thought his chief had been killed instantly. But the doughty fifty-six-year-old lingered in a coma for two days.[38] Just before the fatal bullet struck, he was heard to rally his troops: "Steady, boys! Go ahead; there isn't danger enough to harm a mouse!"[39]

Union Generals Howard, Doubleday, and Robinson stayed on to serve in the peace-time army. So did Colonels Stone, Devin, Gamble, and Morrow.[40] John Calef, Buford's artillery commander at Gettysburg, was still on active duty at the turn of the century. He retired with the rank of lieutenant colonel in 1900, having completed 42 years of service.[41]

Of Oliver Otis Howard, it can be asserted that his post-war army career eclipsed his wartime service. Prestigious assignments followed one after another: Commissioner of the Freedman's Bureau, peace emissary to the Apaches, commander of the Departments of the Columbia and the Platte, Superintendent of West Point, commander of the army's Division of the East. But his greatest contribution was non-political and non-military. In 1867 he founded Howard University, a college for black students in Washington, D. C. Between 1869 and 1874, in addition to his military duties, he served as its president. Finally retiring from the army in 1894—he was then 64—he applied his vast administrative skill and apparently undiminished energy to a number of religious and educational projects.[42]

Abner Doubleday stayed in the army until 1873. Following his retirement he wrote two book-length accounts of his most memorable war experiences. *Reminiscences of Forts Sumter and Moultrie* was published in 1876 and *Chancellorsville and Gettysburg* in 1882.[43]

Among the group of Union officers who played leading roles in the opening fight at Gettysburg and who quickly doffed their uniforms when the war ended, a number of them rose to lofty positions in their respective fields. Three ran for governor and two—Lucius Fairchild in Wisconsin and John L. Beveridge in Illinois—were elected.[44] Former battery commander James A. Hall lost the gubernatorial race in Maine—hardly a surprise since he ran on the Democratic ticket.[45] Fairchild, after three terms as Governor, held diplomatic posts in Liverpool, Paris, and Spain. (In Paris he entertained President Grant, also Mark Twain.)[46] Henry Baxter was appointed U. S. Minister to Honduras.[47] William W. Robinson served twelve years as U. S. Consul in Madagascar.[48] North Carolina native John Benton Callis represented his adopted state of Wisconsin in the 40th U. S. Congress.[49] Edmund L. Dana was elected Judge of the Eleventh Judicial District in Pennsylvania.[50]

While Rufus Dawes himself did not achieve any special prominence after the war, in 1925 his son Charles became Vice President of the United States under Coolidge.[51]

The bibulous Tom Rowley returned to his law practice in western Pennsylvania after his court-martial and subsequent resignation from the army. At various times he served as alderman, clerk of courts, and U. S. Marshal.[52]

"Sol" Meredith, the strapping commander of the Iron Brigade, became Surveyor-General of the Montana Territory. Eventually he settled for the life of a farmer in his native Indiana.[53]

Considering the repressive conditions that existed throughout the South during the Reconstruction period, it is hardly surprising that Heth and the top commanders in his division failed to match the post-war achievements of their Yankee counterparts.

Heth's brigadier Joseph R. Davis resumed his law practice in Biloxi, Mississippi.[54] John Blair (who surrendered to Dawes in the railroad cut) also returned to his law practice in Mississippi.[55] John Connally gained local renown as a preacher in Asheville, North Carolina.[56] Alfred Belo became editor of the *Galveston* [Texas] *News*.[57]

Birkett Fry and his men kept on harassing Yankees in Augusta, Georgia, even after the Confederate armies under Lee and Johnston had surrendered. When circumstances dictated a hasty departure, Fry fled to Cuba. A hard loser, he remained there three years. Once back in the South, however, he did not allow his bitterness to hinder him from having a successful business career in the cotton textile industry.[58]

For Henry Heth there were more reverses in store after Gettysburg. At Falling Waters, on July 14, 1863, his division was overrun in a surprise attack. Three months later, at Bristoe Station, Virginia, his troops were again caught off guard and took heavy losses. In the spring of 1864, his division was routed in the Wilderness Campaign.[59]

The unlucky officer did not fare any better as a businessman in the years immediately following the war. He embarked on a coal mining venture in partnership with a former adversary, Ambrose Burnside. Their hope of handsome profits soon evaporated. Next, Heth tried his hand at selling insurance, but he did so poorly that his wife had to take in boarders. His fortunes seemed to be improving when he accepted the offer to be a director of a fledgling railroad company. But, alas, the company quickly folded when a competitor was granted the government franchise that his railroad needed to survive.

After that, on recommendations from high-placed friends, Heth successively held these government positions: Treasury Department agent in Brownsville, Texas; civil engineer in Georgetown, South Carolina; special agent in the Bureau of Indian Affairs. The last-named entailed constant travel to every western state and territory. In 1892 he presided as chief marshal at the dedication of a monument to his former commander, A. P. Hill. In 1893 he was an honorary pallbearer in the funeral for Jefferson Davis.

Heth died on September 27, 1899, at age 73.[60]

Sergeant Joseph Woods Brunson had fought with the Pee Dee (South Carolina) Light Artillery of Pegram's Battalion on that first morning at Gettysburg. Sixty years later, the then eighty-four-year-old veteran was asked to give the welcoming address at a Confederate reunion to be held on May 3, 1923. But, when the big day arrived, someone else had to read his speech. Brunson was too weak to do so himself.

The old-timers listened raptly, eyes glistening, as Brunson's words evoked the most memorable time in their lives.

...my mind goes back to our fighting days, and the incidents and events of that stormy time seem to pass in panoramic view before me: the long and weary march; the restful bivouac, where the ground was our luxurious couch and the canopy of heaven our covering, sometimes starlit, sometimes stormy; the summer's heat, the winter's cold; the almost intolerable thirst and ever present hunger; the storm of battle, the hissing of the minnies, the screaming of the shell, the whizzing of the solid shot, the doleful whine of the grape shot, the patter of the shrapnel, the steady music of your faithful rifles, and the hoarse chorus of our cannon....

Ah, Boys, then we were young. These time-furrowed faces of ours wore the hue of youth and only the down of adolescence, the jocund tide of youth bounded through our veins, our inspirations were high. We knew then, as we know now, that we were right and that consciousness nerved our arms and exalted our souls when missiles of death flew thickest.[61]

APPENDIX 1

APPROXIMATE ENGAGED STRENGTH AND CASUALTIES

UNION

Morning, July 1, 1863

	Engaged Strength	Casualties	Percent Casualties
CAVALRY CORPS			
1st Division — Brig. Gen. John Buford			
1st Brigade — Colonel William Gamble			
8th Illinois	470	5	1%
12th Illinois	230	15	7%
3rd Indiana	310	30	10%
8th New York	580	30	5%
	1590	80	5%
2nd Brigade — Colonel Thomas Devin			
6th New York	220	10	5%
9th New York	370	10	3%
17th Pennsylvania	460	slight	—
3rd West Virginia	60	slight	—
	1110	20	2%
Division and Brigades Staffs	10	slight	—
Division total	2710	100	4%
Calef — Btry A, 2nd U.S.	70	10	14%

FIRST ARMY CORPS

1st Division — Brig. Gen. James Wadsworth

1st "Iron" Brigade — Brig. Gen. Solomon Meredith

19th Indiana	310	40	13%
24th Michigan	500	70	14%
2nd Wisconsin	300	115	38%
6th Wisconsin	340	130	38%
7th Wisconsin	360	80	22%
	1810	435	24%

2nd Brigade — Brig. Gen. Lysander Cutler

76th New York	380	170	45%
14th Brooklyn (84th NY)	320	105	33%
95th New York	240	80	33%
147th New York	380	220	58%
56th Pennsylvania	250	105	42%
	1570	680	43%
Division and Brigades Staffs	40	slight	—
Division total	3420	1115	33%
Hall — Btry B, 2nd Maine	120	20	17%
TOTALS	6310	1245	20%

Appendix 2

APPROXIMATE ENGAGED STRENGTH AND CASUALTIES

Confederate

Morning, July 1, 1863

	Engaged Strength	Casualties	Percent Casualties
SECOND ARMY CORPS			
Division — Maj. Gen. Henry Heth			
Brigade — Brig. Gen. James Archer			
5th Alabama Bn	140	45	32%
13th Alabama	310	120	39%
1st Tennessee	280	105	38%
7th Tennessee	250	70	28%
14th Tennessee	220	60	27%
	1200	400	33%
Brigade — Brig. Gen. Joseph Davis			
2nd Mississippi	490	330	67%
42nd Mississippi	580	170	29%
55th North Carolina	640	150	23%
	1710	650	38%
Division and Brigades Staffs	20	slight	—
Division totals	2930	1050	36%
Pegram — 5 Batteries	380	10	3%
TOTALS	3310	1060	32%

APPENDIX 3

APPROXIMATE STRENGTH OF INFANTRY ON FIELD, NOT ENGAGED

UNION

Morning, July 1, 1863

FIRST ARMY CORPS	Strength
2nd Division — Brig. Gen. John Robinson	
1st Brigade — Brig. Gen. Gabriel Paul	
13th Massachusetts	280
16th Maine	300
94th New York	410
104th New York	290
107th New York	260
	1540
2nd Brigade — Brig. Gen. Henry Baxter	
12th Massachusetts	260
83rd New York	200
97th New York	240
11th Pennsylvania	270
88th Pennsylvania	270
90th Pennsylvania	210
	1450
Division and Brigades Staffs	20
Division total	3010
3rd Division — Brig. Gen. Thomas Rowley	
1st Brigade — Col. George H. Biddle	
80th New York	290
121st Pennsylvania	260
142nd Pennsylvania	340
150th Pennsylvania	470
	1360
2nd Brigade — Col. Roy Stone	
143rd Pennsylvania	470
149th Pennsylvania	450
151st Pennsylvania	400
	1320
Division and Brigade Staffs	20
Division total	2700

Appendix 4

APPROXIMATE STRENGTH OF INFANTRY ON FIELD, NOT ENGAGED

Confederate

Morning, July 1, 1863

THIRD ARMY CORPS	Strength
Division — Major Gen. Henry Heth	
Brigade — Brig. Gen. James J. Pettigrew	
11th North Carolina	620
26th North Carolina	840
47th North Carolina	570
52nd North Carolina	550
Division total	2580
Brigade — Col. John Brockenbrough	
40th Virginia	250
47th Virginia	210
55th Virginia	270
22nd Virginia	240
Division total	970
TOTAL	3550

Appendix 5

APPROXIMATE STRENGTH OF INFANTRY ARRIVING VICINITY OF GETTYSBURG

Late Morning, July 1, 1863

Union

	Strength
ELEVENTH ARMY CORPS — Maj. Gen. Oliver O. Howard	
1st Division — Brig. Gen. Francis Barlow	
1st Brigade — Col. Leopold von Gilsa	1120
2nd Brigade — Brig. Gen. Adelbert Ames	1340
	2460
2nd Division — Brig. Gen. Adolph von Steinwehr	
1st Brigade — Col. Charles Coster	1160
2nd Brigade — Col. Orlando Smith	1620
	2780
3rd Division — Maj. Gen. Carl Schurz	
1st Brigade — Brig. Gen. Alexander Schimmelfinnig	1670
2nd Brigade — Col. Wladimir Krzyanowski	1410
	3080
Total Union	8320

Confederate

THIRD ARMY CORPS — Lt. Gen. Ambrose Powell Hill	
Division — Maj. Gen. W. Dorsey Pender	
Brigade — Col. Abner Perrin	1880
Brigade — Brig. Gen. James Lane	1730
Brigade — Brig. Gen. Edward Thomas	1330
Brigade — Brig. Gen. Alfred Scales	1410
	6350
SECOND ARMY CORPS	
Division — Maj. Gen. Robert Rodes	
Brigade — Brig. Gen. Junius Daniel	2160
Brigade — Brig. Gen. George Doles	1320
Brigade — Brig. Gen. Alfred Iverson	1380
Brigade — Brig. Gen. Stephen Ramseur	1030
Brigade — Col. Edward O'Neal	1690
	7580
Total Confederate	13930

Appendix 6

ARTILLERY IN ACTION BEFORE 11:00

Morning, July 1, 1863

Battery & Commander	Strength	Guns – Number & Type
	Union	
2nd U.S., Battery A — Calef	70	6 – 3" Rifles
2nd Maine, Battery B — Hall	120	6 – 3" Rifles
Total	**190**	12 – 3" Rifles
	Confederate	
Pegram's Battalion		
Crenshaw Battery — Johnston	80	2 – Napoleons 2 – 12-pdr. Howitzers
Fredericksburg Battery — Marye	70	2 – Napoleons 2 – 3" Rifles
Letcher Battery — Brander	70	2 – Napoleons 2 – 10-pdr. Parrotts
Purcell Battery — McGraw	90	4 – Napoleons
Pee Dee Battery — Zimmerman	70	4 – 3" Rifles
Total	**380**	10 – Napoleons 6 – 3" Rifles 2 – 10-pdr. Parrotts 2 – 12-pdr. Howitzers

APPENDIX 7

ARTILLERY ARRIVING AND IN PLACE BETWEEN 11:00 AND NOON

Morning, July 1, 1863

Battery & Commander	Strength	Guns – Number & Type
	UNION	
2nd Maine, Battery E — Stevens	120	6 – Napoleons
1st N.Y., Batts. E & L — Reynolds	120	6 – 3" Rifles
1st PA., Battery B — Cooper	110	4 – 3" Rifles
4th U.S., Battery B — Stewart	120	6 – Napoleons
Total	**470**	12 – Napoleons 10 – 3" Rifles
	CONFEDERATE	
McIntosh's Battalion		
Danville (VA.) Battery — Rice	100	4 – Napoleons
Hardaway (AL.) Battery — Hurt	80	2 – Whitworths 2 – 3" Rifles
2nd Rockbridge (VA.) Battery — Wallace	80	4 – 3" Rifles
Virginia Battery — Johnson	100	2 – Napoleons 2 – 3" Rifles
Pee Dee Battery — Zimmerman	70	4 – 3" Rifles
Total	**430**	6 – Napoleons 12 – 3" Rifles 2 – Whitworths

NOTES

Abbreviations

The following abbreviations are used in the notes.

B & L Johnson, Robert U. and Clarence C. Buel (Eds.), *Battles and Leaders of the Civil War.*
GNMP Gettysburg National Military Park.
OR 43 Serial No. 43 of Series I (Vol. XXVII, pt. 1) of *The War of the Rebellion: A Compilation of the Official Records of the Union and Confederate Armies*, commonly referred to as the Official Records.
OR 44 Serial No. 44 of Series I (Vol. XXVII, pt. 2) of the Official Records.
OR 45 Serial No. 45 of Series I (Vol. XXVII, pt. 3) of the Official Records.
SHSP *Southern Historical Society Papers.*
USAMHI United States Army Military History Institute, Carlisle Barracks, Pennsylvania.

Names of editors are omitted in citations of the following sources:

Bandy, Ken and Florence Freeland (Eds.), *The Gettysburg Papers.*
Clark, Walter (Ed.), *Histories of the Several Regiments and Battalions from North Carolina in the Great War, 1861-65.*
Fox, William F. (Ed.), *New York at Gettysburg.*
Nicholson, John P. (Ed.), *Pennsylvania at Gettysburg.*

INTRODUCTION

1. Cheek and Pointon, *History of the Sauk County Riflemen*, (Introduction by Alan T. Nolan), ii.
2. Capt. John H. Bassler to Col. J. B. Bachelder, Feb. [?] 1882, copy in GNMP Library.

PROLOGUE

1. *History of Cumberland and Adams County, Pennsylvania*, 21, 23.
2. Georg, "Edward McPherson Farm: Historical Study," unpublished typescript in GNMP Library.
3. Roth, "Tavern with a Past is Brought Up-to-date," *York [Pa.] Sunday News*, July 27, 1986.

CHAPTER I

1. Col. Risden T. Bennett (14th North Carolina) quoted in *Histories of the Several Regiments and Battalions from North Carolina in the Great War, 1861-65*, Vol. I, 717.
2. Maj. James P. Smith (Ewell staff officer), address, *SHSP*, Vol. XXXIII, 136.
3. Quoted in Jones, *A Rebel War Clerk's Diary*, Vol. I, 315.
4. Quoted in *SHSP*, Vol. IV, 151-152.
5. Quoted in Sandburg, *Abraham Lincoln*, Part II, 353.
6. Quoted in Beale, "Gettysburg on July 1, 1863 — by One of Reynold's Corps," manuscript in Samuel P. Bates Papers, Div. of Archives and Manuscripts, State of Pennsylvania, copy in GNMP Library.
7. Boatner, *Civil War Dictionary*, 140; Catton, Glory Road, 255.
8. Sawyer, *Military History of the 8th Regiment Ohio Volunteer Infantry*, 117.

9. Lt. Frank A. Haskell quoted in Byrne and Weaver, Eds., *Haskell of Gettysburg: His Life and Civil War Papers*, 91.
10. Otis, *Second Wisconsin Infantry*, 83.
11. Col. Charles F. Morse, *History of the 2nd Massachusetts Regiment of Infantry: Gettysburg*, 4.
12. Buell, *Cannoneer*, 60.
13. Storrick, *Gettysburg: The Place, the Battles, the Outcome*, 11.
14. *SHSP*, Vol. IV, 156-157. "[I]n the judgement of General Lee," wrote his assistant adjutant general, Lt. Col. Walter H. Taylor, "it was a part of a true defensive policy to take the aggressive when good opportunity offered...." [*Annals of the War by Leading Participants North and South*, 305.]
15. *SHSP*, Vol. XXXIII, 135-136.
16. *SHSP*, IV, 153; *SHSP*, Vol. XXXIII, 135-136; *Confederate Veteran*, Vol. XXV, 209.
17. Storrick, 11.
18. *SHSP*, IV, 153; *SHSP*, Vol. XXXIII, 135-136; Jones (compiler), *Army of Northern Virginia, Memorial Volume*, 94.
19. Steele, *American Campaigns*, Vol. I, 355-356; Spaulding, *U. S. Army in War and Peace*, 298; Tucker, *High Tide at Gettysburg*, 18-20; Grimsley, "The Master General: Frictions of War," *Civil War Times Illustrated*, XXIV (Nov. 1985), 37.
20. De Peyster, *Decisive Conflicts of the Late Civil War*, 5.
21. Stearns, *Three Years with Company K*, 176.
22. *SHSP*, Vol. IV, 56.
23. *SHSP*, Vol. XXVI, 128.
24. Catton, *Glory Road*, 160; Stackpole, *Chancellorsville: Lee's Greatest Battle*, 95. The latter reference contain's Hooker's famous boast: "My plans are perfect, and when I start to carry them out, may God have mercy on General Lee, for I will have none!"
25. Lincoln to Maj. Gen. Joseph Hooker, Jan. 26, 1863, quoted in Sandburg, 268.
26. Nevins (Ed.), *A Diary of Battle: The Personal Journals of Colonel Charles S. Wainwright*, 229; Jepson, "The First Day at Gettysburg. A Tribute to Gen. Reynolds...." *National Tribune*, Oct. 6, 1910; Schildt, *Roads to Gettysburg*, 346-347; Nichols, *Toward Gettysburg: A Biography of John F. Reynolds*, 183-184. According to Wainwright, Reynolds was "unwilling to take Burnside and Hooker's leavings."
27. Address by Joseph G. Rosengarten published (1880) in *Reynolds Memorial — Addresses Before the Historical Society of Pennsylvania*; Rosengarten, "Major-General John F. Reynolds," Gettysburg *Star and Sentinel*, May 5, 1885; Rosengarten, "Reynolds, Hero of the First Day, By One of His Staff," *New York Times Magazine*, June 29, 1913; Nichols, 92.
28. Bates, *Martial Deeds of Pennsylvania*, 467.
29. Nichols, 13.
30. Nichols, *passim.*
31. Boatner, *Civil War Dictionary*, 694; "Unveiling of the Statue of General John F. Reynolds [in Philadelphia, 1884]," pamphlet in GNMP files, 17; inscription on equestrian statue of Reynolds on battlefield.
32. Boatner, 694.
33. *Reynolds Memorial*, 13.
34. *Reynolds Memorial*; 13; Boatner, 694.
35. Nichols, 93,96-97, 99; Bates, 469-470.
36. Bates, 471-472; Boatner, 694.
37. Bates, 472; Sears, *Landscape Turned Red*, 101.

38. Boatner, 694.
39. Schildt, 346-347; Nichols, 183-184.
40. Jepson, "The First Day at Gettysburg. A Tribute to Gen. Reynolds....", *National Tribune*, Oct. 6, 1910; Nevins (Ed.), 229.
41. *Annals of the War*, 447; Coddington, *Gettysburg Campaign*, 12, 51, 53-60; Boatner, 332, 600; Tucker, *High Tide*, 21.
42. Bates, 181.
43. *SHSP*, Vol. IV, 153.
44. Coddington, 87-89, 103; Boatner, 332.
45. Livermore, *Story of the Civil War*, Vol. 2, Part III, 339; Coddington, 250.
46. Nevins (Ed.), 224; Coddington, 75.
47. Tucker, *High Tide*, 42-43.
48. Commager, *The Blue and the Gray*, 595, quotes letter of Col. William S. Christian (55th Virginia) to his wife, June 28, 1863, from his camp near Greenwood, Pennsylvania.
49. Moore (Ed.), *Rebellion Record*, Vol. VII, 109, cites *Richmond Enquirer* account datelined July 8, 1863; Marye, "First Gun at Gettysburg, With the Confederate Advance Guard," *American Historical Register*, July, 1895, 1226. Marye gives a detailed eye-witness account of Heth's Division crossing the Potomac.
50. Robertson, *General A. P. Hill*, 201, cites diary of W. A. Alexander.
51. Freeman, *R. E. Lee*, Vol. III, 52.
52. Dawson, *Reminiscences of Confederate Service*, 90-91.
53. Quoted in *Confederate Veteran*, Vol. XXV, 209.
54. Marye, "First Gun at Gettysburg, With the Confederate Advance Guard," *American Historical Register*, July, 1895, 1227.
55. *OR* 45, 930; Freeman, *R. E. Lee*, Vol. III, 57.
56. Coddington, 154, 176.
57. Dawson, 92.
58. Moore (Ed.), Vol. VII, 325, quotes letter of Col. William S. Christian (55th Virginia) to his wife, June 28, 1863, from his camp near Greenwood, Pennsylvania.
59. Jacobs, *Notes on the Rebel Invasion of Maryland and Pennsylvania*, 11.
60. Coddington, 154-155; *OR* 44, 443.
61. Marye, "First Gun at Gettysburg, With the Confederate Advance Guard," *American Historical Register*, July, 1895, 1227.
62. *OR* 45, 923.
63. Moore (Ed.), Vol. VII, 319; Bates, 183; Coddington, 134-137; Nye, *Here Come the Rebels*, 158.
64. Harman, "The Reaction of the People of Pennsylvania to Lee's Invasion of 1863," unpublished thesis (1959), 139-140, cites *Philadelphia Daily Evening Bulletin*, June 23, 1863.
65. Fremantle, *Three Months in the Southern States*, 246.
66. Jacobs, 18.
67. Hassler, *Crisis at the Crossroads*, 6.
68. Dawson, 93.
69. Pollard, *Southern History of the War*, Vol. III, 24; *Pennsylvania at Gettysburg*, Vol. II, 884.
70. Boyle, *Soldiers True, the Story of the One Hundred and Eleventh Regiment Pennsylvania Volunteers*, 112-113.
71. Tucker, *High Tide*, 28.
72. *Pennsylvania at Gettysburg*, Vol. II, 883; Harman, "The Reaction of the People of Pennsylvania to Lee's Invasion of 1863," unpublished thesis (1959), 59; Nye, 68. The

Reverend Leonard Gardner, who witnessed the flight of the refugees, remembered: "The most useless and cumbersome things were taken. Amid the crowd I saw passing a one-horse wagon filled with household goods and an old baby buggy perched on top."

73. Jacobs, 9.
74. Bates, 1081-1083.
75. Jacobs, 9.
76. Jacobs, 11; Bates, 177; Vanderslice, *Gettysburg Then and Now*, 51.
77. Jacobs, 13-14; *Battles and Leaders of the Civil War*, Vol. III, 289; Nye, 271-273.
78. Myers, 192-193.
79. Jacobs, 14-15.
80. *OR* 44, 465 (Early); *Battles and Leaders of the Civil War*, Vol. III, 289; Jacobs, 15. The first-hand account in *Battles and Leaders* was written in 1886 by H. M. M. Richards, who had served in Company A, 26th Pennsylvania Militia. While he supplied much reliable detail, he conveyed a totally erroneous impression in one regard. Referring to the enemy cavalry, he wrote: "These latter overtook us in the afternoon at Witmer's house...where after an engagement they were repulsed with some loss." Actually, as he surely remembered, it was he and his comrades — thus "we," not "they" — who were repulsed. And "some" hardly suffices for the 26th Pennsylvania's loss at the Witmer farm. Professor Jacobs put the figure at 120. General Early reported (*OR* 44, 465) that White's and French's cavalry combined took 175 prisoners that day. There is sufficient evidence to conclude that the latter accounted for well over half of that number.
81. Myers, 192-193; Jacobs, 15; Bates, 177.
82. Jacobs, 15-18; *OR* 44, 465; Coddington, 167-168; Nye, 275; Bates, 178; Scott, *Story of the Battles at Gettysburg*, Vol. I, 24.
83. Prowell, *History of York County*, 406-410, 588. Prowell's $28,000 figure has been amended to $28,600, as reported by General Early himself [*OR* 44, 466]. Possibly the largest increase in the quantities requisitioned by Early was in the case of shoes — 1,000 pairs in Gettysburg; 2,000, in York [Coddington, 167-168].
84. Prowell, 415, 417; Coddington, 169-170.
85. Freeman, *Lee's Lieutenants*, Vol. III, 76-77, quotes Maj. Gen. W. D. Pender (in Fayetteville) to his wife, June 28, 1863.
86. Stackpole, *They Met at Gettysburg*, 20-21; Nye, 230; Coddington, 188.
87. Harman, "The Reaction of the People of Pennsylvania to Lee's Invasion of 1863," unpublished thesis (1959), 110.
88. Diary of Sarah M. Broadhead, typescript in GNMP Library.
89. *OR* 45, 914.
90. Freeman, *R. E. Lee*, Vol. III, 54-55, 59-60; Nye, 343-344.
91. Hoke, *The Great Invasion of 1863*, 160-164; Coddington, 172.
92. *OR* 45, 942-943. In general, officers tended to wink at Lee's order. Colonel Henry K. Burgwyn, Jr., for example, treated a case of vandalism in his 26th North Carolina far differently than Lee proposed. On learning that some of his men had stolen several bee hives, he sought out the owner and personally reimbursed him for his loss. [*Histories of the Several Regiments and Battalions from North Carolina*, Vol. III, 342.]
93. *SHSP*, Vol. XXVI, 120-121.
94. *OR* 44, 606; Nye, 343-344.
95. *Battles and Leaders of the Civil War*, Vol. III, 244, 249-250 (Longstreet); Pfanz, *Gettysburg: The Second Day*, 3; Tucker, *High Tide*, 80-81. The exact time of Lee's meeting with Harrison is uncertain. According to Colonel E. P. Alexander of the First Corps Artillery Reserve, it was "about midnight" when the spy arrived at Longstreet's headquarters, which would place the meeting with Lee even later. [Alexander, *Military Memoirs*

of a Confederate, 379.] However, Major John W. Fairfax of Longstreet's staff stated that he informed Lee at 10:00 p.m. of Harrison's arrival and that sometime later Lee summoned the spy to his tent. [Freeman, *R. E. Lee*, Vol. III, 60.]

96. Freeman, *R. E. Lee*, Vol. III, 60.
97. *Battles and Leaders of the Civil War*, Vol. III, 250; Alexander, 379; Pfanz, 3-4.
98. Quoted in Dowdey, *Death of a Nation*, 12, and in Coddington, 196.
99. Coddinogton, 681, quotes Brig. Gen. S. D. Ramseur to Nellie, his fiancee, June 28, 1863.
100. *Battles and Leaders of the Civil War*, Vol. III, 241-243; Meade, *Life and Letters of George Gordon Meade*, Vol. 2, 1; *OR* 43, 60.
101. *Battles and Leaders of the Civil War*, Vol. III, 243.
102. *OR* 43, 61.
103. Meade, Vol. 2, 2; *Battles and Leaders of the Civil War*, Vol. III, 243.
104. Guernsey and Alden, *Harper's Pictorial History of the Civil War*, Vol. II, 504.
105. *Report of the Joint Committee on the Conduct of the War*, 175-176 (testimony of Maj. Gen. Joseph Hooker).
106. Swinton, *Campaigns of the Army of the Potomac*, 315-316; Jones (Compiler), *Army of Northern Virginia*, 96.
107. *Battles and Leaders of the Civil War*, Vol. III, 265.
108. *OR* 43, 35.
109. *Report of the Joint Committee on the Conduct of the War*, 260.
110. *Report of the Joint Committee on the Conduct of the War*, 268.
111. *Battles and Leaders of the Civil War*, Vol. III, 243.
112. *OR* 43, 61-62.
113. Schurz, *Autobiography of Carl Schurz*, 255; *Major-General James S. Wadsworth at Gettysburg and Other Fields*, 87.
114. Nevins (Ed.), 227.
115. Byrne and Weaver (Eds.), 93. Lt. Frank A. Haskell served on the staff of Brig. Gen. John Gibbon.
116. Buell, 61, quotes Lt. James Stewart.
117. *Battles and Leaders of the Civil War*, Vol. III, 243; *OR* 45, 415. Hooker initiated the wing arrangement during the second week of June, when he shifted four corps northwest of the army's encampment at Falmouth and placed Reynolds in command. On June 25 — the day the army started crossing the Potomac — Hooker reassigned Fifth Corps to his own wing, with Reynolds retaining command of the other three. [See Coddington, 70, 122].
118. Nichols, 193, 207, quotes Mary Catherine Reynolds to Harriet Reynolds, June 28 and July 1, 1863.
119. Nichols, 189; Eleanor Reynolds to William Reynolds, July 5, 1863, John F. Reynolds Papers, Franklin and Marshall College, copy in Robert L. Brake Collection, USAMHI.
120. Series of maps in *Battles and Leaders of the Civil War*, Vol. III, 262, 264.
121. Chronicles of Capt. Francis B. Jones (149th Pennsylvania), extract covering Gettysburg campaign, typescript copy, USAMHI; *Gettysburg Papers*, Vol. I, 290 (Lt. Francis Wiggin, 16th Maine).
122. *Gettysburg Papers,* 185 (Capt. William Harries, 2nd Wisconsin).
123. Tevis and Marquis, *History of the Fighting Fourteenth,* 77; Lt. Frank A. Haskell quoted in Byrne and Weaver (Eds.), 92.
124. Stearns, 174-175.
125. Swinton, 320; Jacques, *Three Years Campaign of the Ninth New York State Militia*, 152.
126. Tevis and Marquis, 78; Coddington, 125.
127. *Gettysburg Papers*, Vol. I, 185.
128. *Pennsylvania at Gettysburg*, Vol. II, 751.

129. Davis, *Three Years in the Army: Story of the Thirteenth Massachusetts Volunteers*, 223.
130. Smith, *Twenty-fourth Michigan of the Iron Brigade*, 117, quotes Pvt. George Frederick Neff, Company F of that regiment.
131. Nevins (Ed.), 225.
132. Hassler, 11-12; Coddington, map between pps. 180-181; Davis, 223.
133. Coddington, 38, 250; Livermore, Vol. 2, Part III, 339; .
134. *OR* 45, 349.
135. *Annals of the War* ,452.
136. *Annals of the War* , 452-453.
137. *OR* 45, 400; *OR* 43, 926.
138. *Annals of the War* ,453.

CHAPTER 2

1. *OR* 44, 317; Nye, 346.
2. Nye, 347-348 (quotes Jedediah Hotchkiss).
3. Coddington, map between pps. 180-181.
4. Oates, *War Between the Union and the Confederacy*, 201; Bates, 450.
5. Longstreet, *From Manassas to Appomattox: Memoirs of the Civil War in America*, 357; Owen, *In Camp and Battle with the Washington Artillery of New Orleans*, 242.
6. *SHSP*, Vol. IV, 156.
7. *OR* 43, 66-67.
8. Meade, Vol. II, 12, 14.
9. *OR* 45, 416.
10. *OR* 45, 419-420.
11. *OR* 45, 416.
12. *OR* 45, 415.
13. *OR* 45, 458-459; Hassler, *Crisis at the Crossroads*, 9; Fieberger, *Campaign and Battle of Gettysburg*, 31.
14. Hassler, *Crisis* ,19-20.
15. *OR* 45, 417.
16. *Pennsylvania at Gettysburg*, Vol. II, 883.
17. *OR* 43, 143, 913, 1030; OR45, 400.
18. Fuller, "Who Fired the First Shot at the Battle of Gettysburg?" *Journal of U. S. Cavalry Association*, Vol. 24 (1914); Boatner, 238, 322.
19. Cheney, *History of the Ninth Regiment New York Volunteer Cavalry*, 101.
20. *OR* 43, 1030; Fieberger, 31.
21. Hall, Besley, and Wood, *History of the Sixth New York Cavalry*, 132-133.
22. Moyer, *History of the Seventeenth Regiment Pennsylvania Volunteer Cavalry*, 48; *Pennsylvania at Gettysburg*, Vol. II, 883.
23. Biddle, *First Day of the Battle of Gettysburg*, 16.
24. Agassiz (Ed.), *Meade's Headquarters 1863-1865: Letters of Colonel Theodore Lyman*, 21.
25. Moyer, 58.
26. Pratt, "Man on Horseback," *Infantry Journal*, Vol. 47 (1940), 114, 116; Boatner, 97.
27. Weigley, "John Buford," *Civil War Times Illustrated*, Vol. V (June 1966), 15-16.
28. Weigley, 16, 19-20; Boatner, 97.
29. Agassiz (Ed.), 21.
30. Biddle,16; Vanderslice, 52.
31. *OR* 43, 926.
32. *Histories of the Several Regiments and Battalions from North Carolina*, Vol. III, 236; Pickerell, *History of the Third Indiana Cavalry*, 81.

33. Moyer, 49.
34. Moyer, 48; *Pennsylvania at Gettysburg*, Vol. II, 883.
35. Norton, *Deeds of Daring or the History of the Eighth New York Volunteer Cavalry*, 68; Cheney,102; *Gettysburg Papers*, Vol. I, 171; Hard, *History of the Eight Cavalry Regiment Illinois Volunteers*, 255.
36. Hard, 255; Gamble's Brigade monument on the battlefield; *OR* 43, 914.
37. Hard, 255-256. Abner Hard, the 8th Illinois' surgeon, tells the full story of Pvt. Tom Withrow, who, on being unhorsed, became so mad he swore he would have his revenge. Taking cover behind a barn, he kept on sniping at the enemy until he heard a Confederate officer order his men to search the barn. Instantly, Withrow dashed inside and dived into a hay mow. Peeking out, his heart pounding, he saw Rebels looking into every corner and occasionally thrusting their bayonets into the hay. A colonel stopped so close to his hiding place that he could easily have shot him dead. Withrow resisted the temptation, of course, for that would undoubtedly have cost his own life, which, as Hard put it, "he valued more than that of a rebel colonel." Not finding anyone, the Confederates left. Shortly, the farmer whose barn it was came in, checking no doubt for arson or theft. Withrow's sudden appearance gave him a bad scare. But, greatly relieved to see he faced a Yankee, the farmer proposed he come home with him for some dinner. Withrow gratefully accepted, as it would be a long walk to Gettysburg.
38. *OR* 43, 926; DePeyster, 27; Norton, 68; Gamble's Brigade monument on the battlefield.
39. *OR* 43, 986-987, 1008-1009; *OR* 44, 695-697; Prowell, 427-428, 439-440; Nye, 322-323.
40. Nye, 323-324, quotes Major H. B. McClellan's account of the incident as it appeared in *I Rode with Jeb Stuart.*
41. *OR* 43, 986-987; Nye, 324; Prowell, 429.
42. *OR* 44, 696-697; Nye, 324-325.
43. Col. E. P. Alexander ruefully pointed out that Stuart and his troopers could have arrived in Gettysburg on June 30, even ahead of Buford's Brigades. The artillery leader always regretted that that had not been the case. If it had, then (in his words) "Lee's army would have occupied some strong position between Cashtown and Gettysburg, and the onus of the attack would have been upon the Federals, as had been the plan of the campaign." [Alexander, 375-376.]
44. *OR* 45, 434.
45. Hoke, 226; Freeman, *R. E. Lee*, 65.
46. Nye, 365.
47. Owen, 242; June 30, 1863 entry in diary of Lt. John E. Hoffman (Co. C, 3rd West Virginia Cavalry), USAMHI (copy of original in West Virginia University Library); Freeman, *R. E. Lee*, 64.
48. *OR* 44, 607; Hassler, *Crisis*, 19; Coddington, 194, map between pps. 180-181.
49. Morrison (Ed.), *Memoirs of Henry Heth*, 9, 13-14, 26-27, 237, xiii-xv, xviii-xx; Hassler, "Harry Heth — Lee's Hard-Luck General," *Civil War Times Illustrated*, V (July 1966), 13; Boatner, 398.
50. Morrison (Ed.), 57-60, 103, xxiv-xxvii.
51. Morrison (Ed.),129, xxviii-xxx.
52. Morrison (Ed.),139-140, xxx, xxxiii-xxxv, xli-xliv; Boatner, 398.
53. Jacobs, 21.
54. Marye, "The First Gun at Gettysburg, With the Confederate Advance Guard," *American Historical Register*, July 1895, 1228. In his after-action report for Pegram's Battalion, Capt. E. B. Brunson stated the battalion arrived in Cashtown on June 30 [*OR* 44, 677].
55. Fite, *Memoirs of John A. Fite*, 98.
56. Morrison (Ed.),174-175.

57. *OR* 44, 637; *SHSP*, Vol. XXXIII, 142; *Histories of the Several Regiments and Battalions from North Carolina*, Vol. III, 88.
58. *Histories of the Several Regiments and Battalions from North Carolina*, Vol. II, 342-343, Vol. V, 115; Jacobs, 21.
59. Jacobs, 22.
60. Tucker, *High Tide*, 98, cites Shotwell, "Virginia and North Carolina in the Battle of Gettysburg," *Our Living and Dead*, Vol. IV, 82.
61. Jacobs, 21; *OR* 44, 637.
62. Diary of Sarah M. Broadhead, June 30, 1863 entry typescript in GNMP Library.
63. Jacobs, 21; Lt. W. B. Taylor (11th North Carolina) to his mother, July 29, 1863, copy in GNMP Library.
64. *OR* 44, 317.
65. Jacobs, 22.
66. *OR* 43, 923 (Buford report to General Pleasonton, June 30, 1863). The 11:00 a.m. arrival time given here is corroborated in these regimental histories: Cheney, 102, and Hall, *History of the Sixth New York Cavalry*, 133. Buford, in his after-action report [OR43, 926] wrote that his division entered Gettysburg on June 30 "in good season to drive him [the enemy] back before his getting a foothold." Actually, as substantiated in numerous accounts, Pettigrew simply left of his own accord.
67. Cheney, 102; Hall, 133; Moyer, 49.
68. Moyer, 284.
69. Alleman, *At Gettysburg or What a Girl Saw and Heard of the Battle*, 28-29.
70. Article by unnamed 8th Illinois Cavalry veteran, *New York Times*, July 1, 1913.
71. *OR* 43, 923; Bates, 203-204; Col. William. S. Gamble to W. S. Church, Mar. 10, 1864, Chicago Historical Society Library, copy in GNMP Library.
72. Cheney, 102-103; Moyer, 59; Jacobs, 22; Alleman, 28. A comment is in order regarding the 6th New York Cavalry. Its regimental history states that these troops of Devin's brigade camped in the vicinity of McPherson's farm [Hall, 133]. It would therefore have been logical for the regiment to follow Gamble's route through Gettysburg rather than Devin's route.
73. Col. William. S. Gamble to W. S. Church, Mar. 10, 1864, Chicago Historical Society Library, copy in GNMP Library.
74. Georg, *Edward McPherson Farm*, 14-15.
75. Georg, 18, 21, 26, 188.
76. *OR* 43, 926; *New York at Gettysburg*, Vol. I, 7; Lt. W. B. Taylor (11th North Carolina) to his mother, July 29, 1863, copy in GNMP Library. A contemporary account states that Pettigrew made elaborate preparations to ambush Buford's cavalry [Jacobs, 22]. According to Michael Jacobs, then professor of mathematics at Pennsylvania College, the Confederate general placed a regiment on each side of the Chambersburg Pike and sent out another to act as a decoy. Further: After a two-hour wait with no sight of the enemy, Pettigrew's troops returned to Cashtown. (Actually, they bivouacked several miles east of it.) Jacob's account, published in 1864, reappeared almost verbatim three year's later in J. Watts DePeyster's *The Decisive Conflicts of the Civil War* (p. 28). Samuel P. Bates included it in his *Martial Deeds of Pennsylvania* (p. 203), published in 1876. Acceptance by these and subsequent writers notwithstanding, Jacob's account must be considered suspect. Not only is it uncorroborated by any independent source, Confederate or Union, it seems most unlikely that Pettigrew would have sought an engagement with an unknown foe.
77. *OR* 43, 295; Mix, "Experiences at Gettysburg," *National Tribune*, Feb. 22, 1934.
78. Moyer, 49-50; Day, "Veteran of 3d Indiana Cavalry Describes First Day's Fight at Gettysburg," *National Tribune*, July 30, 1903.

79. Mix, "Experiences at Gettysburg," *National Tribune*, Feb. 22, 1934.
80. Nevins (Ed.), 229.
81. Boatner, 244, 704, 711.
82. Boatner, 882-883; *Major-General James S. Wadsworth at Gettysburg and Other Fields*, 45, 52, 79, 84-86; Pearson, *James S. Wadsworth of Geneseo*, 13-14, 22-23, 46-47, 56, 66, 151-165, 168.
83. Pearson, 197, 199; Hill, *Confederate Military History*, Vol. 4, 1000-1001.
84. Smith, *Twenty-Fourth Michigan of the Iron Brigade*, 117, quotes manuscript account by Pvt. George F. Neff of that regiment.
85. *OR* 43, 243. Nineteenth Indiana reported a march of 22 miles [Lt. Col. William W. Dudley to Col. John B. Bachelder, undated letter, copy in GNMP Library]; 2nd Wisconsin, 24 miles [Pvt. Sydney B. Mead, diary entry of June 29, 1863, State Historical Society of Wisconsin, copy in Robert L. Brake Collection, USAMHI]; 147th New York, 26 miles [Lt. H. H. Lyman, diary entry of June 29, 1863, copy in GNMP Library]. Muddy road conditions were mentioned in the Lyman diary entry cited above; also in the official report of the 13th Massachusetts [*OR* 43, 297]. Probably the tiredest troops encamped north of Emmitsburg were those of the 16th Maine. In two days, June 28 and 29 — actually within a period of 26 hours — they had marched a total of 40 miles [*OR* 43, 295].
86. Lt. H. H. Lyman, diary entry of June 29, 1863, copy in GNMP Library.
87. Chamberlin, *History of the 150th Regiment, Pennsylvania Volunteers*, 115.
88. Harris, "With the Iron Brigade Guard at Gettysburg," *Gettysburg*, Issue No. 1 (July 1989), 31. (The account dates from the 1880's, when it was first published in installments in the *Milwaukee Sunday Telegraph*.)
89. *Pennsylvania at Gettysburg*, Vol. II, 751.
90. Lt. H. H. Lyman, diary entry of June 29, 1863, copy in GNMP Library; Coddington, 228.
91. *OR* 43, 243-244; *OR* 45, 417-418; *Pennsylvania at Gettysburg*, Vol. II, 751; Lt. H. H. Lyman, diary entry of June 30, 1863, copy in GNMP Library; Curtis, *History of the Twenty-Fourth Michigan of the Iron Brigade*, 152; *Gettysburg Papers*, Vol. I, 367.
92. Kieffer, *Recollections of a Drummer-Boy*, 106.
93. Nevins (Ed.), 229.
94. Tevis and Marquis, 80-81.
95. *Pennsylvania at Gettysburg*, Vol. I, 340; Strong, *History of the 121st Regiment Pennsylvania Volunteers*, 44; Lt. Col. William W. Dudley to Col. John B. Bachelder, undated letter, copy in GNMP Library; *Gettysburg Papers*, Vol. I, 367.
96. Tevis and Marquis, 80-81.
97. Kieffer, 107-108.
98. *OR* 43, 417-418.
99. *OR* 45, 418.
100. *OR* 45, 417.
101. *OR* 45, 419.
102. *OR* 45, 424
103. *OR* 45, 424-425.
104. *Reynolds Memorial Addresses*, 29 (Joseph G. Rosengarten, member of Reynolds' staff); *OR* 43, 295, 922; *OR* 45, 417, 422.
105. Nichols, 195, cites Maj. Gen. James H. Wilson, *Proceedings of the Buford Memorial Association* (1895), 23-24.
106. *OR* 43, 701.
107. Howard, *Autobiography of Oliver O. Howard*, 402-404; Howard, "Campaign and Battle of Gettysburg, June and July, 1863," *Atlantic Monthly*, July 1876, 52; Coddington, 234, quotes Howard's letter of March 23, 1863 to Prof. Michael Jacobs.

108. *OR* 43, 922.
109. Capt. William Riddle to _____ Le Bouvier, Aug. 4, 1863, John F. Reynolds Papers, Franklin and Marshall College.
110. Coddington, 234, quotes Howard's letter of March 23, 1863 to Prof. Michael Jacobs.
111. *OR* 43, 295.
112. *OR* 43, 244.
113. Howard, 402-403.
114. Nevins (Ed.), 232.
115. *SHSP*, Vol. IV, 157; Morrison (Ed.), 173. The two accounts differ in one detail. In his memoirs, Heth reported Hill's reply as "Do so."
116. *Histories of the Several Regiments and Battalions from North Carolina*, Vol. V, 116-117.
117. *OR* 44, 607; Taylor, *Four Years With General Lee*, 92-93.
118. Coddington, 264, quotes Col. E. P. Alexander's unpublished account of the Battle of Gettysburg.
119. *OR* 44, 444; Nye, 360-361.
120. Coddington, 192.
121. Nye, 36
122. Hassler, *A. P. Hill: Lee's Forgotten General*, 152, cites letter of Third Corps surgeon G. Spencer Welch to his wife.
123. Fite, 98-99.
124. *Histories of the Several Regiments and Battalions from North Carolina*, Vol. II, 342.
125. *Histories of the Several Regiments and Battalions from North Carolina*, Vol. V, 117.
126. Comte de Paris, *History of the Civil War in America*, Vol. 3, 544-545; Hall, 135.
127. *OR* 43, 924; Hall, 135.
128. Lt. A. B. Jerome to Maj. Gen. W. S. Hancock, Oct. 18, 1865, John B. Bachelder Collection, copy in GNMP Library; DePeyster, 151-152.
129. *OR* 43, 295.
130. *OR* 43, 938.
131. *OR* 45, 414.
132. Moyer, 329.
133. Cheney, 105.
134. Calef, "Gettysburg Notes: The Opening Gun," *Journal of the Military Service Institution*, Vol. XL, 47; 2nd United States Artillery, Battery A monument on the battlefield.
135. Gates, *Ulster Guard (20th N. Y. State Militia) and the War of the Rebellion*, 422. Almost identical accounts of the Buford-Devin conversation, as originally reported by Buford's signal officer, Lieutenant A. B. Jerome, also appear in: DePeyster, 151; Moyer, 60; Hall, 136.

CHAPTER 3

1. *Neuer Gemeinnussiger Calender auf das Jahr heilandes Jesu Christi 1873*. (Almanac published in Lancaster, Pennsylvania.)
2. Fite, 99.
3. Freeman, *R. E. Lee*, Vol. III, 65, cites diary entry, July 1, 1863, of John E. Cooke, an officer on Lee's staff. That morning Cooke was in Greenwood, about eight miles west of Cashtown.
4. *OR* 44, 637.
5. *OR* 44, 637.
6. *Annals of the War*, 307.
7. Hassler, *A. P. Hill*, 153.
8. *Gettysburg Papers*, Vol. I, 432-433.

9. Young, *Battle of Gettysburg*, 181.
10. Hassler, *A. P. Hill*, 3; Tucker, *High Tide*, 11.
11. Fremantle, *Three Months in the Southern States*, 203; Dowdey, 91-92.
12. Hassler, *A. P. Hill*, 153.
13. Fremantle, 254.
14. Tucker, *High Tide*, 11.
15. Dowdey, 91-92. James I. Robertson, Jr. has made a study of Hill's recurring illnesses. In his biography of the general, he lists possible causes of Hill's indisposition on July 1,1863, as "upset stomach, diarrhea, simple exhaustion, or a flare-up of the old prostate problem." [*General A. P. Hill: The Story of a Confederate Warrior*, 206.]
16. Dowdey, 79, 87.
17. Boatner, 23.
18. Heth in his battle report did not say his division marched at 5:00, only that he was ordered to do so at that hour (*OR* 44, 637). Hill in his report says Heth "took up the line of march" at 5:00 a.m. (*OR* 44, 607).
19. Marye, "The First Gun at Gettysburg," *The American Historical Register*, July 1895, 1228; *Gettysburg Papers*, Vol I, 432-433; Tucker, *High Tide*, 104-105, cites *Richmond Enquirer*, July 15, 1863. Capt. E. B. Brunson in his report for Pegram's battalion contradicts Marye and Heth, stating that their position was in the rear [*OR* 44, 677]. This is where they should have been, and Brunson's statement may have been a deliberate coverup of Heth's initial blunder (which was soon corrected when at least one, possibly all, of Heth's regiments were moved ahead of the artillery).
20. *Gettysburg Papers*, Vol. I, 432-433.
21. *OR* 44, 649; Brown, *University Grays*, 37.
22. Marye, "The First Gun at Gettysburg," *The American Historical Register*, July 1895, 1228; unnamed captain of Pettigrew's Brigade, "Northern Prison Life," *The Land We Love*, November 1866, 43; Moon, "Beginning of the Battle of Gettysburg," *Confederate Veteran*, Vol. XXXIII (December 1925), 449-450; Freeman, *Lee's Lieutenants*, 78.
23. Hassler, *A. P. Hill*, 153.
24. Boland, "Beginning of the Battle of Gettysburg," *Confederate Veteran*, Vol. XIV (July 1906), 308-309.
25. Marye, "The First Gun at Gettysburg," *The American Historical Register*, July 1895, 1228.
26. Unnamed captain in Pettigrew's Brigade, "Northern Prison Life," *The Land We Love*, November 1866, 43.
27. *The Land We Love*, November 1866, 43.; Belo, "Battle of Gettysburg," *Confederate Veteran*, Vol. VIII (April 1900), 165-168.
28. *SHSP*, Vol. XXIV, 183-184.
29. *Gettysburg Papers*, Vol. I, 432-433.
30. Stackpole, *They Met at Gettysburg*, 2.
31. Coddington, 273, cites Henry Heth, "Gen. Lee's Orders to His Cavalry," *Philadelphia Weekly Times*, Mar. 23, 1878; Theodore W. Bean, "Buford at Gettysburg," *The [Philadelphia] Times*, Sept. 11, 1880, cites the same Heth article.
32. William Riddle to ______ Le Bouvier, Aug. 4, 1863, John F. Reynolds Papers, Franklin and Marshall College, copy in GNMP Library.
33. *OR* 45, 416; Longacre, "John F. Reynolds, General," *Civil War Times Illustrated*, XI (August 1972), 41, cites Gen. Isaac R. Trimble.
34. William Riddle to ______ Le Bouvier, Aug. 4, 1863, John F. Reynolds Papers, Franklin and Marshall College, copy in GNMP Library.
35. *OR* 45, 416.
36. *OR* 45, 457.

37. *OR* 45, 416.
38. Weld, *War Diary*, 229; Coddington, 261.
39. Tevis and Marquis, 81; Cook, *History of 12th Massachusetts*, 100; Nolan, *Iron Brigade*, 233.
40. Bassler, "Reminiscences of First Day's Fight," address given at Albright Collegiate Institute, June 1895, Robert L. Brake Collection, USAMHI; *Pennsylvania at Gettysburg*, 751.
41. Curtis, 155.
42. Chamberlin, *History of 150th Pennsylvania*, 117.
43. *New York at Gettysburg*, Vol. III, 990.
44. Jones, "Chronicles" (excerpt, no page numbers), Robert L. Brake Collection, USAMHI.
45. "Shriver Family Fed Reynolds Last Meal," in Section D, *The Battle of Gettysburg Centennial Edition*, published by *Gettysburg Times* (July 1963); *History of the Shriver Family* (1926), extract in GNMP Library. The newspaper account is based on an interview with Bess and Myrtle Shriver (both unmarried and living in Gettysburg), whose grandparents prepared breakfast for Reynolds and his staff. There is no reference to time except that it was early in the morning. Coddington says they breakfasted "soon after sunrise" [261].
46. *Reynolds Memorial Addresses*, 63; Cook, 100; Strong, 214 — all cite Hall's account in *Brookline [MA] Chronicle*, Feb. 16, 1878. Col. Chapman Biddle, who also heard Reynolds dictate the message to Meade, corroborates Hall's account [Biddle, 24].
47. Nichols, 199.
48. Tevis and Marquis, 81.
49. *OR* 45, 457; Schildt, 458-459.
50. *OR* 43, 701.
51. Coddington, 268-269.
52. Coddington, 261; Nichols, 199.
53. *OR* 45, 457.
54. *OR* 43, 244; Doubleday, *Chancellorsville and Gettysburg*, 124-125; *Report of the Joint Committee on the Conduct of the War*, Part 1, 305; Henry T. Lee to Samuel P. Bates, Feb. 6, 1871, Pa. Historical and Museum Commission, Div. of Archives and Manuscripts, copy in GNMP Library.
55. Chamberlin, 117; Davis, *Story of 13th Massachusetts*, 225; Huidekoper, *Short Story of First Day's Fight*, 4; Fulton, "Gettysburg Reminiscences," *National Tribune*, Oct. 20, 1898. Fulton termed the precipitation "heavy mist," adding that the ground was "slippery" and he got wet "to the skin." With the sun's reappearance both conditions soon would have vanished.
56. M. C. Barnes to William W. Dudley, Mar. 28, 1883, copy in GNMP Library.
57. Curtis, 155.
58. Nevins, (ed.), 232.
59. Buell, 62-63.
60. *Gettysburg Papers*, Vol. I, 172-173; Hard, 256; "Some Stories of the Great Battle," *Gettysburg Compiler*, Jan. 14, 1903.
61. Hall, 136-137.
62. *Gettysburg Papers*, Vol. I, 172; *B & L*, Vol. III, 274; Coddington, 273.
63. Cheney, 107.
64. *Pennsylvania at Gettysburg*, Vol. II, 885.
65. Hall, 138; Coddington, 273; Vanderslice, 67.
66. Moyer, 61-62, 284; *Pennsylvania at Gettysburg*, Vol. II, 885. The size of the force Major Anderson's men encountered was not reported. Whether it was part of Early's or Rodes' division also is not known. From the dispatch intercepted by Buford's scouts [see Chapter

II], it is clear that Early intended a reconnaisance of the Gettysburg area [*OR* 45, 414]. If Early issued a similar order to another commander, the courier may have gotten through. Equally plausible, Rodes — whose division was even closer to Gettysburg than Early's — may have sent a scouting party there.

67. Cheney, 105-106; *New York at Gettysburg*, Vol III, 1153.
68. Cheney, 107.
69. *B & L*, Vol III, 274-275; Moyer, 61.
70. *B & L*, Vol III, 275, cites Newel Cheney's paper prepared for New York State Gettysburg Monument Commission; Cheney, 107-108; *New York at Gettysburg*, Vol.III, 1153. In his regimental history, Cheney gives an erroneous impression. After stating that the enemy was seen approaching from the north (Ewell's men only "half amile away"), he has enemy infantry (Heth's), leaving the Chambersburg Pike "about 8 A. M." and approaching from the south, thus implying that the ensuing action he describes involved Heth's men. As other sources confirm, the action occurred earlier and involved Ewell's men.
71. Norton, *Deeds of Daring*, 147.
72. Cheney, 108; B & L, Vol. III, 275; *New York at Gettysburg*, Vol. III, 1153; Hall, 137. Cheney, in his regimental history, conveys another false impression (see Note 70): that Corporal James was killed before 9:00 by one of Heth's skirmishers. But Heth's troops did not engage Devin's line until sometime after 9:30. And, while Sergeant Holcomb's men could have filled a gap in Devin's line after the attack by Heth's Division, it seems much more likely that he did so in response to Colonel Sackett's call for 6th and 9th New York troopers to strengthen the line to meet the threat from Ewell's skirmishers. Moreover, if Holcomb's action occurred after 9:30, it would certainly weaken (if not negate) the claim that Corporal James was the first Union fatality.
73. Moyer, 61.
74. Theodore W. Bean quoted in Moyer, 61; *Pennsylvania at Gettysburg*, Vol. II, 877.
75. *Gettysburg Papers*, Vol. I, 172; Jacobs, "Meteorology of the Battle," Gettysburg *Star and Sentinel*, Aug. 11, 1885.
76. *OR* 43, 927.
77. Moyer, 60.
78. Calef, "Gettysburg Notes: The Opening Gun," *Journal of the Military Service Institution*, Vol. XL, 47.
79. Mix, "Experiences at Gettysburg," *National Tribune*, July 13, 1934. Mix, who was 92 when he wrote the article, was the last survivor of Company F, 9th New York Cavalry.
80. *SHSP*, Vol. XXIV, 184.
81. Boland, "Beginning of the Battle of Gettysburg," *Confederate Veteran*, Vol. XIV (July 1906), 308-309.
82. Dodge, "Opening the Battle," *National Tribune*, Sept. 24, 1891; *Gettysburg Papers*, Vol. I, 787.
83. Fuller, "Who Fired the First Shot...", *Journal of U. S. Cavalry Association*, Vol. XXIV (1914), 793; Dodge, "Opening the Battle," *National Tribune*, Sept. 24, 1891; monument erected by Jones et al on site of "first shot"; typed notes with accompanying photograph of Jones, Kelley and McCarty, GNMP Library. (These notes substantially duplicate Fuller's account. No author, source, or date are given, but the photograph must have been taken at the Gettysburg reunion in 1890.)
84. This account of the action at the vedette outpost is a composite of the four sources in Note 83 plus Maj. J. L. Beveridge's account in *Gettysburg Papers*, Vol. I, 173-174. Although these sources vary in detail, they dovetail into a consistent narrative. Dodge gives Private Hale's first name as George; however, as both the 8th Illinois roster and Fuller state that it was James, the latter name was used. Fuller and Beveridge state that Jones fired his shot

from the middle of the Pike; Dodge, on the other hand, states it was fired from behind a rail fence. Since Dodge was a participant, his version seems the more plausible one and was used.

85. Dodge, "Opening the Battle," *National Tribune*, Sept. 24, 1891; monument erected by Jones et al on site of "first shot"; anonymous notes in GNMP Library (see Note 83) — all attest to 7:30. This time is consonant with Heth's Division's departure from Cashtown at or shortly after 5:00 and a march of 5-1/2 miles at a moderate pace. Lt. Col. H. E. Dana (quoted in Miers and Brown, eds. *Gettysburg*, 48) surely erred when he said Jones fired at the enemy "a little after sunrise." Maj. J. L. Beveridge (*Gettysburg Papers*, Vol. I, 173-174) and J. D. Vautier (*History of 88th Pennsylvania*, 117) both assert that Jones fired the first shot at Gettysburg, but do not specify the hour.
86. Dodge, "Opening the Battle," *National Tribune*, Sept. 24, 1891; anonymous notes in GNMP Library (see Note 83).
87. Nichols, *Toward Gettysburg*, 200; Scott, *Story of the Battles at Gettysburg*, Vol. I, 138; Coddington, 261-262; Hartwig, "Guts and Good Leadership," *The Morningside Notes*, May 18, 1985, 3.
88. Pearson, *James S. Wadsworth of Geneseo*, 204-205.
89. There is general agreement on the departure time of Reynolds and Wadsworth's Division. Sources include: *OR* 43, 265 (Wadsworth); Weld, *War Diary and Letters*, 230; Hofmann (56th Pennsylvania), "Remarks on the Battle of Gettysburg," address published in 1880; Nathaniel Rollins (2nd Wisconsin), diary entry, July 1, 1863, State Historical Society of Wisconsin.
90. *Pennsylvania at Gettysburg*, Vol. I, 340; Dudley, *Iron Brigade at Gettysburg*, 5; Capt. James A. Hall to Col. John B. Bachelder, Dec. 29, 1869, copy in GNMP Library.
91. Cornelius Wheeler to his parents, July 11, 1863, *Cornelius Wheeler Papers*, Univ. of Wisconsin, copy in GNMP Library; Coddington, 262.
92. *OR* 43, 284; Stine, *History of the Army of the Potomac*, 461.
93. *Pennsylvania at Gettysburg*, Vol. I, 340; *OR* 43, 285; *New York at Gettysburg*, Vol. III, 990; Tevis and Marquis, 132.
94. Tevis and Marquis,, 252.
95. Dudley, *Iron Brigade at Gettysburg*, 5; Dawes, *Service with 6th Wisconsin*, 164.
96. *Pennsylvania at Gettysburg*, Vol. I, 340; Charles H. Veil manuscript written in 1908, Robert L. Brake Collection, USAMHI; Coddington, 262; Nevins, (ed.), 232.
97. Nevins, (ed.), 232.
98. *Gettysburg Papers*, Vol. I, 200.
99. Dawes, 164; Sullivan, "The Charge of the Iron Brigade," dated Feb. 13, 1883, and subsequently published in two parts in *Mauston [Ohio] Star*. James "Mickey" Sullivan, erstwhile private of Company K, quoted these lines from one of the songs the 6th Wisconsin sang:

    On the distant prairie where the heifer wild,
    Stole into the cabbage in the midnight mild,
    Every one that knew her said she was a thief
    And should be killed and quartered and issued out for beef.

100. Curtis, 155-156.
101. Hall, 134; Otis, 83-84.
102. Lt. Col. Rufus R. Dawes to Col. John B. Bachelder, Mar. 18, 1868, copy in GNMP Library; Strong, 119; *Gettysburg Papers*, Vol. I, 185; Kieffer, 108.
103. Weld, 229.
104. Cooke, "The First Day of Gettysburg," *War Talks in Kansas*, 278.
105. Buell, 64.

106. *Gettysburg Papers*, Vol. I, 200.
107. Buell, 63-64.
108. *OR* 43, 244, 265, 348; *Pennsylvania at Gettysburg*, 340; Chamberlin, 117; *New York at Gettysburg*, Vol. III, 677; Jacques, 154; Todd, (ed.), *History of 9th Regiment New York State Militia*, 208.
109. *OR* 43, 326; Slagle, address given at dedication of 149th Pennsylvania monument, Sept. 11, 1889, Robert L. Brake Collection, USAMHI; Jacob F. Slagle to John S. Slagle (brother), Sept. 13, 1863, Robert L. Brake Collection, USAMHI; Biddle, 30-31. The covered bridge still stands, though the present road bypasses it.
110. Jones, "Chronicles" (excerpt, no page numbers), Robert L. Brake Collection, USAMHI; W. R. Ramsey to Capt. J. H. Bassler, Aug. 3, 1906, copy in GNMP Library; *OR* 43, 244.
111. Paul, "Paul's Brigade at Gettysburg," unpublished typescript, GNMP Library; Small, *16th Maine Regiment*, 116; Vautier, *History of 88th Pennsylvania Volunteers*, 105. The starting time given for Robinson's division is supported by Doubleday's official report [*OR* 43, 244], wherein he stated that "from an hour and a half to two hours elapsed before the remaining troops [Second and Third Divisions] were en route."
112. *OR* 43, 244; Slagle, address given at dedication of149th Pennsylvania monument, Sept. 11, 1889, USAMHI.
113. *OR* 45, 416, 457; Howard, "Campaign and Battle of Gettysburg," *The Atlantic Monthly* (July 1876), 52-53; Rosengarten, "Where Reynolds Fell," *Philadelphia Weekly Press*, Jan. 20, 1886; *Gettysburg Papers*, Vol. I, 317.
114. *OR* 43, 701; *OR* 45, 457; Bellah, *Soldiers' Battle: Gettysburg*, 43.
115. *OR* 43, 701; Howard, "Campaign and Battle of Gettysburg," *The Atlantic Monthly* (July 1876), 53; Howard, *Autobiography*, 408; *Gettysburg Papers*, Vol. I, 313.
116. *OR* 44, 317.
117. *OR* 44, 444; G. Campbell Brown, manuscript (undated), Tennessee Historical Commission, copy in Robert L. Brake Collection, USAMHI; Taylor, 93-94; Coddington, 281.
118. Bates, 450.
119. Oates, 201.
120. Young, 157, 159.
121. *OR* 45, 947-948.
122. *SHSP*, Vol. VIII, 515; Vol. XXXVII, 109; Schenck, *Up Came Hill*, 274.
123. Coddington, 236.
124. Haupt, *Reminiscences of General Herman Haupt*, 212-214; *Gettysburg Papers*, Vol. I, 317 (Haupt to Halleck/Schenck); *OR* 45, 427 (Schenck to Halleck); Bates, 197 (Schenck to Meade); *OR* 45, 460 (Meade's belief). Bates, it should be noted, mistakenly attributed Haupt's messages to Maj. Gen. Darius N. Couch (both generals were in Harrisburg). Also, Bates surely erred in stating that Maj. Gen. Schenck telegraphed his message to Meade, although he may have telegraphed the same message to Secretary of War Stanton. If telegraph service to Meade's headquarters in Taneytown had existed, Schenck would not have forwarded Haupt's messages by courier.
125. *OR* 43, 70.
126. *OR* 43, 70; *OR* 45, 458-459.
127. *OR* 45, 458-459.
128. *Report of the Joint Committee on the Conduct of the War*, Part I, 347-348; Fiebeger, 34.
129. *OR* 45, 460-461.
130. *SHSP*, Vol. IV, 99.
131. *SHSP*, Vol. IV, 113.
132. *SHSP*, Vol. IV, 126.
133. *SHSP*, Vol. IV, 157, 159.

134. Fremantle, 256.
135. *Gettysburg Papers*, Vol. I, 431-432.
136. Nofi, *Gettysburg Campaign*, 39, quotes *New York Times*, June 28, 1863.
137. Meade, Vol. II, 18.
138. Meade, Vol. II, 27-29.
139. Catton, 3.
140. Stine, 456.

CHAPTER 4

1. Bates, 188.
2. *Gettysburg Papers*, Vol. I, 432-433.
3. Boland, "Beginning of the Battle of Gettysburg," *Confederate Veteran*, Vol. XIV (July 1906), 308; Fulton, "The Fifth Alabama at Gettysburg," *Confederate Veteran*, Vol. XXXI (Oct. 1923), 379; Moon, "Beginning of the Battle of Gettysburg," *Confederate Veteran*, Vol. XXXIII (Dec. 1925), 449; *Gettysburg Papers*, Vol. I, 174. If Boland is correct there were three 5th Alabama companies (about 90 men) in the skirmish line. I have used Fulton's lower figure of two companies, since Moon refers to a "detail" which connotes a smaller rather than a larger force.
4. Belo, "Battle of Gettysburg," *Confederate Veteran*, Vol. VIII (Apr. 1900), 165-168.
5. Vanderslice, 68; "Some Stories of the Great Battle," *Gettysburg Compiler*, Jan. 14, 1903. Lohr's Hill stood on the farm of Samuel Lohr [Pitzer, *Three Days at Gettysburg*, 19].
6. Marye, "The First Gun at Gettysburg," *American Historical Register*, July 1895, 1228-1229; *OR* 44, 637. Pegram's physical condition is described in Downey, *Guns at Gettysburg*, 18.
7. "Some Stories of the Great Battle," *Gettysburg Compiler*, Jan. 14, 1903.
8. Vanderslice, 68; Fulton, "Fifth Alabama at Gettysburg," *Confederate Veteran*, Vol. XXXI (Oct. 1923), 379; Moon, "Beginning of the Battle of Gettysburg," *Confederate Veteran*, Vol. XXXIII (Dec. 1925), 449; Coddington, 689, cites Col. B. D. Fry's letter to Col. J. B. Bachelder, Feb. 10, 1878. No source gives the time Heth's Division resumed their march, but subsequent events indicate it would have been shortly before 8:00. This determination is consistent with the following time statements: Heth reported he reorganized his troops "somewhere about eight o'clock" [*Gettysburg Papers*, Vol. I, 432-433]; Marye stated he fired the first cannon shot between 7:00 and 8:00 ["First Gun at Gettysburg," *American Historical Register*, July 1895, 1228-1229]; Maj. J. L. Beveridge, 8th Illinois, stated that the enemy skirmish line and the troops behind it resumed the march about 8:00 [*Gettysburg Papers*, Vol. I, 173]; Col. G. H. Chapman, 3rd Indiana, reported his pickets were driven in between 8:00 and 9:00 [in letter to Col. J. B. Bachelder, Mar. 30, 1864].
9. *OR* 44, 637.
10. Miers and Brown, eds., *Gettysburg*, 46-48; *Gettysburg Papers*, Vol. I, 173-175.
11. Moore, "Heth's Division at Gettysburg," Southern Bivouac (May 1885), 385; Swallow, "First Day at Gettysburg," *Southern Bivouac* (Dec. 1885), 437; Coddington, 266.
12. Miers and Brown, eds., 46-48.
13. *SHSP*, Vol. XXXVII, 109; *OR* 43, 934; Col. William Gamble to W. S. Church, Feb. 10, 1864; Vanderslice, 68; *Gettysburg Papers*, Vol. I, 173.
14. Belo, "Battle of Gettysburg," *Confederate Veteran*, Vol. VIII (Apr. 1900), 165-168; 12th Illinois Cavalry monument on battlefield; Vanderslice, 68.
15. Bayly, "Mrs. Joseph Bayly's Story of the Battle," *Gettysburg Compiler* scrapbook, GNMP Library.
16. Bayly, W. J., "Stories of the Battle," *Gettysburg Compiler* scrapbook, GNMP Library.
17. *New York at Gettysburg*, Vol. III, 1134; *OR* 43, 938-939.
18. *B & L*, Vol. III, 274-275; Cheney, 106, 347; Hall, 137.

19. Day, "Veteran of 3d Indiana Cavalry Describes First Day's Fight at Gettysburg," *National Tribune*, July 30, 1903.
20. *OR* 44, 677; *Gettysburg Papers*, Vol. I, 210, 432-433; William M. Rollins, journal entry, Aug. 18, 1894, copy in GNMP Library; *SHSP*, Vol. XXXVII, 109.
21. Fulton, "The Fifth Alabama at Gettysburg," *Confederate Veteran*, Vol. XXXI (Oct. 1923), 379.
22. Day, "Veteran of 3d Indiana Cavalry Describes First Day's Fight at Gettysburg," *National Tribune*, July 30, 1903.
23. Roth, "Tavern with a Past is Brought Up-to-date," *York Sunday News*, July 27, 1986.
24. Turney, "The First Tennessee at Gettysburg," *Confederate Veteran*, Vol. VIII (Dec. 1900), 535-537; Stine, 451.
25. *SHSP*, Vol. IV, 158; *Gettysburg Papers*, Vol. I, 188-189; Moon, "Beginning of the Battle at Gettysburg," *Confederate Veteran*, Vol. XXXIII (Dec. 1925), 449; *Histories of Regiments and Battalions from North Carolina*, Vol. III, 296.
26. *OR* 44, 677-678; Heth quoted in Stine, 451; Hartwig, "Guts and Good Leadership," *Morningside Notes*, May 8, 1985
27. Turney, "The First Tennessee at Gettysburg," *Confederate Veteran*, Vol. VIII (Dec. 1890), 535-537; Moon, "Beginning of the Battle of Gettysburg," *Confederate Veteran*, Vol. XXXIII (Dec. 1925), 449; *SHSP*, Vol. XXIV, 184.
28. *OR* 44, 649 (Davis). According to Heth in 1877, Davis formed his brigade line on the left of the railroad cut [*SHSP*, Vol. IV, 158]; Davis, however, stated in his official report (noted above) that his right then rested on the Chambersburg Pike. Apparently the line obliqued to the left during the advance, as all of his regiments fought north of the railroad cut. The order of Archer's brigade given here disagrees with that shown on the map prepared by Col. J. B. Bachelder and repeated by other historians. According to Bachelder, the 1st Tennessee was on the right and the 7th and 14th Tennesee on the left. The internal evidence of a number of first-hand accounts (as will be evident later in the narrative) points conclusively to the reverse being true.
29. *SHSP*, Vol. XXXIII, 143.
30. Hosmer, *New York Herald*, July 3, 1863.
31. *SHSP*, Vol. XXXVII, 109.
32. Lt. A. B. Jerome to Gen. W. S. Hancock, Oct. 18, 1865, John B. Bachelder Collection, copy in GNMP Library; DePeyster, Decisive Conflicts in Late Civil War, 151-153.
33. *OR* 43, 934, 1030; Col. William Gamble to W. S. Church, Mar. 10, 1864, Chicago Historical Society, copy in GNMP Library.
34. *Gettysburg Papers*, Vol. I, 173.
35. *OR* 43, 278, 934; *Gettysburg Papers*, Vol. I, 173; Col. William Gamble to W. S. Church, Mar. 10, 1864, Chicago Historical Society, copy in GNMP Library; Col. George H. Chapman to Col. J. B. Bachelder, Mar. 30, 1864, GMNP Library; Vautier, 117-118; Hall, 137-138; Vanderslice, 71. Not all sources agree on every point. However, the wealth of sources actually facilitated spotting and rejecting those statements which clashed with the collective body of evidence.
36. Coddington, 266; Tucker, 146.
37. Deeds recorded in Adams County Courthouse: Thaddeus Stevens to Jacob Herbst, Feb. 4, 1827 (Deed Book AA, p. 3) and Sheriff Benjamin Schriver to John B. McPherson, Jan. 24, 1846 (Deed Book Z, p. 466); Georg, "Edward McPherson Farm," 31, typescript, GNMP Library.
38. Calef accounts: OR43, 1030-1031; "Gettysburg Notes: The Opening Gun," *Journal of the Military Service Institution of the U. S.*, Vol. XL (1907), 47-48; "The Regular Artillery in the Gettysburg Campaign," *Journal of the Military Service Institution of the U. S.*, Vol.

XLV (1909), 35. Supplementary accounts: *OR* 43, 934; *OR* 44, 677-678; *Gettysburg Papers*, Vol. I, 174-175, 791; Hall, 138. Calef's Battery A, 2nd United States Artillery, had the unique distinction of firing the opening Union gun in both battles of Confederate invasion, Antietam and Gettysburg ["Gettysburg Notes," 44].

39. *OR* 43, 938-939; *Gettysburg Papers*, Vol. I, 417-418; *B & L*, 275; Mix, "Experiences at Gettysburg," *National Tribune*, Feb. 22, 1934; *Pennsylvania at Gettysburg*, Vol. I, 885; Stine, 453; regimental monuments, GNMP. The 350 skirmishers consisted of two squadrons from the 8th Illinois and one each from the 12th Illinois, 3rd Indiana, and 6th New York.
40. Busey & Martin, *Regimental Strengths at Gettysburg*, 205-206; Coddington, 258.
41. Doubleday, 126.
42. *OR* 43, 927, 1031. Buford underestimated the number of enemy guns at twelve. Actually, as Capt. Ervin B. Brunson noted in the after-action report for Pegram's battalion, seventeen (out of twenty) guns participated in the opening action.
43. *Histories of the Several Regiments and Battalions from North Carolina*, Vol. II, 343.
44. Miers and Brown, eds., 52-53; Frassanito, *Gettysburg: A Journey in Time*, 82.
45. *Gettysburg Papers*, Vol. I, 174-175.
46. Turney, "The First Tennessee at Gettysburg," *Confederate Veteran*, Vol. VIII (Dec. 1900), 535.
47. Moon, "Beginning of the Battle of Gettysburg," *Confederate Veteran*, Vol. XXXIII (Dec. 1925), 449-450; *Gettysburg Papers*, Vol. I, 174-175. Later that day, Moon was captured. As he marched past the disabled gun, he noted its shattered axle. Calef never mentioned this casualty.
48. Day, "Veteran of 3d Indiana Cavalry Describes First Day's Fight at Gettysburg," *National Tribune*, July 30, 1903.
49. Hall, 138; Hard, 257; *OR* 43, 927, 1031.
50. Mills, address at unveiling of Wadsworth statue on Gettysburg battlefield, Oct. 6, 1914, *Major-General James S. Wadsworth at Gettysburg and Other Fields*, 53-54.
51. *Gettysburg Papers*, Vol. I, 174-175.
52. Lt. A. B. Jerome to Maj. Gen. W. S. Hancock, Oct. 18, 1865, John B. Bachelder Collection, copy in GNMP Library.
53. Turney, "The First Tennessee at Gettysburg," *Confederate Veteran*, Vol. VIII (Dec. 1900), 535.
54. *OR* 44, 646; Moon, "Beginning of the Battle of Gettysburg," *Confederate Veteran*, Vol. XXXIII (Dec. 1925), 449.
55. Hoffman, John E., diary entry, July 1, 1863, West Virginia Univ. Library, copy in Robert L. Brake Collection, USAMHI; Jones, ed., *Army of Northern Virginia*, 101; Archer's Brigade and Davis' Brigade monuments on battlefield.
56. Moyer, 50; Mix, "Experiences at Gettysburg," *National Tribune*, Feb. 22, 1934.
57. *New York at Gettysburg*, Vol. III, 1153.
58. *Gettysburg*, Vol. I, 367-368.
59. Bean, "Buford at Gettysburg," *The [Philadelphia] Times*, Sept. 11, 1880.
60. *Indiana at the 50th Anniversary of the Battle of Gettysburg*, 102-103.
61. Based on an analysis of the official reports and battlefield monuments for Buford's brigades and regiments, and for Calef's battery.
62. Calef, "Gettysburg Notes: The Opening Gun," *Journal of the Military Service Institution of the U. S.*, Vol. XL (1907), 48; Hard, 257.
63. Moore, "Heth's Division at Gettysburg," *Southern Bivouac*, Vol. III, (May 1885), 385; Swallow, "First Day at Gettysburg," *Southern Bivouac*, Vol. III (Dec. 1885), 437.
64. Catton, *Glory Road*, 269.

65. "Local Woman Fled With Mother to Seminary Here," clipping dated 1938 from a Gettysburg newspaper (probably *The Gettysburg Times*), GNMP Library. Sarah Slentz was four years old when war came to the McPherson farm. For this article she relied on her mother's account, published in a Phoenixville, Pennsylvania, newspaper in the early 1880s.
66. *OR* 44, 637; Heth's letter published in *The [Philadelphia] Weekly Times*, Mar. 23, 1878 quoted in Bean, "Buford at Gettysburg," *The [Philadelphia] Times*, Sept. 11, 1880; Morrison, ed., 174.
67. Starr, *The Union Cavalry in the Civil War*, Vol. I, 439; Weigley, "John Buford," *Civil War Times Illustrated*, Vol. V (June 1966), 15, 23; Col. B. D. Fry to Col. J. B. Bachelder, Feb. 10, 1878, quoted in Coddington, 689.
68. *OR* 45, 470-471.
69. Battine, *Crisis of the Confederacy*, 187-188; Sgt. Cornelius Wheeler to his parents, July 11, 1863, State Historical Society of Wisconsin, copy in GNMP Library.
70. Jacobs, "Meteorology of the Battle," *Gettysburg Star and Sentinel*, Aug. 11, 1885.
71. *Gettysburg Papers*, Vol. I, 200-201.
72. Comte de Paris, Vol. III, 548.
73. *Annals of the War*, 391.
74. Capt. Charles E. Stubbs to Col. J. B. Bachelder, July 3, 1882, copy in GNMP Library.
75. Lt. Jacob F. Slagle to his brother, John, Sept. 13, 1863, Robert L. Brake Collection, USAMHI; Paul, "Paul's Brigade at Gettysburg," unpublished typescript, GNMP Library.
76. Veil, manuscript (1908), extract quoted in *Philadelphia Public Ledger*, Mar. 19, 1911, copy in Robert L. Brake Collection, USAMHI; Charles H. Veil to David McConaughy, Apr. 7, 1864, Gettysburg College Civil War Institute; Meade, Vol. II, 32; Jepson, "First Day at Gettysburg," *National Tribune*, Oct. 6, 1910; Coddington, 262; Longacre, "John F. Reynolds, General," *Civil War Times Illustrated*, Vol. XI (Aug. 1972), cites Maj. Gen. Isaac R. Trimble.
77. Veil, manuscript (1908), extract quoted in *Philadelphia Public Ledger*, Mar. 19, 1911, copy in Robert L. Brake Collection, USAMHI; Charles H. Veil to David McConaughy, Apr. 7, 1864, Gettysburg College Civil War Institute; Jepson, "First Day at Gettysburg," *National Tribune*, Oct. 6, 1910; Coddington, 262; Stubbs, "2nd Maine Battery at Gettysburg," *National Tribune*, June 2, 1910.
78. Young, 175-176; Comte de Paris, Vol. III, 550;
79. Charles H. Veil to David McConaughy, Apr. 7, 1864, Gettysburg College Civil War Institute; Weld, 229; Stine, 453. The two-story brick Eagle Hotel burned down in 1894.
80. Smith, 236.
81. Curtis, 155-156.
82. McConnell, "First and Greatest Day's Battle — Gettysburg," *National Tribune*, July 13, 1916.
83. Beecham, *Gettysburg: Pivotal Battle of the Civil War*, 61.
84. Lt. Col. R. R. Dawes to Col. J. B. Bachelder, Mar. 18, 1868, copy in GNMP Library.
85. Tevis and Marquis, 164.
86. Smith, 236.
87. *War Talks in Kansas*, 278.
88. Dawes, "Reminiscences of the Battle of Gettysburg," *Gettysburg Star and Sentinel*, Mar. 8, 1872.
89. Curtis, 182.
90. Curtis, 317-318. In the fall of 1863, Culver gave the historic drumsticks to his regimental commander, Col. Henry A. Morrow.
91. Jacob F. Slagle to his brother John, Sept. 13, 1863, Robert L. Brake Collection, USAMHI.

92. Jones, "Chronicles," copy of excerpt covering Battle of Gettysburg, Robert L. Brake Collection, USAMHI.
93. Buell, 63-64.
94. Jepson, "The First Day at Gettysburg," *National Tribune*, Oct. 6, 1910; Veil, manuscript (1908), extract quoted in *Philadelphia Public Ledger*, Mar. 19, 1911, copy in Robert L. Brake Collection, USAMHI.
95. *OR* 44, 924.
96. Lt. A. B. Jerome to Maj. Gen. W. S. Hancock, Sept. 18, 1865, John B. Bachelder Collection, copy in GNMP Library; DePeyster, *Decisive Conflicts of the Late Civil War*, 151-153.
97. Principal sources: Lt. A. B. Jerome to Maj. Gen. W. S. Hancock, Sept. 18, 1865, John B. Bachelder Collection, copy in GNMP Library; DePeyster, 151-153. Supplemental: Moyer, 62; Bates, 208-209; Stine, 453-454; Comte de Paris, Vol. III, 547.
98. *Gettysburg Papers*, Vol. I, 152.
99. Weld, 229-232; Meade, Vol. II, 36-36; *Reynolds Memorial — Addresses Before the Historical Society of Pennsylvania*, address by Joseph G. Rosengarten (1880), 29-30. Weld wrote of his mission: "I naturally felt quite complimented at being chosen, the youngest of the staff, to carry such an important message...."
100. Charles H. Veil to David McConaughy, Apr. 7, 1864, Gettysburg College Civil War Institute.
101. Statements as to the time Reynolds and Buford met at Gettysburg range from 9:00 to "shortly after 10:00." The interrelation of all other events indicates Reynolds must have reached the Seminary about 9:15 and McPherson's Ridge 15-20 minutes later. Vanderslice [p. 72] gives the meeting time as "a little after 9:00."
102. Comte de Paris quoted in "Gettysburg. The Great Battle....", *Gettysburg Star and Sentinel*, July 5, 1885.
103. Bates, 209; DePeyster, 151-153.
104. Flavius J. Bellamy, diary entry, July 1, 1863, F. J. Bellamy Collection, Indiana State Library, copy in Robert L. Brake Collection, USAMHI; Cheney, 110.
105. Cheney, 109; *OR* 44, 646.
106. Mix, "Experiences at Gettysburg," *National Tribune*, Feb. 22, 1934.
107. Calef, "Gettysburg Notes: The Opening Gun," *Journal of the Military Service Institution of the U. S.*, Vol. 40 (1907), 47; Huidekoper, "A Short Story of Gettysburg," *Book of the Royal Blue*, Vol. VI (July 1903), 5.
108. Nichols, 202-203, 253, cites Joseph G. Rosengarten to Prof. Michael Jacobs, Oct. 15, 1863.
109. Charles H. Veil to David McConaughy, Apr. 7, 1864, Gettysburg College Civil War Institute; Maj. Gen. Oliver O. Howard to Capt. William Riddle, Mar. 22, 1864, Howard Collection, Bowdoin College, copy in Robert L. Brake Collection, USAMHI; Coddington, 268-269. According to Veil, Reynolds also sent a message to Sickles, ordering Third Corps to Gettysburg, but there is no confirmation of this. Edwin B. Coddington believed Veil in error on this point: "In view of Reynold's fears about the possibility of a Confederate turning movement starting from Fairfield, it is doubtful whether he would have stripped Emmitsburg of defenders without notifying Meade." [Coddington, 685.]
110. Veil, manuscript (1908), extract quoted in *Philadelphia Public Ledger*, Mar. 19, 1911, copy in Robert L. Brake Collection, USAMHI; Pearson, 206-207. In 1871, it may be noted, Reynolds' aide Joseph G. Rosengarten wrote Col. Samuel P. Bates that Reynolds "went back through town." [Rosengarten to Bates, Jan. 13, 1871, Pennsylvania Historical and Museum Commission, Division of Archives and Manuscripts, copy in Robert L. Brake Collection, USAMHI.] Undoubtedly Rosengarten erred. To take a roundabout route when time was so precious would have been totally illogical. Veil, who rode beside Reynolds,

wrote: "...having sent orders to the head of his column to cut across country from the Emmitsburg road toward the Seminary, he [Reynolds] rode out to meet it."

111. Calef, "Gettysburg Notes: The Opening Gun," *Journal of the Military Service Institution of the U. S.*, Vol. 40 (1907), 48.
112. Halstead-Burns meeting: *Gettysburg Papers*, Vol. I, 152; *B & L*, Vol. III, 284. Burns details: Chamberlin, 121; Battine, 218; Bates, 990; *B & L*, Vol. III, 276. There is a story, believed to have originated with Bates or DePeyster, that Burns led Reynolds back to Wadsworth's Division. In *Martial Deeds of Pennsylvania* (pps. 209, 991), Bates has Reynolds hailing Burns, asking the best way "through the outskirts of the town," then being led by him "down a by-street on a rapid run." A difficult feat, since Reynolds and staff were mounted and Burns was on foot! Moreover, Burns never claimed he performed this service.
113. *Reynolds Memorial Addresses*, 63; Strong, 214 — both cite Capt. James A. Hall's account in *Brookline [MA] Chronicle*, Feb. 16, 1878.
114. Scott, Vol. I, 78; Comte de Paris, Vol. III, 549.
115. *OR* 45, 460.
116. *OR* 45, 462.
117. Nichols, 211.
118. Young, 175-176; *New York at Gettysburg*, Vol. I, 11; Coddington, 267; Nolan, 235.
119. *Annals of the War*, 209.
120. Doubleday, 122.
121. *OR* 43, 244
122. Joseph G. Rosengarten to Col. Samuel P. Bates, Jan. 13, 1871, Pennsylvania Historical and Museum Commission, Division of Archives and Manuscripts, copy in Robert L. Brake Collection, USAMHI.
123. Coddington, 691, cites Wainwright Journals.
124. Battine, 187.
125. *Gettysburg Papers*, Vol. I, 118.
126. Hassler, "First Day's Battle at Gettysburg," *Civil War History*, Vol. VI (Sept. 1960), 265-266.
127. Meade, Vol. II, 35.

CHAPTER 5

1. Huidekoper, 5; Joseph G. Rosengarten to Col. Samuel P. Bates, Jan. 13, 1871, Pennsylvania Historical and Museum Commission, Div. of Archives and Manuscripts, copy in Robert L. Brake Collection, USAMHI; Biddle, 24; *New York at Gettysburg*, Vol. III, 990-991; William Riddle to _____ Le Bouvier, Aug. 4, 1863, John F. Reynolds Papers, Franklin and Marshall College, copy in Robert L. Brake Collection, USAMHI; H. H. Lyman, diary entry, July 1, 1863, typed transcript in GNMP Library; Bates, 991.
2. *OR* 43, 265-266.
3. Pearson, 611. Craig Wadsworth, it may be noted, was not on his father's staff, as Pearson stated. Various sources affirm that he served on Reynolds' staff. It was his brother Charles who served on his father's staff.
4. Curtis, 155-156; Smith, 123; *New York at Gettysburg*, Vol. III, 990-991; H. H. Lyman, diary entry, July 1, 1863, typed transcript in GNMP Library; *OR* 43, 267; Beecham, 62-63; Dudley, 5-6; Lt. Col. William W. Dudley to Col. J. B. Bachelder (n.d.), copy in GNMP Library.
5. Cutler, "Gettysburg — The Great Battle of July 1, 2 & 3, 1863," [Gettysburg] *Star and Sentinel*, May 5, 1885; *OR* 43-273 (report of Maj. John Mansfield, 2nd Wisconsin);

Purifoy, "The Battle of Gettysburg, July 1, 1863" *Confederate Veteran*, Vol. XXXI (Jan. 1923). At ten o'clock, said Cutler, his brigade was climbing the east slope of Seminary Ridge, thereby indicating it had left the Emmitsburg road a short while before. Major Mansfield reported that Meredith's Brigade, which followed Cutler's, turned off that road about 10:00. According to John Purifoy, Wadsworth's Division started across the Codori farm at 10:00.

6. Tucker, *High Tide*, 107.
7. Lt. J. V. Pierce to Col. J. B. Bachelder, Oct. 1, 1882, copy in GNMP Library.
8. *New York at Gettysburg*, Vol. III, 990-991.
9. Tucker, *High Tide*, 107; Lt. Col. William W. Dudley to Col. J. B. Bachelder (n. d.), copy in GNMP Library.
10. *New York at Gettysburg*, Vol. III, 990-991.
11. Nichols, 203, cites Ellie Reynolds' letter to her brother Will, July 5, 1863.
12. Tucker, *Lee and Longstreet*, 215.
13. Beecham, 61-62.
14. *OR* 43, 927, 934; Stine, 453.
15. *B & L*, Vol. III, 275; Moyer, 50.
16. Bean, "Buford at Gettysburg," *The [Philadelphia] Times*, Sept. 11, 1880.
17. Battine, 188.
18. Bean, "Buford at Gettysburg," *The [Philadelphia] Times*, Sept. 11, 1880.
19. Capt. James A. Hall to Col. J. B. Bachelder, Dec. 29, 1869, copy in GNMP Library. There is some confusion as to who delivered Reynolds' summons. Hall said it was Lt. Col. James M. Sanderson. Meredith L. Jones, a Doubleday aide-de-camp, said Sanderson sent him to bring up "the first battery I could find," which turned out to be Hall's. Doubleday said it was Reynolds himself who dispatched Jones to summon Hall. [Jones, "The First Day's Fight," *Blue and Gray*, Vol. 2 (July 1893), 20-21; Doubleday, 130].
20. *OR* 43, 1031; Calef, "Gettysburg Notes: The Opening Gun," *Journal of the Military Service Institution of the U. S.*, Vol. 40 (1907), 48; Downey, 22-23.
21. Jacobs, 23; Parkhurst, "At Gettysburg. Heroism of the 147th New York," *National Tribune*, Nov. 1, 1888; Lt. H. H. Lyman to Col. J. B. Bachelder (n. d.), copy in GNMP Library; John Bartlett's account (see details in footnote 23).
22. *New York at Gettysburg*, Vol. III, 990-991; Parkhurst, "At Gettysburg. Heroism of the 147th New York," *National Tribune*, Nov. 1, 1888; Lt. H. H. Lyman to Col. J. B. Bachelder (n. d.), copy in GNMP Library.
23. John Bartlett's (notarized) account on November 23, 1889 of his experiences at Gettysburg, as a private in Co. C, 147th New York (copy in GNMP Library).
24. *New York at Gettysburg*, Vol. III, 990-991.
25. *Gettysburg Papers*, Vol. I, 152; *New York at Gettysburg*, Vol. III, 990-991.
26. Snyder, *Oswego County, New York, in the Civil War*, 63.
27. *New York at Gettysburg*, Vol. III, 990-991.
28. *War Talks in Kansas*, 278. Lt. Sidney G. Cooke (147th New York), who reported the incident, stopped short of identifying the man as Burns, but there can be no doubt it was he. According to A. P. Smith's 1867 history of the 76th New York, men of that regiment also saw Burns. While this is probably true, Smith's statement that the old man, failing to catch up with the New Yorkers, fought instead with the 56th Pennsylvania must be dismissed as fiction. [Smith, *History of the Seventy-Sixth Regiment New York Volunteers*, 243.] Not only is there no evidence from anyone in that regiment that a civilian fought with them, but Burns himself said he "pitched in with them Wisconsin fellers." [Byrne and Weaver, eds., 97.]
29. Bates, 991.

30. *Gettysburg Papers*, Vol. I, 175-176; *New York at Gettysburg*, Vol. III, 990-991; John Bartlett's account, Nov. 23, 1889 (see details in footnote 22); Scott, Vol. I, 146.
31. Lt. Col. Wiliam W. Dudley to Col. J. B. Bachelder (n. d.), copy in GNMP Library; Dudley, 5-6.
32. Beecham, 62-63.
33. Lt. Col. Wiliam W. Dudley to Col. J. B. Bachelder (n. d.), copy in GNMP Library; Dudley, 5-6; *Annals of the War*, 64.
34. Beecham, 62-63; Lucius Fairchild to R. K. Beecham, Apr. 3, 1864, copy in Robert L. Brake Collection, USAMHI; Sgt. Cornelius Wheeler to his parents, July 11, 1863, copy in Robert L. Brake Collection, USAMHI.
35. *OR* 43, 267.
36. *OR* 43, 279; Dawes, 164.
37. Dawes; Lt. Col. Rufus R. Dawes to Col. J. B. Bachelder, Mar. 18, 1868, copy in GNMP Library.
38. Day, "Veteran of 3d Indiana Cavalry Describes First Day's Fight at Gettysburg," *National Tribune*, July 30, 1903.
39. *OR* 43, 1031; Calef, "Gettysburg Notes: The Opening Gun," *Journal of the Military Service Institution of the U. S.*, Vol. 40 (1907), 48.
40. *Gettysburg Papers*, Vol. I, 175-176.
41. Mills, address at unveiling of Wadsworth statue on Gettysburg battlefield, Oct. 6, 1914, *Major-General James S. Wadsworth at Gettysburg and Other Fields*, 53-54.
42. Swett, "The Eighth New York Cavalry at Gettysburg," *National Tribune*, Apr. 3, 1884.
43. *OR* 43, 927.
44. Hard, 257.
45. *OR* 43, 927.
46. Beecham, 64.
47. *New York at Gettysburg*, Vol. II, 733.
48. Joseph G. Rosengarten to Col. Samuel P. Bates, Jan. 13, 1871, Pennsylvania State Archives, copy in Robert L. Brake Collection, USAMHI.
49. Bachelder maps, GNMP Library; Huidekoper, 4; Moyer, 63; *Gettysburg Papers*, Vol. I, 175-177;
50. Flavius J. Bellamy, diary entry of July 1, 1863, Indiana State Library, copy in Robert L. Brake Collection, USAMHI. Although not definitely known, it is believed this particular school stood on the southeast corner of Washington and High Streets.
51. *OR* 43, 914.
52. Nichols, 52.
53. Capt. James A. Hall to Col. J. B. Bachelder, Feb. 27, 1868 and Dec. 29, 1869, copies in GNMP Library; *Maine at Gettysburg*, 16.
54. *Maine at Gettysburg*, 15, 19; Capt. James A. Hall to Col. J. B. Bachelder, Dec. 29, 1869, copy in GNMP Library; Lt. H. H. Lyman to Col. J. B. Bachelder (n.d.), copy in GNMP Library; *OR* 43, 359.
55. Capt. James A. Hall to Col. J. B. Bachelder, Feb. 27, 1868 and Dec. 29, 1869, copies in GNMP Library.
56. *OR* 43, 265-266; Huidekoper, 7 [quoted]; Pierce, "Gettysburg. Last Words as to What Regiment Opened the Battle," *National Tribune*, Apr. 3, 1884; Capt. John A. Kellogg to Col. J. B. Bachelder, Nov. 1, 1865.
57. *New York at Gettysburg*, Vol. I, 12.
58. *New York at Gettysburg*, Vol. III, 990-991; *Gettysburg Papers*, Vol. I, 175-176; Doubleday, 128; Coey, "Cutler's Brigade," *National Tribune*, July 15, 1915; Snyder, 59.
59. Lt. H. H. Lyman to Col. J. B. Bachelder (n.d.); Hill, Vol. 4, 1001; Scott, Vol. I, 146.

60. *New York at Gettysburg*, Vol. III, 990-991.
61. John Bartlett's account, Nov. 23, 1889 (see details in footnote 22).
62. Bartlett's account; Hill, Vol. 4, 1001, 1003; Parkhurst, "At Gettysburg. Heroism of the 147th New York," *National Tribune*, Nov. 1, 1888; Lt. H. H. Lyman to Col. J. B. Bachelder (n. d.); Coey, "Cutler's Brigade," *National Tribune*, July 15, 1915.
63. *Maine at Gettysburg*, 16.
64. Joseph G. Rosengarten to Col. Samuel P. Bates, Jan. 13, 1871.
65. *OR* 43, 281-282; Vautier, 118.
66. Tevis and Marquis, (recollections of Col. Edward B. Fowler), 132.
67. *OR* 43, 244. Apparently the meeting of Reynolds and Marten took place just minutes before the infantry battle commenced. Joseph G. Rosengarten believed the command to Doubleday to hold the Fairfield road was the last order Reynolds gave. [Rosengarten, "Reynolds, Hero of the First Day," *New York Times Magazine*, June 29, 1913.]
68. Doubleday, 130. It may be noted that Doubleday quoted Reynolds in slightly different words in his testimony before the Joint Committee on the Conduct of the War. It is a bit less dramatic than the later version but essentially the same. [*Report of the Joint Committee....*, Vol. I, 306.]
69. *OR* 43, 244; Doubleday, 130; Georg, monograph on the McPherson farm, 35. Col. Chapman Biddle [*Reynolds Memorial Addresses*, 65] and others believed Reynolds had referred to the Mummasburg Road, on the right of the line. This is disproved by Doubleday himself, who in his after-action report [*OR* 43, 244] wrote that Marten returned "with orders for me to attend to the Millerstown [Fairfield] road, *on the left of the line* [italics added]."
70. Bates, 210, and Hofmann, "The 56th Pennsylvania at Gettysburg," *National Tribune*, Mar. 20, 1884, both cite Brig. Gen. Lysander Cutler's letter to Pennsylvania Governor Andrew G. Curtin, Nov. 5, 1863; Rosengarten, "Where Reynolds Fell," *Philadelphia Weekly Press*, Jan. 20, 1886.
71. Hofmann, "The 56th Pennsylvania at Gettysburg," *National Tribune*, Mar. 20, 1884. In this account Colonel Hofmann corrected his earlier misstatement [*OR* 43, 288] that his regiment became engaged at eleven o'clock.
72. *OR* 43, 285.
73. Bates, 210; 56th Pennsylvania Infantry Regiment monument, GNMP.
74. *OR* 43, 285; Abner Doubleday to Samuel P. Bates, Oct. 18, 1875, Pennsylvania Historical and Museum Commission, Div. of Archives and Manuscripts, copy in Robert L. Brake Collection, USAMHI; Vautier, 119.
75. *Histories of the Several Regiments and Battalions from North Carolina*, Vol. III, 297.
76. Lt. H. H. Lyman to Col. J. B. Bachelder (n. d.); Hill, Vol. 4, 1001.
77. *OR* 43, 359. Herein Hall reported his battery opened fire at 10:45. Certain infantry reports indicate it was closer to 10:30. Support for the earlier time is implicit in the inscription on the battery's monument on the battlefield. Stating, as it does, that Hall's Battery relieved Calef's Battery shortly after ten o'clock means that Hall's gunners could have been firing by 10:30.
78. Daniel Hall to Gen. O. O. Howard, May 20, 1882; Coddington, 268, cites Hall's letter to Col. L. Livermore, Feb. 17, 1877; Howard, 411.
79. Tremain, *Two Days of War: A Gettysburg Narrative and Other Experiences*, 14; *OR* 43, 1031.
80. *OR* 43, 268; Curtis, 156-157; McConnell, "First and Greatest Day's Battle of Gettysburg," *National Tribune*, July 13, 1916; Sgt. Cornelius Wheeler to his parents, July 11, 1863, copy in Robert L. Brake Collection, USAMHI; John R. Callis to Col. J. C. Bachelder (n. d.), copy in GNMP Library; Dawes, 165 (diagram).

81. Pvt. Sydney Mead (Co. F, 2nd Wisconsin), diary entry for Jul 1, 1863, State Historical Society of Wisconsin, copy in USAMHI.
82. Coddington, 269.
83. Veil, manuscript (1908), extract quoted in *Philadelphia Public Ledger*, Mar. 19, 1911, copy in Robert L. Brake Collection, USAMHI; Gates, *"Ulster Guard" (20th N. Y. State Militia) and the War of the Rebellion*, 427; "He Shot Reynolds," *Pittsburgh Leader* [n.d.], GNMP scrapbook; Hopkins, "Death of Reynolds. It Came From a Volley and Not From a Sharpshooter," *National Tribune*, Apr. 14, 1910.
84. Veil, manuscript (1908), extract quoted in *Philadelphia Public Ledger*, Mar. 19, 1911, copy in Robert L. Brake Collection, USAMHI; Bates, 212.
85. Bates, 212; Veil, manuscript (1908), extract quoted in *Philadelphia Public Ledger*, Mar. 19, 1911, copy in Robert L. Brake Collection, USAMHI; Beecham, 62-66; *OR* 43, 268.
86. Bates, 212; Gates, 427. While Reynolds' fervid exhortation to the 2nd Wisconsin appears in identical words in these two sources, there are other versions. Eleanor Reynolds, in a letter to William Reynolds, quoted their brother as saying: "Forward, forward, men! Drive those fellows out of that. Forward! For God's sake forward!" On July 4, 1863, a shorter version appeared in the *New York Herald*: "For God's sake! forward, my brave boys — forward!"
87. Henry T. Lee to Samuel P. Bates, Feb. 6, 1871, Pennsylvania Historical and Museum Commission, Division of Archives and Manuscripts, copy in USAMHI.
88. *OR* 43, 273; Col. William Gamble to W. S. Church, Mar. 10, 1864, Chicago Historical Society, copy in GNMP Library; 8th New York Cavalry monument. Gamble wrote Church that his brigade was engaged until 10:30. The inscription on the 8th New York Cavalry monument confirms that the Iron Brigade relieved Gamble's troopers at that hour.
89. Sgt. Cornelius Wheeler to his parents, July 11, 1863, copy in Robert L. Brake Collection, USAMHI; OR44, 646.
90. *OR* 43, 273; *Gettysburg Papers*, Vol. I, 186.
91. *OR* 43, 273; *Gettysburg Papers*, Vol. I, 186.; Nolan, 238.
92. Sgt. Cornelius Wheeler to his parents, July 11, 1863, copy in Robert L. Brake Collection, USAMHI; *Gettysburg Papers*, Vol. I, 186.
93. Charles H. Veil to David McConaughy, Apr. 7, 1864, Gettysburg College Civil War Institute.
94. William Riddle to _____ Le Bouvier, Aug. 4, 1863, John F. Reynolds Papers, Franklin and Marshall College, copy in Robert L. Brake Collection, USAMHI.
95. Comte de Paris, Vol. III, 548; Coddington, 277; Nichols, 211.
96. Veil, manuscript (1908), extract quoted in *Philadelphia Public Ledger*, Mar. 19, 1911, copy in Robert L. Brake Collection, USAMHI; Captain William H. Wilcox to Editor, *The Philadelphia Inquirer*, July 4, 1863 (published July 7, 1863); Bates, 474; Doubleday, 131; Nichols, 205.
97. Veil, manuscript (see footnote 96); Eleanor Reynolds to William Reynolds, July 5, 1863, John F. Reynolds Papers, Franklin and Marshall College, copy in Robert L. Brake Collection, USAMHI; Bates, 474; Joseph G. Rosengarten to Col. Samuel P. Bates, Jan. 13, 1871, Pennsylvania Historical and Museum Commission, Div. of Archives and Manuscripts, copy in Robert L. Brake Collection, USAMHI.
98. Veil, manuscript (see footnote 96); Bates, 474; Joseph G. Rosengarten to Col. Samuel P. Bates, Jan. 13, 1871 (see footnote 97); *Reynolds Memorial — Addresses Before the Historical Society of Pennsylvania*, 24.
99. Charles H. Veil to David McConaughy, Apr. 7, 1864, Gettysburg College Civil War Institute; William Riddle to _____ Le Bouvier, Aug. 4, 1863, John F. Reynolds Papers, Franklin and Marshall College, copy in Robert L. Brake Collection, USAMHI; Miers, E.

S. and Brown, R. A., eds., *Gettysburg*, 57; Rosengarten, "Reynolds' Last Battle," *Philadelphia Weekly Times*, Mar. 17, 1877; Lt. H. H. Lyman to Col. J. B. Bachelder (n.d.), copy in GNMP Library; Doubleday, 131. According to accounts in the *New York Herald* and the *New York World*, Reynolds fell into the arms of Captain W. H. Wilcox, exclaiming, "Good God, Wilcox, I am killed." Dramatic, yes; but not one iota of truth in it. Wilcox was not even within sight of his chief when the fatal shot was fired. ["The Battle of Wednesday," *New York Herald*, July 4, 1863; the *New York World* account is cited in two anthologies: Miers and Brown, 57-58, and Moore, Vol. III, 117.]

100. Charles H. Veil to David McConaughy, Apr. 7, 1864, Gettysburg College Civil War Institute; Eleanor Reynolds to her brother William, Jul. 5, 1863, John F. Reynolds Papers, Franklin and Marshall College, copy in Robert L. Brake Collection, USAMHI.
101. Weld, 233.
102. *Gettysburg Papers*, Vol. I, 209.
103. Nichols, 209.
104. Veil, manuscript (see footnote 96); Rosengarten, "Reynolds, Hero of the First Day, by One of His Staff," *New York Times*, Jun. 29, 1913.
105. Veil, manuscript (see footnote 96).
106. Captain William H. Wilcox to Editor, *The Philadelphia Inquirer*, Jul. 4, 1863 (published Jul. 7, 1863); Hopkins, "Death of Reynolds," *National Tribune*, Apr. 14, 1910; Nichols, 253. Capt. James A. Hall and Lt. Frank Carr of Hall's Battery may have joined the group around Reynolds' body, as another battery member, Charles E. Stubbs, stated in the Jun. 2, 1910 issue of the *National Tribune*. It seems doubtful, however, since Hall never mentioned it.
107. "The Battle of Wednesday," *New York Herald*, Jul. 4, 1863; Hopkins, "Death of Reynolds," *National Tribune*, Apr. 14, 1910. The latter account focuses on the role of John Carson, whom the writer knew personally. What he, Thomas S. Hopkins, wrote about his friend is, in the main, believable. However, his statement that Carson "eased Reynolds from the saddle and laid him upon the ground" is obviously false.
108. Eleanor Reynolds to William Reynolds, Jul. 5, 1863, and Jennie (Reynolds) Gildersleeve to William Reynolds, same date, John F. Reynolds Papers, Franklin and Marshall College, copies in Robert L. Brake Collection, USAMHI; Bates, 475; Nichols, 206.
109. Baird quoted in Bates, 474-475; Veil, manuscript (see footnote 96); Eleanor Reynolds to William Reynolds, Jul. 5, 1863 (see footnote 108).
110. Veil, manuscript (see footnote 96); DePeyster, 14; Jennie (Reynolds) Gildersleeve to William Reynolds, Jul. 5, 1863 (see footnote 108).
111. Veil, manuscript (see footnote 96).
112. Eleanor Reynolds to William Reynolds, Jul. 5, 1863 (see footnote 108).
113. Rosengarten, "Where Reynolds Fell," *Philadelphia Weekly Press*, Jan. 20, 1886.
114. *Reynolds Memorial—Addresses Before the Historical Society of Pennsylvania*, 24; Charles H. Veil to David McConaughy, Apr. 7, 1864, Gettysburg College Civil War Institute.
115. *New York at Gettysburg*, Vol. II, 688; Stine, 455.
116. Hopkins, "Death of Reynolds," *National Tribune*, Apr. 14, 1910. According to Hopkins, Captain Carson rode Reynolds' horse. More likely he took orderly Veil's mount, since Veil reported that after the tragedy he himself rode the general's horse.
117. Henry T. Lee to Samuel P. Bates, Feb. 6, 1871, Pennsylvania Historical and Museum Commission, Division of Archives and Manuscripts, copy in USAMHI.
118. Joseph G. Rosengarten quoted in *Annals of the War*, 63.
119. *B & L*, Vol. III, 277.

CHAPTER 6

1. *OR* 44, 649; *Histories of Regiments and Battalions from North Carolina*, Vol. III, 297; Belo, "Battle of Gettysburg," *Confederate Veteran*, Vol. VIII (Apr. 1900), 165-168.
2. Cheek and Pointon, *History of the Sauk County Riflemen*, 39.
3. Doubleday, 128-129.
4. *New York at Gettysburg*, Vol. II, 734.
5. Lt. A. B. Jerome to Maj. Gen. W. S. Hancock, Oct. 18, 1865, copy in GNMP Library.
6. *Histories of Regiments and Battalions from North Carolina*, Vol. III, 297.
7. Hill, Vol. 4, 1001; Stine, 462.
8. *OR* 43, 285; *New York at Gettysburg*, Vol. I, 12, Vol. II, 616.
9. Belo, "Battle of Gettysburg," *Confederate Veteran*, Vol. VIII (Apr. 1900), 165-168; *Histories of Regiments and Battalions from North Carolina*, Vol. III, 288, 297. Both Colonel Connally and the unnamed Union prisoner are quoted in the Belo article. Another version of Connally's reply to Belo appeared in the 1899 *Confederate Military History* (Vol. IV, 174). It reads: "Yes, but do not pay any attention to me. Take the colors and keep ahead of the Mississippians." Not surprisingly, this version, with its appealing emphasis on Connally's selflessness, has been included in some later accounts. But Belo's recollection of Connally's words, being at first-hand, seems more likely to be accurate.
10. Captain Herschel W. Pierce quoted in Bellah, 242.
11. *OR* 44, 638, 650.
12. *OR* 44, 649.
13. *OR* 43, 245; *Pennsylvania at Gettysburg*, Vol. I, 341.
14. Belo, "Battle of Gettysburg," *Confederate Veteran*, Vol. VIII (Apr. 1900), 165-168.
15. Doubleday, 135; Abner Doubleday to Samuel P. Bates, Oct. 18,1875, Pennsylvania Historical Commission, Division of Archives and Manuscripts, copy in USMHI.
16. Dawes quoted in Tucker, *High Tide*, 114-115. Cutler, it may be noted, reported that his regiments retired in good order (*OR* 43, 266). Belo, Dawes, and Doubleday all attested, varying only in degree, that such was not the case. Lacking Cutler's natural bias, they can be believed.
17. Bates, 210, cites Brig. Gen. Lysander Cutler's letter to Pennsylvania Governor Andrew G. Curtin, Nov. 5, 1863; W. B. Murphy to Dr. F. A. Dearborn, June 29, 1900, State Historical Society of Wisconsin, copy in GNMP Library.
18. *OR* 43, 285; *Pennsylvania at Gettysburg*, Vol. I, 341; Vautier, 120.
19. *OR* 43, 288 ("twenty minutes"); *OR* 43, 282-283 ("within thirty minutes"); Hill, Vol. 4, 1001 ("about fifteen minutes"). As stated in these sources, the casualties by unit were:

169	- 76th New York
70+	- 56th Pennsylvania
12	- Provost Guard
251+	

20. *OR* 43, 282; *New York at Gettysburg*, Vol. I, 12.
21. *OR* 43, 288.
22. *OR* 43, 253-254, 282-283.
23. Belo, "Battle of Gettysburg," *Confederate Veteran*, Vol. VIII (Apr. 1900), 165-168.
24. John Bartlett, notarized account, Nov. 23, 1889, copy in GNMP Library; Snyder, 59.
25. Hartwig, "Guts and Good Leadership: The Action at the Railroad Cut, July 1, 1863," *Morningside Notes*, May 8, 1985, cites Lt. Henry H. Lyman to Col. J. B. Bachelder, Dec. 28, 1888.
26. John Bartlett, notarized account, Nov. 23, 1889, copy in GNMP Library; Snyder, 59; Dr. O. S. Coe to Col. J. B. Bachelder, Dec. 28, 1888, copy in GNMP Library.

27. Parkhurst, "At Gettysburg. Heroism of the 147th New York," *National Tribune*, Sept. 24, 1891; Pearson, 208-209.
28. Lt. J. Volney Pierce to Col. J. B. Bachelder, Oct. 1, 1882, copy in GNMP Library; Parkhurst, "At Gettysburg. Heroism of the 147th New York," *National Tribune*, Sept. 24, 1891; Snyder, 59-60. The two 147th New York soldiers who were killed in the same instant were Corporal Fred Rife and Private Hiram Stowell, both of Company G.
29. *New York at Gettysburg*, Vol. III, 991-992; Parkhurst, "At Gettysburg. Heroism of the 147th New York," *National Tribune*, Sept. 24, 1891.
30. *National Tribune*, Sept. 24, 1891; John Bartlett, notarized account, Nov. 23, 1889, copy in GNMP Library.
31. *New York at Gettysburg*, Vol. III, 991-992.
32. Coey, "Cutler's Brigade. The 147th New York's Magnificent Fight on the First Day at Gettysburg," *National Tribune*, July 15, 1915.
33. Parkhurst, "At Gettysburg. Heroism of the 147th New York," *National Tribune*, Sept. 24, 1891.
34. Francis Pease (diary entry of July 7, 1863) quoted in Snyder, 63.
35. Coey, "Cutler's Brigade. The 147th New York's Magnificent Fight on the First Day at Gettysburg," *National Tribune*, July 15, 1915.
36. Parkhurst, "At Gettysburg. Heroism of the 147th New York," *National Tribune*, Sept. 24, 1891.
37. *New York at Gettysburg*, Vol. III, 991-992; John Bartlett, notarized account, Nov. 23, 1889, copy in GNMP Library.
38. Hartwig, "Guts and Good Leadership: The Action at the Railroad Cut, July 1, 1863," *Morningside Notes*, May 8, 1985, cites Lt. Henry H. Lyman to Col. J. B. Bachelder, Dec. 28, 1888.
39. John Bartlett, notarized account, Nov. 23, 1889, copy in GNMP Library.
40. Bartlett account, Nov. 23, 1889.
41. *New York at Gettysburg*, Vol. III, 991-992; Snyder, 60, 62.
42. *OR* 43, 281-282.
43. *OR* 43, 245.
44. Stine, 464-465, quotes speech of J. V. Pierce (1888); *New York at Gettysburg*, Vol. III, 991-992. Two independent sources — a lieutenant in Company C and a private in Company F — agree in the matter of how long the 147th New York was engaged before being flanked. According to Lt. H. H. Lyman it was "about 15 minutes." So he wrote in his diary and again in an undated letter to Col. J. B. Bachelder (copies of both in GNMP Library). Pvt. Francis M. Pease noted in his diary, on July 7, 1863, that it was "some 15 or 20 minutes." (The entry for that date is quoted in Snyder, 63).
45. Hill, Vol. 4, 1001; Lt. H. H. Lyman to Col. J. B. Bachelder, (n. d.), copy in GNMP Library; Stine, 464-465, quotes speech of J. V. Pierce; Scott, Vol. I, 148; Mulholland, "Percentage of Losses at Gettysburg," *Philadelphia Public Ledger*, Apr. 2, 1902.
46. Stine, 464-465, quotes speech of J. V. Pierce; *New York at Gettysburg*, Vol. III, 991-992; Scott, Vol. I, 148; Coey, "Cutler's Brigade. The 147th New York's Magnificent Fight on the First Day at Gettysburg," *National Tribune*, July 15, 1915.
47. Lt. J. V. Pierce to Col. J. B. Bachelder, Oct. 1, 1882, copy in GNMP Library.
48. Stine, 464-465, quotes speech of J. V. Pierce.
49. *OR* 43, 359.
50. Capt. James A. Hall to Col. J. B. Bachelder, Feb. 27, 1868, copy in GNMP Library.
51. *OR* 44, 678.
52. Downey, 21.

53. Capt. Charles E. Stubbs to Col. J. B. Bachelder, July 3, 1882, copy in GNMP Library; *OR* 44, 678.
54. Capt. James A. Hall to Col. J. B. Bachelder, Dec. 29, 1869, New Hampshire Historical Society, copy in GNMP Library; *OR* 43, 229, 245-246, 359. Both Hall and Doubleday stated in their after-action reports that when Confederates suddenly appeared on the battery's front and right, they were "within 60 yards."
55. *OR* 43, 359. Hall's statement in his official report that his battery commenced firing at 10:45 conflicts with a large body of testimony dealing with the interaction of the artillery with the infantry. These accounts point to an earlier starting time — about 10:30. On the other hand, Hall's time statement in the same report that his battery fired for 25 minutes can be readily accepted. Not only does it fit the circumstances, it was supported in the report of the other Union battery commander on the scene, Lt. John H. Calef (*OR* 43, 1031).
56. Capt. James A. Hall to Col. J. B. Bachelder, Dec. 29, 1869, New Hampshire Historical Society, copy in GNMP Library; *Maine at Gettysburg*, 17-18.
57. Capt. Charles E. Stubbs to Col. J. B. Bachelder, July 3, 1882, copy in GNMP Library.
58. *OR* 43, 359, 245-246; *Maine at Gettysburg*, 17.
59. Capt. James A. Hall to Col. J. B. Bachelder, Dec. 29, 1869, New Hampshire Historical Society, copy in GNMP Library; *Maine at Gettysburg*, 17-18.
60. Stine, 464-465, quotes speech of J. V. Pierce.
61. Capt. James A. Hall to Col. J. B. Bachelder, Dec. 29, 1869, New Hampshire Historical Society, copy in GNMP Library.
62. *OR* 43, 359.
63. *OR* 43, 359; Capt. James A. Hall to Col. J. B. Bachelder, Dec. 29, 1869, New Hampshire Historical Society, copy in GNMP Library.
64. *OR* 43, 359; Capt. James A. Hall to Col. J. B. Bachelder, Dec. 29, 1869, New Hampshire Historical Society, copy in GNMP Library; *OR* 43, 359.
65. Stine, 464-465, quotes speech of J. V. Pierce.
66. Doubleday, 129; Lt. J. V. Pierce to Col. J. B. Bachelder, Oct. 1, 1882, copy in GNMP Library.
67. Stine, 464-465, quotes speech of J. V. Pierce.
68. *OR* 44, 649.
69. Bates, 213.
70. Stine, 464-465, quotes speech of J. V. Pierce.

CHAPTER 7

1. Col. J. B. Bachelder's notes (n. d.) of his conversation with Col. Lucius Fairchild, copy in GNMP Library.
2. *OR* 43, 273.
3. *OR* 43, 273, 245, 273; Lucius Fairchild to R. K. Beecham, Apr. 11, 1884, copy in USAMHI; Capt. Nathaniel Rollins (Co. H), diary entry of July 1, 1863, State Historical Society of Wisconsin, copy in USAMHI; Pvt. Sydney B. Mead (Co. F), diary entry of July 1, 1863, State Historical Society of Wisconsin, copy in USAMHI; *Gettysburg Papers*, Vol. I, 186; Otis, 84-85; Thomas, *Ready...Aim... Fire!*, 59, cites Quarterly Summary Statements of Ordnance and Ordnance Stores, June 30, 1863; Tucker, *High Tide*, 146.
4. *Gettysburg Papers*, Vol. I, 186; Col. J. B. Bachelder's notes (n. d.) of his conversation with Col. Lucius Fairchild, copy in GNMP Library.
5. *OR* 43, 274; *OR* 44, 646; Lucius Fairchild to R. K. Beecham, Apr. 11, 1884, copy in USAMHI.
6. Col. J. B. Bachelder's notes (n. d.) of his conversation with Col. Lucius Fairchild, copy in GNMP Library.

7. *OR* 43, 273; Lucius Fairchild to R. K. Beecham, Apr. 11, 1884, copy in USAMHI; Ross, *The Empty Sleeve: Biography of Lucius Fairchild*, 48-49; Stine, 457.
8. Stine, 730-731.
9. Beecham, 63-64. Maj. Gen. Abner Doubleday, in *Chancellorsville and Gettysburg* (p. 132), quotes the Confederates' sally on recognizing the Iron Brigade, as follows: "There are those d____d black-hatted fellows again! 'Tain't no militia. It's the Army of the Potomac.'" Although the wording differs from Beecham's, the gist is the same.
10. Turney, "The First Tennessee at Gettysburg," *Confederate Veteran*, Vol. VIII (1900), 535.
11. *OR* 44, 646; Dowdey, 93, 96.
12. Kimble, "Tennesseans at Gettysburg — The Retreat," *Confederate Veteran*, Vol. XVIII (1910), 460.
13. Boland, "Death of Gen. Reynolds," *National Tribune*, May 20, 1915.
14. Turney, "The First Tennessee at Gettysburg," *Confederate Veteran*, Vol. VIII (1900), 535.
15. Moon, "Beginning of the Battle at Gettysburg," *Confederate Veteran*, Vol. XXXIII (1925), 449.
16. *OR* 43, 281-282, 287; battlefield monument of 14th Brooklyn Regiment; Col. E. B. Fowler's recollections (July 28, 1863) quoted in Tevis and Marquis, 132.
17. Tevis and Marquis, 132-133.
18. Tevis and Marquis, 132-133; *New York at Gettysburg*, Vol. I, 13.
19. Lt. Col. John R. Callis to Col. J. B. Bachelder (n. d.), copy in GNMP Library. Callis' inept punctuation of the dialogue has been changed to better indicate the inflections of the speakers.
20. *OR* 43, 279.
21. Lt. Col. William W. Dudley to Col. J. B. Bachelder (n. d.), copy in GNMP Library; M. C. Barnes to Lt. Col. William W. Dudley, Mar. 28, 1883, copy in GNMP Library.
22. Aubery, *Echoes From the Marches of the Famous Iron Brigade*, 37.
23. Tucker, *High Tide*111, cites "The 19th Indiana at Gettysburg," manuscript, Indiana State Library.
24. M. C. Barnes to Lt. Col. William W. Dudley, Mar. 28, 1883, copy in GNMP Library.
25. Tucker, *High Tide*, 111, cites "The 19th Indiana at Gettysburg," manuscript, Indiana State Library.
26. Smith, *The Twenty-fourth Regiment of the Iron Brigade*, 120.
27. *OR* 43, 270.
28. *OR* 43, 927; *Gettysburg Papers*, Vol. I, 177; Cheney, 109; various regimental monuments on battlefield.
29. *OR* 43, 927.
30. *OR* 43, 927, Day, "Veteran of 3rd Indiana Cavalry Describes First Day's Fight at Gettysburg," *National Tribune*, July 30, 1903.
31. *OR* 43, 927, Day, "Veteran of 3rd Indiana Cavalry Describes First Day's Fight at Gettysburg," *National Tribune*, July 30, 1903.
32. Norton, *Deeds of Daring*, 68-69.
33. Day, "Veteran of 3rd Indiana Cavalry Describes First Day's Fight at Gettysburg," *National Tribune*, July 30, 1903.
34. *OR* 43, 275-276; Lt. Col. Rufus R. Dawes to Col. J. B. Bachelder, Mar. 18, 1868, copy in GNMP Library; Dawes, 164-165. The account of the 6th Wisconsin in this stage of the battle relies primarily on the first source; the other two provided supplementary detail. Only in the Official Report did Dawes explicitly state that his regiment was twice ordered into battle and twice halted prior to its charge on the railroad cut. Unfortunately, he did not state who ordered the first halt or who ordered the second advance (nor did anyone else).

Edwin B. Coddington considered it "pretty certain" that Meredith ordered the first halt (*Gettysburg Campaign*, 276); however, a case can certainly be made for Wadsworth. As to who issued the second order to advance, Coddington wrote that it was Meredith "or someone else." In all probability it was Meredith; though winning his fight, he had lost many men and therefore had the best reason to call up additional troops. Doubleday (as will be related later in the narrative) ordered the second halt and the subsequent charge.

35. Nevins, (ed.), 232-233; Boatner, 825.
36. *OR* 43, 354; Nevins, (ed.), 232-233.
37. Nevins, (ed.), 233.
38. *OR* 43, 245; Doubleday, 131; Jepson, "The First Day at Gettysburg. A Tribute to General Reynolds," *National Tribune*, Oct. 6, 1910;
39. Buell, 65.
40. Buell, 65.
41. Biddle, F27; Stine, 458-459; Sgt. Cornelius Wheeler to his parents, July 11, 1863, State Historical Society of Wisconsin, copy in USAMHI.
42. Moon, "Beginning of the Battle at Gettysburg," *Confederate Veteran*, Vol. XXXIII (Dec. 1925), 449.
43. Fite, 99.
44. Boland, "Beginning of the Battle of Gettysburg," *Confederate Veteran*, Vol. XIV (July 1906), 308-309.
45. Buell, 65.
46. Quoted in Moore, ed., 117.
47. Among the numerous references: Col. W. W. Robinson's report in the Official Records (*OR* 43, 279). George E. Jepson, in a speech before the 13th Massachusetts Association, said the Iron Brigade on McPherson's Ridge emitted a "wild West yell." (The speech was published in 1902 in the Association's Circular No. 15.)
48. *OR* 43, 267; Stine, 457.
49. M. C. Barnes to Lt. Col. William W. Dudley, Mar. 28, 1883, copy in GNMP Library.
50. Beecham, 63-64.
51. Lt. Col. William W. Dudley to Col. J. B. Bachelder (n. d.), copy in GNMP Library.
52. *OR* 43, 274; Hassler, *Crisis*, 52.
53. Hassler, *Crisis*, 52; Smith, *Twenty-fourth Michigan*, 126; Coddington, 271.
54. Stine, 451, 458-459.
55. Moon, "Beginning of the Battle at Gettysburg," *Confederate Veteran*, Vol. XXXIII (1925), 450.
56. *OR* 44, 646; Dudley, 6-7; Stine, 458-459; Curtis, 157.
57. Lt. Col. John R. Callis to Col. J. B. Bachelder (n. d.), copy in GNMP Library.
58. *OR* 43, 245.
59. *OR* 43, 279; M. C. Barnes to Lt. Col. William W. Dudley, Mar. 28, 1883, copy in GNMP Library.
60. Beecham, 63-64; *OR* 43, 274.
61. Turney, "The First Tennessee at Gettysburg," *Confederate Veteran*, Vol. VIII (1900), 535.
62. Lt. Col. John R. Callis to Col. J. B. Bachelder (n. d.), copy in GNMP Library.
63. *OR* 43, 267.
64. Lt. Col. William W. Dudley to Col. J. B. Bachelder (n. d.), copy in GNMP Library. Dudley, it should be noted, identified the 19th Indiana's prisoners as belonging to the 1st Tennessee. But that could not have been the case: That Tennessee regiment, as Confederate sources attest, was on the opposite (left) end of Archer's line. The 19th Indiana engaged the 7th and 14th Tennessee on Archer's right. (Dudley's error — a memory slip, no doubt — was inadvertently perpetuated in Col. Bachelder's map.)

65. Boland, "Beginning of the Battle of Gettysburg," *Confederate Veteran*, Vol. XIV (July 1906), 308-309; Moon, "Beginning of the Battle at Gettysburg," *Confederate Veteran*, Vol. XXXIII (1925), 450; Stine, 458-459.
66. Stine, 458-459; Mulholland, "Percentage of Losses at Gettysburg — Greatest in History," *Philadelphia Public Ledger*, Apr. 2, 1902. Brigadier General St. Clair Mulholland's article contains the only known contemporary reference as to how Maloney subdued Archer. It has been used in the narrative, though it is conceded that Maloney may have grabbed some part of Archer's anatomy other than his throat.
67. Stine, 458-459.
68. Beecham, 65-67.
69. Beecham, 65-67; Stine, 458-459; [Dailey quotation] *Gettysburg Papers*, Vol. I, 186-187 (Capt. William H. Harries, 2nd Wisconsin). An explanation is in order regarding Major Mansfield's report for the 2nd Wisconsin [*OR* 43, 274]. After crediting Maloney with the capture of Archer, he wrote that Archer surrendered his sword to Maloney and that the sword eventually passed to Lieutenant Dailey. Taken at face value, this tends to discredit the accounts of Beecham, Stine, and Harries (which collectively are compatible). The accounts are vindicated, however, by virtue of the following: (1) Mansfield did not actually see Archer hand over his sword and therefore could have been misinformed or made a wrong assumption; (2) it is improbable that a general would surrender his sword to a mere private; (3) Captain Harries actually saw Archer surrender his sword to Lieutenant Dailey.
70. Stine, 458-459.
71. *Gettysburg Papers*, Vol. I, 186-187 (Capt. William H. Harries, 2nd Wisconsin).
72. *B & L*, Vol. III, 285. (Major E. P. Halstead's account of the Doubleday- Archer conversation also appears in *Gettysburg Papers*, Vol. I, 153.)
73. *Gettysburg Papers*, Vol. I, 186-187 (Capt. William H. Harries, 2nd Wisconsin).
74. *B & L*, Vol. III, 285.
75. Otis, 84-85.
76. Capt. Nathaniel Rollins (Co. H, 2nd Wisconsin), diary entry of July 1, 1863, State Historical society of Wisconsin, copy in USAMHI.
77. Otis, Second Wisconsin Infantry, 84-85; Beecham, 69; Pvt. Sydney Mead, diary entry of July 1, 1863, State Historical Society of Wisconsin, copy in USAMHI. All three sources agree on the number of casualties; the first two state there were 302 men engaged, with the third tacit on the subject.
78. Peter F. Arndt to Thomas and Mary Dobell, Sept. 3, 1863, copy in GNMP Library.
79. Lt. Col. John R. Callis to Col. J. B. Bachelder (n.d.), copy in GNMP Library.
80. "Hon. William W. Dudley, Commissioner of Pensions," *National Tribune*, Aug. 20, 1881. How many colorbearers became casualties during the morning of July 1 is not known, but before the day ended the 19th Indiana had lost eight.
81. *OR* 43, 270; Curtis, 157; Smith, *Twenty-fourth Michigan*, 126.
82. Curtis, 182.
83. Estimated casualties by regiment:

116	- 2nd Wisconsin
80	- 7th Wisconsin
40	- 19th Indiana
70	- 24th Michigan
306	- Total

84. Heth quoted in Stine, 451.

85. Estimated casualties by regiment/battalion:

	Killed/Wounded	Captured	Total
1st Tennessee	45	60	105
7th Tennessee	40	30	70
14th Tennessee	35	25	60
5th Alabama	25	20	45
13th Alabama	55	65	120
	200	200	400

86. *OR* 44, 637.
87. Doubleday, 132.
88. Dudley, 6-7.
89. *OR* 44, 646.
90. Stine, 458-459; M. C. Barnes to Lt. Col. William W. Dudley, Mar. 28, 1883, copy in GNMP Library.
91. Boland, "Beginning of the Battle of Gettysburg," *Confederate Veteran*, Vol. XIV (July 1906), 308-309.
92. Jepson, speech published in Thirteenth Massachusetts Circular No. 15 (1902), 16; Jepson, "The First Day at Gettysburg. A Tribute to General Reynolds," *National Tribune*, Oct. 6, 1910.
93. Moon, "Beginning of the Battle at Gettysburg," *Confederate Veteran*, Vol. XXXIII (1925), 450; *Philadelphia Inquirer*, July 3, 1863.
94. Hosmer, dispatch dated July 1, 1863, *New York Herald*, July 3, 1863; Moon, "Beginning of the Battle at Gettysburg," *Confederate Veteran*, Vol. XXXIII (1925), 450. Of the five officers in Archer's Brigade above the rank of major, four were captured in the three-day battle: Archer and Aiken on the first day; Col. Birkett D. Fry of the 13th Alabama, the third day; Lt. Col. Newton J. George of the 1st Tennessee, either the first or the third day.
95. Rosengarten, "Reynolds' Last Battle," *Philadelphia Weekly Times*, Mar. 17, 1877; Rosengarten, "Major-General John F. Reynolds," Gettysburg *Star & Sentinel*, May 5, 1885.
96. Nevins, (ed.), 233; Joseph G. Rosengarten to Col. Samuel P. Bates, Jan. 13, 1871, Pennsylvania Historical and Museum Commission, Division of Archives and Manuscripts, copy in GNMP Library.
97. Dawes, 167-168.
98. *Gettysburg Papers*, Vol. I, 367-368.
99. Lucius Fairchild to R. K. Beecham, Apr. 11, 1884, copy in USAMHI; Ross, 48-49.
100. Lt. Col. William W. Dudley to Col. J. B. Bachelder (n. d.), copy in GNMP Library; *SHSP*, Vol. XXXVII, 109.
101. Charles H. Veil to David McConaughy, Apr. 7, 1864, Gettysburg College Civil War Institute.
102. Lt. H. H. Lyman to Col. J. B. Bachelder (n. d.), copy in GNMP Library.
103. Rosengarten, address, *Reynolds Memorial — Addresses Before the Historical Society of Pennsylvania*, 24; Veil, manuscript (1908), extract quoted in *Philadelphia Public Ledger*, Mar. 19, 1911, copy in Robert L. Brake Collection, USAMHI. Rosengarten neglected to mention just when he joined the the men accompanying Reynolds. Veil indicated, however, that it was before the group reached the George house. In his next sentence after describing the arrival there, he wrote that (presumably within minutes) he and Rosengarten rode together into Gettysburg to obtain a casket.
104. Veil, manuscript (1908), extract quoted in *Philadelphia Public Ledger*, Mar. 19, 1911, copy in Robert L. Brake Collection, USAMHI.
105. "Death of General Reynolds," *Gettysburg Compiler*, July 28, 1934. Later Mrs. Sheads

retrieved the shawl. The heirloom passed to succeeding generations of the distaff side of the Sheads family. In 1934 it was in the possession of Mrs. Leo Bushman of Gettysburg.

106. Veil, manuscript (1908), extract quoted in *Philadelphia Public Ledger*, Mar. 19, 1911, copy in Robert L. Brake Collection, USAMHI; Joseph G. Rosengarten to Col. Samuel P. Bates, Jan. 13, 1871, Pennsylvania Historical and Museum Commission, Division of Archives and Manuscripts, copy in GNMP Library; Charles H. Veil to David McConaughy, Apr. 7, 1864, Gettysburg College Civil War Institute; William Riddle to _____ Le Bouvier, Aug. 4, 1863, John F. Reynolds Papers, Franklin and Marshall College, copy in GNMP Library.
107. Jacobs, 19.
108. Jacobs, 19; Nichols, 202; Schildt, 455.
109. The Gettysburg description incorporates details found in the sources listed in footnotes 107 and 110-112.
110. Storrick, 42.
111. C. J. Tyson quoted in Preston, *History of the Tenth Regiment of Cavalry, New York State Volunteers*, 126-127 (also quoted in Schildt, 457-458); Frassanito, 41, 236.
112. Sallie Robbins Broadhead, diary entry of July 1, 1863, quoted in Miers & Brown, eds., 52-53.
113. *OR* 44, 646; Turney, "The First Tennessee at Gettysburg," *Confederate Veteran*, Vol. VIII (1900), 535-537; Lt. Col. John R. Callis to Col. J. B. Bachelder (n. d.), copy in GNMP Library.
114. *OR* 43, 245, 267; Doubleday, 132; M. C. Barnes to Lt. Col. William W. Dudley, Mar. 28, 1883, copy in GNMP Library.
115. Beecham, 66-67.
116. Beecham, 66-67, 67; *OR* 43, 268; Curtis, 157; McConnell, "First and Greatest Day's Battle — Gettysburg," *National Tribune*, July 13, 1916. According to Beecham, Sergeant Bryan was the 24th Michigan's only fatality west of Willoughby Run.
117. *OR* 43, 266 (Wadsworth). Doubleday gave two accounts of the time he arrived on the field. Both conflict with his own testimony and that of others as to his actions before and after his arrival. In one account, he said he "reached the ground just as the head of Wadsworth's Division [Cutler's Brigade] was going into action" [*Report of the Joint Committee on the Conduct of the War*, Part I, 306]. In the other, he said he "overtook the Iron Brigade just as it was going into action" [*Chancellorsville and Gettysburg*, 128]. Evidently he wished to give the impression he arrived on the scene earlier than he actually did. Wadsworth, who had no reason to dissemble, stated that Doubleday "arrived on the ground about the time, or shortly after General Reynolds fell."
118. *OR* 43, 245; *Report of the Joint Committee on the Conduct of the War*, Part I, 306; Bates, 212.
119. *Report of the Joint Committee on the Conduct of the War*, Part I, 306.
120. *OR* 43, 279; Stine, 460-461.
121. Pvt. Sydney Mead (Co. F, 2nd Wisconsin), diary entry of July 1, 1863, State Historical Society of Wisconsin, copy in USAMHI.
122. McConnell, "First and Greatest Day's Battle — Gettysburg," *National Tribune*, July 13, 1916.
123. *Gettysburg Papers*, Vol. I, 202; *OR* 43, 274.
124. *OR* 43, 279.
125. Lt. Col. William W. Dudley to Col. J. B. Bachelder (n. d.), copy in GNMP Library; *Gettysburg Papers*, Vol. I, 190.
126. *OR* 43, 268.

127. Beecham, 68-69; Otis, Second Wisconsin Infantry, 84-85; Sgt. Cornelius Wheeler to his parents, July 11, 1863, copy in Robert L. Brake Collection, USAMHI.
128. *OR* 43, 244, 268; Doubleday, 130.
129. *OR* 43, 244.
130. *OR* 43, 274-76, 279; Beecham, 68-69.
131. *OR* 43, 245.
132. Hopkins, "Death of Reynolds," *National Tribune*, Apr. 14, 1910.
133. *OR* 43, 245.
134. *OR* 43, 275-276; Doubleday, 131; Lt. Col. Rufus R. Dawes to Col. J. B. Bachelder, Mar. 18, 1868, copy in GNMP Library; Dawes, 164-165.
135. Beecham, 68-69; Sgt. Cornelius Wheeler to his parents, July 11, 1863, copy in Robert L. Brake Collection, USAMHI.
136. Curtis, 157-158.
137. *OR* 44, 646.

CHAPTER 8

1. *OR* 43, 359 (Hall's report dated July 16, 1863); Capt. James A. Hall to Col. J. B. Bachelder, Dec. 29, 1869, copy in GNMP Library. A discrepancy between these accounts deserves passing mention. In 1863 Hall reported the horses pulling the last gun were shot; in 1869 he said they were bayonetted. In all likelihood Hall was right the first time. Bachelder evidently thought so. The horses were shot, he stated unequivocally in his 1886 article, "Hall's Maine Battery at Gettysburg" (clipping in GNMP Library files).
2. *OR* 43, 359; Capt. James A. Hall to Col. J. B. Bachelder, Dec. 29, 1869, copy in GNMP Library; Coddington, 270, cites Capt. James A. Hall to Col. J. B. Bachelder, Feb. 27, 1868.
3. *OR* 43, 359; Capt. James A. Hall to Col. J. B. Bachelder, Dec. 29, 1869, copy in GNMP Library.
4. *OR* 43, 246.
5. Dawes, 166; Lt. Earl M. Rogers to Col. J. A. Watrous (n. d.), State Historical Society of Wisconsin, copy in GNMP Library; Lt. Col. Rufus R. Dawes to Col. J. B. Bachelder, Mar. 18, 1868, copy in GNMP Library.
6. *OR* 43, 275-276; Lt. Col. Rufus R. Dawes to Col. J. B. Bachelder, Mar. 18, 1868, copy in GNMP Library; Sullivan, "Gettysburg. Member of 6th Wisconsin Takes Issue with 'Carleton'," *National Tribune*, May 14,1885.
7. Dawes, 166-167.
8. Dawes, 166-167, 167; *OR* 43, 275-276; Lt. Col. Rufus R. Dawes to Col. J. B. Bachelder, Mar. 18, 1868, copy in GNMP Library; Sullivan, "Gettysburg. Member of 6th Wisconsin Takes Issue with 'Carleton'," *National Tribune*, May 14, 1885.
9. Dawes, , 167; Lt. Col. Rufus R. Dawes to Col. J. B. Bachelder,Mar. 18, 1868, copy in GNMP Library; Tevis and Marquis, 133 (Col. E. B. Fowler quoted).
10. Tevis and Marquis, 83, 133; *OR* 43, 286-287; *New York at Gettysburg*, Vol. I, 13.
11. Tevis and Marquis, 83, 134; *OR* 43, 286-288; New York at Gettysburg, Vol. I, 13; Doubleday, 129.
12. Tevis and Marquis, 133.
13. Tevis and Marquis, 83, 133.
14. Hill, Vol. 4, 1001; *OR* 43, 245; Stine, 464-465.
15. *New York at Gettysburg*, 992; Lt. J. V. Pierce to Col. J. B. Bachelder, Oct. 1, 1882, copy in GNMP Library.
16. *New York at Gettysburg*, Vol. III, 1005; Hill, Vol. 4, 1001.
17. *New York at Gettysburg*, Vol. III, 992-993 (Capt. J. V. Pierce quoted), 1005; Vol. I, 12.
18. Lt. J. V. Pierce to Col. J. B. Bachelder, Oct. 1, 1882, copy in GNMP Library; Coey, "Cutler's Brigade,"*National Tribune*, July 15, 1915; Stine, 464-465 (Capt. J. V. Pierce

quoted). From the participants' accounts, the question arises: What did Capt. Ellsworth vigorously wave in the air — his sword or his hat? Pierce said it was the former; Coey, the latter. While either could have been right, Pierce's version (antedating Coey's by 33 years) seems the more likely.

19. Coey, "Cutler's Brigade," *National Tribune*, July 15,1915.
20. Lt. H. H. Lyman to Col. J. B. Bachelder (n. d.), copy in GNMP Library. According to Lyman, the 147th New York had nothing to eat until July 4, "except small issues of fresh beef which was eaten without salt."
21. Stine, 464-465 (Major Harney quoted by Lt. J. V. Pierce).
22. Snyder, 62 (Major Harney quoted by Lt. H. H. Lyman).
23. Snyder, 62; Hill, Vol. 4, 1001-1002; Lt. J. V. Pierce to Col. J. B. Bachelder, Oct. 1, 1882, copy in GNMP Library; Lt. H. H. Lyman to Col. J. B. Bachelder (n. d.), copy in GNMP Library; Coey, "Cutler's Brigade," *National Tribune*, July 15, 1915.
24. Hill, Vol. 4, 1001-1002.
25. Coey, "Cutler's Brigade," *National Tribune*, July 15, 1915.
26. *New York at Gettysburg*, Vol. III, 992-993.
27. Lt. H. H. Lyman to Col. J. B. Bachelder (n. d.), copy in GNMP Library; Coey, "Cutler's Brigade," *National Tribune*, July 15, 1915; *New York at Gettysburg*, Vol. I, 12.
28. *New York at Gettysburg*, Vol. III, 992-993; Lt. J. V. Pierce to Col. J. B. Bachelder, Oct. 1, 1882, copy in GNMP Library.
29. Snyder, 62.
30. Hill, Vol. 4, 1001-1002.
31. Coey, "Cutler's Brigade," *National Tribune*, July 15, 1915.
32. Harris, "The Second Mississippi at Gettysburg, " *Confederate Veteran*, Vol. XXV (Nov. 1917), 527.
33. *New York at Gettysburg*, Vol. III, 992-993; Lt. H. H. Lyman to Col. J. B. Bachelder (n. d.), copy in GNMP Library; Coey, "Cutler's Brigade," *National Tribune*, July 15, 1915; *OR* 43, 254, 282-283.
34. *OR* 43, 359.
35. Parkhurst, "At Gettysburg. Heroism of the 147th New York," *National Tribune*, Nov. 1, 1888.
36. Hofmann, "Gettysburg Again. Gen. Hofmann on the Action of the 147th New York at the Opening of the Battle," *National Tribune*, June 5, 1884.
37. Coey, "Cutler's Brigade," *National Tribune*, July 15, 1915.
38. Doubleday, 132-133; Lt. H. H. Lyman to Col. J. B. Bachelder (n. d.), copy in GNMP Library; *New York at Gettysburg*, Vol. III, 992-993.
39. *Gettysburg Papers*, Vol. I, 280.
40. *OR* 43, 282; 147th New York monument on the battlefield; *New York at Gettysburg*, Vol. III, 1003.
41. Harris, "The Second Mississippi at Gettysburg, " *Confederate Veteran*, Vol. XXV (Nov. 1917), 527.
42. *Gettysburg Papers*, Vol. I, 280.
43. *New York at Gettysburg*, Vol. III, 1006; Tucker, *High Tide*,115.
44. Freeman, *Lee's Lieutenants*, Vol. III, 78.
45. *New York at Gettysburg*, Vol. III, 1006; Bellah, 38, 41.
46. *Histories of the Several Regiments and Battalions from North Carolina*, Vol. III, 288; Dawes, 169; Tucker, *High Tide*, 115.
47. *Histories of the Several Regiments and Battalions from North Carolina*, Vol. III, 297-298.
48. Coddington, 272.
49. Capt. J. A. Kellogg to Col. J. B. Bachelder, Mar. 31, 1868, copy in GNMP Library.

50. Belo, "Battle of Gettysburg," *Confederate Veteran*, Vol. VIII (Apr. 1900); *New York at Gettysburg*, Vol. III, 1006.
51. *OR* 44, 649; *Histories of the Several Regiments and Battalions from North Carolina*, Vol. III, 297-298.
52. *OR* 43, 1031.
53. Calef, "Gettysburg Notes: The Opening Gun," *Journal of the Military Service Institution of the United States*, Vol. 40 (1907), 49.
54. Dawes, 167. The position of the brigade guard is indicated in Dawes' note at the bottom of page 171.
55. Dawes, 167.
56. *Histories of the Several Regiments and Battalions from North Carolina*, Vol. III, 297-298.
57. Dawes, 167-168; *OR* 43, 275-276; Capt. J. A. Kellogg to Col. J. B. Bachelder, Mar. 31, 1868, copy in GNMP Library. While there is compelling documentation that Dawes approached Pye, it may be noted that, at one point, Dawes (possibly in a lapse of memory) indicated the reverse. In his letter of March 18, 1868 to Col. J. B. Bachelder (copy in GNMP Library), he said Major Pye "came toward me." Also in this letter, instead of the dramatic "We must charge!" which appears in his book, he said his first words to the 95th New York's commander were "Let's go for them, Major."
58. Dawes, 168; Lt. Earl M. Rogers to Col. J. A. Watrous (n. d.), State Historical Society of Wisconsin, copy in GNMP Library; Sullivan, "Gettysburg. Member of 6th Wisconsin Takes Issue with 'Carleton'," *National Tribune*, May 14, 1885; Lt. Col. Rufus R. Dawes to Col. J. B. Bachelder, Mar. 18, 1868, copy in GNMP Library. Lt. Rogers, after confirming Dawes' statement that he (Dawes) continually exhorted his troops to stay closed up, went on to credit him with twice recovering the fallen regimental colors and carrying it until relieved by a color guard. This seems highly improbable, since Dawes — not one to be reticent about his actions — never mentioned it.
59. Dawes, 168.
60. Lt. Col. Rufus R. Dawes to Col. J. B. Bachelder, Mar. 18, 1868, copy in GNMP Library.
61. Dawes to Bachelder, Mar. 18, 1868.
62. Tevis and Marquis, 83, 133. Some misleading statements by Colonel Fowler need to be addressed here. In his official report (*OR* 43, 286-287) and in his recollections (quoted in Tevis and Marquis, 132-135), he gave the strong impression that he exercised overall command of the charge. He wrote, for example, that Dawes' 6th Wisconsin "advanced bravely to our assistance." (In point of time, the reverse was true.) He continued: "I then gave the order to advance the whole line," implying inclusion of the 6th Wisconsin, which simply was not so. Further: "When nearing the cut, I sent my Adjutant to the 6th Wisconsin, directing them to flank the enemies' position, which they did...." Again, not so. That regiment's commander, Lt. Col. Rufus Dawes, set the record straight. In a footnote in his Service With the Sixth Wisconsin Volunteers [p. 167], he flatly declared: "He [Fowler] gave us no orders whatever. I did not know he was on the field until the charge was over."
63. Coey, "Cutler's Brigade," *National Tribune*, July 15, 1915.
64. Dawes, 168.
65. Sullivan, "Gettysburg. Member of 6th Wisconsin Takes Issue with 'Carleton'," *National Tribune*, May 14, 1885. Subsequently, a minie ball struck Private Sullivan in the shoulder, knocking him down. Sergeant Albert Tarbox rushed to his side. "They've got you down, Mickey, have they?" he said, and with that, pitched forward — dead. Sullivan, though feeling "sick and faint," thought he was still able to guard prisoners. He soon found out otherwise, for "the blood was running down inside my clothes and dropping from my pants leg and my shoe was full and running over." He went to the hospital set up in the Court

House in Gettysburg. There he saw doctors, both civilian and military, "busy cutting up and patching up" the wounded. Luckily, he could be patched up. [Sullivan, "The Charge of the Iron Brigade at Gettysburg," account dated Feb. 13, 1883, and subsequently published in two installments in *Mauston [Ohio] Star.*]

66. Dawes, 168.
67. Sullivan, "Gettysburg. Member of 6th Wisconsin Takes Issue with 'Carleton'," *National Tribune*, May 14, 1885; Lt. Col. Rufus Dawes to his wife Mary, July 4, 1863, State Historical Society of Wisconsin, copy in GNMP Library; Fox, *Regimental Losses in the American Civil War*, 439; 6th Wisconsin monument. According to Sullivan, the 6th Wisconsin lost 40 men killed and 82 wounded in the charge. The day after the battle, Dawes wrote his wife that his regiment's losses in the morning and afternoon engagements on July 1 were 154, with only six more casualties incurred over the next two days. William Fox, after careful study of all available data, concluded that total casualties in the 6th Wisconsin in the three-day battle were 168. This figure appears on the regiment's monument on the battlefield. As the brigade guard fought alongside the 6th Wisconsin, it can be assumed its percent of loss closely matched that of Dawes' regiment. Those men killed or wounded while serving in the brigade guard would have been included in the reports of the respective regiments from which they were drawn.
68. Dawes, 168; Lt. Col. Rufus R. Dawes to Col. J. B. Bachelder, Mar. 18, 1868, copy in GNMP Library. The two accounts agree except for the size of Brooks' force: "about twenty men" versus "about fifty men." The smaller figure (in Dawes' book) is probably more nearly correct, inasmuch as a majority of the Confederates seem not to have been aware of the enfilade fire coming from their right flank. In fact, W. B. Murphy (Co. A, 2nd Mississippi) went so far as to aver that no enemy infantry ever flanked their position in the cut. [Murphy to Dr. F. A. Dearborn, June 29, 1900, State Historical Society of Wisconsin, copy in GNMP Library.] Murphy was wrong, of course. Dawes' account of the action of Brooks' men is corroborated in Doubleday's *Chancellorsville and Gettysburg* (pp. 132-133) and in Cheek and Pointon's *Sauk County Riflemen* (p. 74).
69. Tevis and Marquis, 84.
70. Lt. Earl M. Rogers to Col. J. A. Watrous (n. d.), State Historical Society of Wisconsin, copy in GNMP Library.
71. Sullivan, "Gettysburg. Member of 6th Wisconsin Takes Issue with 'Carleton'," *National Tribune*, May 14, 1885.
72. Lt. Earl M. Rogers to Col. J. A. Watrous (n. d.), State Historical Society of Wisconsin, copy in GNMP Library.
73. Belo, "Battle of Gettysburg," *Confederate Veteran*, Vol. VIII (Apr. 1900); *Histories of the Several Regiments and Battalions from North Carolina*, Vol. III, 298.
74. Dawes, 172; Dawes, "Reminiscenses of the Battle of Gettysburg," [Gettysburg] *Star and Sentinel*, Mar. 8, 1872.
75. W. B. Murphy to Dr. F. A. Dearborn, June 29, 1900, State Historical Society of Wisconsin, copy in GNMP Library; Aubery, 62-65.
76. W. B. Murphy to Dr. F. A. Dearborn, June 29, 1900, State Historical Society of Wisconsin, copy in GNMP Library.
77. Dawes, 168-169; Lt. Col. Rufus R. Dawes to Col. J. B. Bachelder, Mar. 18, 1868, copy in GNMP Library; C. W. Okey quoted in Aubery, 62-65. These accounts differ on two details. Okey misidentified Remington as "Pennington." And Okey said it was he (not Eggleston, as Dawes claimed) who was shot by the Rebel that was killed a moment later by "Rocky Mountain" Anderson. Incidentally, W. B. Murphy, 2nd Mississippi's color-bearer, doubted that Anderson clubbed a Southerner to death at this time. Writing to a Dr. Dearborn (full reference in footnote 78), he did allow, however, that "If he did I did not see it."

78. W. B. Murphy to Dr. F. A. Dearborn, June 29, 1900, State Historical Society of Wisconsin, copy in GNMP Library.

79. Murphy to Dearborn, June 29, 1900. The inscription on the Cutler Brigade monument states that the three regiments in the charge captured two battle flags. The assertion may have stemmed from Cutler's report (*OR* 43, 266), in which he wrote (quite inaccurately) that "two entire regiments" were taken prisoner, adding "with their flags." If a second flag was captured, no clue exists as to its identity.

80. Lt. Earl M. Rogers to Col. J. A. Watrous (n. d.), State Historical Society of Wisconsin, copy in GNMP Library; Dawes, 169; *OR* 43, 276. An account in Cheek and Pointon's *Sauk County Riflemen* (p. 74) has Waller depreciating his own actions and giving credit to a 6th Wisconsin private for the capture of the 2nd Mississippi's colors. Purporting to be Waller's own words, it reads:

> Bodley Jones of A Company had made for the flag in the charge and had captured it and had it in his possession when killed. I (Waller) grabbed it as Jones fell and carried it back and surrendered it to our proper officers and I got the medal of honor for the capture. But if he had not been killed, he and not I would have had the medal.

Three considerations point to the quotation being spurious: (1) the claim that Jones captured the flag is totally unsupported; (2) the account is at odds with the consistent testimony in the sources listed above; (3) the degree of modesty and selflessness here attributed to Waller is not quite believable. Then too, one is reminded that *Sauk County Riflemen* is devoted exclusively to the exploits of 6th Wisconsin's Company A and Pvt. Jones belonged to that company.

81. Lt. Earl M. Rogers to Col. J. A. Watrous (n. d.), State Historical Society of Wisconsin, copy in GNMP Library.

82. Tevis and Marquis, 84; Sullivan, "Gettysburg. Member of 6th Wisconsin Takes Issue with 'Carleton'," *National Tribune*, May 14, 1885.

83. *OR* 43, 246; Dawes cited in Stine, 468.

84. Sullivan, "Gettysburg. Member of 6th Wisconsin Takes Issue with 'Carleton'," *National Tribune*, May 14, 1885; Lt. Earl M. Rogers to Col. J. A. Watrous (n. d.), State Historical Society of Wisconsin, copy in GNMP Library.

85. *OR* 43, 287; Dawes, 173.

86. *Histories of the Several Regiments and Battalions from North Carolina*, Vol. III, 298.

87. Dawes, 169. Substantially the same account appears in Dawes' letter of March 18 , 1868, to Col. J. B. Bachelder (copy in GNMP Library).

88. Dawes, 169; Lt. Col. Rufus R. Dawes to Col. J. B. Bachelder, Mar. 18, 1868, copy in GNMP Library.

89. W. B. Murphy to Dr. F. A. Dearborn, June 29, 1900, State Historical Society of Wisconsin, copy in GNMP Library.

90. Lacking any casualty details restricted to the morning hours, the number of officers and men killed or wounded in Davis' Brigade had to be determined by a series of deductions. Thus, the figure 350 represents the difference between the brigade strength before and after the 3-day battle minus the estimated casualties on July 3 and the approximately 300 officers and men captured on July 1.

91. *OR* 44, 649.

92. *OR* 44, 637-638.

93. *OR* 43, 246.

94. Nevins, (ed.), 267. Wainwright noted that the charge began about 11:00.

95. Dawes, 170.

96. Dawes, 170; Dawes, "Reminiscences of the Battle of Gettysburg," [Gettysburg] *Star and Sentinel*, Mar. 8, 1872; *OR* 43, 278.

97. Dawes, 170.
98. Inferred from the reports of Heth (*OR* 44, 637-638) and Davis (*OR* 44, 649-650). Davis reported his troops "all much exhausted by the excessive heat."
99. Dawes, 170; *OR* 43, 288, 360.
100. Tevis and Marquis, 84-85. Another poignant incident is related in J. C. Storrick's *Gettysburg: The Place, the Battles, the Outcome* (published in 1932). When the fighting was over in the railroad cut, a 6th Wisconsin officer came up to Lt. Col. Dawes and gasped, "Tell them at home I died like a man and a soldier." Whereupon he opened his coat, revealing a massive chest wound, and then dropped dead. Storrick's source is not known and the story may be apochryphal. Since Dawes wrote voluminously about his war experiences, it seems unlikely he would not have mentioned such a dramatic incident had it occurred.
101. Tevis and Marquis, 148-149.
102. *OR* 43, 246, 359-360; Capt. James A. Hall to Col. J. B. Bachelder, Dec. 29, 1869, copy in GNMP Library.
103. *OR* 43, 356.
104. *OR* 43, 266, 356, 1031; Calef, "Gettysburg Notes: The Opening Gun," *Journal of the Military Service Institution of the United States*, Vol. 40 (1907), 49; Coddington, 687, cites an unpublished portion of Col. C. S. Wainwright's journals (manuscript pages 213-214); Pearson, 212. According to Wainwright, Calef downright refused and Wadsworth was so incensed he ordered him to the rear in arrest. That did not happen, however, as Calef's eyewitness account of his battery in action *after the argument* attests.
105. *OR* 43, 1031-1032.
106. *OR* 43, 359-360; Pearson, 212.
107. *OR* 43, 246, 276, 287-288; Tevis and Marquis, 84, 134-135.
108. Abner Doubleday to Samuel P. Bates, Oct. 18, 1875, Pennsylvania Historical and Museum Commission, Division of Archives and Manuscripts, copy in USAMHI.

CHAPTER 9

1. Longstreet, 351; Alexander, 381.
2. *OR* 44, 358, supplemented by sources in footnote 1. Harry W. Pfanz, in *Gettysburg — The Second Day* (p. 22), cites the delay of Longstreet's Divisions as proof that Lee was not expecting a battle on July 1. If he were, he would not have allowed the Second Corps wagon train to precede those troops.
3. Owen, 243.
4. *SHSP*, Vol. XLIII, 143; Freeman, *R. E. Lee*, Vol. III, 65.
5. Freeman, Vol. III, 66; Scott, Vol. I, 123. Unfortunately, Scott did not indicate his source for the Lee quotation. Although its origin could not be found, the quotation is nonetheless plausible; it sounds exactly like Lee.
6. *SHSP*, Vol. XLIII, 56.
7. Taylor, 91-92; *Annals of the War*, 420; Freeman, *R. E. Lee*, Vol. III, 66; Stackpole, 156-157.
8. *SHSP*, Vol. XXXIII, 143.
9. Alexander, 381; Coddington, 280.
10. Maj. G. Campbell Brown, manuscript (n. d.), Tennessee Historical Commission archives, copy in Robert L. Brake Collection, USAMHI; Pfanz, 20.
11. *OR* 44, 444.
12. Taylor, 91-92.
13. *OR* 44, 638. Heth reported his division rested in line of battle "an hour or more" before being ordered to attack.

14. *OR* 44, 638; Vanderslice, 79; Doubleday, 133; *Histories of the Several Regiments and Battalions from North Carolina*, Vol. II, 346; Coddington, 280.
15. *Histories of the Several Regiments and Battalions from North Carolina*, Vol. III, 236.
16. *Histories of the Several Regiments and Battalions from North Carolina*, Vol. II, 368. (Periods were substituted for Burgwyn's inappropriate semi-colons.)
17. *SHSP*, Vol. VIII, 515-516.
18. Battine, 190.
19. *OR* 44, 656-657, 668; Scott, Vol. I, 163-164, 232; Stine, 480.
20. *OR* 44, 674-675. The 88th Pennsylvania's historian slightly exaggerated the number of Confederate guns firing around noon. About forty, he claimed, and no doubt it seemed that many! [Vautier, 122.]
21. Diary of Jedediah Hotchkiss, entry of July 1, 1863, Library of Congress; Jacobs, 24-25.
22. Cheney, 110.
23. *The Confederate Soldier in the Civil War*, 164 (report of Gen. Robert E. Lee, June 6, 1864); Battine, 191.
24. Coddington, 280. Lee, in his June 6, 1864 report (see footnote 23), implied that he had not been consulted. He wrote: "General Heth then prepared for action, and as soon as Pender arrived to support him, was ordered by General Hill to advance."
25. *SHSP*, Vol. V, 196.
26. Biddle, 27.
27. *Pennsylvania at Gettysburg*, Vol. I, 664-665.
28. *OR* 43, 326-327; Lt. Col. George F. McFarland (151st Pennsylvania) to Maj. Gen. Abner Doubleday, June 15,1864, copy in GNMP Library; Biddle, 30.
29. *OR* 43, 320, 326-327; Lt. Col. George F. McFarland to Maj. Gen. Abner Doubleday, June 15, 1864, copy in GNMP Library; *Pennsylvania at Gettysburg*, Vol. I, 664-665.
30. *Pennsylvania at Gettysburg*, Vol. I, 664-665.
31. *OR* 43, 320; Gates, 432-433; Lt. Col. George F. McFarland (151st Pennsylvania) to Maj. Gen. Abner Doubleday, June 15, 1864, copy in GNMP Library; Scott, Vol. I, 159-160.
32. *OR* 43, 326-327; Lt. Col. George F. McFarland to Maj. Gen. Abner Doubleday, June 15, 1864, copy in GNMP Library.
33. Lt. Col. George F. McFarland (151st Pennsylvania), in his after-action report (*OR* 43, pp.326-327) and also in his letter to Doubleday (see footnote 31), stated that his regiment arrived on the Fairfield road at 10:30. Col. Chapman Biddle, in his *First Day of the Battle of Gettysburg* (p.30), stated that his brigade formed a battle line "a little before eleven A.M." From these time statements and those of subsequent events, it can be concluded that the brigade was moving into position on McPherson's Ridge at or shortly after eleven o'clock. Maj. Alexander Biddle claimed that as the 121st Pennsylvania marched up McPherson's Ridge, he and his men saw General Reynolds — "in the open fields near a woods" — just before he was mortally wounded. [Strong, 120; *Pennsylvania at Gettysburg*, Vol. I, 665.] In point of time, assuming the regiment moved out from the Fairfield Road somewhat earlier than Col. Chapman Biddle indicated, it is just barely possible. On the other hand, at a distance of at least 500 yards, it could have been a case of mistaken identity. The report of 151st Pennsylvania troops seeing Reynolds' body being carried to the rear is believable. [*Pennsylvania at Gettysburg*, Vol. II,768-769.]
34. Regiment, brigade, and battery monuments on McPherson's Ridge; *OR* 43, 323; Biddle, 30-31; *Pennsylvania at Gettysburg*, 768-769.
35. Transcript of Court Martial of Gen. Thomas A. Rowley, National Archives, copy in USAMHI.
36. Gates, 432-433; *OR* 43, 320.
37. *OR* 43, 323.

38. Ashhurst, "Remarks on Certain Questions Relating to the First Day's Fight at Gettysburg," 9-10.
39. Tucker, *High Tide*, 118.
40. *OR* 43, 331-332; *Pennsylvania at Gettysburg*, Vol. II, 745.
41. Bassler, "Reminiscences of the First Day's Fight at Gettysburg," address given at Albright Collegiate Institute, June 1895, copy in GNMP Library.
42. Bassler, "Reminiscences of the First Day's Fight at Gettysburg," address given at Albright Collegiate Institute, June 1895, copy in GNMP Library.
43. Quoted in Bates, 215.
44. *OR* 43, 331-332; *Pennsylvania at Gettysburg*, Vol. II, 745.
45. Chamberlin, 117.
46. Bassler, "Reminiscences of the First Day's Fight at Gettysburg," address given at Albright Collegiate Institute, June 1895, copy in GNMP Library.
47. Chamberlin, 117-118.
48. Huidekoper, 6; *Pennsylvania at Gettysburg*, Vol. II, 745, 751; Chamberlin, 118; W. R. Ramsey (150th Pennsylvania) to J. H. Bassler, Aug. 3, 1906, copy in GNMP Library.
49. *Pennsylvania at Gettysburg*, Vol. II, 751.
50. Bassler, "Reminiscences of the First Day's Fight at Gettysburg," address given at Albright Collegiate Institute, June 1895, copy in GNMP Library; Chamberlin, 118; *Pennsylvania at Gettysburg*, Vol. II, 751; Bates, 215; Huidekoper, 6.
51. Bassler, "Reminiscences of the First Day's Fight at Gettysburg," address given at Albright Collegiate Institute, June 1895, copy in GNMP Library; *OR* 43, 331-332.
52. Chamberlin, 119.
53. Chamberlin, 119; *Pennsylvania at Gettysburg*, Vol. II, 752.
54. *OR* 43, 332; *SHSP*, Vol. XXXVII 267-268; Lt. Col. H. S. Huidekoper (150th Pennsylvania) to Col. J. B. Bachelder (n. d.), copy in GNMP Library; Hubler (143rd Pennsylvania), "Just the Plain, Unvarnished Story of a Soldier in the Ranks," *New York Times Magazine*, June 29, 1913; Biddle, 29; detailed sketch (Oct. 1977) of McPherson farm by Kathleen Georg Harrison, GNMP Library.
55. Chamberlin, 119; *Pennsylvania at Gettysburg*, Vol. II, 745.
56. Hubler, "Just the Plain, Unvarnished Story of a Soldier in the Ranks," *New York Times Magazine*, June 29, 1913.
57. *Report of the Joint Committee on the Conduct of the War*, Part I, 307; *Pennsylvania at Gettysburg*, Vol. II, 745. (The famous quotation also appears in the writings of Doubleday, Comte de Paris, and many others.)
58. Chamberlin, 112; Scott, Vol. I, 198; *OR* 43, 329.
59. *Pennsylvania at Gettysburg*, Vol. II, 752.
60. Bassler, "Reminiscences of the First Day's Fight at Gettysburg," address given at Albright Collegiate Institute, June 1895, copy in GNMP Library.
61. *OR* 43, 279; Curtis, 159; Cornelius Wheeler to his parents, July 11, 1863, copy in Robert L. Brake Collection, USAMHI; McConnell, "First and Greatest Day's Battle — Gettysburg," *National Tribune*, July 30, 1903.
62. Beecham, 71.
63. *OR* 43, 266, 282, 285; *Pennsylvania at Gettysburg*, Vol. I, 341; Doubleday, 135; Abner Doubleday to Samuel P. Bates, Oct. 18, 1875, in Pennsylvania Historical and Museum Commission, Division of Archives and Manuscripts, copy in Robert L. Brake Collection, USAMHI.
64. *OR* 43, 276.
65. *OR* 43, 287-288; Tevis and Marquis, 132-135.
66. Dawes, 173.

67. *OR* 43, 354-355, 362; *New York at Gettysburg*, Vol. III, 1256.
68. Nevins, (ed.), 234.
69. *OR* 43, 355; Coddington, 687, cites an unpublished portion of Col. C. S. Wainwright's journals (manuscript pages 213-214).
70. *OR* 43, 356; Vautier, 124. According to Wainwright (in the unpublished portion of his journals) the flight of the two batteries was simultaneous, but there is no indication that such was the case in the official reports for either battery.
71. *OR* 43, 229; *New York at Gettysburg*, Vol. III, 1256; Downey, 32-33.
72. *OR* 43, 1032.
73. Buford quoted in Stine, 452.
74. *OR* 43, 1032.
75. *OR* 43, 360; *Maine at Gettysburg*, 20-21. When Hall's battery reached Cemetery Ridge, General Howard ordered the three operable guns be placed "on the left of the cemetery" [*OR* 43, 360].
76. Buell, 65; *Maine at Gettysburg*, 82-84.
77. Nevins, (ed.), 232-233.
78. Chamberlin, 120. In the 19th Indiana Lieutenant Colonel William W. Dudley also reported seeing the enemy "forming in plain sight" [*Iron Brigade at Gettysburg*, 11].
79. Dudley, 11.
80. Boatner, 740.
81. Davis, *Three Years in the Army: The Story of the Thirteenth Massachusetts Volunteers*, 225; Thirteenth Massachusetts Circular No. 15 (1902), 15-17.
82. Davis, 225; *OR* 43, 311.
83. Stearns, 178.
84. Jacob F. Slagle to his brother John, Sept. 13, 1863, copy in Robert L. Brake Collection, USAMHI; Davis, 225.
85. Vautier, 105.
86. *OR* 43, 311; *Gettysburg Papers*, Vol. I, 265; Davis, 226; Stearns, 178-179.
87. Stearns, 178-179.
88. Vautier, 105, 114; Locke, *Story of the Regiment [11th Pennsylvania]*, 228-229. In the lead brigade (Baxter's), the 83rd New York reported arriving at the Seminary about 11:00 [Todd, ed., *History of the Ninth Regiment New York State Militia [83rd New York]*, 268]. It seems likely it arrived a short time after 11:00, as the 104th New York, in the same brigade, reported that at that hour the regiment was just "in sight of Seminary Ridge"[*New York at Gettysburg*, Vol. II, 752]. In the rear brigade (Paul's), the 88th Pennsylvania reported its position at 11:00 as "some two miles" from its destination [*OR* 43, 311].
89. Cheney, 110.
90. *OR* 43, 292, 307; Vautier, 105, 114; Locke, 228-229.
91. Doubleday, 136; Davis, 226; Maine at Gettysburg, 46; *New York at Gettysburg*, Vol. II, 723; Todd, ed., 269; *OR* 43, 295,299.
92. Kieffer, 112; Paul, "Paul's Brigade at Gettysburg," unpublished manuscript (n. d.), typed copy in GNMP Library; Pindell, "Our Technological Inheritance," *Civil War Times Illustrated*, Vol. XXVI (Summer, 1987), 53.
93. Davis, 226.
94. Battine, 189.
95. *OR* 43, 329, 332, 345.
96. Chamberlin, 120, quotes diary of Sgt. William R. Ramsey.
97. Sgt. John C. Kensill (150th Pennsylvania) to Capt. John H. Bassler (149th Pennsylvania), Feb. 14, 1882, copy in GNMP Library.
98. Kieffer, 112-113.

99. *OR* 43, 332, 341, 345; Chamberlin, 122.
100. *Pennsylvania at Gettysburg*, Vol. II, 768-769.
101. Mulholland, *Percentage of Losses at Gettysburg — Greatest in History*, 3.
102. Tevis and Marquis, 132-135, quotes Col. E. B. Fowler; Hill, Vol. 4, 1002.
103. Jacob F. Slagle to his brother John, Sept. 13, 1863, copy in GNMP Library.
104. *OR* 43, 279, 315.
105. *OR* 43, 329; Vol. II, 752; Chamberlin, 119.
106. M. C. Barnes to Lt. Col. William W. Dudley, Mar. 28, 1883, copy in GNMP Library.
107. McConnell, "First and Greatest Day's Battle — Gettysburg," *National Tribune*, July 13, 1916.
108. Cornelius Wheeler to his parents, July 11, 1863, copy in Robert L. Brake Collection, USAMHI.
109. *OR* 43, 315, 320; Gates, 433; Biddle, 31.
110. Mulholland, 3; Chamberlin, 121.
111. Bates, 988-989. Although some accounts give Burns' age as seventy and others say over seventy, he was actually two months short of his seventieth birthday at the time of the battle. He was born September 5, 1793, in Burlington, New Jersey, to Joseph and Polly Burns. Through his father, born in Scotland near the River Dee, he is reputed to have been kin to poet Robert Burns. His mother (nee Dobson) was English.
112. Cheney, 112. If Lt. Newel Cheney of the 9th New York did not personally witness the incident he recounted, it can be assumed that his source was a comrade who did. The point is made because a later version by historian Samuel P. Bates is somewhat different. His account in *Martial Deeds of Pennsylvania* (p. 991) and Cheney's basically agree; that is, both have Burns acquiring a firearm and bullets from a wounded soldier. However, accordingto Bates, Burns approached two wounded cavalrymen and cajoled one of them into giving up his weapon. Also different is the dialogue between the participants. In the case of Bates, it smacks of invention. For instance, he has Burns saying, "Ah, my lads, your guns are needed over yonder; but you are bleeding and are too weak to carry them...." The brief verbal exchange as reported by Cheney seems much more plausible.
113. *B & L*, Vol. III, 276.
114. Bates, 990.
115. Bates, 990, 988-990; Boatner, 107.
116. Chamberlin, 121. Samuel P. Bates and St. Clair Mulholland also reported this meeting in detail. With the exception of the quoted words of Burnsand Wister, these accounts closely match Chamberlin's. (See Bates, p. 991, and Mulholland, p. 3.)
117. Sgt. John C. Kensill (150th Pennsylvania) to Capt. John H. Bassler (149th Pennsylvania), Feb. 14, 1882, copy in GNMP Library.
118. Lt. Col. John R. Callis to Col. J. B. Bachelder (n. d.), copy in GNMP Library. The mindless punctuation (or lack of it) in the original has been remedied in the text.
119. Callis to Bachelder; Callis quoted in Auberry, 78-79. An account in *Pennsylvania at Gettysburg* (Vol. II, 936) has Burns saying to Callis: "There are three hundred cowards back in that town who could come out of their cellars and fight. I will show you that there is one man who is not afraid." While it is true that Burns had to convince Callis to allow him to fight, it seems quite improbable that he made such a melodrammatic speech.
120. *B & L*, Vol. III, 276.
121. Callis quoted in Auberry, 78-79.
122. Cheney, 112.
123. Cook, 106; *Reynolds Memorial — Addresses Before theHistorical Society of Pennsylvania*, 68-69.

124. Diary of Capt. John Irvin (149th Pennsylvania), entry for July 1, 1863, Robert L. Brake Collection, USAMHI.
125. Hubler, "Just the Plain, Unvarnished Story of a Soldier in the Ranks," *New York Times Magazine*, June 29, 1913.
126. *Gettysburg Papers*, Vol. I, 259-260.
127. *Gettysburg Papers*, Vol. I, 294; Small, 117. According to both sources, Paul's brigade left Seminary Ridge about 1:00 p.m. to enter combat.
128. Biddle, 27-28.
129. *Report of the Joint Committee on the Conduct of the War*, Part I, 307.
130. Boatner, 193; Tucker, *High Tide*, 68; Cornelius Wheeler to his parents, July 11, 1863, copy in Robert L. Brake Collection, USAMHI.
131. Boatner, 413; Tucker, *High Tide*, 125; Sears, 222-223, 227.
132. Howard, "Campaign and Battle of Gettysburg, June-July, 1863," *Atlantic Monthly*, July, 1876; Coddington, 278.
133. O. O. Howard to Capt. William Riddle, Mar. 22, 1864, Howard Collection, Bowdoin College, copy in Robert L. Brake Collection, USAMHI; *Gettysburg Papers*, Vol. I, 314.
134. *Gettysburg Papers*, Vol. I, 314; Howard, "Campaign and Battle of Gettysburg, June-July, 1863," *Atlantic Monthly*, July, 1876, 53; O. O. Howard to T. H. Davis and Company, Sept. 14, 1875, Pennsylvania Historical and Museum Commission, Division of Archives and Manuscripts, copy in Robert L. Brake Collection, USAMHI; *OR* 43, 701-702. While these accounts are complementary and largely corroborative, minor differences in detail had to be resolved in favor of the most likely possibility. Oddly enough, none of these accounts contain the name of the aide whom Howard sent with Major Riddle to find General Reynolds. That it was his own brother Charles is attested in a speech given by that officer in 1903. [*Gettysburg Papers*, Vol. I, 314.]
135. Howard, "Campaign and Battle of Gettysburg, June-July, 1863," *Atlantic Monthly*, July, 1876, 53-54; O. O. Howard to T. H. Davis and Company, Sept. 14, 1875, Pennsylvania Historical and Museum Commission, Division of Archives and Manuscripts, copy in Robert L. Brake Collection, USAMHI. The incident, with slight modifications, is also recounted in Howard's autobiography (p. 410) and in *Gettysburg Papers*, Vol. I (p. 314).
136. O. O. Howard to Capt. William Riddle, Mar. 22, 1864, Howard Collection, Bowdoin College, copy in Robert L. Brake Collection, USAMHI; Daniel Hall to O. O. Howard, May 20, 1882, Howard Collection, Bowdoin College, copy in Robert L. Brake Collection, USAMHI.
137. Howard to Riddle, Mar. 22, 1864.
138. Howard, "Campaign and Battle of Gettysburg, June-July, 1863," *Atlantic Monthly*, July, 1876, 53-54; *Autobiography of Oliver O. Howard*, 412.
139. Bentley, "Howard at Gettysburg," *National Tribune*, Feb. 25, 1885; Howard, "Campaign and Battle of Gettysburg, June-July, 1863," *Atlantic Monthly*, July, 1876, 53-54; *Gettysburg Papers*, Vol. I, 316; Frassanito, 82. Maj. Charles H. Howard identified the messenger as George Gwinn, a Pennsylvania cavalry officer. [*Gettysburg Papers*, Vol. I, 316.]
140. *Autobiography of Oliver O. Howard*, 412.
141. Howard, "Campaign and Battle of Gettysburg, June-July, 1863," *Atlantic Monthly*, July, 1876, 53-54; O. O. Howard to T. H. Davis and Company, Sept. 14, 1875, Pennsylvania Historical and Museum Commission, Division of Archives and Manuscripts, copy in Robert L. Brake Collection, USAMHI; Bentley, "Howard at Gettysburg," *National Tribune*, Feb. 25, 1885.
142. *National Tribune*, Feb. 25, 1885.
143. Howard, "Campaign and Battle of Gettysburg, June-July, 1863," *Atlantic Monthly*, July,

1876, 53-54; *OR* 43, 701-702. Historian William R. Livermore erred when he wrote (in 1913) that "from roof of a building [Howard] saw Ewell's men coming down on Doubleday's right flank." [*Story of the Civil War*, Vol. 2, Part III, 419.] From the Fahnestock building Howard could indeed see for a great distance — but not that far!

144. *OR* 43, 701-702; O. O. Howard to T. H. Davis and Company, Sept. 14, 1875, Pennsylvania Historical and Museum Commission, Division of Archives and Manuscripts, copy in Robert L. Brake Collection, USAMHI.
145. Howard, "Campaign and Battle of Gettysburg, June-July, 1863," *Atlantic Monthly*, July, 1876, 53-54.
146. *OR* 43, 696; O. O. Howard to T. H. Davis and Company, Sept. 14, 1875, Pennsylvania Historical and Museum Commission, Division of Archives and Manuscripts, copy in Robert L. Brake Collection, USAMHI. In the report Howard stated he assumed command "a little past eleven." In the letter he said he reached the observatory "just before 11 A.M." and then, "Not ten minutes later his [Reynolds'] death was reported, and I assumed command of the field...." This time frame accords with the action he saw from the observatory as well as his own actions afterward, thus negating his earlier statement, which appears in the official records (*OR* 43, 702), that Riddle delivered the message about 11:30.
147. Bentley, "Howard at Gettysburg," *National Tribune*, Feb. 25, 1885.
148. Howard, "Campaign and Battle of Gettysburg, June-July, 1863," *Atlantic Monthly*, July, 1876, 53-54; *Gettysburg Papers*, Vol. I, 316, 320 (Maj. Charles H. Howard). In addition to those named by the general, Maj. Howard stated that his brother also notified Doubleday and Buford at this time. He may have, though there is no supporting evidence that he did. With one exception, the aides dispatched to the various commanding officers were not identified. Maj. Howard noted only that it was Capt. Edward Pearson who rode to Schurz.
149. Abner Doubleday to Samuel P. Bates, Oct. 18, 1875, in Pennsylvania Historical and Museum Commission, Division of Archives and Manuscripts, copy in Robert L. Brake Collection, USAMHI. (A similar account appears in Doubleday's *Chancellorsville and Gettysburg*, p. 135.)
150. A number of writers, it should be noted, have accepted the existence of the dispatch as described by Doubleday. This writer is not alone in holding the opposite opinion, however. See, for example, John A. Carpenter's excellent critique of Doubleday's *Chancellorsville and Gettysburg*, in *Military Affairs*, Vol. 27 (Summer, 1963), pps. 84-88.
151. *OR* 43, 702; Coddington, 279.
152. *OR* 43, 702; *Autobiography of Carl Schurz*, 256; Howard, "Campaign and Battle of Gettysburg, June-July, 1863," *Atlantic Monthly*, July, 1876, 53-54.
153. *Atlantic Monthly*, July, 1876, 53-54; *Gettysburg Papers*, Vol. I, 320 (Maj. Charles H. Howard).
154. *Gettysburg Papers*, Vol. I, 320. This source cites Capt. Edward Pearson's letter of Jan. 22, 1886 to Maj. Gen. Howard, in which Pearson recalled the general's exact words.
155. *OR* 43, 702; Howard, "Campaign and Battle of Gettysburg, June-July, 1863," *Atlantic Monthly*, July, 1876, 53-54.
156. De Peyster, 153.
157. *Gettysburg Papers*, Vol. I, 314.
158. *Report of the Joint Committee on the Conduct of the War*, Part I, 307.
159. *Report of the Joint Committee on the Conduct of the War*, Part I, 307.; *OR* 43, 247.
160. *Autobiography of Carl Schurz*, 256.
161. *Autobiography of Carl Schurz*, 257; Doubleday, 138.
162. Abner Doubleday to Samuel P. Bates, Oct. 18, 1875, in Pennsylvania Historical and Museum Commission, Division of Archives and Manuscripts, copy in Robert L. Brake Collection, USAMHI.

163. *Gettysburg Papers*, Vol. I, 316.

164. Meade, Vol. II, 35-36; Weld, 230-232; Coddington, 283-285, 694; *OR* 45, 461.

CHAPTER 10

1. Swallow, "First Day at Gettysburg," *Southern Bivouac*, Vol. I (Dec. 1885), 439.
2. An undated letter of Col. John S. Mosby, which Edwin B. Coddington cites in his *Gettysburg Campaign* (p. 274), supports this view. According to Mosby, although A. P. Hill referred to the mission as a "reconnaisance," what he really intended was a foray in which he hoped to capture a great many Yankees.
3. Doubleday, 132.
4. Fremantle, 254.
5. Morrison (Ed.), lviii; Dowdey, 87-88.
6. Freeman, *Lee's Lieutenants*, Vol. III, xxiv.
7. Morrison (Ed.), lvii.
8. Bates, 450.
9. Morrison (Ed.), xliv-xlv; Coddington, 274.
10. *OR* 43, 114.
11. Quoted in Bean, "Buford in Gettysburg," *The [Philadelphia] Times*, Sept. 11, 1880.
12. Calef, "Gettysburg Notes: The Opening Gun," *Journal of the Military Service Institution of the United States*, 53.
13. Quoted in Bean, "Buford in Gettysburg," *The [Philadelphia] Times*, Sept. 11, 1880. Rosengarten's statement also appears in *Annals of the War*, (p. 62).
14. *Gettysburg Papers*, Vol. I, 433-434.
15. Lt. A. B. Jerome to Maj. Gen. W. S. Hancock, Oct. 18, 1865, copy in GNMP Library.
16. *New York at Gettysburg*, Vol. II, 22-23.
17. Buckeridge, *Lincoln's Choice*, 55.
18. Quoted in Young, 177.
19. *OR* 45, 349; Coddington, 127-128.
20. Coddington, 128, quotes Alfred Pleasonton to Joseph Hooker, Aug. 17, 1876.
21. Hill, Vol. 4, 175.
22. Scott, Vol. I, 155.
23. Steele, Vol. I, 392.
24. Quoted in *Gettysburg Papers*, Vol. I, 438.
25. Sypher, *History of the Pennsylvania Reserve Corps*, 493, cites Meade's remarks on being presented a sword by this organization.
26. Sypher, 493. (Meade's tribute to Reynolds has been included in numerous accounts since it first appeared in Sypher's history in 1865.)
27. McClellan, *McClellan's Own Story*, 140.
28. Weld, 230.
29. Bates, 475-476.
30. Nevins (Ed.), 239; Battine, 187.
31. Quoted in *Gettysburg Papers*, Vol. I, 118.
32. Rosengarten, "Where Reynolds Fell," *Philadelphia Weekly Press*, Jan. 20, 1886.
33. Quoted in Young, 177.
34. Coddington, 277, quotes Howard's letter to Prof. Michael Jacobs, Mar. 23, 1864.
35. Nevins (Ed.), 239.
36. Rosengarten, "Reynolds, Hero of the First Day, by One of his Staff," *New York Times Magazine*, June 29, 1913.
37. Quoted in Stine, 457.
38. Tucker, *Lee and Longstreet*, 217.

39. Hassler, "The First Day's Battle at Gettysburg," *Civil War History*, Vol. VI (Sept. 1960), 265-266.
40. Buell, 61.
41. Coddington, 37.
42. Nevins (Ed.), 233.
43. Coddington, 690, cites Rawle's letter to Capt. G. S. L. Ward, Apr. 2, 1883.
44. Ashhurst, *Remarks on Certain Questions Relating to the First Day's Fight at Gettysburg*, 13.
45. *OR* 43, 246-247; Doubleday, 134.
46. Oliver O. Howard to T. H. Davis and Company, Sept. 14, 1875, Pennsylvania Historical and Museum Commission, Division of Archives and Manuscripts, copy in Robert L. Brake Collection, USAMHI.
47. Pearson, 213, quotes "Dawes with the Sixth Wisconsin at Gettysburg," *Sketches of War History, Ohio Commandery of the Loyal Legion*, Vol. III, 373.
48. *OR* 43, 288.
49. Stine, 464-465, quotes speech of J. V. Pierce.
50. *OR* 43, 245.
51. Calef, "The Regular Artillery in the Gettysburg Campaign," *Journal of the Military Service Institution of the United States*, Vol. 45 (1909), 35.
52. *B & L*, Vol. III, 276.
53. *OR* 43, 927.
54. *OR* 43, 1032.
55. Quoted in *Maine at Gettysburg*, 19.
56. Quoted in *New York at Gettysburg*, Vol. III, 1133.
57. Jones (compiler), *Army of Northern Virginia, Memorial Volume*, 101, quotes address of Maj. John W. Daniels to Army of Northern Virginia Association, Richmond, Va., Oct. 29, 1875.

CHAPTER 11

1. Marcot, *Spencer Repeating Arms*, 83.
2. Boatner, 782.
3. Coddington, 258.
4. Coddington, 258-259; Busey & Martin, *Regimental Strengths at Gettysburg*, 206.
5. *Major-General James S. Wadsworth at Gettysburg....*, 53.
6. Miers & Brown, eds., 48.
7. *Gettysburg Papers*, 421.
8. Scott, Vol. I, 135.
9. Moyer, 328.
10. Scott, Vol. 1, 135.
11. *B & L*, Vol. III, 275; *New York at Gettysburg*, Vol. I, 10; Vol. III, 1153; regimental histories of 9th New York [Cheney, 108] and 6th New York [Hall, 137].
12. Minnigh, *Gettysburg: What They Did Here*, 168.
13. Calkins, letter to editor of *National Tribune*, reprinted in *Gettysburg Times* [1913?], GNMP.
14. Tucker, *High Tide*, 106, cites Weaver, 4-5.
15. *Indiana at the 50th Anniversary of the Battle of Gettysburg*, 102-103.
16. Moore, "Heth's Division at Gettysburg," *Southern Bivouac*, Vol. 3 (May 1885), 385.
17. Swallow, "The First Day at Gettysburg," *Southern Bivouac*, Vol. 4 (Dec. 1885), 487.
18. Vautier, 117; Hoke, *The Great Invasion*, 266; etc.
19. Beach, *The 1st New York (Lincoln) Cavalry*, 249.
20. Storrick, 31-32.

21. Kenneth P. Williams [*Lincoln Finds a General*, Vol. II, 682] and Russell F. Weigley ["John Buford," *Civil War Times Illustrated* (Jun. 1966), 22] both found this to be the case, and both concluded the dispatch was written sometime before 10:10.
22. Reynolds' ordnance officer, J.G. Rosengarten, elucidated Buford's 9:30 time statement thus: "...he must have meant [the fighting] of the infantry of the Confederate force with his own dismounted men serving as infantry, for the skirmishing had been going on for an hour or more...." ["Where Reynolds Fell," *Philadelphia Weekly Press*, Jan. 20, 1886].
23. Lt. A.B. Jerome to Maj. Gen. W.S. Hancock, Sep. 18, 1865; DePeyster, 151-153.
24. Charles H. Veil to David McConaughy, Apr. 7, 1864.
25. *Gettysburg Campaign*, 682.
26. Doubleday, 126, among others.
27. Veil, manuscript (1908) quoted in *Philadelphia Public Ledger*, Mar. 19, 1911.
28. Weld, *War Diary and Letters*, 229.
29. Rosengarten to Samuel P. Bates, Jan. 13, 1871.
30. Rosengarten, "Major-General John F. Reynolds," Gettysburg *Star and Sentinel*, May 5, 1885.
31. Rosengarten, "Reynolds, Hero of the First Day," *New York Times Magazine*, Jun. 29, 1913, 251.
32. *OR* 43, 930.
33. Brown, *The Signal Corps, U.S.A., in the War of the Rebellion*, 589, 804.
34. Nichols.
35. Jepson, "First Day at Gettysburg," *National Tribune*, Oct. 6, 1910.
36. *Gettysburg Papers*, Vol. I, 152.
37. Doubleday to Samuel P. Bates, Oct. 18, 1875; Doubleday, 126.
38. DePeyster quoted in Smith, 36.
39. Doubleday to Samuel P. Bates, Oct. 18, 1875.
40. Jepson, "Thirteenth Massachusetts Circular No. 15" (1905), 15; Stine, 453.
41. Lt. A.B. Jerome to Maj. Gen. W.S. Hancock, Sep. 18, 1865; DePeyster, 151-153.
42. *Gettysburg Papers*, Vol. I, 294.
43. *Gettysburg Papers*, Vol. I, 367-368.
44. Biddle, 26-27; Catton, *Glory Road*, 274.
45. *New York Times*, Jul. 4, 1863.
46. Downey, *Guns at Gettysburg*, 26.
47. Rosengarten, "Reynolds' Last Battle," *Philadelphia Weekly Times*, Mar. 17, 1877; Rosengarten, "Where Reynolds Fell," *Philadelphia Weekly Press*, Jan. 20, 1886; Coddington, 687.
48. Swallow, "The First Day at Gettysburg," *Southern Bivouac*, Vol. I (Dec. 1885), 439.
49. "He Shot General Reynolds," *Pittsburgh Leader*, c. 1903, clippings in scrapbook No. 1, 127, GNMP Library.
50. Kingston, "The Man Who Shot Reynolds," *The [Lancaster] Sunday News*, Nov. 23, 1952, cites *Lancaster Intelligencer*, Nov. 7, 1902; Nichols, 253-254.
51. Charles Veil to "Friend Conevery," Nov. 11, 1902, John F. Reynolds Papers, Franklin and Marshall College.
52. Boland, "Death of Gen. Reynolds," *National Tribune*, May 20, 1915.
53. Moon, "Beginning of the Battle of Gettysburg," *Confederate Veteran*, Vol. XXXIII (Dec. 1925), 449-450.
54. Tolley, "Campaigns by Army of Northern Virginia," *Confederate Veteran*, Vol. III (Mar. 1900), 109.
55. Boland, "Death of Gen. Reynolds," *National Tribune*, May 20, 1915.
56. *OR* 44, 637; *SHSP*, Vol. XXXVII (1909), 109.

57. Pollard, *Southern History of the War*, Vol. III, 24-25.
58. Doubleday, 131; Biddle, 26-27.
59. Dudley, 9; *Gettysburg Papers*, Vol. I, 187.
60. Capt. E. C. Baird quoted in Bates, Martial Deeds of Pennsylvania, 474; Eleanor Reynolds to William Reynolds, Jul. 5, 1863, John F. Reynolds Papers, Franklin and Marshall College.
61. Histories by Cheney, Hall, Livermore, Comte de Paris, Fox, etc.
62. *OR* 43, 266.
63. *Gettysburg Papers*, Vol. I, 176; W. R. Ramsey (150th Pennsylvania) to J. H. Bassler, Aug. 3, 1906, copy in GNMP Library; Nichols, 205.
64. *OR* 43, 696.
65. Eleanor Reynolds to William Reynolds, July 5, 1863, John F. Reynolds Papers, Franklin and Marshall College.
66. Biddle, 26; Strong, 216; Purifoy, "The Myth of the Confederate Hollow Square," *Confederate Veteran*, Vol. XXXIII (Feb. 1925), 53; Coddington, 279.
67. DePeyster, 14.
68. Joseph G. Rosengarten to Col. Samuel P. Bates, Jan. 13, 1871, copy in USAMHI.
69. Biddle, 26.
70. Strong, 216; *New York at Gettysburg*, Vol. I, 11-12.
71. Lt. Col. William W. Dudley to Col. John B. Bachelder [n.d.], copy in GNMP Library.
72. Hofmann, "The 56th Pennsylvania at Gettysburg," and Reed, "The 2nd Wisconsin Sticks to Its Claim," *National Tribune*, Mar. 20, 1884.
73. Captain E. M. Rogers quoted in "Gettysburg. The Great Battle of July 1, 2 & 3, 1863," Gettysburg *Star & Sentinel*, May 5, 1885.
74. Pierce, "Gettysburg. Last Words as to What Regiment Opened the Battle," *National Tribune*, Apr. 3, 1884.
75. Phillips, "The Second Wisconsin at Gettysburg," *National Tribune*, May 29, 1884; Otis, The Second Wisconsin Infantry, 84.
76. Hofmann, "Gettysburg. Gen. Hofmann Replies to 2nd Wisconsin Claim," *National Tribune*, Jun. 19, 1884.
77. Lucius Fairchild to R. K. Beecham, Apr. 11, 1884, copy in USAMHI.
78. *Gettysburg Papers*, Vol. I, 209-211.
79. Doubleday quoted in *War Talks in Kansas*, 281-282; *OR* 43, 265; Biddle, 27.
80. *OR* 43, 245; *OR* 44, 637.
81. Doubleday, 132.
82. Comte de Paris, Vol. 3, 554; Bates, 212; *Confederate Military History*, Vol. 8, 199; Purifoy, "Battle of Gettysburg, July 1, 1863," *Confederate Veteran*, Vol. XXXI (Jan. 1923), 22.
83. Gates, 428.
84. Meade, Vol. 2, 46; *OR* 43, 266.
85. *OR* 43, 267, 274; Dudley, 6-7; John R. Callis to J. B. Bachelder (n.d.), copy in GNMP Library.
86. *OR* 44, 646.
87. Coddington, 688, cites B. D. Fry to J. B. Bachelder, Dec. 27, 1877, *New Hampshire Historical Society.*
88. Turney, "The First Tennessee at Gettysburg," *Confederate Veteran*, Vol. VIII (1900), 535.
89. Swallow, "First Day at Gettysburg," *Southern Bivouac*, Vol. I (Dec. 1885), 439.
90. Pvt. Sydney Mead, diary entry of Jul. 1, 1863, State Historical Society of Wisconsin, copy in USAMHI.
91. Sgt. Cornelius Wheeler to his parents, Jul. 11, 1863, copy in Robert L. Blake Collection, USAMHI.

92. Stine, 462.
93. Vanderslice, 79.
94. *OR* 43, 246, 282.
95. Tevis and Marquis, 134.
96. Dudley, 9.
97. Quiner, *Military History of Wisconsin*, 461.
98. Cooke, "First Day of Gettysburg," *War Talks in Kansas*, 279 [also in *Gettysburg Papers*, Vol. I].
99. Lt. J. V. Pierce to Col. J. B. Bachelder, Oct. 1, 1882, copy in GNMP Library.
100. *New York at Gettysburg*, Vol. III, 994-996.
101. Coey, "Cutler's Brigade. The 147th New York's Magnificent Fight on the First Day at Gettysburg," *National Tribune*, Jul. 15, 1915.
102. *Confederate Military History*, Vol. 4, 1002.
103. Hofmann, "Gettysburg Again. Gen. Hofmann on the Action of the 147th New York on the Opening of the Battle," *National Tribune*, Jun. 5, 1884.
104. *OR* 43, 246.
105. *OR* 43, 266.
106. *OR* 43, 282.
107. Swallow, "First Day at Gettysburg," *Southern Bivouac*, Vol. I (Dec. 1885), 439.
108. J. R. Davis to J. A. Early,Mar. 12, 1878, cited in Coddington, 689.
109. W. B. Murphy to F. A. Dearborn, Jun. 29, 1900, State Historical Society of Wisconsin, copy in GNMP Library.
110. Ashe, "First Day at Gettysburg," *Confederate Veteran*, Vol. XXXVIII (Oct. 1930), 379.
111. *OR* 43, 276; Dawes, 169.
112. Purifoy, "Battle of Gettysburg, July 1, 1863," *Confederate Veteran*, Vol. XXXI (Jan. 1923), 139.
113. Tevis and Marquis, 134.
114. Hassler, "First Day's Battle at Gettysburg," *Civil War History*, Vol. VI (Sep. 1960), 267; Hassler, 48-49.
115. Coddington, 272; Young, *Battle of Gettysburg*, 184.
116. Transcript of Court-Martial, National Archives, copy in USAMHI.
117. Coddington, 307-308, 706, cites General Court Martial Orders No. 120, Judge Advocate General J. Holt to [Lincoln], May 6, 17, 1864.
118. Boatner, 711.
119. Doubleday, 126.
120. Abner Doubleday to Samuel P. Bates, Oct. 18, 1875, Pa. Historical and Museum Commission, Div. of Archives and Manuscripts, copy in USAMHI.
121. Joseph G. Rosengarten to Samuel P. Bates, Jan. 13, 1871, Pa. Historical and Museum Commission, Div. of Archives and Manuscripts, copy in USAMHI.
122. Maj. Gen. O. O. Howard to Maj. William Riddle, Mar. 22,1864, Howard Collection, Bowdoin College, copy in USAMHI.
123. Maj. William Riddle to Maj. Gen. O. O. Howard, Apr. 3, 1864, Howard Collection, Bowdoin College, copy in USAMHI.
124. Daniel Hall to Maj. Gen. O. O. Howard, May 20, 1882, Howard Collection, Bowdoin College, copy in USAMHI.
125. O. O. Howard to T. H. Davis and Co., Sep. 14, 1875, Pa. Historical and Museum Commission, Div. of Archives and Manuscripts, copy in USAMHI.

EPILOGUE

1. William Riddle to _____ Le Bouvier, Aug. 4, 1863, John F. Reynolds Papers, Franklin and Marshall College, copy in Robert L. Brake Collection, USAMHI.

2. Nichols, 211-212; Maloney, "General Reynolds and Dear Kate," *American Heritage*, Vol. 15 (Dec. 1963), 62.
3. Jennie Gildersleeve to her brother, William Reynolds, July 5, 1863, in John F. Reynolds Papers, Franklin and Marshall College, copy in Robert L. Brake Collection, USAMHI; Joseph G. Rosengarten to Samuel P. Bates, Jan. 13, 1871, Pennsylvania Historical and Museum Commission, Division of Archives and Manuscripts, Harrisburg, copy in Robert L. Brake Collection, USAMHI.
4. Veil, manuscript (1908), extract quoted in *Philadelphia Public Ledger*, Mar. 19, 1911, copy in Robert L. Brake Collection, USAMHI; Eleanor Reynolds to her brother, William Reynolds, July 5, 1863, in John F. Reynolds Papers, Franklin and Marshall College, copy in Robert L. Brake Collection, USAMHI.
5. William Riddle to _____ Le Bouvier, Aug. 4, 1863 (see Note l); Veil, manuscript (see Note 4); Joseph G. Rosengarten to Samuel P. Bates, Jan. 13, 1871 (see Note 3).
6. Weld, 233, 236.
7. Weld, 233; Jennie Gildersleeve to William Reynolds, July 5, 1863 (see Note 3).
8. William Riddle to _____ Le Bouvier, Aug. 4, 1863 (see Note l).
9. Jennie Gildersleeve to William Reynolds, July 5, 1863 (see Note 3). Jennie, in this letter, gave no indication as to who found the letters, or when. M. R. Maloney, writing in 1963, states it was Riddle and Veil [*American Heritage*, Vol. 15 (Dec. 1963), 62].
10. Weld, 233-234, 237; Jennie Gildersleeve to William Reynolds, July 5, 1863 (see Note 3); Eleanor Reynolds to William Reynolds, July 5, 1863 (see Note 4); Nichols, 211.
11. Jennie Gildersleeve to William Reynolds, July 5, 1863 (see Note 3); Nichols, 212.
12. Maloney, "General Reynolds and Dear Kate," *American Heritage*, Vol. 15 (Dec. 1963), 62.
13. Eleanor Reynolds to William Reynolds, July 5, 1863 (See Note 4).
14. Jennie Gildersleeve to William Reynolds, July 5, 1863 (see Note 3); Nichols, 212, 255; Maloney, "General Reynolds and Dear Kate," *American Heritage*, Vol. 15 (Dec. 1963), 64; Longacre, "John F. Reynolds, General," *Civil War Times Illustrated*, Vol. XI (Aug. 1972), 43; Rosengarten, address, *Reynolds Memorial — Addresses Before the Historical Society of Pennsylvania*, 22.
15. Eleanor Reynolds to William Reynolds, July 5, 1863 (See Note 4); Jennie Gildersleeve to William Reynolds, July 5, 1863 (see Note 3); Nichols, 212-213.
16. Weld, 237; Jennie Gildersleeve to William Reynolds, July 5, 1863 (see Note 3); Rosengarten, address, *Reynolds Memorial — Addresses Before the Historical Society of Pennsylvania*, 24.
17. Jennie Gildersleeve to William Reynolds, July 5, 1863 (see Note 3). That the two Kates did not make the trip from Philadelphia to Lancaster can be inferred from the absence of their names on Jennie's inclusive list of those who did.
18. Eleanor Reynolds to William Reynolds, July 5, 1863 (See Note 4).
19. Weld, 237; Jennie Gildersleeve to William Reynolds, July 5, 1863 (see Note 3); Nichols, cites *Lancaster Daily Inquirer*, July 6, 1863, 212-213.
20. Joseph G. Rosengarten to Samuel P. Bates, Jan. 13, 1871 (see Note 3); Weld, 237.
21. Weld, 237, Jennie Gildersleeve to William Reynolds, July 5, 1863 (see Note 3).
22. Nichols, 255.
23. Maloney, "General Reynolds and Dear Kate," *American Heritage*, Vol. 15 (Dec. 1963), 64.
24. *American Heritage*, Vol. 15 (Dec. 1963), 64-65; Nichols, 255; Longacre, "John F. Reynolds, General," *Civil War Times Illustrated*, Vol. XI (Aug. 1972), 43.
25. Curtis, 183; Biddle, 29.
26. *B & L*, 276.

27. *Pennsylvania at Gettysburg*, Vol. II, 936.
28. Bates, 992-995; Curtis, 183.
29. Hassler, 61.
30. Bates, 995-996; *Reynolds Memorial — Addresses Before the Historical Society of Pennsylvania*, 68.
31. Bates, 996-997.
32. Bates, 997.
33. Boatner, 284, 400, 631, 649, 706-707.
34. Hopkins (Ed.), "The James J. Archer Letters: A Marylander in the Civil War," *Maryland Historical Magazine*, Vol 56 (1961), 352-354, 356; Harris, "Gen. Jas. J. Archer," *Confederate Veteran*, Vol. III (Jan. 1895), 18-19. The private who captured General Archer did not live to tell his grandchildren about it. Within a few hours after his coup, he, Patrick Maloney, was killed in action [*OR* 43, 274]. The sword that Archer had reluctantly surrendered, shortly after his capture, to the arrogant Lieutenant D. B. Dailey came close to being recovered by Confederates before the day ended. Wounded about 4:00 p.m., Dailey had gone to the home of a Mr. Scott in Gettysburg. When the Rebels swept into town, they discovered his hiding place and took him prisoner. Only minutes before — apparently wary that this just might happen — he had asked the young lady attending him to hide Archer's belt and sword. She had quickly obliged by stashing them in the parlor wood box and covering them with a newspaper. Four days later Dailey managed to escape. Returning to the Scott home to retrieve the sword, he was dismayed to learn that it had already been given to the 24th Michigan's Colonel Morrow. [See Stine, 459-460.].
35. Boatner, 716.
36. Boatner, 216-217; Nolan, 276.
37. Weigley, "John Buford," *Civil War Times Illustrated*, Vol. V (June 1966), 15, 23; Pratt, "Man on Horseback," *Infantry Journal*, Vol. 47 (1940), 119; Young, 355.
38. *Major-General James S. Wadsworth at Gettysburg and Other Fields*, 116; Steere, *Wilderness Campaign*, 400; Boatner, 882-883.
39. Hill, Vol. 4, 1008.
40. Boatner, 238-239, 244, 322, 413-414, 570, 704, 800.
41. Fuller, "Who Fired the First Shot at the Battle of Gettysburg," *Journal of U. S. Cavalry Association*, Vol. 24 (1914), 791.
42. Boatner, 413-414. A full account of Howard's post-war activities appears in his autobiography, published in 1907.
43. Boatner, 244.
44. Boatner, 62, 272.
45. Wert, "Little Stories of Gettysburg," newspaper clipping datelined July 3, 1907, GNMP Library.
46. Ross, viii, 169.
47. Boatner, 51.
48. Nolan, 276.
49. John B. Callis to Col. J. B. Bachelder, n.d., copy in GNMP Library.
50. Bates, 809.
51. Scott, Vol. I, 149, 471.
52. Bates, 791-792; Boatner, 711.
53. Boatner, 543.
54. Wheeler and Hooker, *Confederate Military History*, Vol. 12, 249-250; Young, 442.
55. Davis, *Recollections of Mississippi and Mississippians*, 175-176.
56. Young, 443.
57. Young, 443.

58. Wheeler and Hooker, Vol. 12, 409, 411; McBrien, *Tennessee Brigade*, 112.
59. Hassler, "Harry Heth — Lee's Hard Luck General," *Civil War Times Illustrated*, Vol. V (July 1966), 19-20; Boatner, 87.
60. Morrison (Ed.), lix-lxiii.
61. Brunson, *Pee Dee Light Artillery*...., 12, 36. (The original punctuation has been slightly altered for the sake of clarity.)

BIBLIOGRAPHY

BOOKS AND PAMPHLETS

Agassiz, George R. (Ed.). *Meade's Headquarters 1863-1865: Letters of Colonel Theodore Lyman from The Wilderness to Appomattox.* Boston: The Atlantic Monthly Press, 1922.

Alexander, E. P. *Military Memoirs of a Confederate.* New York: C. Scribner's Sons, 1907.

Alleman, Mrs. Tillie (Pierce). *At Gettysburg or What a Girl Saw and Heard of the Battle.* New York: W. Lake Borland, 1889.

The Annals of the War, by Leading Participants North and South. Philadelphia: The Times Publishing Co., 1879.

Ashhurst, R. L. *Remarks on Certain Questions Relating to the First Day's Fight at Gettysburg.* Philadelphia: Press of Allen, Lane & Scott, 1897.

Aubery, Doc (Cullen B.). *Echoes from the Marches of the Famous Iron Brigade, 1861-1865.* Milwaukee, 1900.

Bandy, Ken and Florence Freeland (Eds.). *The Gettysburg Papers,* 3 vols. Dayton: Press of Morningside Bookshop, 1978.

Bassler, John H. *Reminiscences of the First Day's Fight at Gettysburg.* Address at Albright Collegiate Institute [Pa.], June, 1895. Pamphlet, n.p., n.d.

Bates, Samuel P. *Martial Deeds of Pennsylvania.* Philadelphia: T. H. Davis & Co., 1876.

Battine, Cecil. *The Crisis of the Confederacy: A History of Gettysburg and the Wilderness.* London, Longmans, Green & Co., 1905.

Beach, William H. *The First New York (Lincoln) Cavalry From April 19, 1861 to July 7, 1865.* New York: The Lincoln Cavalry Association, 1902.

Beale, James. *The Statements of Time on July 1, 1863 at Gettysburg, Pa.* Philadelphia: James Beale, Printer, 1897.

Beecham, R. K. *Gettysburg, the Pivotal Battle of the Civil War.* Chicago: A. C. McClurg & Co., 1911.

Bellah, James Warner. *Soldiers' Battle: Gettysburg.* New York: David McKay Co., 1962.

Biddle, Chapman. *The First Day of the Battle of Gettysburg.* Philadelphia: J. B. Lippincott & Co., 1880.

Boatner, Mark M., III. *The Civil War Dictionary.* New York: David McKay Co., 1959.

Boyle, John Richards. *Soldiers True: The Story of the One Hundred and Eleventh Regiment Pennsylvania Veteran Volunteers and of its Campaigns in the War for the Union, 1861-1865.* New York: Eaton & Mains, 1903.

Brown, J. Willard. *The Signal Corps, U.S.A. in the War of the Rebellion.* Boston: U. S. Signal Corps Association,1896.

Brown, Maud Morrow. *The University Grays* (Co. A, 11th Mississippi Infantry Regiment). Richmond: Garrett and Massie, 1940.

Brunson, Sgt. Joseph Woods. *Pee Dee Light Artillery of Maxcy Gregg's (Later Samuel McGowan's) Brigade, First South Carolina Volunteers (Infantry) C.S.A.* Winston- Salem: Stewart Printerws, 1927.

Buckeridge, J. O. *Lincoln's Choice.* Harrisburg: The Stackpole Co., 1956.

Buell, Augustus. *The Cannoneer.* Washington: The National Tribune, 1890.

Busey, John W. and David G. Martin. *Regimental Strengths at Gettysburg.* Baltimore: Gateway Press, 1982.

Byrne, Frank L. and Andrew T. Weaver (Eds.). *Haskell of Gettysburg: His Life and Civil War Papers*. Madison, Wis: State Historical Society of Wisconsin, 1970.

Catton, Bruce. *Gettysburg: The Final Fury*. Garden City, N. Y.: Doubleday & Co., 1974 (Berkley Books Edition, 1982).

---. *Glory Road*. Garden City, N.Y.: Doubleday & Co., 1952.

Chamberlin, Thomas. *History of the One Hundred and Fiftieth Regiment, Pennsylvania Volunteers, Second Regiment, Bucktail Brigade*. Philadelphia: F. McManus, Jr. & Co., 1905.

Cheek, Philip and Mair Pointon. *History of the Sauk County Riflemen, Known as Company "A", Sixth Wisconsin Veteran Volunteer Infantry, 1861-1865*. Madison: Democrat Printing Co., 1909.

Cheney, Newel. *History of the Ninth Regiment New York volunteer Cavalry*. Jamestown, N. Y.: Poland Center, 1901.

Clark, Walter (Ed.). *Histories of the Several Regiments and Battalions from North Carolina in the Great War, 1861-65*, 5 vols. Raleigh: State of North Carolina, 1901 (Broadfoot's Bookmart reprint, 1982).

Coddington, Edwin B. *The Gettysburg Campaign: A Study in Command*. New York: Charles Scribner's Sons, 1968 (paperback edition, 1984).

Commager, Henry Steele (Ed.). *The Blue and the Gray*. Indianapolis: Bobbs-Merrill Co., 1950.

The Confederate Soldier in the Civil War. (A compilation of campaign and battle accounts by Lee, Jackson, Longstreet, and other top Confederate leaders.) Published by The Fairfax Press, n.d.

Confederate Veteran, 40 vols. Nashville: S. A. Cunningham, 1893-1932 (Broadfoot's Bookmart reprint n.d.).

Cook, Benjamin F. *History of the 12th Massachusetts Volunteers*. Boston: 12th (Webster) Massachusetts Regimental Association, 1882.

Curtis, O. B. *History of the Twenty-Fourth Michigan of the Iron Brigade, Known as the Detroit and Wayne County Regiment*. Detroit: Winn & Hammond, 1891 (Butternut Press edition, 1984).

Davis, Charles E., Jr. *Three Years in the Army: The Story of the Thirteenth Massachusetts Volunteers from July 16, 1861, to August 1, 1864*. Boston: Estes & Lawnat, 1864.

Davis, Reuben. *Recollections of Mississippi and Mississippians*. Boston and New York: Houghton, Mifflin & Co., 1889.

Dawes, Rufus R. *Service with the Wisconsin Volunteers*. Marietta, Ohio: E. R. Alderman & Sons, 1890.

Dawson, Francis W. *Reminiscences of Confederate Service, 1861-1865*. Charleston, S.C.: The News and Courier Book Presses, 1882 (Louisiana State University Press reprint, 1980).

De Peyster, J. Watts. *The Decisive Conflicts of the Late Civil War*. New York: MacDonald & Co., 1867.

Doubleday, Abner. *Chancellorsville and Gettysburg*. New York: C. Scribner's Sons, 1882.

Dowdey, Clifford. *Death of a Nation*. New York: Alfred A. Knopf, 1958.

Downey, Fairfax. *The Guns at Gettysburg*. New York: David McKay Co., 1958.

Dudley, William W. *The Iron Brigade at Gettysburg*. Cincinnati: n.p., 1879.

Fiebeger, G. J. *The Campaign and Battle of Gettysburg*. West Point, N.Y.: United States Military Academy Press, 1915.

Fite, John A. *Memoirs of Colonel John A. Fite, 7th Tennessee Infantry, C.S.A.* Sarasota, Fla.: n.p., 1935.

Fox, William F. *Regimental Losses in the American Civil War*. Albany: J. B. Lyon Co., 1889 (Morningside Bookshop reprint, 1974).

Fox, William F. (Ed.). *New York at Gettysburg*, 3 vols. Albany: J. B. Lyon Co., 1902.

Frassanito, William A. *Gettysburg: A Journey in Time*. New York: Charles Scribner's Sons, 1975.

Freeman, Douglas Southall. *Lee's Lieutenants, A Study in Command*, 3 vols. New York: Charles Scribner's Sons, 1949-51.

---. *R. E. Lee, a Biography*, 4 vols. New York: Charles Scribner's Sons, 1934-35.

Fremantle, James A. L. *Three Months in the Southern States, April-June, 1863*. New York: J. Bradburn, 1864.

Gates, Theodore B. *The "Ulster Guard" (20th N.Y. State Militia) and the War of the Rebellion*. New York: B. H. Tyrrel, 1879.

Guernsey, Alfred H. and Henry M. Alden. *Harper's Pictorial History of the Civil War*, 2 vols. New York: Harper & Brothers, 1866-1868 (Fairfax Press reprint, n.d.).

Hall, Hillman, W. B. Besley and Gilbert G. Wood. *History of the Sixth New York Cavalry, Second Ira Harris Guard, Second Brigade, First Division, Cavalry Corps, Army of the Potomac, 1861-1865*. Worcester, Mass.: The Blanchard Press, 1908.

Hall, Isaac. *History of the 97th Regiment New York Volunteers in the War for the Union*. Utica, N.Y.: L. C. Childs & Son, 1890.

Hard, Abner, M.D. *History of the Eighth Cavalry Regiment Illinois Volunteers during the Great Rebellion*. Aurora, Ill: n.p., 1868.

Hassler, William W. *A. P. Hill: Lee's Forgotten General*. Richmond: Garrett & Massie, 1957.

Hassler, Warren W., Jr. *Crisis at the Crossroads: The First Day at Gettysburg*. University, Ala.: University of Alabama Press, 1970.

Haupt, Herman. *Reminiscences of General Herman Haupt*. Milwaukee: Wright & Joys Co., 1901.

Hill, D. H., Jr. Volume 4 (N.C.) of 12-volume *Confederate Military History: A Library of Confederate States History... Written by Distinguished Men of the South*. Atlanta: Confederate Publishing Co., 1899 (Thomas Yoseloff reprint, 1962).

History of Cumberland and Adams Counties, Pennsylvania. Chicago: Warner, Beers & Co., 1886.

Hofmann, John W. *Remarks on the Battle of Gettysburg*. Address before the Historical Society of Pennsylvania, March 8, 1880. n.p.: A. W. Auner, 1880.

Hoke, Jacob. *The Great Invasion of 1863, or General Lee in Pennsylvania*. Dayton, Ohio: W. J. Shuey, 1887 (Thomas Yoseloff reprint, 1959).

Hotchkiss, Major Jedediah. Volume 3 (Va.) of 12-volume *Confederate Military History: A Library of Confederate States History... Written by Distinguished Men of the South*. Atlanta: Confederate Publishing Co., 1899 (Thomas Yoseloff reprint, 1962).

Howard, Oliver O. *Autobiography of Oliver O. Howard*. New York: The Baker & Taylor Co., 1907.

Huidekoper, Henry S. *A Short Story of the First Day's Fight at Gettysburg*. Philadelphia: Bicking Print, 1906.

Indiana at the 50th Anniversary of the Battle of Gettysburg. Indianapolis: n.p., 1913.

Jacobs, Michael. *Notes on the Rebel Invasion of Maryland and Pennsylvania and the Battle of Gettysburg*. Philadelphia: J. B. Lippincott & Co., 1864.

Jacques, John W. *Three Years Campaign of Ninth New York State Militia [83rd New York Regiment]*. New York: Hilton & Co., 1865.

Johnson, Robert U. and Clarence C. Buel (Eds.). *Battles and Leaders of the Civil War*, 4 vols. New York: The Century Co., 1884-89 (Castle reprint, 1985).

Jones, John B. *A Rebel War Clerk's Diary*, 2 vols (Howard Swiggett, Ed.). New York: n.p., 1935.

Jones, J. William (Compiler). *Army of Northern Virginia, Memorial Volume*. Richmond: J. W. Randolph & English, 1880 (Morningside Bookshop reprint, 1976).
Kieffer, Harry M. *The Recollections of a Drummer-Boy*. Boston: Ticknor & Co., 1889.
Livermore, William R. *The Story of the Civil War*, 2 vols. New York: G. P. Putnam's Sons, 1913.
Locke, William Henry. *The Story of the Regiment [11th Pennsylvania]*. Philadelphia: J. B. Lippincott & Co., 1872.
Longstreet, James. *From Manassas to Appomattox: Memoirs of the Civil War in America*. Philadelphia: J. B. Lippincott Co., 1896.
McClellan, George B. *McClellan's Own Story*. New York: Charles L. Webster & Co., 1889.
_____. *Maine at Gettysburg*. Portland: The Lakeside Press, 1898.
Marcot, Roy M. *Spencer Repeating Firearms*. Irvine, Cal.: Northwood Heritage Press, 1983.
Meade, George G. (Ed.). *The Life and Letters of George Gordon Meade*, 2 vols. New York: C. Scribner's Sons, 1913.
Miers, Earl Schenck and Richard A. Brown (Eds.). *Gettysburg*. New Brunswick, N.J.: Rutgers University Press, 1948.
Minnigh, L. W. *Gettysburg: What They Did Here*. Gettysburg: Tipton & Blocher, 1920.
Moore, Frank (Ed.). *The Rebellion Record: A Diary of American Events, with Documents, Narratives, Illustrative Incidents, Poetry, etc.*, Vol. VII. New York: D. Van Nostrand, 1864.
Morrison, James L., Jr (Ed.). *The Memoirs of Henry Heth*. Westport, Conn.: Greenwood Press, 1974.
Morse, Charles F. *History of the 2nd Massachusetts Regiment of Infantry*. Boston: n.p., 1882.
Moyer, Henry P. *History of the Seventeenth Regiment Pennsylvania Volunteer Cavalry*. Lebanon, Pa.: Sowers Printing Co., 1911.
Mulholland, St. Clair A. *Percentage of Losses at Gettysburg*. Gettysburg: W. H. Tipton, 1911.
Myers, Frank M. *The Comanches: A History of White's Battalion, Virginia Cavalry, Laurel Brig., Hampton Div., A.N.V.* Baltimore: Kelly, Piet & Co., 1871.
Neuer Gemeinnussiger Calendar auf Jahr heilandess Jesu Christi 1873. Farmers' almanac published in Lancaster, Pa.
Nevins, Allan (Ed.). *A diary of Battle: The Personal Journals of Colonel Charles S. Wainwright 1861-1865*. New York: Harcourt, Brace & World, 1962.
Nichols, Edward J. *Toward Gettysburg: A Biography of John F. Reynolds*. University Park, Pa.: Pennsylvania State University Press, 1958.
Nicholson, John P. (Ed.). *Pennsylvania at Gettysburg*, 2 vols. Harrisburg: William Stanley Ray, 1914.
Nofi, Albert E. *The Gettysburg Campaign, June and July, 1863*. New York: Gallery Books, 1986.
Nolan, Alan T. *The Iron Brigade: A Military History* (3rd Edition). Berrien Springs, Mich: Hardscrabble Books, 1983.
Norton, Henry. *A Sketch of the Eighth New York* [Cavalry]. Norwich, N.Y.: n.p., 1888.
---. *Deeds of Daring or History of the Eighth N.Y. Volunteer Cavalry*. Norwich, N. Y.: Chenango Telegraph Printing House, 1889.
Nye, Wilbur Sturtevant. *Here Come the Rebels!* Baton Rouge: Louisiana State University Press, 1965.
Oates, William C. *The War Between the Union and the Confederacy and Its Lost Opportunities*. New York: Neale Publishing Co., 1905 (Morningside Bookshop reprint, 1974).
Otis, George H. *The Second Wisconsin Infantry*. Dayton, Ohio: Press of Morningside Bookshop, 1984. (First published, in installments, in *The* [Milwaukee] *Sunday Telegraph*, in 1880.)
Owen, William M. *In Camp and Battle With the Washington Artillery of New Orleans*. Boston:

Tichnor & Co., 1885.
Paris, Comte de. *History of the Civil War*, 4 vols. Philadelphia: Porter & Coates, 1883.
Pearson, Henry Greenleaf. *James S. Wadsworth of Geneseo*. New York: Charles Scribner's Sons, 1913.
Pfanz, Harry W. *Gettysburg — The Second Day*. Chapel Hill: University of North Carolina Press, 1987.
Pickerill, W. N. *History of the Third Indiana Cavalry*. Indianapolis: Aetna Printing Co., 1906.
Pitzer, John. *Three Days at Gettysburg*. Gettysburg: by author, n.d.
Pollard, Edward A. *A Southern History of the War*, Vol. 3 (*The Third Year of the War*). New York: Charles B. Richardson, 1865.
Prowell, George R. *History of York County, Pennsylvania*, 2 vols. Chicago: J. H. Beers & Co., 1907.
Quiner, E. B. *Military History of Wisconsin*. n.p., 1866.
Report of the Joint Committee on the Conduct of the War at the Second Session, Thirty-Eighth Congress. Washington: Government Printing Office, 1865.
Reynolds Memorial — Addresses Before the Historical Society of Pennsylvania. Philadelphia: J. B. Lippincott & Co., 1880.
Robertson, James I., Jr. *General A. P. Hill: The Story of a Confederate Warrior*. New York: Random House, 1987.
Ross, Sam. *The Empty Sleeve: A Biography of Lucius Fairchild*. Madison: The State Historical Society of Wisconsin, 1964.
Sandburg, Carl. *Abraham Lincoln*, 3 vols. New York: Harcourt Brace Jovanovich, 1926 (First Harvest/HBJ edition, 1982).
Sawyer, Franklin. *A Military History of the 8th Regiment Ohio Volunteer Infantry*. Cleveland: n.p., 1881.
Schenck, Martin. *Up Came Hill*. Harrisburg: The Stackpole Co., 1958.
Schildt, John W. *Roads to Gettysburg*. Parsons, W. Va.: McClain Printing Co., 1978.
Schurz, Carl. *The Reminiscences of Carl Schurz*. New York: Charles Scribner's Sons, 1961.
Scott, James K. P. *The Story of the Battles at Gettysburg*. Harrisburg: Telegraph Press, 1927.
Sears, Stephen W. *Landscape Turned Red*. New Haven and New York: Ticknor & Fields, 1983.
Slagle, Jacob F. *Address at dedication of 149th Pennsylvania monument, Sept. 11, 1889*. Pamphlet, n.p., 1889.
Small, A. R. *The Sixteenth Maine Regiment in the War of the Rebellion*. Portland: B. Thurston & Co., 1886.
Smith, A. P. *History of the Seventy-Sixth Regiment New York Volunteers*. Cortland, N.Y.: Truair, Smith, and Miles, 1867.
Smith, Donald L. *The Twenty-Fourth Michigan of the Iron Brigade*. Harrisburg: The Stackpole Co., 1962.
Snyder, Charles McCool. *Oswego County, New York in the Civil War*. Oswego: The Oswego County Historical Society and the Oswego County Civil War Centennial Commission, 1962.
Southern Historical Society Papers, 50 vols. Richmond: 1876-1953.
Spaulding, Oliver L. *The U.S. Army in War and Peace*. New York: G. P. Putnam & Sons, 1937.
Stackpole, Edward J. *They Met at Gettysburg*. Harrisburg: The Stackpole Co., 1956.
---. *Chancellorsville: Lee's Greatest Battle*. Harrisburg: The Stackpole Co., 1958.
Starr, Stephen Z. *The Union Cavalry in the Civil War*, Vol. I. Baton Rouge: Louisiana State University Press, 1979.
Stearns, Austin C. *Three Years With Company K* [13th Massachusetts]. Cranbury, N.J.: Fairleigh Dickinson Press, 1976.

Steele, Mathew Forney. *American Campaigns*, Vol. I. Washington: Byron S. Adams, 1909.
Steere, Edward. *The Wilderness Campaign*. Harrisburg: The Stackpole Co., 1960 (Bonanza Books edition, n.d.).
Stine, J. H. *History of the Army of the Potomac*. Washington: Gibson Bros., 1903.
Storrick, W. C. *Gettysburg: The Place, The Battles, The Outcome*. Harrisburg: J. Horace McFarland Co., 1932.
Strong, William W. *History of the 121st Regiment Pennsylvania Volunteers*. Philadelphia: Burk & McFetridge Co.,1893.
Swinton, William. *Campaigns of the Army of the Potomac: A Critical History of Operations in Virginia, Maryland and Pennsylvania from the Commencement to the Close of the War, 1861-1865*. New York: Charles B. Richardson, 1866.
Sypher, J. R. *History of the Pennsylvania Reserve Corps*. Lancaster: E. Barr & Co., 1865.
Taylor, Walter H. *Four Years With General Lee*. New York: D. Appleton & Co., 1878.
Tevis, C. V. and D. R. Marquis. *The History of the Fighting Fourteenth* [Brooklyn Regiment]. New York: Brooklyn Eagle Press, 1911.
Thirteenth Massachusetts Circular No. 15. Boston (?): Thirteenth Massachusetts Association, 1902.
Thomas, Dean S. *Ready...Aim...Fire! Small Arms Ammunition in the Battle of Gettysburg*. Gettysburg, Pa.: Thomas Publications, 1981.
Todd, William (Ed.). *History of Ninth Regiment New York State Militia* [83rd New York]. New York: Veterans of the Regiment, 1889.
Tremain, Henry Edwin. *Two Days of War, A Gettysburg Narrative and Other Excursions*. New York: Bonnell, Silver & Bowers, 1905.
Trobriand, Regis de. *Four Years With the Army of the Potomac*. Boston: Ticknor & Co., 1889.
Tucker, Glenn. *High Tide at Gettysburg: The Campaign in Pennsylvania*. Indianapolis: Bobbs-Merrill Co., 1958 [Morningside Bookshop revised edition, 1973].
---. *Lee and Longstreet at Gettysburg*. Indianapolis: Bobbs-Merrill Co., 1968.
Unveiling of the Statue of General John F. Reynolds. Philadelphia: Reynolds Memorial Association, 1884.
Vanderslice, John M. *Gettysburg Then and Now*. New York: G. W. Dillingham Co., 1899.
Vautier, John D. *History of the 88th Pennsylvania Volunteers in the War of the Union, 1861-1865*. Philadelphia: J. B. Lippincott Co., 1894.
Wadsworth, Major-General James S., at Gettysburg and Other Fields. Albany: J. B. Lyon Co., 1916.
The War of the Rebellion: A Compilation of the Official Records of the Union and Confederate Armies, 128 vols. Washington: U.S. Government Printing Office, 1880-1901.
War Talks in Kansas: A Series of Papers Read before the Kansas Commandery of the Loyal Legion of the United States. Kansas City, Mo.: Franklin Hudson Publishing Co., 1906.
Weld, Stephen Minot. *War Diary and Letters of Stephen Minot Weld, 1861-1865* (2nd edition). Boston: Massachusetts Historical Society, 1979.
Wheeler, Lt. Gen. Joseph and Col. Charles E. Hooker. Volume 12 (Alabama and Mississippi) of 12-volume *Confederate Military History: A Library of Confederate States History...Written by Distinguished Men of the South*. Atlanta: Confederate Publishing Co., 1899 (The Blue & Grey Press reprint, n.d.)
Williams, Kenneth P. *Lincoln Finds a General: A Military Study of the Civil War*, 5 vols. New York: The MacMillan Co., 1949-1959.
Young, Jesse Bowman. *The Battle of Gettysburg: A Comprehensive Narrative*. New York: Harper & Bros., 1913.

ARTICLES

National Tribune:

Bentley, W. A. "Howard at Gettysburg," Feb. 12, 1885.
Boland, E. T. "Death of Gen. Reynolds. An Ex-Confederate Who Was a Witness Describes the Event," May 20, 1915.
Coey, James. "Cutler's Brigade. The 147th New York's Magnificent Fight on the First Day at Gettysburg," July 15, 1915.
Day, Thomas G. "Veteran of 3d Indiana Cavalry Describes First Day's Fight at Gettysburg," July 3, 1903.
Dodge, H. O. "Opening the Battle....", Sept. 24, 1891.
Fulton, Dr. James. "Gettysburg Reminiscenses. A Surgeon's Story," Oct. 20, 1898.
Hofmann, John W. "The 56th Pennsylvania at Gettysburg," March 20, 1884.
---. "Gettysburg Again. Gen. Hoffman on the Action of the 147th New York at the Opening of the Battle," June 5, 1884.
Hopkins, Thomas S. "Death of Reynolds. It Came from a Volley and Not from a Sharpshooter," April 14, 1910.
Jepson, George E. "The First Day at Gettysburg. A Tribute to Reynolds....", Oct. 6, 1910
McConnell, Charles H. "First and Greatest Day's Battle of Gettysburg" [2 parts], July 13 and July 20, 1916.
Mix, A. R. "Experiences at Gettysburg," Feb. 22, 1934.
Parkhurst, B. E. "At Gettysburg. Heroism of the 147th New York," Nov. 1, 1888.
Pierce, J. V. "Last Words as to What Regiment Opened the Battle," April 3, 1884.
Stubbs, Charles E. "2nd Maine Battery at Gettysburg," June 2, 1910.
Sullivan, James P. "Gettysburg. Member of 6th Wisconsin Takes Issue with 'Carleton,'" May 14, 1885.
Swett, Joel B. "The Eighth New York Cavalry at Gettysburg," April 3, 1884.

Confederate Veteran:

Ashe, Samuel A. "The First Day at Gettysburg," Vol. XXXVII (Oct. 1930), 378-381.
Belo, A. H. "Battle of Gettysburg," Vol. VIII (April 1900), 165-168.
Boland, E. T. "Beginning of the Battle of Gettysburg," Vol. XIV (July 1906), 308-309.
Fulton, W. F. "The Fifth Alabama at Gettysburg," Vol. XXXI (Oct. 1923), 379-380.
Harris, F. S. "Gen. Jas. J. Archer," Vol. III (Jan. 1895), 18-19.
Harris, T. C. "The Second Mississippi at Gettysburg," Vol. XXV (Nov. 1917), 527
Kimble, June. "Tennesseans at Gettysburg — The Retreat," Vol. XVIII (1910), 460-463.
Moon, Dr. W. H. "Beginning of the Battle at Gettysburg," Vol. XXXIII (Dec. 1925), 449-450.
Purifoy, John. "The Battle of Gettysburg, July 1, 1863" [2 parts] Vol. XXXI (Jan. and Apr. 1923), 22-25 and 138-142.
---. "The Myth of the Confederate Hollow Square," Vol. XXXIII (Feb. 1925), 53-55.
Tolley, William P. "Campaigns by Army of Northern Virginia," Vol. VIII (March 1900), 109.
Turney, J. B. "The First Tennessee at Gettysburg," Vol VIII (Dec. 1900), 535-537.

Other:

Bean, Theodore W. "Buford at Gettysburg," *The* [Philadelphia] *Times*, Sept. 11, 1880.
Calef, John H. "Gettysburg Notes: The Opening Gun," *Journal of the Military Service Institution of the United States*, Vol. 40 (1907), 40-58. . "The Regular Artillery in the Gettysburg Campaign," *Journal of the Military Service Institution of the United States*, Vol. 45 (1909), 32-38.

Carpenter, John A. "Doubleday's Chancellorsville and Gettysburg" [book review], *Military Affairs*, Vol. 27 (Summer 1963), 84-88.
Cutler, Lysander, et al. "Gettysburg. The Great Battle of July 1, 2 & 3, 1863," Gettysburg *Star and Sentinel*, May 5, 1885.
Dawes, Rufus R. "Remininiscences of the Battle of Gettysburg," Gettysburg *Star and Sentinel*, March 8, 1872.
Fuller, Ezra B. "Who Fired the First Shot at the Battle of Gettysburg?" *Journal of the U.S. Cavalry Association*, Vol. 24 (1914), 784-796.
Grimsley, Mark. "The Master General [Lee]," *Civil War Times Illustrated*, Vol. XXIV (Nov. 1985), 12-51.
Harris, Loyd G. "With the Iron Brigade Guard at Gettysburg," *Gettysburg*, Issue No. 1 (July 1989), 29-34.
Hartwig, D. Scott. "Guts and Good Leadership: The Action at the Railroad Cut, July 1, 1863," *The Morningside Notes*, May 8, 1985, 3-13.
Hassler, Warren W., Jr. "The First Day's Battle at Gettysburg," *Civil War History*, Vol. VI (Sept. 1960), 259-276.
Hassler, William W. "Harry Heth — Lee's Hard-Luck General," *Civil War Times Illustrated*, Vol. V (July 1966), 12-20.
Hopkins, C. A. Porter (Ed.). "The James J. Archer Letters: A Marylander in the Civil War," *Maryland Historical Magazine*, Vol. 56 (1961), 72-93, 125-149, 353-383.
Howard, Oliver O. "Campaign and Battle of Gettysburg, June and July, 1863," *Atlantic Monthly*, July 1876.
Hubler, Simon. "Just the Plain, Unvarnished Story of a Soldier in the Ranks," *New York Times Magazine*, June 29, 1913.
Huidekoper, H. S. "A Short Story of Gettysburg Forty Years After the Battle," *Book of the Royal Blue*, Vol. VI, No. 10 (July 1903).
Jacobs, Michael. "Meteorology of the Battle," Gettysburg *Star and Sentinel*, Aug. 11, 1885.
Jones, Meredith L. "The First Day's Fight," *Blue and Gray*, Vol. 2 (July 1893), 20-21.
Kingston, Joseph T. "The Man Who Shot Reynolds," *The* [Lancaster, Pa.] *Sunday News*, Nov. 23, 1952.
Longacre, Edward G. "John F. Reynolds, General," *Civil War Times Illustrated*, Vol. XI (Aug. 1972), 26-43.
Maloney, M. R. "General Reynolds and Dear Kate," *American Heritage*, Vol. 15 (Dec. 1963), 62-65.
Marye, John L. "The First Gun at Gettysburg, With the Confederate Advance Guard," *The American Historical Register*, July 1885, 1225-1232.
McClean, James L., Jr. "The First Union Shot at Gettysburg," *Lincoln Herald*, Vol. 82 (Spring 1980), 319-323.
Moore, A. H. "Heth's Division at Gettysburg," *Southern Bivouac*, Vol. III (May 1885).
"Northern Prison Life," *The Land We Love*, Nov. 1866. (By unnamed officer of Pettigrew's brigade.)
Pindell, Richard. "Our Technological Inheritance," *Civil War Times Illustrated*, Vol. XXVI (Summer 1987), 53-55.
Pratt, Fletcher. "Man on Horseback" [Buford], *Infantry Journal*, Vol. 47 (1940), 112-119.
Rosengarten, Joseph G. "Reynolds Last Battle," *Philadelphia Weekly Times*, March 17, 1877.
---. "Major-General John F. Reynolds," Gettysburg *Star and Sentinel*, May 5, 1885.
---. "Where Reynolds Fell," *Philadelphia Weekly Press*, Jan. 20, 1886.
---. "Reynolds, Hero of the First Day, by One of His Staff," *New York Times Magazine*, June 29, 1913.

Roth, Jeffrey B. "Tavern with a Past is Brought Up-to-date," *York* [Pa.] *Sunday News*, July 27, 1986.

Swallow, William H. "The First Day at Gettysburg," *Southern Bivouac*, Vol. I (Dec. 1885), 436-444.

Weigley, Russell F. "John Buford," *Civil War Times Illustrated*, Vol. V (June 1966).

Wilcox, William H. "Where Reynolds Fell" [letter to the Editor], *The Philadelphia Inquirer*, July 7, 1863.

NEWSPAPERS

Gettysburg Compiler
Gettysburg Times
Gettysburg Star and Sentinel
National Tribune
New York Herald
New York Times
Philadelphia Public Ledger
Scrapbook of newspaper clippings, GNMP Library

MISCELLANEOUS

Letters, diaries, and other unpublished sources in the Gettysburg National Military Park Library, Civil War Institute of Gettysburg College, and U.S. Army Military History Institute (including the Robert L. Brake Collection).

INDEX

-A-

Adams County Court House, 193, 194
Aiken, James, 128, 140, 200
Alabama
 5th, 70, 72, 77, 135
 13th, 58, 70, 72, 77, 128, 135, 136, 139, 140
Aldie, Va., 8, 29, 214
Alexander, Edward P., 44, 68
American Revolution, 90
Anderson, Richard H., 170, 174
Anderson, J.Q., 54, 64, 238
Annapolis, Md., 38
Antietam, Battle of, 5, 29, 127, 190, 192
Archer, James J., 45, 49, 69, 70, 71, 72, 75, 77, 83, 84, 85, 86, 95, 102, 104, 126, 127, 128, 129, 133, 134, 136, 137, 138, 139, 142, 146, 147, 148, 171, 175, 200, 201, 202, 205, 208, 209, 223, 225, 226, 238
Army of Northern Virignia, 1, 8, 63, 69, 98, 169, 174, 198, 202, 207
Army of the Cumberland, 3
Army of the Potomac, 1, 2, 3, 5, 15, 17, 19, 21, 22, 25, 26, 44, 69, 94, 98, 112, 198, 207
Army of the Tennessee, 3
Arndt, Peter, 138
Ashe, Samuel, 229
Ashhurst, R.L., 208
Auberry, C.B., 130
Aylesworth, Edwin, 154

-B-

Baird, E.C., 110, 112, 113, 221
Baldwin, Ambrose N., 185
Baltimore, Md., 2, 15, 18, 19, 25, 65, 196, 233
Bankhead, Henry C., 69
Barksdale, William, 4
Barlow, Francis C., 63, 193, 195, 196
Bartlett, John, 107, 120
Bassler, John H., 176, 177, 178
Bates, James L., 189
Baxter, Henry, 181, 182, 183, 189, 239
Bean, Theodore, 57, 101
Beecham, Robert K., 89, 100, 102, 105, 127, 224
Bell, Robert, 10, 11
Bellore, Charles, 139
Belo, Alfred H., 116, 117, 119, 157, 158, 162, 164, 201, 240
Berryville, Va., 6
Beveridge, John L., 72, 78, 83, 84, 104, 239
Biddle, Alexander, 61, 62, 90, 128, 147
Biddle, Chapman, 40, 97, 175, 176, 179, 184, 185, 219, 221, 222, 224
Biddle, George, 152, 200
Blair, John A., 157, 158, 164, 165, 200, 201, 229, 240
Blue Ridge Mountains, 6, 21
Blue Water Creek, 29, 32
Boland, E.T., 58, 139, 220
Boonsboro, Md., 28
Brace, France, 225
Brandy Station, Va., 5, 29
Bridgeport, Md., 42, 53
Broadhead, Sarah, 14, 35, 83, 142
Brockenbrough, John, 50, 58, 77, 131, 135, 144, 145, 146, 171, 201
Brooklyn, 14th, 41, 59, 102, 107, 114, 128, 129, 144, 150, 151, 152, 159, 160, 161, 163, 165, 166, 167, 168, 177, 178, 179, 184, 199, 203, 224, 225, 227, 229, 230
Brokaw, Theodore, 89
Brown, G. Campbell, 64, 170, 171
Brunson, Joseph Woods, 240
Bryan, Jonathan, 143
Buchanan, Felix, 220
Buck, Daniel, 71, 72, 78
Buckles, Abraham, 130
Buell, Augustus, 2, 62, 90, 132, 133, 207
Buena Vista, Battle of, 106
Buford, John, 23, 26, 28, 29, 30, 36, 37, 42, 43, 45, 47, 52, 57, 58, 67, 68, 69, 72, 73, 78, 81, 82, 84, 85, 86, 87, 88, 92, 93, 94, 95, 96, 97, 98, 99, 100, 101, 104, 105, 106, 158, 179, 180, 182, 192, 196, 200, 201, 202, 203, 204, 205, 207, 209, 213, 215, 216, 217, 218, 230, 231, 238
Bullfrog road, 62
Bull Run, First Battle of, 38, 61, 127
Bull Run, Second Battle of, 4, 21, 29, 127
Burgwyn, Henry, 83, 171

Burns, John, 96, 102, 186, 187, 188, 236, 237
Burnside, Ambrose E., 190, 240
Butterfield, Daniel, 19, 41, 197, 198

-C-

Calef, John H., 28, 46, 57, 81, 82, 92, 95, 96, 100, 101, 104, 109, 158, 167, 168, 179, 180, 200, 203, 209, 210, 239
Calkins, Homer, 214
Callis, John B., 129, 136, 188, 226, 239
Carlisle, Pa., 9, 24, 31, 43, 65
Carlisle road, 54, 57, 64, 105, 171, 174
Carr, Frank, 106, 123
Carson, John P., 112, 114, 146
Cashtown, Pa., 24, 31, 32, 33, 34, 43, 44, 45, 48, 49, 50, 63, 64, 65, 69, 70, 71, 78, 87, 144, 169, 170, 201, 202, 230
Cat Tail Branch, 42
Catoctin Mountains, 22
Cavetown, Md., 28
Cemetery Ridge, 96, 97, 98, 168, 180, 193, 195, 196, 197, 203, 204, 206, 297, 207, 208, 218, 231, 232
Chamberlin, Thomas, 181, 185, 187
Chambersburg, Pa., 6, 14, 15, 32, 64, 65, 66, 67, 69
Chambersburg Pike, 11, 24, 35, 46, 49, 53, 54, 58, 70, 71, 72, 73, 77, 78, 81, 82, 88, 92, 97, 98, 99, 101, 102, 106, 107, 108, 109, 110, 128, 131, 132, 133, 138, 139, 140, 143, 145, 146, 147, 148, 149, 151, 152, 155, 159, 160, 166, 168, 169, 171, 172, 174, 176, 177, 180, 183, 184, 186, 212, 217
Chancellorsville, Va., 5, 18, 49
Chancellorsville, Battle of, 1, 2, 3, 5, 19, 21, 29, 33, 127, 190, 205
Cheney, Newel, 182, 212
Christian, William S., 6, 8
Cincinnati, Oh., 3
Codori farm, 92, 99, 100, 177, 182
Coey, James, 228
Comstock, Asa, 182
Connally, John, 115, 116, 157, 200, 240
Cook, John E., 108, 116, 119
Cooke, Sidney G., 61, 228
Cornish, Daniel, 56, 214
Couch, Darius N., 10, 25, 31, 66, 67
Crawford, Will, 70
Culp, Peter, 89
Culp's Hill, 203
Culpeper, Va., 5, 6, 18, 230
Culver, Anson, 90
Cumberland Valley, 2, 9, 65
Cunningham, Burlington, 130
Curtain, Andrew G., 4, 8, 9, 223
Cutler, Lysander, 40, 59, 89, 92, 99, 100, 101, 102, 106, 108, 110, 114, 117, 152, 156, 157, 158, 167, 183, 189, 208, 221, 223, 224, 227, 228, 229, 230, 238

-D-

Daily, D.B., 137, 138, 223
Dana, E.L., 71, 72, 213, 239
Daney, Andrew, 184
Davidson, R.E., 127
Davies, Alfred W., 56
Davis, Jefferson, 2, 33, 240
Davis, Joseph, 49, 50, 70, 71, 72, 75, 77, 83, 85, 86, 95, 108, 110, 117, 119, 121, 124, 128, 145, 148, 150, 151, 152, 156, 157, 158, 161, 163, 165, 166, 201, 202, 221, 225, 228, 229, 240
Dawes, Charles G., 239
Dawes, Rufus R., 61, 89, 104, 117, 131, 140, 146, 151, 159, 160, 161, 163, 164, 165, 179, 208, 227, 229, 239
Dawson, Francis, 8, 9
Day, Tom, 74, 83
Devin, Thomas C., 28, 37, 47, 78, 81, 82, 85, 95, 100, 105, 106, 174, 182, 219, 239
De Trobriand, P. Regis, 97
De Witt, J. Wilson, 57
Dickey, Gilbert A., 130, 139
Dinnin, James, 174, 182
Dodge, H.O., 58, 59
Doubleday, Abner, 38, 39, 53, 59, 62, 88, 90, 94, 96, 98, 107, 108, 114, 117, 121, 132, 138, 139, 143, 144, 145, 146, 150, 151, 152, 163, 167, 168, 176, 177, 178, 179, 181, 182, 183, 190, 195, 196, 197, 201, 207, 208, 209, 217, 218, 221, 224, 225, 227, 228, 229, 230, 231, 239
Dougal, William, 177
Douglas, Martin, 122
Dover, Pa., 31
Dudley, William W., 130, 134, 136, 139, 145, 200, 221, 222, 227
Dumfries, Va., 21
Durham, Gabriel B., 214

-E-

Early, Jubal A., 3, 11, 13, 24, 32, 44, 46, 63, 64, 169, 170, 174, 187, 207

East Berlin, Pa., 24
Edwards Ferry, 22, 26
Eggleston, Lewis, 163
Eleventh Corps, 22, 26, 41, 43, 50, 52, 53, 63, 68, 88, 95, 109, 174, 190, 192, 193, 196, 197, 207, 232
Ellsworth, Timothy, 154, 156
Emmitsburg, Md., 23, 26, 28, 40, 41, 42, 51, 52, 53, 59, 62, 63, 69, 109, 195, 205, 236
Emmitsburg road, 30, 35, 39, 40, 42, 51, 52, 59, 62, 63, 88, 89, 90, 92, 95, 96, 99, 100, 102, 132, 140, 141, 174, 176, 177, 182, 186, 189, 193, 197, 203
Eustice, George, 188
Evans, William, 166
Ewell, Richard S., 5, 6, 8, 14, 15, 24, 31, 32, 43, 44, 54, 63, 64, 69, 169, 170, 171, 197, 201
Everett, Edward, 204

-F-

Fairchild, Lucius, 102, 126, 127, 138, 140, 200, 224, 239
Fairfield, Pa., 8, 30, 40, 41, 54, 108
Fairfield road, 40, 62, 97, 98, 99, 100, 101, 102, 104, 105, 107, 108, 109, 130, 131, 151, 171, 174, 175, 176
Fayetteville, Pa., 14, 32, 49, 64, 169
Fifth Corps, 22, 26, 51
First Corps, 5, 6, 15, 22, 24, 26, 32, 38, 39, 40, 41, 45, 50, 51, 53, 68, 92, 95, 96, 97, 174, 192, 193, 195, 196, 206, 207, 208
Fite, John , 34, 45, 48, 133
Flanigan, Mark, 143
Follett, 131
Forney farm, 56
Forrester, George, 166
Fort Delaware, 140, 238
Fort McHenry, 238
Fountaindale, Md., 28, 29, 30
Fowler, Edward B., 41, 52, 61, 128, 129, 151, 152, 160, 165, 179, 184, 227, 229
Frederick, Md., 15, 16, 21, 22, 25, 29, 39
Fredericksburg Va., 4, 5, 18, 21, 71
Fredericksburg, Battle of, 5, 29, 190
Fremantle, James A.L., 1, 9, 49, 69
French, W.H., 12, 68
Fry, Birkett D., 58, 87, 142, 171, 226, 240

-G-

Gaines' Mill, Battle of, 4, 162
Gamble, William, 28, 37, 72, 78, 81, 95, 96, 100, 102, 105, 109, 126, 128, 133, 176, 200, 239
Gates, Theodore B., 175, 185
George, George, 141, 233
George, Newton J., 128
Genesee Valley, 38
Gildersleeve, George, 233, 234
Glenber, Matt, 130, 131
Globe Tavern, 238
Goltermann, William, 166
Gordon, John B., 11, 13, 14
Grant, Tom, 85
Greencastle, Pa., 215
Greenmount, 40, 51, 59, 62
Greenwood, 31, 64, 169, 170
Gregg, David M., 23, 205
Grover, Andrew J., 89, 108, 115, 116, 119, 200

-H-

Hagerstown, Md., 187
Hale, James, 58
Hall, Daniel, 109, 192, 193, 200, 209, 232
Hall, James A., 52, 53, 88, 92, 99, 100, 101, 106, 109, 148, 149, 150, 156, 239
Hall, Marcus, 54, 56
Halleck, Henry W., 4, 5, 16, 17, 18, 19, 25, 65, 66
Haller, Granville, 10
Halstead, E.P., 94, 96, 138, 217
Hancock, Winfield S., 97, 198, 204, 217
Hanley, Timothy, 56
Hanover, Pa., 30, 51, 66
Hard, Abner, 105
Hardie, James A., 16, 17, 18, 19
Harland, John, 161, 162
Harman farm, 185
Harney, George, 121, 147, 152, 154, 156, 227
Harpers Ferry, Va., 18
Harries, William H., 126, 138, 221
Harris, Loyd G., 39, 40
Harrisburg, Pa., 2, 5, 9, 10, 14, 15, 24, 25, 31, 51, 63, 65, 66, 69
Harrisburg Pike, 14, 46, 54, 64, 95, 105
Harrison, Henry, 15, 16, 24
Haupt, Herman, 65, 66, 69
Hauser, John F., 165
Heermance, William, 73, 213
Heidlersburg, Pa., 24, 32, 43, 44, 46, 63, 64, 65, 69, 92
Hendrix, Tom, 218, 220
Herbst, John, 81

Herbst's Woods, 78, 81, 82, 97, 101, 107, 109, 110, 113, 126, 127, 128, 129, 134, 145, 168, 171, 175, 176, 177, 178, 180, 183, 185, 188, 209, 220
Herr, Frederick, 75
Herr Ridge, 74, 75, 77, 81, 82, 83, 84, 86, 92, 94, 106, 123, 135, 143, 146, 166, 171, 172, 175, 177, 183, 185
Herr Tavern, 75
Heth, Henry, 1, 2, 5, 14, 25, 30, 32, 33, 34, 35, 43, 44, 48, 49, 50, 58, 63, 64, 65, 68, 69, 70, 71, 74, 75, 77, 83, 86, 87, 94, 100, 135, 139, 165, 168, 169, 171, 174, 201, 202, 204, 205, 209, 215, 220, 225, 226, 240
Hewitt, Catherine, "Kate," 233, 234, 235, 236
Hill, Ambrose P., 5, 6, 14, 15, 32, 33, 43, 44, 48, 49, 63, 64, 65, 68, 69, 74, 92, 95, 169, 170, 171, 174, 197, 201, 202, 238, 240
Hill, Daniel H., 205, 228
Hinchcliff, John, 154
Hodges, Alpheus, 73, 74, 212
Hoffman farm, 56
Hofmann, John W., 108, 119, 223, 224, 228
Holland, John, 133
Holt, Joseph, 230
Hood, John B., 32, 64, 169
Hooker, Joseph, 2, 3, 4, 5, 6, 15, 16, 18, 19, 21, 23, 190, 204, 205
Horner's mill, 63
Hosmer, G.W., 77, 140
Howard, Charles, 193, 197
Howard, Oliver O., 41, 42, 43, 52, 63, 88, 95, 109, 190, 192, 193, 194, 195, 196, 197, 198, 204, 206, 207, 208, 218, 221, 231, 232, 239
Hubler, Simon, 178, 189
Humphreys, Andrew A., 68
Hunt, Henry, 109
Hunterstown, Pa., 11, 44, 46, 54
Hunterstown road, 46, 54

-I-

Illinois
- 8th, 36, 53, 54, 72, 78, 81, 83, 104, 105
- 12th, 54, 72, 78, 105

Imboden, John D., 32, 64
Indiana
- 3rd, 29, 54, 74, 78, 83, 104, 105, 130
- 7th, 59
- 19th, 53, 61, 104, 109, 113, 129, 130, 133, 134, 135, 136, 138, 144, 145, 146, 168, 222

Iron Brigade, 40, 108, 109, 133, 134, 136, 138, 143, 144, 148, 150, 151, 175, 178, 180, 199, 208
Irvin, John, 189

-J-

Jackson, Thomas J., 1, 2, 49, 135, 190, 205
James, Cyrus W., 57, 214
Jefferson, Md., 26, 31
Jenkins, 6, 14
Jennings, William W., 11
Jepson, George E., 217, 218
Jerome, A.B., 78, 92, 93, 94, 115, 196, 204, 216, 217, 218
Johnson, Edward, 24, 32, 63, 64, 169, 170
Johnson's Island, 238
Joint Committee on the Conduct of War, 67, 144, 190, 197, 203
Jones, F.B., 51
Jones, Gorge W., 178
Jones, Marcellus E., 58, 59, 70, 71, 211, 212
Jones, Meredith, 150

-K-

Kelley, T.B., 58
Kellogg, John A., 158
Kellogg, Josiah, 54
Kempster, Walter, 69, 203
Kendlehart, D., 13
Kieffer, Harry, 41, 183, 184
Kilpatrick, Judson, 23, 30, 205
Kimble, June, 128
Kress, John A., 82

-L-

Lancaster, Pa., 3, 219, 233, 236
Landis, Harry, 234
Lane, James H., 171, 172
Lane, John, 45, 171
Lee, Henry T., 110
Lee, Robert E., 1, 2, 3, 5, 6, 7, 8, 14, 15, 16, 24, 25, 31, 43, 44, 48, 50, 58, 63, 64, 65, 66, 68, 69, 169, 170, 171, 174, 201, 202, 205, 207
Leesburg, Va., 22, 26
Legate, George H., 88
Lemon, Charles, 86, 200, 214
Lewisburg, Va., 33
Libby Prison, 4
Liberty Mills, 238
Lincoln, Abraham, 3, 5, 16, 18, 31, 188, 207, 230, 237

Littlestown, Pa., 26
Livermore, Thomas L., 98, 206
Lohr's Hill, 72
Longstreet, James, 1, 3, 5, 6, 15, 32, 43, 69, 169, 170
Lundy's Lane, Battle of, 187
Lutheran Theological Seminary, 11, 37, 78, 86, 89, 92, 93, 94, 96, 101, 102, 132, 140, 151, 177, 182, 183, 186, 216, 217
Lyman, H.H., 157

-M-

MacMillan house, 101
Maine
  2nd, 40, 99, 106, 120, 122, 148
  5th, 180
  16th, 181
Maloney, Patrick, 137
Malvern Hill, Battle of, 162
Manassas, Battle of, 162
Manchester, Md., 26, 51, 66
Mansfield, John, 127, 226
Marsh Creek, 40, 41, 52, 58, 59, 62, 70, 78, 86, 88, 181, 204
Marston, J.H., 160
Marten, Benjamin, 107, 146
Martinsburg, Va., 18
Marye, Edward A., 8, 33, 49, 71, 74
Massachusetts
  12th, 181, 189, 190
  13th, 181, 183
Mayo, Robert, 58
McCabe, Joseph, 46, 214
McCarty, W. Marion, 59
McClellan, George B., 4, 61, 190, 192, 205
McDowell, Irvin, 38
McIntosh, David G., 77, 172, 174, 220
McLaws, 5, 32, 64, 169
McPherson farm, 37, 78, 81, 86, 101, 102, 107, 119, 155, 177, 178, 180, 184, 237
McPherson's Ridge, 37, 73, 74, 77, 78, 81, 82, 83, 85, 92, 94, 95, 96, 97, 98, 100, 101, 102, 104, 105, 106, 108, 109, 110, 112, 119, 120, 122, 126, 127, 128, 129, 130, 131, 133, 139, 144, 145, 146, 148, 151, 152, 166, 167, 175, 176, 177, 179, 180, 181, 182, 183, 185, 187, 188, 189, 190, 199, 201, 203, 204, 206, 208, 209, 210, 216, 218, 219, 222, 224, 225
McSherrystown, Pa., 30
Mead, Sydney, 144, 227
Meade, George, 98
Meade, George G., 5, 16, 17, 18, 19, 20, 21, 23, 24, 25, 26, 31, 42, 43, 51, 52, 53, 63, 64, 65, 66, 67, 69, 88, 92, 94, 95, 96, 97, 195, 196, 197, 198, 203, 205, 206, 207, 215, 221, 226
Mechanicsburg, Pa., 14
Mechanicstown, Md., 23, 46
Mechanicsville, Battle of, 4
Medal of Honor, 163
Meredith, J.M., 50, 58, 89, 92, 99, 100, 101, 102, 104, 107, 109, 114, 131, 139, 143, 144, 145, 146, 175, 179, 180, 184, 208, 223, 224
Meredith, Solomon, 40, 126, 150, 240
Merritt, Wesley, 26, 46
Mexican War, 3, 32, 38, 90, 106, 181, 187
Meysenburg, Theodore, 193
Michigan, 24th, 39, 51, 53, 61, 90, 102, 104, 109, 113, 130, 133, 134, 135, 136, 138, 139, 144, 145, 146, 168, 237
Middleburg, Md., 8, 25, 29, 44, 66
Middletown, Md., 19, 26, 64
Miller, Francis C., 107, 119, 120, 121, 152, 200
Miller, Hugh R., 157
Mills, Albert, 84, 104, 213
Mississippi
  2nd, 77, 108, 124, 153, 157, 158, 162, 164, 199
  11th, 49
  42nd, 77, 109, 120, 121, 122, 123, 124, 153, 157, 164
Mitchell, William G., 110, 112, 233
Mix, A.R., 37, 38, 57, 58, 81, 95
Monterey, Battle of, 106
Monterey Pass, 10, 28
Moon, W.H., 83, 85, 135, 220
Moore, A.H., 215
Morgan, Milo, 225
Moritz Tavern, 41, 42, 50, 51, 53, 59, 62, 63
Morrow, Henry A., 102, 130, 134, 146, 200, 226, 239
Morton's Ford, 238
Mulholland, St. Clair A., 184
Mummasburg, Pa., 13, 34, 44, 46, 67
Mummasburg road, 37, 54, 56, 82, 95, 108, 190
Murphy, W.B., 117, 162, 163, 165, 229

-N-

Napier, Sir William, 114
Newton, John, 196, 207

Newville road, 105
New York
1st, 175, 180
6th, 54, 56, 72, 81, 82
8th, 54, 78, 81, 104, 105, 131
9th, 37, 46, 54, 56, 57, 73, 82, 85, 95, 182, 186, 189
76th, 59, 89, 102, 106, 107, 108, 114, 115, 117, 119, 120, 124, 129, 143, 152, 156, 168, 179, 195, 199, 224, 225
80th, 176, 185
83rd, 181, 189, 190
94th, 181
95th, 59, 105, 106, 107, 128, 129, 144, 150, 151, 152, 159, 160, 161, 163, 165, 166, 168, 177, 178, 179, 199, 203, 208, 227, 229, 230
97th, 181, 182
104th, 181
107th, 181
142nd, 109
147th, 39, 40, 51, 59, 102, 106, 107, 119 120, 121, 123, 124, 125, 129, 147, 148, 150, 152, 153, 154, 155, 156, 157, 160, 168, 179, 184, 186, 199, 200, 209, 227, 228, 229
Nichols, Perry, 56
North Carolina
11th, 35
52nd, 29
55th, 70, 72, 77, 108, 115, 116, 124, 153, 157, 158, 164
Norton, Henry, 131

-O-

Oak Ridge, 119, 156, 157, 196, 197
Oates, William C., 64
Okey, Cornelius, 163
Osborn, Thomas W., 196
Otis, George H., 223
Oyster Point, 14

-P-

Parkhurst B.E., 120
Parr's Ridge, 26
Paul, Gabriel R., 181, 183, 190
Pease, Francis M., 102, 155
Peck, Abel, 139
Pegram, William J., 33, 49, 70, 71, 72, 77, 81, 82, 83, 94, 106, 109, 120, 122, 123, 128, 141, 146, 168, 169, 200, 209, 238
Pender, William D., 14, 32, 33, 43, 64, 65, 77, 169, 171, 174, 238
Pendleton, W.N., 174
Pennsylvania College, 11, 37, 83, 186
Pennsylvania
1st, 40, 53, 180
17th, 28, 30, 36, 46, 54, 57, 82, 85
11th, 181, 182
21st, 10, 11
56th, 59, 102, 106, 107, 108, 114, 116, 119, 120, 124, 129, 143, 152, 156, 168, 179, 195, 199, 222, 223, 224, 225
88th, 181, 189, 190
90th, 181, 189
121st, 176, 185
143rd, 176, 177, 183, 184
149th, 51, 176, 177, 178, 183, 184
150th, 22, 39, 40, 41, 51, 176, 177, 178, 183, 184, 237
151st, 184
Pennsylvania Militia
26th, 10, 11, 13
Pennsylvania Reserves, 4
Pergel, Charles, 81
Perrin, Abner, 171, 172
Petersburg (York Springs), Pa., 43
Petersburg pike, 65
Pettigrew, James J., 33, 35, 43, 44, 45, 48, 49, 50, 69, 77, 82, 131, 144, 145, 146, 169, 171, 201, 238
Philadelphia, Pa., 2, 15, 25, 51, 66, 69, 234, 236
Philadelphia City Troop, 10
Phillips, Frederick L., 223
Pickett, George E., 6, 32, 64
Pierce, Herschel, 116, 121, 123, 124, 125
Pierce, J. Volney, 51, 101, 102, 120, 154, 155, 156, 209, 223, 224, 228
Pierce, Tillie, 36
Pipe Creek, 26, 66, 67, 69, 97, 198
Plattsburg, Battle of, 187
Pleasonton, Alfred, 23, 30, 46, 69, 87, 106, 203, 205, 215
Poolesville, Md., 22, 98
Port Royal, SC, 234
Potomac River, 6, 15, 16, 18, 22, 26, 49
Pye, Edward, 152, 159, 160, 208

-Q-

Queenston Heights, Battle of, 187

-R-

Raison, Henry, 86
Ramseur, Stephen D., 16
Rappahannock River, 2, 5, 18, 21
Rawle, William, 207
Rea, Will, 130, 131
Reed, E.R., 223
Reed, Melvin, 225
Remington, William, 163
Rexford, William H., 143
Reynolds, Gilbert H., 179, 180, 183
Reynolds, John F., 3, 4, 5, 17, 19, 20, 21, 25, 38, 41, 42, 43, 45, 46, 50, 51, 52, 53, 57, 59, 61, 63, 67, 68, 74, 78, 87, 88, 89, 92, 93, 94, 95, 96, 97, 98, 99, 100, 101, 104, 106, 107, 109, 110, 112, 113, 114, 122, 126, 132, 140, 141, 143, 144, 146, 150, 152, 167, 179, 190, 192, 193, 194, 195, 196, 197, 198, 200, 203, 204, 205, 206, 207, 208, 210, 215, 216, 217, 218, 219, 220, 221, 222, 224, 225, 231, 232, 233, 234, 235, 236
Reynolds, Mary, 21
Reynolds, Samuel, 233, 234, 236
Reynolds, William, 234, 235
Richardson, Hollon, 144
Richmond, Va., 4, 18, 32
Riddle, William, 43, 50, 52, 63, 95, 110, 192, 193, 195, 231, 232, 233
Rider, John, 139
Rihl, William H., 215
Riker, Edward, 166, 167
Rison, 214
Robertson, A.C., 56
Robinson, John C., 38, 88, 90, 94, 181, 182, 200, 207, 239
Robinson, William W., 129, 145, 239
Rockville, Md., 31
Roder, John, 81, 158
Rodes, Robert, 14, 24, 32, 43, 44, 63, 64, 65, 169, 170, 174, 184, 189
Rogers, C.E., 150
Rollinson, William, 56
Rosengarten, Joseph G., 95, 98, 100, 113, 114, 140, 141, 142, 203, 206, 217, 219, 222, 225, 231, 233
Rowley, Thomas A., 38, 90, 94, 174, 175, 176, 177, 200, 230, 231, 239

-S-

Sackett, William, 54, 56, 238
Sager, George, 58, 59
Sandoe, George W., 215
Scales, Alfred M., 171, 172
Schenck, Robert C., 65
Schimmelfennig, Alexander, 196
Schurz, Carl, 19, 63, 193, 195, 196, 197
Scotland, Pa., 32, 63, 64, 169
Scott, K.P., 205
Second Corps, 5, 6, 8, 15, 22, 24, 26, 44, 51, 190
Seddon, James A., 2
Sedgwick, John, 97
Seminary Ridge, 35, 46, 82, 92, 96, 98, 99, 100, 101, 102, 104, 114, 124, 126, 127, 130, 131, 132, 133, 149, 151, 154, 158, 167, 168, 174, 177, 179, 180, 182, 183, 189, 190, 197, 206, 216, 224, 225
Seminole War, 181, 187
Seven Pines, Battle of, 162
Seymour, Horatio, 38
Shafer, Levi, 58, 59
Shenandoah Valley, 2, 5
Shepard, Samuel, 139, 226
Shepherdstown, Va., 6
Shippensburg, Pa., 24
Shriver, Christian, 51
Shriver, Jacob, 51
Shultz house, 101
Shuttz, Peter, 154
Sickles, Daniel E., 41, 42, 53, 109, 195, 198
Sigler, John, 51
Sixth Corps, 22, 26, 51
Skelly, Daniel, 193, 194
Slagle, Jacob, 88, 90, 182, 184
Slattery, Tom, 158
Slentz, John, 37, 86
Slocum, Henry, 195
Smith, James P., 170
Smith, Maurice T., 116
Smith, Tom, 54, 56
Soch's mill, 62
South Moutain, 9, 10, 11, 24, 28, 32, 64, 77, 170, 172
Stannard, George J., 40, 62
Stanton, Edwin M., 5, 16, 18, 31, 65
Stearns, Austin, 182
Stevens, George H., 110, 127, 138, 179
Stevens, Thaddeus, 37
Stewart, James, 85, 132, 140, 179, 219
Stillman, J.T., 140

Stone, Roy, 40, 62, 90, 132, 147, 157, 174, 175, 176, 177, 178, 179, 180, 183, 184, 185, 189, 200, 239
Stoneman, George, 238
Strong, William W., 221
Stuart, J.E.B., 5, 8, 15, 16, 23, 24, 30, 31, 68, 90, 170, 171, 202
Sullivan, James, 161
Susquehanna River, 2, 13, 15, 25, 66
Swallow, William H., 215, 219, 226, 227, 229
Sweeney, Thomas, 75
Swett, Joel, 104
Sykes, George, 132

-T-

Taneytown, Md., 25, 41, 42, 43, 50, 51, 52, 63, 64, 67, 87, 195, 197
Taneytown road, 174, 233
Taylor, Benjamin, 225
Taylor, Walter H., 48, 68
Tennessee
  1st, 77, 84, 110, 128, 135, 136, 139
  7th, 34, 45, 48, 77, 85, 129, 130, 135, 136
  14th, 77, 128, 129, 135, 136
Third Corps, 5, 6, 15, 22, 24, 26, 41, 42, 51, 53, 109
Thomas, Albert, 106
Thomas, Edward L., 171, 172
Thoroughfare Gap, 29
Thorpe, Ben, 218, 219, 220
Ticknor, John, 159
Tolley, William, 220
Tongue, Levi, 161, 162
Torresdale, Pa., 234, 235
Tremain, Henry E., 109
Trevilian Station, Va., 238
Trimble, Isaac R., 3, 6, 14, 15, 44
Turney, J.B., 84, 128, 136, 226, 227
Twelfth Corps, 22, 26, 51
Two Taverns, 51, 195
Tyler, John, 32

-U-

Ulmer, Frank, 148
Ulmer, William, 106, 122, 124
Union Mills, Md., 26
Uniontown, Md., 26
U.S. Artillery
  2nd, 46, 81
  4th, 133, 180
U.S. Infantry
  4th, 40, 53
  5th, 181
  10th, 187
  14th, 4
U.S. Military Academy, 4, 32, 235
Upperville, Va., 8, 29
Ushuer, Ferdinand, 214

-V-

Veil, Charles H., 94, 112, 114, 140, 141, 216, 217, 220, 233, 236
Vicksburg, Ms., 2
Virginia Cavalry
  17th, 12
  35th, 11, 12, 13
von Amsberg, George, 196
von Steinwehr, A.W.A.F., 63, 193, 195, 196, 231

-W-

Wadsworth, Craig, 99, 129, 132, 230
Wadsworth, James S., 19, 38, 39, 40, 52, 53, 59, 62, 73, 86, 87, 88, 90, 92, 93, 95, 96, 97, 99, 100, 104, 106, 107, 117, 126, 131, 132, 144, 150, 152, 154, 158, 167, 168, 174, 179, 182, 185, 194, 201, 203, 204, 206, 208, 209, 215, 218, 221, 223, 224, 226, 229, 238, 239
Wainwright, Charles S., 3, 19, 22, 38, 40, 53, 61, 98, 132, 140, 167, 179, 180, 206, 207
Walkersville, 22
Waller, Francis A., 163, 165
Walton, J.B., 170
War of 1812, 90, 96, 187
Washington, D.C., 2, 4, 6, 15, 18, 23, 25, 65, 238, 239
Watrous, Robert, 158
Watson, James, 189
Way, William, 53
Waynesboro, Pa., 30
Webb, Henry, 219, 220
Weber, John, 183
Weld, Stephen, 61, 94, 197, 198, 205, 216, 233
Westminster, Md., 65, 140, 189, 233
West Virginia
  3rd, 82
Wheeler, Cornelius, 61, 62, 87, 88, 112, 224, 227
Whisler, Ephraim, 71
Whisler's Ridge, 53, 71, 72, 73, 172
White, E.V., 11, 12, 13, 44
White House, the, 3
Whitney, F.W., 212

Wiggin, Francis, 219
Wilcox, Cadmus M., 68, 112, 233
Wilderness, Battle of the, 239, 240
Williams, Joseph O., 87, 88
Williams, Seth, 68
Williamsport, 6
Willoughby Run, 53, 54, 62, 73, 74, 75, 78, 82, 83, 84, 85, 86, 100, 105, 126, 128, 131, 133, 135, 137, 142, 143, 144, 145, 146, 158, 166, 171, 185, 188, 189, 198, 199, 203, 209, 210, 212, 215, 225
Winchester, Va., 6
Winegar, William, 138
Wisconsin
2nd, 61, 90, 102, 104, 108, 109, 110, 112, 113, 114, 126, 127, 128, 129, 130, 133, 134, 136, 138, 144, 145, 146, 168, 199, 209, 221, 222, 223, 224, 237
6th, 40, 61, 90, 131, 140, 146, 150, 151, 152, 157, 158, 159, 160, 161, 162, 163, 165, 166, 168, 177, 179, 189, 199, 203, 208, 227, 228, 229, 230
7th, 61, 104, 109, 112, 129, 133, 134, 138, 145, 168, 185, 188, 237
Wister, Langhorne, 177, 178, 187, 188
Witmer Farm, 12
Wood, J.D., 150
Woodsborough, 22
Woodward, G.M., 223, 224
Wright, Than, 120
Wrightsville bridge, 13, 15
Wrightsville, Va., 13, 14, 15
Wyburn, William, 155, 156

-Y-

York, Pa., 13, 15, 31, 41, 43, 65, 66, 67
York Pike, 13, 54
Young, Jesse B., 64
Young, Louis G., 43, 44, 45